Antique Trader®

Bottles

IDENTIFICATION & PRICE GUIDE

8th Edition

Michael Polak

Copyright ©2016 Michael Polak

Published by

Krause Publications, a division of F+W Media, Inc.
700 East State Street • Iola, WI 54990-0001
715-445-2214 • 888-457-2873
www.krausebooks.com

To order books or other products call toll-free 1-800-258-0929
or visit us online at www.krausebooks.com.

ISBN-13: 978-1-4402-4614-2
ISBN-10: 1-4402-4614-9

Cover Design by Dane Royer
Designed by Sharon Bartsch
Edited by Kristine Manty

Printed in China

10 9 8 7 6 5 4 3 2 1

Dedication

Between the 6th and 7th editions, we've lost a number of our bottle collecting friends and mentors, who were dedicated staunch supporters and pioneers of the hobby of bottle collecting, leaving behind great stories and long-lasting legacies. The hobby will miss, but not forget, their passionate dedication and strong commitment and support toward the continued growth of the hobby of antique bottle collecting. I'm sure they will find some great digging in "Bottle Heaven."

—*Mike Polak*

Introduction

Acknowledgments

Peter Bleiberg: Thank you for your contribution of the great war slogan milk bottle photographs along with all of the background information, and for your overall support of the project.

Dave Carvalho: Thanks for your contribution of the violin bottle photos and your overall support of the project.

Collector Books/Schroeder Publishing: Thank you for the Avon photographs.

Blake and Brent Cousins (Bottle Hunters of Hawaii): Thank you for the photos for the great Hawaiian bottles and "Digging for Bottles" chapter and your overall support of the project. Aloha.

Penny Dolnick: Thank you for writing the great introduction article for the "Perfume & Cologne Bottles" chapter along with pricing inputs and background information.

Michael and Lori Eckles, Showtime Auction Services (www.showtimeauctions.com; mikeckles@aol.com): Thank you for the photographs and overall support of the project.

Lindsay Evans: Thank you for your contribution of the ceramic pot lid photographs along with all of the background and pricing information, and for your overall support of the project and assistance with the new "Pot Lids (Ceramic)" chapter.

Chuck Gildea: Thanks for your contribution of the Roman bottle photographs and overall support of the project.

Jim Hagenbuch, Jessie Sailer and Josh Reinhart, Glass Works Auctions (www.glswrk-auction.com; glswrk@enter.net): Thank you for the great assortment of photographs, pricing information and support.

Dave Hall: Thanks for your contribution of the W.E. Garret & Sons "Scotch Snuff" advertising pamphlet for the "Snuff" bottles chapter and the overall support of the project.

Bud Hastin (Avon Collector's Encyclopedia): Thanks for the great photographs and your help with the Avon collectibles pricing.

Hawaiian Bottle Club (Mike Leong/Brennan Leong/Brandon Lee): Thank you to the entire club and all of its members for the great photos and description of Hawaiian bottles and providing valuable background information, and for all of your support for the project. Aloha.

Norm Heckler/Jason Heckler (Heckler Auctions; www.hecklerauction.com; info@hecklerauction.com): Thank you for your contribution of photographs and your overall support of the project.

George Hedemann: Thanks for your contribution of the great Hawaiian bottle photos, providing the detailed background Hawaiian history and pricing information, and your friendship. Aloha.

Fred Holabird: Thanks for your great friendship and never ending help with understanding the "Bottles of Nevada," and your continued support of the book.

David Graci: Thanks for your contribution of photographs and background information on soda and beer bottle closures.

International Association of Jim Beam Bottle & Specialties Club: Thanks for your contribution of photographs and background information on Jim Beam bottles.

Bob Kay: Thanks for your contribution of pricing inputs on miniature bottles and your support of the project.

Ray Klingensmith (Glass Discoveries Auction; www.glassdiscoveries.com; ray@poletop.com): Thanks for your contribution of historical bottle background information and your overall support of the project.

Eva LaRue (Curator, Central Nevada Historical Museum, Tonapah, Nevada): Thank you for all your help, support, historical input, and overall contribution toward the writing of the chapter on the Central Nevada Historical Museum.

Ken Leach (Auctions Director, International Perfume Bottle Association; www.perfumebottlesauction.com; ken@perfumebottlesauction.com): Thank you for your contribution of photographs of perfume bottles and your overall support of the project.

Gary and Vickie Lewis: Thanks for your contribution of photographs of ACL soda bottles and your overall support of the project.

John Loose: Thanks for your contribution of the photos for use in the "Digging for Bottles" chapter and the story of Charlie Cook and Terry Guidroz.

Gary Moeller (Director, National Bottle Museum): Thanks for all of your help, support, contributions and photographs toward the overall hobby of bottle collecting and your valuable input on the history of mineral and soda water bottle manufacturers.

Dan Morphy (president and founder, Morphy Auctions, www.morphyauctions.com): Thanks for your contribution of photographs and background description and pricing information, and support of the overall project.

Jacque Pace Polak: A special thank you to my wife for her continued patience and valuable moral support.

Steve Ritter (Steve Ritter Auctioneering; www.ritterauction.com; ritterauction@earthlink.net): Thanks for your help in obtaining the ACL soda bottle photographs and your help with pricing.

Jan Rutland, Director, National Bottle Museum: Thanks for all your help, support, and contributions to the overall hobby of bottle collecting and your valuable input on the history of mineral and soda water bottle manufacturers. (Note: Jan passed away on Oct. 26, 2010.)

Bob Snyder: Thanks for all of your help and support with the photos and information for the miniature bottles chapter.

David Spaid: Thanks for your help with understanding the world of miniature bottles and your support of the project.

Rick Sweeney: Thanks for your help and understanding with the pricing inputs and photographs for the "Soda: Applied Color Label" chapter.

Jennifer Tai: Thanks for helping your dad take photos and for your moral support for the entire book project.

Glenn Takase: Thanks for your contribution of the great Hawaiian bottle photos, providing the detailed background Hawaiian history and pricing information, your friendship, and making me walk the plank regarding the "Hana Ice" soda bottle. Aloha.

Kim Thompson (Public Relations Specialist, The Corning Museum of Glass): A super big thank you for all of your assistance with museum photos, history, and background information for the chapter featuring The Corning Museum of Glass, and your overall support of the project.

John Tutton: Thank you for your contribution of photographs of milk bottles and your overall support of the project.

Judy Voss, Vice President/Matthew Parise, Graphics Design (Rock Island Auction Company (www.rockislandauction.com; info@rockislandauction.com): Thank you for your contribution of photographs from the Richard Ellis Collection of Anna Pottery and pottery examples, as well as your overall support of the project.

Violin Bottle Collectors Association and members: Thanks for all of your help with the contribution of photographs and an overall understanding of violin bottles. A special thank you to Bob Linden, Frank Bartlett, Samia Koudsi, and Bob Moore for their time and effort providing photographs, pricing data, and resource information.

Vicki and Bruce Waasdorp (American Pottery Auctions, www.antiques-stoneware.com; waasdorp@antiques-stoneware.com): Thank you for your contribution of photographs of crocks and stoneware, and your overall support of the project.

Rick Weiner: Thanks for your contribution and use of detailed information from your bottle digging story "The Crescent City Connection" dated August 2014, for inclusion in the "Digging for Bottles" chapter.

Jeff Wichman (American Bottle Auctions, www.americanbottle.com; info@americanbottle.com): Thank you for your contribution to the 8th edition cover photographs, your great assortment of bottle photographs for the various book chapters, the detailed background and pricing information, and your overall support of the book.

Contents

Introduction

Old (Pre-1900)

New (Post-1900)

Reference

About the Cover

With the development of every new edition, a huge part of the fun is working on the new cover and trying to decide what types of bottles and colors will make the cut. If I had it my way, there would probably be at least 100 covers since I like all the bottles and their bright and brilliant colors. As always, we wanted the bottles and their colors to jump off the page, and continue to get the collector excited and ignite their passions for antique bottle collecting.

For the 8th edition of *Antique Trader Bottles: Identification & Price Guide*, that's exactly what we've done by featuring a great grouping of rare and unique historical bottles. And as with all of the other editions, we always work with a different auction company. For the 8th edition grouping of photos, Jeff Wichman of American Bottle Auctions and the entire staff went the extra mile and provided a great selection of photos.

Moving from left to right on the cover, the first bottle is a brilliant yellow straw amber, "Mrs. S. A. Allen – World's Hair Restorer – New York," circa 1865-1875, valued at approximately $900-$1,000; the second bottle is a dark "old" amber, "Dr. Wonser's – U.S.A. – Indian Root Bitters," circa 1871-1873, valued at approximately $11,000 to $12,000; the third bottle is a brilliant emerald green, "Major Ringold – Rough and Ready," circa 1825-1835, valued at approximately $13,000-$14,000; the fourth bottle is a deep cherry puce, pattern-molded pocket flask, circa 1820-1835, valued at approximately $500-$600; the fifth bottle behind the flask is a medium amber, "WM. H. Spear & Co, – Old Pioneer Whiskey – Fenkhausen & Braunscheweiger – Sole Agents, S.F.," circa 1878-1882, value at approximately $1,000-$1,200; and the sixth bottle is a deep cobalt blue, "E.C. & M Insulator," valued at $2,000-$2,200.

Following the completion of American Bottle Auction No. 61 on April 27, 2015, Jeff Wichman summarized the overall auction and his thoughts about the hobby:

"From all accounts, the bottle market is still filled with good-natured laughter and effervescent moods, depending on condition. At what point it goes from

Introduction

rollicking fun to serious business, we may never be able to tell. We can't have an auction without the collector base that's out there today. Veteran collectors as well as the eager and ready-to-learn new faces are in full force throughout the country. We see so many new and younger people getting interested in the bottle collecting hobby, is it a sign of things to come? Sons and daughters of collectors, friends of collectors, and people who see what we all see in the glass and in the people that collect it. There are so many websites and books new and old that collectors can spend their days and nights checking it out. The hobby is a big deal now, with more core collectors than ever before. As digging becomes a lost art, we now have all the chips on the table. There is no buying new chips from the bank, what we have now is going to have to last forever," Jeff said.

"Sure, there'll be new bottles dug and boxes and collections uncovered, but I think we can safely say that the rarity of certain bottles will stay pretty constant from here on out. That is probably a good thing, in the art world and other places of 'collecting things,' inventory is pretty finite. We know how many Van Goghs and Renoirs there are. We know which stamps were made and where and how many Flintstones lunch boxes there probably are. With bottles now, it seems like we are closing in on the variants, rarity, and established collections around the country. It brings a little pause to the hobby, but there will always be a new find or bottle for sale," he said.

As I have pointed out elsewhere in the book, interest in bottle collecting, and high interest in extremely rare and scarce bottles, continues to grow and draw the attention of many antiques collectors throughout the United States and Europe. Enjoy the 8th edition of the "Bottle Bible," and always have fun with the hobby of antique bottle collecting.

— *Mike Polak*

Introduction

Welcome again to the fun hobby of antique bottle collecting with the new 8th edition of *Antique Trader Bottles: Identification and Price Guide*. Once again, I need to say **thank you** to all of my readers for your support in making the 7th edition a huge success. With the publication of each edition, the positive and valuable input and helpful comments from bottle collectors, clubs, and dealers across the United States, Europe, and Asia-Pacific continues to be overwhelming. I have enjoyed writing and updating the 8th edition as much as the first seven editions, incorporating all of the positive feedback, and living up to the nickname the "Bottle Bible" given the book by collectors, clubs, and dealers.

In order to continue making this book the most informative reference and pricing guide available, and to provide the beginner and veteran collector with a broad range of detailed pricing information and reference data, major updates and additions are included in this edition. The 8th edition also introduces a special new chapter on one of the fastest growing segments of bottle collecting, pot lids.

This edition also includes extensive updates and revisions to essentials of the hobby, such as the history and origin of glass and bottles, how to start a collection, basic bottle facts, bottle sources, bottle handling techniques, and one of my favorites, digging for bottles, which features the digging adventures of Charlie Cook and Terry Guidroz and their crew from New Orleans. In addition to a number of valuable illustrations, this edition also features hundreds of color photographs throughout the book. The 8th edition also provides complete pricing updates and revisions for both the old bottles (pre-1900) and new bottles (post-1900) sections. To help you better understand the details of how to price and evaluate a bottle, the chapter titled "Determining Bottle Values" has also been updated and expanded, along with the reference and research sections on trademarks, bibliography, and the glossary of common terminology.

Interest in bottle collecting continues to grow, and more collectors are spending their free time digging through old dumps and foraging through

Introduction

ghost towns, digging out old outhouses (that's right), exploring abandoned mine shafts, and searching their favorite bottles or antiques shows, swap meets, flea markets, and garage sales. In addition, the Internet has greatly expanded, offering collectors numerous opportunities and resources to buy and sell bottles with many new auction websites, without even leaving the house. Many bottle clubs now have websites providing even more information for the collector. These new technologies and resources have helped bottle collecting to continue to grow and gain interest.

Most collectors, however, still look beyond the type and value of a bottle to its origin and history. I find that researching the history of a bottle is almost as interesting as finding the bottle itself. I enjoy both pursuits for their close ties to the rich history of the settling of the United States and the early methods of merchandising.

My goal has always been to enhance the hobby of bottle collecting for both beginning and expert collectors, to help you experience the excitement of antique bottle collecting, especially the thrill of making that special find. I hope the 8th edition continues to bring you an increased understanding and enjoyment of the hobby.

If you would like to provide additional information or input regarding the 8th edition, to order books, or just talk bottles, contact me by e-mail at bottleking@ earthlink.net or through my website, www.bottlebible.com. Good bottle hunting and have fun.

How to Use This Book

The 8th edition of *Antique Trader Bottles: Identification & Price Guide* is formatted to assist all collectors, from the novice to the seasoned veteran. The table of contents clearly indicates those chapters that the experienced collector may want to skip, such as "The Beginning Collector." Other introductory sections, including "Bottles: History & Origin," "Bottle Facts," "Bottle Sources," "Bottle Handling," and a new chapter on pot lids, will contribute valuable information and resource materials to even an expert's store of knowledge about bottles and collecting.

The pricing information has been divided into two sections. The first section, "Old Bottles (Pre-1900)," beginning on P. 78, covers older collectibles, those manufactured almost exclusively before 1900, categorized by physical type and the bottle's original contents. Trade names, where applicable, are listed alphabetically within these sections. In some categories, such as flasks, trade names were not embossed on the bottles, so pieces are listed by embossing or other identification that appears on the bottle. Descriptive terms used to identify these pieces are explained in the introductory sections and are also listed in the glossary at the end of the book.

The second pricing section, "New Bottles (Post-1900)," beginning on P. 418, is a guide to pieces produced after the turn of the century, broken down by manufacturer, such as Avon bottles, Jim Beam bottles, applied painted soda label (ACL) bottles, and miniature bottles.

Since it is difficult to list prices for every bottle, I've produced a detailed cross-section of bottles in various price ranges with dollar amounts for each listing, indicating the value of that particular piece. Similar but not identical bottles could be more or less valuable than those mentioned. These listings will provide a good starting point for pricing pieces in your collection or for those you are considering to add.

The reference section at the back of the book, which has been updated, includes trademark identification, auction companies, glossary, bibliography, and museum and research resources, and will provide additional assistance to all collectors.

Bottle Collecting News

Since the 7th edition was published, there continues to be non-stop exciting action and major events happening in the world of antique bottle collecting. In addition to numerous bottle auctions, along with 15 to 20 antique bottle shows held each month by bottle clubs across the United States, England, Australia, and Europe, there have been major archeological finds, shipwreck discoveries in the Gulf of Mexico and the Baltic Sea, bottles found in attics, and of course many great bottle digs across the country.

All of this good news demonstrates that the hobby is not only strong, but continues to gain popularity while bringing an overall greater awareness to a wider spectrum of antiques collectors. While attending shows and talking with collectors and dealers from across the country, the consensus is that the hobby is doing well and growing stronger. During these shows, there were large crowds of collectors with dealers from all over the United States and foreign countries experiencing brisk sales, trading, and swapping digging stories.

Recent auctions have continued to excite and provide collectors with a varied selection of bottles from every category to fit anyone's budget. It's important to remember that a $50 or $100 bottle can be as valuable to one collector as a $30,000 or $50,000 bottle may be to another.

As always, Norm Heckler Auctions, Woodstock Valley, Connecticut, continues to tantalize collectors with rare, scarce, quality historical bottles. Between January 2015 and October 2015, Norm Heckler conducted five auctions that produced astonishing results for sales of these bottles in all categories.

Auction No. 119, Jan. 28, 2015

- A bright medium amethyst "Eagle-Grapes Historical Flask," GII-55, quart, with a sheared top and pontiled scarred base, possibly from Coffin & Hay Manufactory, Winslow, New Jersey (1836-1847), sold for $3,218. This particular flask had a strong mold impression and a rare and unique color.

Auction No. 120, March 18, 2015

- An early, rare medium yellow amber with olive tone, 8-7/8-inch "G.W. Stone's Liquid – Cathartic & Family Physic – Lowell Mass" medicine bottle with an applied double collared top, smooth base, rectangular shape with beveled corners, and three embossed indented panels, Stoddard Glasshouse, New Hampshire (1860-1870), sold for $18,720. Rare with whittled and crude glass.

- An extremely rare and historically important deep emerald green, 5-5/8-inch "North Bend" – "Tippecanoe" Historical Cabin Bottle," GVII-1, log cabin form, pontiled scarred base, applied round collared top, long stovepipe neck (which is unique for this cabin), Mount Vernon Glass Works, Vernon, New York (1840), sold for $25,740.

Auction No. 122, May 27, 2015

- A rare medium blue green "Geo Eagle" soda water bottle, 6-7/8-inch cylindrical shape with diagonal rib pattern, applied sloping collared top, iron pontil mark, with a sheared top and pontiled scarred base (1845-1860), sold for $3,218.

Auction No. 125 – July 22, 2015

- A scarce medium red amber "Eagle-Willington Glass Co." historical flask, GII-64, pint, applied double collared top, smooth base, Willington Glass Works, West Willington, Connecticut (1860-1872), sold for $5,850.

Jeff Wichmann and his crew at American Bottle Auctions, Sacramento, California, were making some noise of their own with sales of bitters, sarsaparillas, and western whiskeys.

Auction No. 61, April 26, 2015

- A rare olive yellow amber "Thos. Taylor & Co. Importers Viginia. N." Western whiskey, 11-3/4-inches, applied drippy top (1874-1880), sold for $10,500. This is a great example of the only known San Francisco-made whiskey bottle for a Nevada business.
- A medium cobalt blue "Dr. Wynkoop's Katharismic Honduras Sarsaparilla New York" medicine, 10 inches, with an applied top and open pontil (1840-1860), sold for $8,500.
- A medium amber with an olive tone "Dr. Wonser's USA Indian Root Bitters," 11 inches, with applied top and smooth base (1871-1873), sold for $13,500. A popular western bitters.
- A medium green "Alex Von Humboldt's Stomach Bitters," 11" inches, with applied tapered collar top, smooth base (1868-1871), sold for $8,000. This bitters bottle is considered one of the rarest western "square"-shaped bitters and is the only true green example known.

Introduction

Jim Hagenbuch and his crew at Glass Works Auction, East Greenville, Pennsylvania, have been busy enticing bottle collectors with a selection of flasks, bitters, and medicine bottles:

Auction No. 106, March 23, 2015

- A rare yellowish "old" amber "New Granite Glass Works – Stoddard – N.H. – American Flag" flask, pint, GX-27, sheared and tooled top, open pontil, New Granite Glass Works, Stoddard, New Hampshire (1860-1855), sold for $21,500.
- A rare dark reddish amber "American Life Bitters – P.E. ILER – Manufacturer/Omaha, NEB – American Life Bitters," cabin shape, 9-1/8" inches, smooth base, applied tapered collar top (1865-1875), sold for $14,000.
- A medium blue green "DWD – E. Dexter Loveridge – Wahoo Bitters" PATD (motif of eagle with arrow) – "DWD" –E – Dexter Loveridge – Wahoo Bitters – 1863," 10-1/8 inches, smooth base, applied ring top (1863-1870), sold for $20,000.

Auction No. 107 – July 13, 2015

- An extremely rare deep emerald green "Scott & Stewart – United States Syrup – New York" medicine, 9-1/2" inches, iron pontil, applied tapered collar top (1845-1860) sold for an astonishing $27,000.

I think it's safe to assume that everyone's heard of Wyatt Earp and his brothers Virgil and Morgan of Tombstone, Arizona, who, along with Doc Holiday, shot it out with Tom and Frank McLaury and Billy Clanton, killing all three at the OK Corral on Oct. 26, 1881. From May 4 to June 10, 2013, with digging resuming in 2014, there was a lot of action happening again because of Wyatt Earp, and the good news is no one was shot.

A great digging adventure at Wyatt Earp's Northern Saloon in Tonopah, Nevada, had amazing results and brought increased attention and excitement to both bottle collectors and Western history enthusiasts. When all the dust literally settled, there was a total of 618 bottles found, including two rare ones: an aqua "Tonopah Soda Works – Tonopah, Nevada" valued at $1,500-$2,000; and a clear "Washington Bar – Coleman and Granger" whiskey flask valued at $2,000-$2,500. There were also numerous coins, tokens, marbles, poker chips, and glass stoppers found.

There was also plenty of pottery and stoneware buzz happening at the Red Wing Collectors Society Convention Auction on July 11, 2013 in Red Wing, Minnesota. One of the top highlights was an eight-gallon Red Wing pantry jar, which is difficult to find, that sold for $4,200. Other special items included a two-gallon elephant ear ice water cooler for $2,100, a

Red Wing Gray Line cake stand for $1,300, and a 20-gallon butterfly crock backstamped "Red Wing Stoneware Company" in mint condition for $1,050.

The International Perfume Bottle Association kept the action rolling at its 26th annual convention and auction from May 1-4, 2014, in Pittsburgh, Pennsylvania, and the 27th convention and auction from April 30-May 30, 2015, in Spartanburg, South Carolina. The 26th annual auction offered 301 lots of vintage perfume bottles and vanity items that resulted in some impressive sales. The highlights included an extremely rare 1922 Rosine bottle, *Antinea ou au Fond de la Mer* (Bottle of the Sea) that sold for $18,000, a 1920s sapphire blue Czechoslovakian perfume bottle with an Egyptian theme that sold for $12,000, and a rare DeVilbiss bottle that sold for $9,600. But the star of the auction was a boxed 1917 Egyptian-style Baccarat perfume bottle complete with cover and inner stopper, "Toute l'Egypt" for Monne, selling for an astonishing $38,400.

Not to be outdone, the 27th annual convention auction offered 302 lots of a quality selection of bottles and other objects by notable designers and glassmakers and broke all previous records, with a total of $533,724. Highlights included a rare Julian Viard bottle for Colmy's "C'est Un Secret" for $19,000; an Australian scent brooch of 18k gold set with rubies, emeralds, and sapphires for $10,800; the first completed bottle that Rene Lalique designed for a perfumer, the 1909 "Cyclamen" for Coty, for $19,200; and the star of the evening, a rare 16-inch Christian Dior Silk Doghouse with a figural bottle designed in 1956 marking the 10th anniversary of the House of Dior for an astounding $67,000. The 28th annual convention is scheduled for April 27-May 5, 2016 at the Marriott in Portland, Oregon.

The Federation of Historical Bottle Collectors, in conjunction with various bottle clubs, sponsors a yearly two-day National Antique Bottle Show, with an average of 300 sales tables, educational displays, educational seminars and programs, and a banquet. Since the 7th edition of this book, there have been three additional shows: The Manchester, New Hampshire, Show & Auction in July 2013, the Lexington, Kentucky, Show & Auction in August 2014, and the Chattanooga, Tennessee, Show & Sale in July 2015. The next Federation national show will be Aug. 4 -7, 2016 in Sacramento, California, at the McClellan Conference Center, with the Lions Gate Hotel as the event host. If you are interested in obtaining additional information, contact Richard Siri, show chairman, as rtsiri@sbglobal.net.

The Corning Museum of Glass also had the largest exhibition to date between May 16, 2015 through January 4, 2016. Devoted to ancient mold-blown glass, this exhibition featured examples from the early first century to the 7th century A.D. More than 120 works of glass, including the museum's collection of ancient glass, along with loans from the Metropolitan

Introduction

Museum of Art and other international public and private collections, demonstrated the relationship between mold-blown glass vessels and their counterparts in ceramic and metal, which had to be shaped in molds for centuries. The Corning Glass Museum is located in the Finger Lakes Wine Country of New York and is open daily. For more information on this historic exhibition and the museum in general, visit www.cmog.org.

In downtown Los Angeles, the 32-acre Los Angeles State Historic Park is currently undergoing a year-long renovation that will reshape the entire landscape and provide a visitor's center, restrooms, and restored wetlands. During renovation work in October 2014, the construction crews, working with an archeologist, uncovered the last remnants of a historic building, several trash pits, and a 19th century utility system. The remnants are from the park when it was a Southern Pacific Railroad station and yard, which opened in 1875. The trash pits contained decorative glass inkwells, vintage bottles, fragments of old tools, buttons, and a variety of shattered china. It's thought the refuse was most likely dumped into the pits from shops and restaurants and the 1879 Pacific Hotel, which served train passengers.

Would you like a little shot of centuries-old seltzer water to spruce up your drink? In August 2014, while divers were conducting an ongoing salvage operation of a cargo ship believed to have sunk between 1800 and 1830 in Gdansk Bay, at the bottom of the Baltic Sea close to the Polish coast, a 200-year-old stoneware seltzer bottle was recovered intact with the alcohol contents. According to Tomasz Bednarz, an underwater archaeologist from the National Maritime Museum leading the research on the shipwreck, the bottle dates back to 1806-1830. It is embossed with "Selters," the name of a supplier of high-quality carbonated water from the Taunua Mountains area in Germany, and was manufactured in Ranschbach, Germany, located 25 miles from the springs of Selters water. Preliminary laboratory tests have shown that the bottle contains a 14% alcohol distillate, which may be vodka or a type of gin called Jenever, most likely diluted with water. You never know what delectable delights will be given up by old shipwrecks.

Since we're on the subject of bottles found in waterways, here are a couple of fishing stories that just happen to be true. Have you ever found a beer bottle more than 100 years old while fresh-water fishing? It's never happened to me, but it did happen to Steve Kay of West Bloomfield, Michigan, while taking his four-year-old twin boys fishing at Walnut Lake. As Steve was getting ready to throw out his line, he spotted an amber-colored bottle floating in the lake. As he scooped up the bottle to put it in the trash, he noticed that it was heavily embossed with "Detroit Brewing Company," "Registered," and two marks on the base of the bottle embossed "SB & C CO." After Steve made a few phone calls and searched the Internet, he found out that the bottle is 121 years old and was made in 1893 by the Steagal Bottle & Glass Co. of Chicago.

The second fishing adventure happened in April 2014. While a fisherman was trying his luck in the Baltic Sea near the city of Kiel, Germany, he pulled out a brown beer bottle that contained a postcard with a message asking the finder to return the postcard to the bottle owner in Berlin. That was difficult to do, since the International Maritime Museum traced the bottle to a then 20-year-old named Richard Platz, who threw it into the water in 1913. According to the *Guinness Book of World Records*, the previous record for a bottle with a message was dated 1914 and had been in the water for nearly 98 years.

Here's a recent event that was set in motion in 1864, when the iron-hulled sidewheel steamship *Mary-Celestia* was leaving Bermuda with supplies for the Confederate states. As the ship was leaving port, it struck a reef and sank within six minutes, with there being some conjecture that the ship was blown up by the Union. In 2011, Philippe Rouja and his brother Jean-Pierre were diving around the shipwreck and found a sealed bottle of wine in a locker in the bow. They later found additional wine bottles as well as two sealed bottles of perfume embossed with Piesse and Lubin–London, women's shoes, hairbrushes, and pearl shell buttons. The bottle was uncorked and tested on March 6, 2015, and tasted by sommeliers at a wine and food event, "From Deep Below: A Wine Event 150 Years in the Making," in Charleston, South Carolina. The verdict? Wine chemist Pierre Louis Teissedre said, "The sample smelled like camphor, stagnant water, hydrocarbons, turpentine, and sulphur," with an analysis reflecting 37% alcohol. Some of the other tasters said, "It smelled and tasted like crab water, gasoline, salt water, vinegar, and hints of citrus and alcohol."

Regarding the perfume bottles, Piesse and Lubin was a popular London perfume establishment during the 19th century. Now Drom Fragrances is trying to re-create history and reproduce the scent in its New Jersey laboratory. During this process, the liquid from the two bottles was analyzed by gas chromatography. The two bottles were identical, meaning they were extremely well preserved while being buried beneath the sea for 150 years.

Although these wine and perfume bottles were manufactured prior to the Civil War, they have significant historical value related to the war based on the where they were found and the circumstances surrounding the sinking of the ship. You never know where good bottles will surface, and when the drinking will begin, literally.

As all of the recent discoveries show, the hobby is strong, with an increasing interest and excitement by collectors, and everyone is having fun with antique bottle collecting.

Bottles: History & Origin

Glass bottles are not as new as some people believe. In fact, the glass bottle has been around for about 3,000 years. During the second century B.C., Roman glass was free-blown with metal blowpipes and shaped with tongs that were used to change the shape of the bottle or vessel. The finished item was then decorated with enameling and engraving. The Romans even get credit for originating what we think of today as the basic "store bottle" and early merchandising techniques.

In the late first century B.C., the Romans, with the assistance of glassworker craftsmen from Syria and Egypt, began making glass vials that local doctors and pharmacists used to dispense pills, healing powders, and miscellaneous potions. The vials were three to four inches long and very narrow. The majority of early bottles made after the Romans were sealed with a cork or a glass stopper, whereas Romans used a small stone rolled in tar as a stopper. The finished vials contained many impurities such as sand particles and bubbles because of the crude manufacturing process. The thickness of the glass and the crude finish, however, made Roman glass very resilient compared to glass of later times, which accounts for the survival and good preservation of some Roman bottles as old as 2,500 years. The Roman glass techniques and manufacturing methods eventually influenced all of the European art and industrial complexes.

While a second unsuccessful pattern was made in 1621, the first attempt to manufacture glass in America is thought to have taken place at the Jamestown settlement in Virginia around 1608 by the London Company. It is interesting to note that the majority of glass produced in Jamestown was earmarked for shipment back to England (due to its lack of resources) and not for the new settlements. As it turned out, the Jamestown glass house enterprise ended up a failure almost before it got started. The poor quality of glass produced and the small quantity simply couldn't support England's needs.

The first successful American glasshouse was opened in 1739 in New Jersey by Caspar Wistar, a brass button manufacturer who immigrated from Germany to Philadelphia in 1717. During a trip to Salem County, New Jersey, Wistar noticed the abundance of white sand along with a proximity to clay, wood, and water transportation. He soon bought 2,000 acres of the heavily wooded land and made arrangements for experienced glass workers to come from Europe; the factory was completed in the fall of 1739.

Roman bottles, jars, and glass objects, 1st-3rd centuries A.D.,
found in the baths and necropolises of Cimiez Nice, France.

Since English law did not permit the colonists to manufacture anything in competition with England, Wistar kept a low profile. In fact, most of what was written during the factory's operation implied that it was less than successful. Caspar Wistar died in 1752 a very wealthy man and left the factory to his son, Richard. The Wistar glass operation, however, closed in 1779 as a result of lost markets, a result of the Revolutionary War.

Henry Stiegel started the next major glasshouse operation in Manheim, Pennsylvania, between 1763 and 1774, and eventually went on to establish several more. The Pitkin Glass Works was opened in East Hartford, Connecticut, around 1783 and was the first American glasshouse to provide figured flasks and also the most successful of its time until it closed around 1830 due to the high cost of wood for fuel. By 1850, there were approximately 40 glass manufacturing factories in New York alone, producing millions of bottles and jars.

To understand the early successes and far more numerous failures of early glasshouses it is essential that the reader get an overview of the challenges that glass workers faced in acquiring raw materials and constructing the glasshouse. The glass

Introduction

factory of the 19th century was usually built near abundant sources of sand, wood, or coal and close to roads, rivers, and other waterways for transportation of raw materials and finished products to the major East Coast markets of Boston, New York, and Philadelphia. Finding a suitable location was usually not a problem, but once production was underway resources quickly diminished.

The majority of furnaces burned wood until the middle of the 19th century. The first American glasshouse to use soft coal was built by Isaac Craig and James O'Hara in Pittsburgh in 1776-1797. Bituminous coal became available after 1810, and during the 1850s anthracite was used. By 1860 only one furnace in New England continued to burn wood, and by 1880 the fuel used in glassmaking in the United States was mainly coal. The next major problem was constructing the glasshouse building, a large wooden structure housing a primitive furnace that was about nine feet in diameter and shaped like a beehive.

A major financial drain on the glass companies – and one of the causes of so many business failures – was the large melting pots inside the furnace that held the molten glass. The melting pot, which cost about $100 and took eight months to build, was formed by hand from a long coil of clay and was the only substance known that would not melt when the glass was heated to 2,700 degrees F. The pots lasted about eight weeks, as exposure to high temperature over a long period of time caused the clay itself to turn to glass. The cost of regularly replacing melting pots proved to be the downfall of many an early glass factory.

Throughout the 19th century, glasshouses opened and closed because of changes in demand and technological improvements. Between 1840 and 1890, an enormous demand for glass containers developed to satisfy the demands of the whiskey, beer, medical, and food-packing industries. Largely due to this steady demand, glass manufacturing in the United States evolved into a stable industry. Western expansion and the great gold and silver rush between 1850 and 1860 contributed a great deal to this increase in demand.

While the East Coast glasshouses had been in production since 1739, the West didn't begin its entry into glass manufacturing until 1858 when Baker & Cutting started the first glasshouse in San Francisco. Until then the West depended on glass bottles from the East. The glass manufactured by Baker & Cutting, however, was considered to be poor quality, and production was eventually discontinued.

In 1862, Carlton Newman and Patrick Brennan founded Pacific Glass Works in San

Roman Unguentaria bottle,
1st-3rd centuries, A.D.

Elegant Roman vase in different color of
iridescence, 3rd-4th centuries, A.D.

Late Roman Empire mold blown flask,
4th-5th centuries, A.D.

Roman Unguentaria bottle,
1st-2nd centuries, A.D.

Introduction

Francisco. In 1876, San Francisco Glass Works bought Pacific Glass Works and renamed the company San Francisco and Pacific Glass Works (SFPGW). Today these early bottles manufactured in San Francisco are the most desired by Western collectors.

Unlike other businesses of the time that saw major changes in manufacturing processes, producing glass bottles remained unchanged. The process gave each bottle character, producing unique shapes, imperfections, irregularities, and various colors.

That all changed at the turn of the century when Michael J. Owens invented the first fully automated bottle making machine. Although many fine bottles were manufactured between 1900-1930, Owens' invention ended an era of unique bottle design that no machine process could ever duplicate.

To better understand the history and origin of antique bottles, it is important to take a look at the development of the manufacturing process.

Free Blown Bottles: B.C.-1860 (Figure 1)

Around the 1st century B.C., the blowpipe, a long hollow metal rod, was invented. The tip was dipped into molten glass and the glass blower blew into the rod to form the molten glass into the desired form, bowls, and other glass containers.

Pontil Marks: 1618-1866

Once the bottle was blown, it was removed from the rod through the use of a three-foot metal pontil rod that was dipped into the tank of molten glass and applied to the bottom of the bottle. The neck of the bottle was then touched with a wet rod to break it from the blowpipe. There are four general types of pontil marks:

- **Glass Tipped or Open Pontil** – This type of pontil mark was left by the use of a solid iron bar as the pontil rod, leaving a jagged broken glass circular scar on the bottom of the bottle.
- **Blowpipe or Ring Pontil** – This mark was created similarly to the glass-tipped pontil. It was thought to be less expensive to just use another blowpipe as the pontil.
- **Sand Pontil** – This mark was created when the glass blower dipped the glass-tipped pontil in sand before attaching to the bottom of the bottle. This was done to keep the pontil rod from sticking to the bottle and making removal easier.
- **Bare Iron Pontil** – One of the most sought bottles has the "iron" pontil mark. The residual red, reddish-black, gray, or black deposits are iron, usually oxidized iron, commonly know as "rust."

FIGURE 1—Free-Blown Bottles: B.C.-1860

1 The blowpipe was inserted into the pot of hot "metal" (liquid glass) and twisted to gather the requisite amount onto the end of the pipe.

2 The blowpipe was then rolled slowly on a metal table to allow the red-hot glass to cool slightly on the outside and to sag.

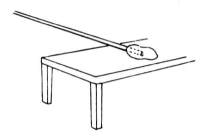

3 The blower then blew into the pipe to form an internal central bubble.

4 The glass was further expanded and sometimes turned in a wooden block that had been dipped in cold water to prevent charring, or possibly rolled again on the metal table.

5 The body and neck were then formed by flattening the bottom of the bottle with a wooden paddle called a battledore, named after the glassblower who developed the technique.

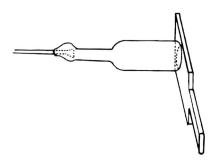

6 One of the irons (called a pontil) was attached to the bottom of the bottle for easy handling during the finishing of the bottle neck and lip. A "kick-up" could be formed in the bottom of the bottle by pushing inward when attaching the iron.

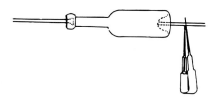

7 The bottle was whetted, or cracked off the blowpipe, by touching the hot glass at the end of the pipe with a tool dipped in cold water.

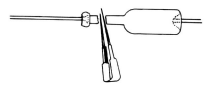

8 With the bottle held on a pontil, the blower reheated the neck to polish the lip and further smoothed it by tooling. Bottles were created with a variety of applied and tooled ring and collar tops.

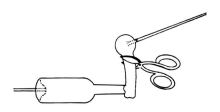

Snap Cases: 1860-1903 (Figure 2)

Between 1850 and 1860, the snap case was developed to replace the pontil rod. This represented the first major invention for bottle making since the blowpipe. The snap case was a five-foot metal rod that had claws to grasp the bottle. A snap locked the claw into place in order to hold the bottle more securely while the neck was being finished. Each snap case was tailor-made to fit bottles of a certain size and shape. These bottles have no pontil scars or marks, which left the bases of the bottle free for lettering or design. There may, however, be some minor grip marks on the side as a result of the claw device.

The snap case instrument was used for small mouth bottle production until the automatic bottle machine came into existence in 1903.

FIGURE 2—Snap Cases: 1860-1903

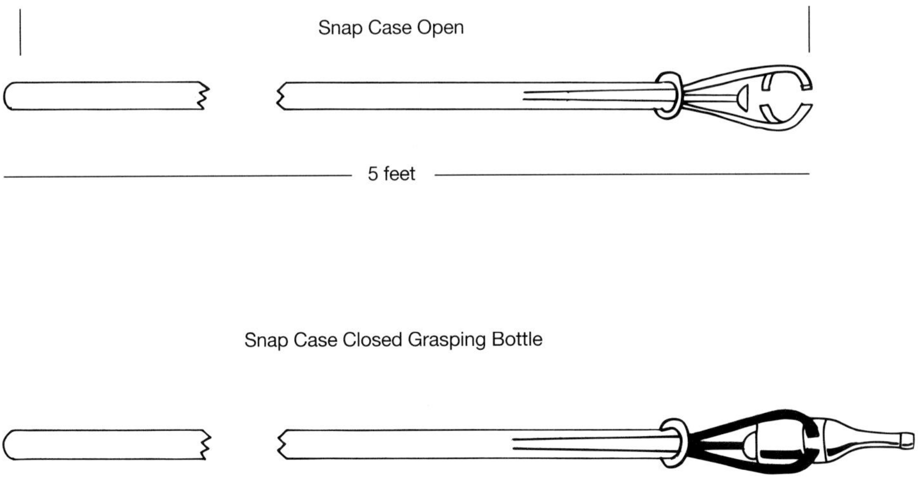

Snap Case Open

5 feet

Snap Case Closed Grasping Bottle

Molded Bottles: B.C.-1900 (Figure 3)

The use of molds in bottle making, which really took hold in the early 1800s, actually dates back to the 1st century with the Romans. As detailed earlier in the free-blown process, the glass blower shaped the bottle, or vessel, by blowing and turning it in the air. When using a mold, the glass blower would then take a few puffs while lowering the red-hot shaped mass into the hollow mold. The blower continued blowing air into the tube

FIGURE 3—Molds: First century B.C., 1900

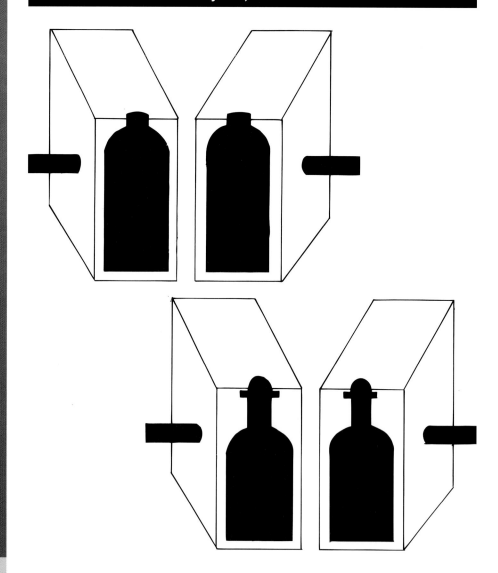

until the glass compressed itself against the sides of the mold to acquire the finished shape. Most of these bottle molds were made of clay or wood, and formed only the base and body of the container. The neck had to be drawn out utilizing the skill of the glassblower.

Molds were usually made in two or more sections to enable the mold to come apart. The hardened bottle was then easily removed. Since it was impossible to create perfectly fitted molds, the seams showed on the surface of the finished article, providing a clue as to the manufacturing methods used in the production of the bottle. Molds were categorized as "open," in which only the body of the bottle was forced, with the neck and lip being added later, or "closed," in which the neck and lip were part of the original mold (Figure 3). The average life for a wooden mold was between 100 to 1,000 castings, depending of the thickness of the glass blown into them. The most common mold in use after 1860 was the cast iron mold, which proved to be the best and more economical way to manufacture cheap bottles.

By 1900, a number of improvements, such as tightly locking molds components, allowed for vent holes to be drilled into the mold to allow air within to escape while being replaced with hot glass. These vent holes were bored in the shoulders and bases of the mold. Then the hot glass penetrated part way into the holes, leaving a mark on the glass about the size of a pin head. These marks are very noticeable on the shoulder of quart whisky bottles of the 1900s. Often the vent mark was incorporated into the design on the bottles. Later two types of molds came into use:

(1) The three-piece mold, used between 1809 and 1880, which consisted of two main kinds: the three-piece dip mold and the full-height mold.

(2) The turn mold or paste mold, used between 1880 and 1900.

The introduction of the three-piece mold helped the bottle industry become stronger in the 19th century by increasing production to keep up with demand.

Three-Piece Molds (Figure 4)

Three-Piece Dip Mold:

The bottom section of the bottle mold was one piece, while the top, from the shoulder up, was two separate pieces. The mold seams circled the bottle at the shoulder and on each side of the neck.

FIGURE 4—Three-Piece Mold

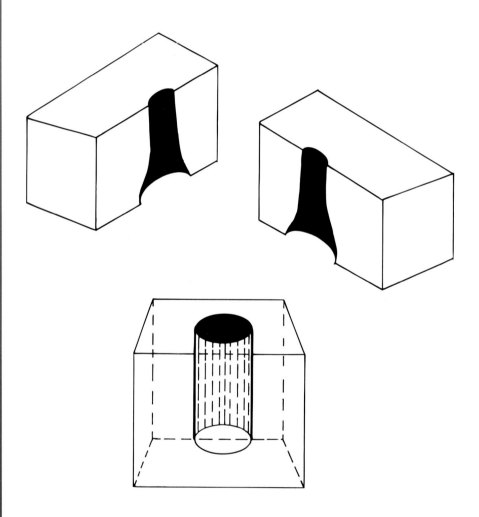

Full Height Mold:

The entire bottle was formed in the mold, forming vertical seams on both sides that ran from the bottom of the bottle to below the lip.

Full height metal mold: front view.   Full height metal mold: side view.

Full height metal bottle mold: "Quick Death – Insecticide – And Disinfectant – REG. U.S. Pat. Office – Victory – Chemical Co. – 312 No. 15th St. – Philada. Pa.," 1880-1900. Heavy hinged cylindrical metal mold with handles made to create bottles, top diameter 6" x 8-1/2", not including handles. Shown are an 1890 "Quick Death" bottle made from the mold, a bottle in the large size of the same product (this mold is in the collection of Richard Watson), a cobalt blue bottle blown recently by Frank Stebbens, and a "Dead Stuck for Bugs" bottle.

Turn Mold or Paste Mold

Wooden molds were kept wet to prevent the hot glass from igniting or charring the wood. Turning the bottle in the wet mold erased all seams and mold marks, and gave the glass a high luster. After metal molds replaced wooden molds, manufacturers used a paste inside the mold, allowing the bottle to slide easily during the turning process, which explains the origin of the terms "turn mold" and "paste mold."

Mason Jars: 1858

In 1858, John L. Mason invented the wide-mouth jar that became famous as a food preservative container. The new screw-top jar was formed in the same mold as the body. The jar was then broken from the blowpipe and sent to the annealing oven to temper the glass, making it more resistant to breakage. Then the jagged edges of the rims were ground down. Earlier jars can be distinguished from later ones by the rough and sharp edges produced by the grinding process.

Press and Blow Process: 1892

In 1892, a semi-automatic process called "press and blow" was invented to produce wide-mouth containers such as fruit jars and milk bottles. First molten glass was pressed into the mold to form the mouth and lip. Then a metal plunger was inserted through the mouth and air pressure was applied to form the body of the bottle.

Press and blow milk mold used by Thatcher milk bottles,
Lockport Glass Company, Lockport, N.Y., circa 1927.

The Automatic Bottle Making Machine: 1903

Michael J. Owens, recognized as the inventor of the first automatic bottle-making machine, started as a glass blower in 1874 at the young age of 15. Owens proved to be a capable inventor and in 1888, while working in Toledo, Ohio, for the American Lamp Chimney Company, he invented a semi-automatic machine for tumblers and lantern chimneys. Utilizing his engineering talent and his glassmaking experience, he developed his first bottle-making machine in 1899 (Figure 1). After experimenting with three machines, he perfected the process with his fourth in 1903 (Figures 2, 3, and 4). Owens continued to make additional improvements and introduced Machine No. 5 (Figure 5) in 1904. This final improvement allowed the continuous movement of the machine that eliminated the intermittent stopping of the rotation of both machine and glass tank and increased the quantity and quality of bottles. A major advantage with these new machines was that the neck and top of the bottle no longer required hand finishing.

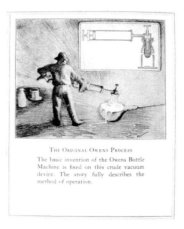

THE ORIGINAL OWENS PROCESS

The basic invention of the Owens Bottle Machine is fixed on this crude vacuum device. The story fully describes the method of operation.

1 **The Original Owens Process:** The basic invention of the Owens Bottle Machine is fixed on this crude vacuum device.

At first Owens' machine made only heavy bottles because they were in the greatest demand but, in 1909, improvements to the machine made it possible to produce small prescription bottles. Between 1909 and 1917, numerous other automatic bottle-making machines were invented, and soon all bottles were formed automatically throughout the world.

In 1904, Owens' first machine produced 13,000 bottles a day. By 1917 machine No. 5 was producing approximately 60,000 bottles a day. In 1917, the "gob feeder" was developed, which produced a measured amount of molten glass from which a bottle could be blown. In this process, a gob of glass is drawn from the tank and cut off by shears.

Early in 1910, the Owens Bottle Company installed an automatic conveyor system in its factories, eliminating the need for "carry in" boys who gathered bottles from the machine and carried them to the annealer oven.

Introduction

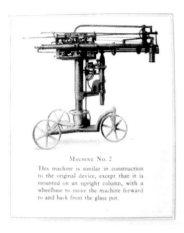

MACHINE No. 2

This machine is similar in construction to the original device, except that it is mounted on an upright column, with a wheelbase to move the machine forward to and back from the glass pot.

MACHINE No. 3

This was the first rotating machine, and was very novel in construction. It was for the requirements of this machine that the revolving glass tank was developed.

2 **Machine No. 2:** This machine is similar in construction to the original device, except that it is mounted on an upright column, with a wheelbase to move the machine forward to and back from the glass pot.

3 **Machine No. 3:** This was the first rotating machine, and was novel in construction. It was for the requirements of this machine that the revolving glass tank was developed.

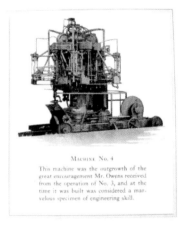

MACHINE No. 4

This machine was the outgrowth of the great encouragement Mr. Owens received from the operation of No. 3, and at the time it was built was considered a marvelous specimen of engineering skill.

MACHINE No. 5

This machine shows a great improvement over No. 4. It formed the foundation for the general type in use at the present day.

4 **Machine No. 4:** This machine was the outgrowth of the great encouragement Mr. Owens received from the operation of No. 3, and at the time it was built was considered a marvelous specimen of engineering skill.

5 **Machine No. 5:** This machine shows a great improvement over No. 4. It formed the foundation for the general type in use at the present day.

Screw-Topped Bottles

One last note about bottle making concerns the process of producing screw-topped bottles. Early glass blowers produced bottles with inside and outside screw caps long before the bottle making machines mechanized the process. Because early methods of production were so complex, screw-topped bottles produced before the 1800s were considered specialty bottles and expensive to replace. Today they are considered to be rare and collectible. In fact, the conventional screw-top bottle did not become common until after 1924 when the glass industry standardized the threads.

The Beginning Collector

Now that you have learned some things about the history, origin and the process of producing a bottle, it's time to provide information about how to approach the hobby of bottle collecting, as well as suggestions on books and reference guides, startup costs, old vs. new bottles, and information on bottle clubs and dealers.

The first thing to understand about antique bottle collecting is that there aren't set rules. Everyone's finances, spare time, storage space and preferences are different, so tailor your collecting methods to your own individual circumstances. As a collector you will need to think about whether to specialize and focus on a specific type of bottle or group of bottles, or you may want to be more of a general or maverick collector who acquires everything that becomes available.

The majority of bottle collectors I have known over the years, myself included, took the maverick approach as new collectors. We grabbed everything in sight, ending up with bottles of every type, shape and color. Now, after 40 plus years of collecting, my recommendation to newcomers is to do a small amount of maverick collecting and focus on a specific or specialized bottle or group of bottles. Taking the more general approach in the early years has given me a detailed breadth of knowledge about bottles and glass, but specializing has the following distinct advantages over the maverick approach:

- It reduces the field of collection, which will provide more time for organization, study and research.
- It allows a collector to become an authority on bottles in a particular or specific field.
- Trading becomes easier with other specialists who may have duplicate or unwanted bottles.
- By becoming more of an authority within a specialized area, the collector can negotiate a better deal by spotting bottles that are underpriced.

I need to mention, however, that the specialized collector may be tempted by bottles that don't quite fit into their collections. So they cheat a little and give into that maverick urge. This occasional cheating sometimes results in a smaller side collection or, in some cases, turns the collector away from a specialty and back to being a maverick. But that's OK. Remember, there are no set rules, with the exception of having a lot of fun.

Now what does it cost to start a collection and how can you determine the value of a bottle? Aside from digging excursions of which the cost includes travel and daily expenses, starting a collection can be accomplished by spending just a few dollars or maybe just a few cents per bottle. I find digging for bottles the ultimate way of adding to your collection and it is how I started my addiction to the hobby.

Knowing what and where to find the best deals obviously takes time and experience. But the beginner can do well with just a few pointers. Let's start with the approach of buying bottles, instead of digging for bottles, since this is a quicker method with more sources available for the new bottle collector.

Over the years, I've developed a quick-look technique for buying bottles and group my finds into one of three categories:

- **Low end or common bottles:** Bottles in this category reflect noticeable wear and the labels are usually missing or not very visible. In most cases the label is completely gone and there is no embossing or identification markings. The bottle is dirty (which can usually be cleaned) with some scrapes and is free of chips. These bottles are usually clear without any trace of color.

- **Average grade/common bottles:** Bottles of this type show some wear, and a label may be visible but usually is faded. They are generally clear or aqua in color and free of scrapes or chips. Some may have minimal embossing but not likely.

- **High-end and unique bottles:** These bottles can be empty, partially empty or full with the original stopper and label or embossing. Bottle color can be clear but usually is green, teal blue, cobalt blue, amber, yellow, yellow-green, or shades of each of these colors. The bottle will have no chips, scrapes and very little wear. If it has been stored in a box the bottle is most likely in good or excellent condition. Also, the box must be in very good condition.

Price ranges will be discussed briefly here since pricing and values are covered in detail in the "Determining Bottle Values" chapter. Usually low-end bottles can be found for $1 to $5; an average bottle will range from $5 to $20; and the high-end bottle will range from $20 to $100, although some high-end bottles can sell for $1,000 or more. Anything above $100, and most certainly any bottle above $500, should be looked at closely by someone who has been collecting for a while and is knowledgeable.

As a general rule, I try not to spend more than $2-$5 per bottle for the low-end and $5 to $10 for average bottles. It's easier to stick to this rule when you've done your homework but sometimes you just get lucky. As an example, during a number of bottle and antiques shows, I have found tables where the seller had shopping bags full of bottles for $2 a bag called "grab bags." I consider this a bargain and I can't pass up the lure of the unknown. When I examined my treasures after one show, I discovered nine bottles, some purple, all

Introduction

pre-1900 and in great shape with embossing for a total cost of 22 cents per bottle. Now what could be better than that? Well, what was better was that I found a Tonopah, Nevada, medicine bottle worth $100 at that time, now worth $225.

In the high-end category, deals are usually made after some good old horse trading and bartering. But hey, that's part of the fun. Always let the seller know that you are a new collector with a limited budget. It really helps. I have never run across a bottle seller who wouldn't work with a new collector to try to give the best deal for a limited budget.

Collectors should be aware of the characteristics of an old bottle versus a new bottle and what defines an antique bottle. Quite often, new collectors assume that any old bottle is an antique and if a bottle isn't old it is not a collectible. A collectible bottle is defined as an item that is rare or valuable, or holds a special interest to the collector, such as historical. In the world of bottle collecting that's not necessarily the case. In the antiques world, an antique is typically defined as being more than 100 years old. But quite a number of bottles listed in this book are less than 100 years old and are quite valuable. History, origin, background, use, and bottle rarity all factor into the equation.

The number and variety of old and antique bottles is greater than the new collectible items in today's market. On the other hand, the Jim Beams, Ezra Brooks, Avons, recent Coke bottles, figurals and miniature soda and liquor bottles manufactured more recently are very desirable and collectible and are, in fact, made for that purpose. If you decide you want to collect new bottles, the best time to buy is when the first issue comes out on the market. When the first issues are gone, the collector market is the only available source, which limits availability and drives the price up considerably.

An example of a company that has done this repeatedly is the Coca-Cola Company. When Coca-Cola reissued the 8-ounce junior size Coke bottle in the Los Angeles area in an attempt to garner the attention in a marketplace full of cans, the word spread fast among collectors. This 8-ounce bottle had the same contour as the 6-1/2-ounce bottle that was a Coke standard from the 1920s into the 1950s and has also been issued as a special Christmas issue every year since 1992. The 6-1/2-ounce bottle is available in a few part of the United States, most noticeably in Atlanta where Coca-Cola is headquartered. When these reissued 8-ounce bottles were issued, the "heavy duty collectors" paid in advance and picked up entire case lots from the bottling operations before they hit the retail market. A recent example occurred in December 2008 when Coca-Cola issued a replica of the 1899 Hutch Coca-Cola in a six-pack. They sold as a novelty for $3.99 and disappeared as soon as they hit the shelves. Some of the dealers are now selling them for $20 to $25.

But Coca-Cola never stops. A recent example of this is when Coca-Cola launched a new "natural" and "healthy" soda line called "Coca-Cola Life" with a 60% reduction in calories, which hit the store shelves on Jan. 1, 2015. For the final green touch, the stevia-sweetened soda is sold in Coca-Cola's "Plant Bottle," which is a fully recyclable bottle composed of 30% vegetable fiber, with green label, and still in the traditional hobble skirt design. As of this writing, the introductory price was $2.99 for a six-pack, but that won't last for long.

For the beginner collector, and even the old-timer, books, references guides, magazines, and other similar literature is readily available at libraries and book stores, and even more online. Check out the bibliography in this book to get started. Also, joining a bottle club can be of great value and will provide numerous new sources of information, as well as an occasional digging expedition.

I want to finish with a final note on reproductions and repaired bottles. Recently, the market has been flooded with reproductions, especially fruit jar bottles, from China and India. Recently, as early as 2012 and 2013, China has been producing good examples of commonly collected bitters bottles. One is "Drake's Plantation Bitters" and another is "Old Sachem Bitters and Wigwam Tonic." While both bottles are similar to the originals, the Drake's is slightly smaller, has poor embossing, and the tooled top is poorly done. The most noticeable difference on the Sachem's is the embossing that is not only poorly done, but does not stand out from the bottle like the original. Also, the original has a mold seam running across the base while the reproduction does not.

Bottom line: If you are not sure about what you are buying, ask another more knowledgeable collector for help. Or just walk away. Always check the bottle, jar, or pottery carefully to make sure that there have been no repairs or special treatments. It is best to hold the item up to the light or take it outside with the dealer to look for cracks, nicks, or dings. Be sure to check for scratches that may have happened during cleaning. There are also a number of bottles and jars that have reproduction closures. The proper closure can make a difference in the value of the bottle so it's important to make sure the closure fits securely and the metal lid in stamped with the correct patent dates or lettering.

Remember: If you need help, don't hesitate to ask an experienced collector. In order to better understand the hobby, new bottle collectors should learn certain aspects such as age identification, bottle grading, labeling, and glass imperfections and peculiarities. There are no dumb questions.

Bottle Facts

As mentioned in the introduction, the first question from a new collector is either, "How do you know how old a bottle is?" or "How can you tell it is really an antique bottle?" A few of the most common methods for determining the age are by the mold seams, color variations, condition, crudity and imperfection. Details on the lip, or top of the bottle, and how they were applied, will provide further identification.

Trademarks also provide excellent help for determining bottle age. Trademarks not only help determine history, age and value, but also provide a deeper knowledge of the many glass manufacturers that produced bottles and the companies that provided the contents. There is an excellent chapter on trademarks (see page 517) with in-depth information.

Mold Seams (Figure 1)

Prior to 1900, bottles were manufactured using either a blowpipe (free-blown) until 1860 or with a mold until 1900. In this process, the mouth or lip of the bottle was formed last

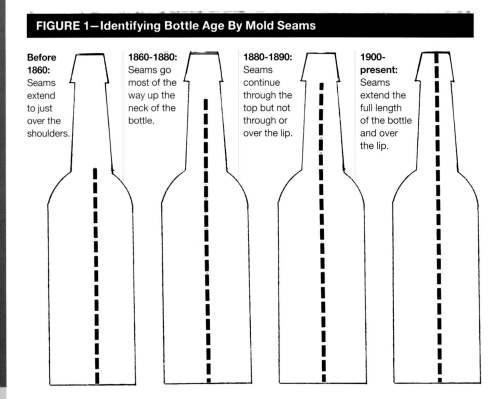

FIGURE 1—Identifying Bottle Age By Mold Seams

Before 1860: Seams extend to just over the shoulders.

1860-1880: Seams go most of the way up the neck of the bottle.

1880-1890: Seams continue through the top but not through or over the lip.

1900-present: Seams extend the full length of the bottle and over the lip.

and applied to the bottle after completion (applied lip). An applied lip can be identified by observing the mold seam, which runs from the base up to the neck and near the end of the lip. On a machine-made bottle, the lip is formed first and the mold seam runs over the lip. Therefore, the closer to the top of the bottle the seam extends, the more recent the bottle.

On the earliest bottles manufactured before 1860, the mold seams will end low on the neck or at the shoulder. On bottles made between 1860 and 1880, the mold seam stops right below the mouth and makes it easy to detect that the lip was separately formed. Around 1880, the closed mold began to be used. With the closed mold, the neck and lip were mechanically shaped. Then the bottle was severed from the blowpipe and the ridge evened off by hand sanding or filing. The mold seam usually ends within one-quarter inch from the top of the bottle. After 1900, the seam extends all the way to the top.

Lips and Tops (Figures 2A, 2B, 3 and 4)

Since the lip, or top, was an integral part the bottle-making process, it is important to understand that process. One of the best ways to identify bottles manufactured prior to 1840 is by the presence of a "sheared lip." This type of lip was formed by cutting or snipping the glass free of the blowpipe with a pair of shears, a process that leaves the lip with a stovepipe look. Since hot glass can be stretched, some of these stovepipes have a very distinctive appearance.

Around 1840, bottle manufacturers began to apply a glass ring around the sheared lip, forming a "laid-on-ring" lip. Between 1840 and 1880, numerous variations of lips or tops were produced using a variety of tools. After 1880, manufacturers started to pool their processing information, resulting in a more evenly finished and uniform top. As a general rule, the more uneven and crude the lip or top, the older the bottle.

Introduction

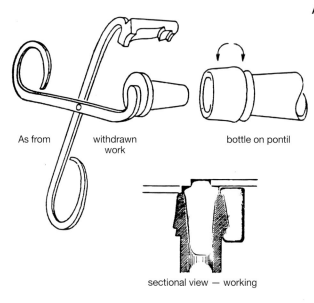

As from / withdrawn work

bottle on pontil

sectional view — working

A. The line drawings were developed from a description that appeared in the seventh edition (1842) of the *Encyclopedia Britannica*, vol. X, p. 579: "The finisher then warms the bottle at the furnace, and taking out a small quantity of metal on what is termed a ring iron, he turns it once round the mouth forming the ring seen at the mouth of bottles. He then employs the shears to give shape to the neck. One of the blades of the shears has a piece of brass in the center, tapered like a common cork, which forms the inside of the mouth, to the other blade is attached a piece of brass, used to form the ring." This did not appear in the sixth edition (1823), though it is probable the method of forming collars was practiced in some glasshouses at that time.

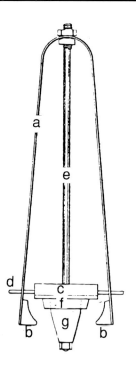

a

e

d

c

f

g

b   b

B. The exact period in which neck finishing tools evolved having metal springs with two jaws instead of one, to form collars, is undetermined. It doubtless was some time before Amosa Stone of Philadelphia patented his "improved tool," which was of simpler construction, as were many later ones. Like Stone's, the interior of the jaws [was] made in such shape as to give the outside of the nozzle of the bottle or neck of the vessel formed the desired shape as it [was] rotated between the jaws in a plastic state..." U.S. Patent Office. From specifications for (A. Stone) patent No. 15,738, September 23, 1856.

Bottle Facts

FIGURE 3—Tooled Bottle Lips / Tops Identification

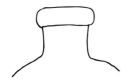

1 Tooled, rounded, rolled-over collar

2 Tooled, flanged, with flat top and squared edges

3 Tooled, rounded above 3/4" flat band

4 Tooled, flat ring below thickening plain lip

5 Tooled, narrow beveled fillet below thickened plain lip

6 Tooled, broad sloping collar above beveled ring

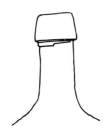

7 Tooled, plain broad sloping collar

8 Tooled, broad sloping collar with beveled edges at top and bottom

9 Tooled, broad flat collar sloping to heavy rounded ring

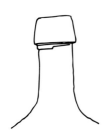

10 Tooled, broad flat vertical collar with uneven lower edge

11 Tooled, double rounded collar, upper deeper than lower; neck slightly pinched at base of collar

12 Tooled, broad round collar with lower level

Introduction

FIGURE 4—Bottle Lips/Other Tops Identification

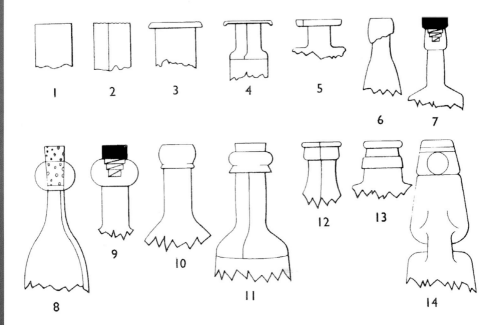

1. Free-blown
2. Sheared
3. Rolled
4. Flared
5. Laid-on ring
6. Applied top
7. Internal threads
8. Blob-top (cork use)

9. Blob-top (internal thread)
10. Improved applied lip on the two-piece mold bottle
11. Improved applied lip on a three-piece mold bottle
12. 20th century lip
13. Collar below lip
14. Hiram Codd lip

Closures / Stoppers

As mentioned in the "Bottles: History & Origin" chapter, the Romans used small stones rolled in tar as stoppers. The following centuries saw little advance in the methods of closure. During most of the 15th and 16th centuries, the closure consisted of a sized cloth tied down with heavy thread or string. Beneath the cover was a stopper made of wax or bombase (cotton wadding). Cotton wool was also dipped in wax to be used as a stopper, along with coverings of parchment, paper, or leather. Corks and glass stoppers were still used in great numbers, with the cork sometimes being tied or wired down for effervescent liquids. When the closed mold came into existence, however, the shape of the lip was more accurately controlled, which made it possible to invent and manufacture many different capping devices.

Glass stoppers,
1850-1900.

Introduction

Example of glass stopper with cork as insulator for
poison bottles, 1890-1910.

S.A. Whitney, who owned Whitney Glass Works in Glasborough, New Jersey, introduced an early closure device when he received Patent No. 31,046 on Jan. 1, 1861, for an internal screw stopper (Figure 5). A unique closure was developed on July 23, 1872, when a British inventor, Hiram Codd, invented a bottle made with a groove inside the neck and was granted Patent No. 129,652 (Figure 6). A glass marble was inserted and then a ring of cork or rubber was fitted into the groove to confine the marble within the neck. The gas released by an effervescing liquid forced the marble to the top of the neck, sealing the bottle. A second patent, No. 138,230, issued April 29, 1873, contained the interior lug, which was a ball-holding element (Figure 7). It is interesting to note that many young boys broke the bottle to get the marble.

More interesting is that the Codd stopper closure isn't dead. The Sangaria Corporation, a Japanese company that distributes carbonated soft drinks in the United States, has re-issued and duplicated this same stopper design with the glass marble. In

FIGURE 5—S.A. Whitney Bottle Stopper

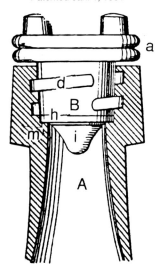

No. 31046   Patented Jan. 1, 1861

From Samuel A. Whitney's specification for his "Bottle Stopper," Patent No. 31,046, Jan. 1, 1861. The drawing on the left shows grooves in the neck of the bottle. In the drawing on the right, in which "h" is a cork washer, the stopper is in place. "The stopper is formed by pressing or casting the molten...glass in molds of the desired shape... Although...applicable to a variety of bottles and jars, it is especially well adapted to and has been more especially designed for use in connection with mineral-water bottles, and such as contain effervescing wines, malt liquors, &c., the corks in this class of bottles, if not lost, being generally so mutilated as to be unfit for second use when the bottles are refilled." (U.S. Patent Office)

fact, a warning note on the back of the bottle reads, "Do not try to remove the marble from the bottle to avoid injury."

The Hutchinson stopper was awarded Patent No. 213,992 on April 8, 1879, and was a popular closure until the early 1900s (Figure 8). The stopper incorporated a heavy wire loop to control a rubber gasket that remained inside the neck of the bottle. After filling the bottle, the gasket was pulled up against the shoulders and was kept in place by the carbonation. Since it was simple to use, the Hutchinson stopper was easily adaptable to a number of other bottle types.

The lightning stopper (Figure 9), used from 1880 to the early 1900s, was the best closure for beer bottles before the invention of the crown cap. The lightning stopper featured a porcelain or rubber plug anchored to the outside of the bottle by means of a permanently attached wire. The wire formed a bar that controlled the opening and closing of the bottle. Since the lightning stopper cost more than the Hutchinson stopper, it wasn't used for soft drinks.

In 1892, William Painter invented the crown cap, which revolutionized the soft drink and beer bottling industry (Figure 10). By 1915 all major bottlers had switched to the crown-type cap. It was reported that Painter's "crown cork" system had taken him three years of constant work to perfect and cost $100,000, a considerable amount of money in 1892. It wasn't until 1960, with the introduction of the screw cap for beer and soda pop bottles, that the crown-type cap began to disappear.

Finally, in 1902, threads were manufactured on the outside of the lip to enable a threaded cap to be

FIGURE 6

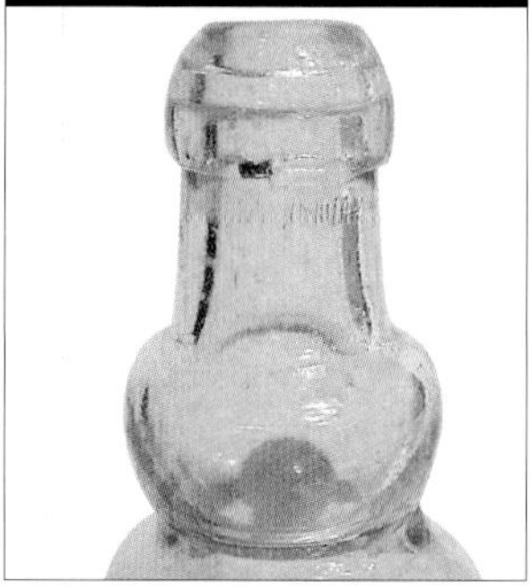

Hiram Codd interior ball stopper, Patent #129,652, July 23, 1872.

FIGURE 7

Hiram Codd interior ball stopper, Patent #138,230, April 29, 1873.

FIGURE 8

Charles G. Hutchinson stopper, Patent #213,992, April 8 (year uncertain).

FIGURE 9

Lightning stopper,
used from 1880 to
early 1900s.

FIGURE 10

William Painter crown cap,
Patent #468,226, Feb. 2,
1890.

FIGURE 11

Dumfries Ale (English)
depicting inside
threads.

FIGURE 12

Dumfries Ale (English),
full bottle depicting inside
threads.

screwed onto the mouth of the bottle. This was not a new idea. Early glassblowers produced bottles with inside and outside screw caps long before bottle-making machines came along. Early methods of production were so complex, however, that screw-topped bottles produced before the 1800s were considered specialty bottles. They were expensive to replace and today are considered rare and quite collectible. In fact, the conventional screw-top bottle did not become common until after 1924 when the glass industry standardized the threads.

In 1875 some glass manufacturers introduced an inside screw-neck whiskey bottle that used a rubber stopper (Figures 11 and 12). This invention wasn't very popular because the alcohol interacted with the rubber, discoloring the rubber and making the whiskey bitter. The following table lists some of the brands of embossed whiskeys that featured the inside threaded neck and the approximate dates of circulation:

Introduction

WHISKEY COMPANY	DATE OF CIRCULATION
Adolph Harris	1907-1912
Chevalier Castle	1907-1910
Crown (squatty)	1905-1912
Crown (pint)	1896-1899
Donnelly Rye	1910-1917
El Monte	1910-1918
H.L. Nye	1900-1905
Hall Luhrs	1880-1918
Hanley	1905-1911
J.C. Donnelly	1907-1915
McDonald/Cohn	1903-1912
Mini Taylor/Williams	1881-1900
Old Gilt Edge	1907-1912
O'Hearns	1907-1916
Posner	1905-1915
Roth (aqua)	1903-1911
Roth (amber sq.)	1898-1909
Roth (amber fluted shoulder)	1903-1911
Roth (amber qt.)	1903-1911
Rusconi-Fisher	1902-1915
Taussig (clear)	1915-1918
Weeks/Potter	1860-1875
Whitney	1860-1875
Wilmerding/Loewe	1907-1917

Glass Color

The next most common method for determining the age of a bottle is by examining the color of the glass. The basic ingredients for glass production (sand, soda, and lime) have remained the same for 3,000 years. These ingredients, when mixed together, are collectively called the batch. When the batch is heated to a molten state, it is referred to as the metal. In its soft or plastic stage, the metal can be molded into objects, which when cooled, become the solid material we know as glass.

Producing colored and perfectly clear glass were both major challenges for glass manufactures for centuries. In the 13th and 14th centuries, the Venetians produced clear glass by using crushed quartz in place of sand. In 1668, the English tried to improve on this process by using ground flint to produce clear glass, and by 1675 an Englishman named George perfected lead glass. Today, this lead glass is referred to as "flint glass." Before 1840, intentionally colored or colorless glass was reserved for fancy figured flasks and vessels.

In naturally colored glass, the color was considered unimportant until 1880, when food preservation packers began to demand clear glass for food products. Since most glass produced previously was green, glass manufacturers began using manganese to bleach out the green tinge produced by the iron content to satisfy the increased demand for clear glass. Only then did clear bottles become common.

Iron slag was used up to 1860 and produced a dark olive green or olive amber glass that has become known as "black glass" and was used for wine and beverage bottles that needed protection from light. Natural glass colors are brown, amber, olive green, and aqua.

The true colors of blue, green and purple were produced by the metallic oxides added to the glass batch. Cobalt was added for blue glass; sulfur for yellow and green; manganese and nickel for purple; nickel for brown; copper or gold for red; and tin or zinc for milk-colored glass (for apothecary vials, druggist bottles, and pocket bottles). The Hocking Glass Company discovered a process for making a brilliant red-colored glass described as copper-ruby. The color was achieved by adding copper oxide to a glass batch as it was cooling and then immediately reheating the batch before use. Since these bright colors were expensive to produce, they are very rare and sought after by most collectors.

Many bottle collectors consider purple glass the most appealing and, therefore, it is prized above other glass. As discussed earlier, the iron contained in sand caused glass to take on a color between green and blue. Glass manufacturers used manganese, which counteracted the aqua to produce clear glass. Glass with manganese content was most common in bottle production between 1880 and 1914. When exposed to the ultraviolet

Introduction

rays of the sun, the manganese in the glass oxidizes, or combines with oxygen, and turns the glass purple. The longer the glass is exposed to the ultraviolet rays from the sun, the deeper the purple color. Purple glass is also known as "desert glass" or "sun-colored" glass because the color is activated as a result of exposure to UV rays in intense sunlight.

Because Germany was the main source of manganese, the supply ceased with the outbreak of World War I. By 1916 the glassmaking industry began to use selenium as a neutralizing agent. Glass that was produced between 1914 and 1930 is glass that is most likely to change to an amber or straw color.

The following chart shows how color is achieved by adding various oxides to the batch:

COLOR	PRODUCED BY ADDING OXIDE
Aqua	Iron oxide in sand
Black	Iron oxide, manganese, cobalt, iron
Clear	Selenium
Yellow	Nickel
Red	Gold, copper, or selenium
Blue	Cobalt oxide
Blue-Green	Iron in silicate-based glass
Amber	Manganese oxide, sulfur, carbon oxide
Dark Brown	Sulphide of copper and sulphide of sodium
Amethyst (Purple)	Sulphide of nickel
Rose Tinted	Adding selenium directly into the batch
Orange Red	Selenium mixed first with cadmium sulphide
Dark Reddish-Brown	Sodium sulphide
Reddish Yellow	Sulphide of sodium and molybdenite
Yellow Green	Uranium oxide
Green	Iron oxide
Milk Glass	Tin or zinc oxide
Olive Green	Iron oxide and black oxide of manganese
Purple	Manganese
Orange	Oxide of iron and manganese

Imperfections

Imperfections and blemishes also provide clues to how old a bottle is and often add to the charm and value of an individual piece. Blemishes usually show up as bubbles or "seeds" in the glass. In the process of making glass, air bubbles form and rise to the surface where they pop. As the "fining out" (elimination process) became more advanced around 1920, these bubbles or seeds were eliminated.

Another peculiarity of the antique bottle is the uneven thickness of the glass. Often one side of the base has a one-inch thick side that slants off to paper thinness on the opposite edge. This imperfection was eliminated with the introduction of the Owens bottle-making machine in 1903.

In addition, the various marks of stress and strain, sunken sides, twisted necks, and whittle marks (usually at the neck where the wood mold made impressions in the glass) also give clues that a bottle was produced before 1900.

Labeling and Embossing

While embossing and labeling were common practices in the rest of the world for a number of centuries, American bottle manufacturers did not adopt the inscription process until 1869. These inscriptions included information about the contents, manufacturer, distributor, and slogans or other messages advertising the product. Raised lettering on various bottles was produced with a plate mold, sometimes called a "slug plate" fitted inside the casting mold. This plate created a sunken area that makes them a special value to collectors. Irregularities such as a misspelled name add to the value of a bottle, as will any name embossed with hand etching or other method of crude grinding. These bottles are very old and valuable.

Inscription and embossing customs came to an end with the production of machine-made bottles in 1903 and with the introduction of paper labels. In 1933, with the repeal of prohibition, the distilling of whiskey and other spirits was resumed under strict government regulations. One of the major regulations was that the following statement was required to be embossed on all bottles containing alcohol: "Federal Law Forbids Sale or Re-Use of this Bottle." This regulation was in effect until 1964 and is an excellent method of dating spirit bottles from 1933 to 1964.

Determining Bottle Values

Collectors and dealers typically use the following factors to determine a bottle's value: supply and demand, condition, rarity, historic and geographic appeal, embossing/labeling and design, age, and color.

Supply and Demand

As with any product, when demand increases and supply decreases, the price goes up, and having some knowledge of what is in demand adds to determining value. Since demand for certain bottles can change over time, it's important to stay aware and up to date of what is in demand.

Condition

Mint: An empty or full bottle (preferably full) with a label or embossing. Bottle must be clean and have vibrant color, with no chips, cracks, scrapes, or wear of any type. While a chip can significantly reduce the value of a bottle, a crack will reduce the value to nearly zero. If the bottle comes in a box, the box must be in perfect condition, too. There should be absolutely no damage. It should be noted that many collectors do not consider tumbled bottles to be in Mint condition even though they will appear to be in Mint condition.

Extra Fine/Near Mint: An empty or full bottle with slight wear on the label or embossing. Slight wear or damage is defined as tiny nicks, light scratches, small open bubbles, and light stains, with no chips or cracks. The bottle must be clean with clear color, and no chips or scrapes. There is usually no box, or the box is only in fair condition.

Very Good/Excellent: Bottle has some light or minor wear and label is usually missing or not very visible. Usually there is embossing but it may show extra wear.

Good: Bottle shows additional wear, no embossing, and a label is barely recognizable or completely absent. Color is usually faded and the bottle is difficult to clean to an acceptable standard. There are usually some scrapes and minor chips. Most likely there is no box.

Fair or Average: Bottle shows considerable wear, label is missing, and embossing is damaged.

Poor/Damaged: Bottle has large cracks and large pieces chipped away.

Rarity

It is important to know that while rarity is a strong factor in establishing a high price for a bottle, there is no guarantee that a bottle will always retain its "rare" status. There have been occurrences in which only one to five bottles of a particular bottle were known to be in existence until an estate went to auction, or, a quantity of additional rare or scarce bottles were discovered or surfaced that affected the previous total known amount.

Unique: A bottle is considered to be unique if only one is known to exist. These bottles are also the most valuable and expensive.

Extremely Rare: Only 5 to 10 known specimens.

Very Rare: Only 10 to 20 known specimens.

Rare: Only 20 to 40 known specimens.

Very Scarce: No more than 50 known specimens.

Scarce: No more than 100 known specimens.

Common: Common bottles, such as clear 1880 to 1900 medicine bottles, are abundant, easy to acquire, usually very inexpensive, and great bottles for the beginning collector.

Historic and Geographic Appeal

These bottles are valuable because of the significance of where they were made. For example, territorial bottles have higher values because they were produced prior to the territory achieving statehood. Another good example is collectors of Western whiskey bottles who focus especially on bottles from San Francisco, and, in general, northern California, while collectors in the East focus on historical flasks portraying figures and events that are relevant to East Coast states. Another good example is Hawaiian soda bottles that are unique to Hawaii and therefore popular to Hawaiian collectors.

Embossing Labeling and Design

Bottles without embossing are common and have little dollar value to many collectors. Exceptions are hand-blown bottles made before 1840, which usually do not have embossing.

Embossing describes the name of the contents, manufacturer, state, city, dates, trademarks, and other valuable information. Embossed images and trademarks can also enhance and increase the value of the bottle.

Labeling found intact with all the specific information about the bottle also enhances and increases the value of the bottle.

Age

While age can play an important role in the value of a bottle, there's not always a direct correlation. As a guideline, there are four time frames that are commonly used when determining value.

1. 1650-1820: Hand blown and formed with a pontil scar on the base.

2. 1820-1865: Blown into an iron mold with a pontil scar on the base.

3. 1865-1900: No pontil scar on the base.

4. 1900-present: Machine-made bottles with a mold seam running over the top of the lip.

As stated in "The Beginning Collector" section, the history, rarity, and use of a bottle need to factored in with the age of the bottle to determine the proper overall value.

Color

To collectors, rare colors are the major factor in determining the value of bottles within a specific bottle category. In fact, quite often you will hear the expression "color is king." There are many shades of the colors listed here, but these are the basic color patterns that will point you in the right direction.

Low Price: clear, aqua, light amber

Average Price: milk glass, green, black, basic olive green, teal blue-green

High Price: dark teal blue, cobalt blue, purple (amethyst), yellow, yellow-green, straw yellow, puce, darker shades of amber

Unique Features

The following characteristics can also significantly affect value:

• Pontil marks

• Whittle marks

• Glass imperfections (thickness and bubbles)

• Slug plates

• Crudely applied lips and tops

Summary

Even with these guidelines, it's often necessary and important to consult and check out more detailed references, especially concerning rare and scarce bottles that tend to be more valuable. The bibliography and other resource listings in the back of this book will provide some of that extra help and assistance. And remember, never miss a chance to ask other collectors and dealers for advice and assistance.

Bottle Sources

Antique and collectible bottles can be found in a variety of places and sometimes where you least expect them. The following provides a listing of abundant sources and potential hiding places for those much sought-after bottles, whether you are a beginner or veteran collector.

Digging for Bottles

Digging is a relatively inexpensive way to collect bottles and one heck of a lot of fun. While the "Digging for Bottles" chapter starting on page 69 provides excellent detailed digging information, especially on privy or outhouse digging, the following information is an edited excerpt on specifics of where to find bottles.

Usually, settlers and store owners hauled and dumped their garbage within a mile of the town limits, or they would dig a hole about 25 yards from the back of their home or business for garbage and refuse. Many hotels and saloons had a basement or underground storage area where empty bottles were kept. Ravines, ditches, and washes at the bottom of foothills are also prime digging spots because heavy rains or melting snow often washed debris down from other areas.

Residents would store or throw their bottles under their porches when porches were common building features in the late 19th and 20th centuries, so bottles can often be found beside house and under porches. Explore abandoned roads where houses or cabins once stood, wagon trails, old railroad tracks, and sewers. If it is legal, old battlegrounds and military encampments are excellent places to dig. Cisterns and wells are other good sources of bottles and period artifacts.

Introduction

Ghost Towns

The first love of this bottle guy, and high on the list of many collectors, is an expedition to a ghost town. It's always fun and usually a great history lesson. The best places to search in ghost towns are near saloons, ravines, and washes where miners dumped their trash, trade stores, abandoned buildings and shacks (look under the floors), old cellars and basements, the "red light district," train stations, and town dumps. Most of these sites usually have the original pre-1900 trash dump, but it's also a good idea to check out any newer trash dumps phased in during the 1920s-1930s.

Lakes, Rivers, and Oceans

Scuba diving for bottles has become popular in recent years. Just as settlers and store owners hauled their trash out to dumps, many settlers, tavern owners, and trading post owners who lived near waterways piled their trash on a barge, took it out to the deepest part of the river or lake, and pushed the trash into the water. By doing this, they left behind great bottles that in many cases are rare or scarce and in excellent condition.

The ocean has always been a vast dumping ground for all sorts of trash, including bottles. Today there are many 17th and 18th century shipwrecks being found that are producing huge quantities of rare and scarce quality bottles. As more collectors become proficient in the skill of diving, the bottle-collecting world will see many new quality finds from the past.

The Internet and Social Media

In the 40 years that I've been collecting, I have never seen anything impact the hobby of bottle collecting as much as the Internet and social media sites. Open a search engine, type in "antique bottle collecting," and you'll be amazed at the amount of data immediately at your fingertips. Numerous websites throughout the United States, Canada, Europe, Asia, Central America, and Mexico provide detailed information about bottle clubs, dealers, sellers, antiques publications and books, auction companies, and eBay and other online auction sites. All these Internet and social media sites have exposed bottle collecting to the entire world and are a convenient and inexpensive resources tool for all collectors.

Flea Markets, Swap Meets, and Other Sources

For beginning collectors, these sources will likely be the most fun (next to digging) and yield the most bottles at the best prices. The majority of bottles found at these sources will fall into the common or common-above average category. But you might find that occasional gem hidden buried under the common stuff. The bottles are out there; you just need to look long and hard.

Flea Markets, Swap Meets, and Thrift Stores: Target areas where household goods are being sold. It's a good bet they will have bottles.

Garage Sales: Focus on the older areas of town because the items will be older, more collectible, and more likely to fall into a rare or scarce category. Often these homes are up for sale through estate or probate sales and potentially can produce great finds. To make a point, here's a great garage sale experience that actually occurred in 2013 in Phoenix: A garage sale junkie, but not a bottle collector, walked into a seller's garage on a Saturday morning and noticed five bottles on a shelf. They looked interesting, so he asked the seller if he would consider selling them. The seller said, "Sure, $1 takes all." After the buyer did some research, he discovered that one bottle was a rare late 1800s Hutchinson "Phoenix A.T. (Arizona Territory)" bottle produced before Arizona became a state in 1912, which he sold for $1,100. Another rare bottle in the grouping was a milk bottle with Donald Duck on the front, which sold for $400. Finally, the buyer sold a third bottle, an amber Coca-Cola, for $25. Bottom line: A $1,525 profit for a $1 purchase. Stay alert!

Salvage Stores or Salvage Yards: These are great places to search for bottles, since these businesses buy from companies that tear down old houses, apartments, and businesses. A New York salvage company discovered an untouched illegal Prohibition-era distillery complete with bottles, unused labels, and equipment. What a find!

Local Bottle Clubs and Collectors

By joining a local bottle club or working with other collectors, you will find more ways to add your collection, gather information, and participate in more digging. Members usually have quantities of unwanted or duplicate bottles, which they will sell reasonably, trade, or sometimes even give away, especially to an enthusiastic new collector. Quite often many of the club collectors are also dealers. If you make these collectors/dealers aware of what you are looking for, they will try to find it. Since most dealers usually have a varied number of contacts, it works to a collector's advantage to know as many dealers as possible.

Bottle Shows

Bottle shows not only expose collectors to bottles of every type, shape, color, and variety, but also provide them the opportunity to talk with experts in specialized fields. In addition, publications dealing with all aspects of bottle collecting are usually available for sale or even free. Bottle shows can be rewarding learning experiences not only for beginning collectors but also for veteran collectors. They take place almost every weekend all across the country, and they always offer something new to learn or share and, of course, bottles to buy or trade.

Make sure you look under the tables at these shows because many great bargains in the form of duplicates and unwanted items may be lurking where you least expect it. Quite often, diggers find so many bottles that they don't even bother to clean them. Instead, they offer them as is for a very low price. Hey, for a low price, I'll clean bottles!

Auction Companies

Auction companies have become a great source of bottles and glassware over the last few years. There are a number of auction houses that specialize only in bottles. (Check out the "Auction Companies" section in the back of the book.) When evaluating auction houses, look for one that specializes in antiques and estate buyouts. To promote itself and provide buyers with a better idea of what will be presented for sale, an auction house usually publishes a catalog that provides detailed bottle descriptions, conditions, and photographs. I recommend, however, that you first visit an auction as a spectator to learn how the process works before you decide to participate. When buying, be sure to check the color and condition of the bottle and terms of the sale. There are usually buyer and/or seller premiums in addition to the actual sale price. These guidelines also apply to all Internet auctions. Use caution and follow these general rules. Note: If you are not sure about an item or what you are doing, ask someone in your club or another collector for advice.

BUYING AT AUCTIONS

- Purchase the catalog and review all the items in the auction. At live auctions, a preview is usually held for customers to inspect the items.
- After reviewing the catalog and making your choice, phone or mail your bid. A 10 to

20 percent buyer's premium is usually added to the sale price.

- Callbacks allow bidders to increase the previous high bid on certain items after the close of the auction.
- The winning bidder receives an invoice in the mail. After the bidder's check clears, the bottles are shipped.
- Most auction houses have a return policy as well as a refund policy for items that differ from the description in the catalog.

SELLING AT AUCTIONS

- Check and evaluate the auction source before consigning any merchandise. Make sure that the auction venue is legitimate and has not had any problems with payments or product.
- Package the item with plenty of bubble wrap, insure your bottle, and mail the package by certified mail, signed receipt requested.
- Allow 30 days to receive payment and be aware that most firms charge a 15 percent commission on the sales price.

Estate Sales

An estate sale is a great source for bottles if the home is in a very old neighborhood or section of a city that has historical significance. These sales are a lot of fun, especially when the people running the sale let you look over and handle the items to be able to make careful selections. Prices are usually good and are always negotiable. In addition, always try to obtain the name of the company or person that is running the sale, and make sure to give them your name and number for information of future sales that may contain bottles.

Knife and Gun Shows

Bottles at a knife and gun shows? Yes. Quite a few gun and knife enthusiasts are also great fans of the West and keep an eye open for related artifacts. Every knife and gun show I've attended has had a large number of dealers with bottles on their tables (or under the tables) for sale. And the prices were about right, since they were more interested in selling their knives and guns than the bottles. Plus, these dealers will often provide information on where they made their finds, which you can put to good use later.

Introduction

Retail Antique Dealers

This group includes dealers who sell bottles at or near full market prices. Buying from dealers has advantages and disadvantages. They usually have a large selection and will provide helpful information and details about the bottles. And it's a safe bet that the bottles for sale are authentic. On the other hand, it can be very expensive to build a collection this way. But these shops are a good place to browse and learn.

General Antiques and Specialty Shops

The difference between general and retail antiques shops is that general shops usually have lower prices and a more limited selection than retail shops. This is partly because merchants in general shops are not as well informed about bottles and may overlook critical characteristics. If a collector is well informed, general antique dealers can provide the opportunity to acquire under-priced quality merchandise.

Ward's Lemon Crush soda fountain syrup dispenser, 13-1/2", American 1900-1930, $1,210.

Digging for Bottles

There are many ways to begin your search for collectible bottles, but few searches are as satisfying and fun as digging up bottles yourself. While the goal is to find a bottle, the adventure of the hunt is as exciting as the actual find. From a beginner's viewpoint, digging is a relatively inexpensive way to start your collection. The efforts of individual and bottle club digging expeditions have turned up numerous important historical finds. These digs revealed valuable information about the early decades of our country and the history of bottle and glass manufacturing in the United States. The following discussion of how to plan a digging expedition covers the essentials: locating the digging sites, equipment and tools, general rules and helpful hints, as well as a section on privy/outhouse digging for the real adventurer.

Locating the Digging Site

Prior to any dig, you will need to learn as much as possible about the area you plan to explore. Do not overlook valuable resources in your own community. You will likely be able to collect important information from your local library, local and state historical societies, various types of maps, and city directories (useful for information about people who once lived on a particular piece of property). The National Office of Cartography in Washington, D.C. and the National Archives are excellent resources as well.

In my experience, old maps are the best guides for locating digging areas with good potential. These maps show what the town looked like in an earlier era and provide clues to where stores, saloons, hotels, red light districts, and the town dump were located. All are ripe for exploring. The two types of maps that will prove most useful are plat maps and Sanborn Fire Insurance maps.

A plat map, which will show every home and business in the city or area you wish to dig, can be compared to current maps that identify the older structures or determine where they once stood. The Sanborn Insurance maps are the most detailed, accurate, and helpful of all for choosing a digging site. These maps, which have also been published under other names, provide detailed information on each lot illustrating the location of houses, factories, cisterns, wells, privies, streets, and property lines. These maps were produced for nearly every city and town between 1867 to 1920 and are dated so that it's possible to determine the age of the sites you're considering. Another new tool in the hunt

Introduction

for surveying remote digging sites is Google Earth. It allows you to view the entire site from space. Hey, we've got the Internet, let's use it.

Figure 1 depicts an 1890 Sanborn Perris map section of East Los Angeles. This map section was used to locate an outhouse in East Los Angeles dated between 1885 and 1905. A dig on that site turned up more than 50 bottles. Knowing the approximate age of the digging site also helps to determine the age and types of bottles or artifacts you find there.

Local chambers of commerce, law enforcement agencies, and residents who have lived in the community for a number of years can be very helpful in your search for information. Other great resource for publications about the area's history are local antique and gift shops, which often carry old books, maps, and other literature about the town, county, and surrounding communities.

Since most early settlers handled garbage themselves, buried bottles can be unearthed almost anywhere, but a little knowledge of past customs can narrow the search to a location that's likely to hold some treasures. Usually, the garbage was hauled and dumped within one mile of the town limits. Often, settlers or storeowners would dig a hole about 25 yards out from the back of their home or business for garbage and refuse. Many hotels and saloons had a basement or underground storage area where empty bottles were kept.

Ravines, ditches, and washes are also prime digging spots because heavy rains or melting snow often washed debris down from other areas. Bottles can quite often be found beside houses and under porches. Residents would store or throw their bottles under their porches when porches were common building features in the late 19th and 20th centuries. Explore wagon trails, old railroad tracks, sewers, and abandoned roads where houses or cabins once stood. Old battlegrounds and military encampments are excellent places to dig, when legal. Cisterns and wells are other good sources of bottles and period artifacts.

The first love of this bottle hound, and high on the list of most collectors, is an expedition to a ghost town. It's fun and a lesson in history. The best places to search in ghost towns are near saloons, trade stores, train stations, the "red light district," and the town dump (prior to 1900). The Tonopah, Nevada, town dump was the start of my digging experiences and is still a favorite spot.

FIGURE 1

Sanborn Perris map section of East Lost Angeles, 1885-1905.

Introduction

Privy / Outhouse Digging

"You've dug bottles out of an old outhouse? You've got to be kidding!" Telling your family and friends about this unique experience will usually kick the conversation into high gear. I'm quite serious when I say that one of the best places to find old bottles—old bottles that can be very rare and in great condition—is in an old outhouse. Prior to 1870, most bottles were not hauled out to the dump. Why would anybody bother when they could simply toss old bottles down the outhouse hole in the back of a house or business? In fact, very few pontil age (pre-Civil War) bottles are ever found in dumps. At that time people either dug a pit in their backyard for trash, or used the outhouse. These outhouses, or privies, have been known to yield all kinds of other artifacts such as guns, coins, knives, crockery, dishes, marbles, pipes, and other household items.

To develop a better sense of where privies can be found, it is important to have an understanding of their construction and uses. The privies of the 19th century (which produce the best results) were deep holes constructed with wood, brick, or sides called "liners." You'll find privies in a variety of shapes: square, round, rectangular, and oval. The chart below summarizes the different types of privies, their locations, and depth.

In general, privies in cities are fairly deep and usually provide more bottles and

TYPES OF PRIVIES

CONSTRUCTION	SHAPE	LOCATION	DEPTH
BRICK	Oval, round, rectangular, square	Big towns and cities, behind brick buildings	Not less than six feet deep
STONE	Round, square, rectangular	Limestone often used in areas where stone is common	Rectangular, less than 10 feet deep; round, often 20 feet or more
WOOD	Square or rectangular	Farms, small towns	May be one privy on plot not more than 10 to 15 feet deep; often very shallow
BARREL	Round	Cities and towns	8 to 12 feet deep

artifacts. Privies in rural areas are shallower and do not contain as many bottles. Outhouses on farms are very difficult to locate and digs often produce few results.

How long was an outhouse used? The lifespan of a privy is anywhere from 10 to 20 years. It was possible to extend its useful life by cleaning it out or relining it with new wood, brick, or stone. In fact, nearly all older privies show some evidence of cleaning.

At some point, old privies were filled and abandoned. The materials used to fill them included ashes, bricks, plaster, sand, rocks, building materials, and soil, which had been dug out when a new or additional privy was added to the house. Often, bottles or other artifacts were thrown in with the fill. The depth of the privy determined the amount of the fill required. In any case, the result was a privy containing layers of various materials, with the bottom layer being the "use" layer or "trash" layer as shown in Figure 2.

It is possible to locate these old outhouses due to the characteristic differences in density and composition of the undisturbed earth. Because of the manner of construction, it is fairly easy to locate them by probing the area with a metal rod or "probe."

FIGURE 2—Older Privies

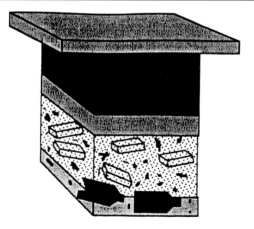

Your own community is a great place to begin the hunt for a privy. A good starting point is to find an old house. Those dating from 1880 to 1920 usually had a least one privy in the backyard. Try to locate a small lot with few buildings or obstructions to get in the way of your dig. First look for depressions in the ground, since materials used to fill privies have a tendency to settle. A subtle depression may indicate where a septic tank, well, or privy was once located. In addition, like most household dumps, outhouses were

Introduction

usually located 15 to 30 yards behind a residence or business. Another good indicator of an old privy site is an unexpected grouping of vegetation such as bushes or trees, which flourishes above the rich fertilized ground. Privies were sometimes located near old trees for shade and privacy.

The most common privy locations were (1) directly outside the back door, (2) along a property line, (3) in one of the back corners or the rear middle of the lot, and (4) the middle of the yard. Figure 3 depicts patterns of typical outhouse locations.

FIGURE 3—Typical Privy Configurations

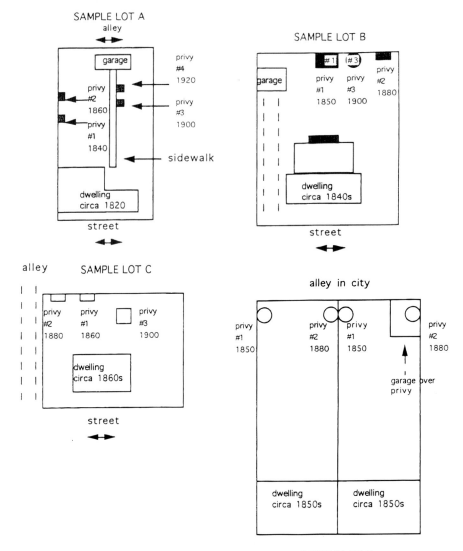

Now that you've located that privy (with luck it's full of great bottles), it's time to open up the hole. The approximate dimensions of the hole can usually be determined with your probe. If you know, or even suspect, that the hole is deeper than you are tall, it is extremely important to open the entire hole to avoid a cave-in. Never try to dig half a hole in hopes of getting to the trash layer quicker. Remember that the fill is looser than the surrounding ground and could come down on you. Also, always dig to the bottom and check the corners carefully. Privies were occasionally cleaned out, but very often bottles and artifacts were missed in the corners or on the sides. If you are not sure whether you've hit the bottom, check with the probe. It's easier to determine if you can feel the fill below what you may think is the bottom. In brick and stone-lined holes, if the wall keeps going down, you are not on the bottom.

Quite often it is difficult to date a privy without the use of detailed and accurate maps. But it is possible to determine the age of the privy by the type and age of items found in the hole. The chart on the following page lists some types of bottles you might find in a dig and shows how their age relates to the age of the privy.

MATERIAL	1920+	1900-1919	1880-1900	1860-1880	1840-1860	PRE-1840
Crown Tops	Yes	Yes	No	No	No	No
Screw Tops	Yes	Yes	No	No	No	No
Aqua Glass	Yes	Some	Yes	Yes	Yes	Yes
Clear Glass	All	Most	Some	Some	Some	Some
Ground Lip Fruit Jar	No	Rare	Yes	Yes	Rare	No
Hinge Mold	No	No	No	Yes	Yes	No
Pontiled	No	No	No	Yes	Yes	Yes
Free-Blown	No	No	No	No	No	Yes
Historical Flasks	No	No	No	Yes	Yes	Yes
Stoneware (Crockery)	No	No	Yes	Yes	Yes	Yes

Introduction

While finding a prized bottle is great, digging and refilling the hole can be hard work and very tiring. To help make this chore easier, put down a tarp on the ground surrounding the hole as you dig, and shovel the dirt on the tarp. Then, shovel the dirt off the tarp and fill five-gallon plastic buckets. The first benefit of this method is the time and energy you'll save filling the hole. The second benefit, and maybe the biggest, is that you'll leave no mess. This becomes important for building a relationship with the property owner. The less mess, the more likely you'll get permission to dig again.

Also, the dig will be safer and easier if you use a walk board. Place an 8-foot long 2 x 8 plank over the hole. The digger, who is standing on the board pulling up buckets of dirt (let's all take turns), can do so without hitting the sides. This also reduces the risk of the bucketman falling in or caving in a portion of the hole. Setting up a tripod with a pulley

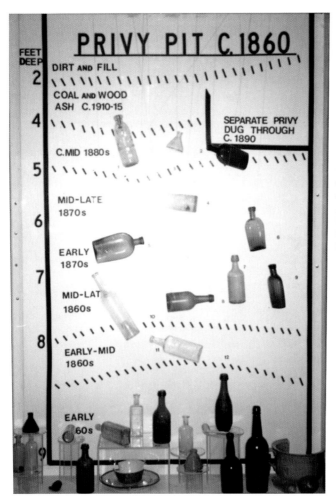

Privy pit display, circa 1860 (actual dug pit), National Bottle Museum, Ballston, Spa, New York.

over the hole will help save time and prevent strain on the back.

The short few paragraphs presented here are really just an outline of privy/outhouse digging. There are two books that discuss the art of privy/outhouse digging in detail, and I recommend everyone obtain them for their library: *The Secrets of Privy Digging* by John Odell and *Privy Digging 101* by Mark Churchill. See the bibliography for complete publishing information on these fine works. Now, let's have some "outhouse" fun.

The Probe

Regardless of whether you're digging in outhouses, old town dumps, or beneath a structure, a probe is an essential tool. The probe, shown in Figure 4, is a simple device, usually five to six feet long (a taller person may find that a longer probe works better) with a handle made of hollow or solid pipe, tapered to a point at the end so it's easier to penetrate the ground. Welding a ball bearing on the end of the rod will help in collecting soil samples. As discussed earlier, examining the soil samples is critical to finding privies. To make probing easier, add weight to the handle by filing the pipe with lead or welding a solid steel bar directly under the handle. The additional weight will reduce the effort needed to sink the probe.

While probing, press down slowly and try to feel for differences in the consistency of the soil. Unless you are probing into sand, you should reach a point where it becomes difficult to push, which means you have hit a natural bottom. If you find you can probe deeper in an adjacent spot, you may have found an outhouse. When this happens, pull out the probe and plunge it in again, this time at an angle to see if you feel a brick or wood liner. After some practice, you'll be able to determine what type of material you are hitting. Glass, brick, crockery, and rocks all have their own distinctive sound and feel. While you can purchase probes in a number of places, you might want to have one custom made to conform to your body height and weight for more comfortable use.

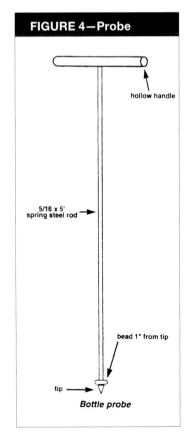

FIGURE 4—Probe

hollow handle

5/16 x 5'
spring steel rod

bead 1" from tip

tip

Bottle probe

Introduction

Digging Equipment and Tools

When I first started digging, I took only a shovel and my luck. Since then, I've refined my list of tools and equipment. The following list includes those items I have found useful and recommended by veteran diggers.

General Digging Equipment

- Probe
- Long-handled shovel
- Short-handled shovel
- Long-handled potato rake
- Small hand rake
- Old table knives
- Old spoons
- Hard and soft bristle brushes
- Gloves/boots/eye protection/durable clothes
- Insect repellent, snake bite kit, first aid kit
- Extra water and hat
- Dirt sifter (for coins or other items): 2' x 2' wooden frame with chicken wire
- Hunting knife
- Boxes for packing and storing bottles

Privy/Outhouse Digging Equipment

- Long handled shovel*
- Five-foot probe*
- Slam probe
- Pick*
- Root cutters*
- Short handled garden scratcher*
- Rope, 1" x 15'+ with clip
- Tripod with pulley
- Walk board*
- Short-handled shovel
- Ten-foot probes*
- Posthole digger

- Pry bar
- Ax
- Five-gallon buckets
- Heavy tarps
- Hardhat and gloves

Indicates essential item

General Rules and Helpful Hints

Although I said there were no rules to bottle collecting, when digging there are two major rules you always need to follow.

Rule No. 1:

Always be responsible and respectful and ask for permission to dig. As a safety precaution, do not leave any holes open overnight. Do not damage shrubs, trees, or flowers unless the owner approves. When the digging is complete, always leave the site looking better than when you started. I can't stress this enough. That means filling in all holes and raking over the area. Take out your trash as well as any trash left by previous prospectors or others. Always offer to give the owner some of the bottles. They may not want any, but they will appreciate the gesture. If you adhere to these few rules, the community or owner will thank you, and future bottle diggers will be welcomed. The following is a summary of the "Bottle Digger's Code of Ethics" (compliments of the San Diego Bottle Club).

- Respect property rights and all warning signs.
- To respect both public and private property, always obtain valid permission to search, probe, or dig on the property.
- Do not park illegally and do park so that other vehicles can get out.
- Upon entering public or private property, do not damage or destroy any property improvements on the site.
- After digging on a site, try to leave all land and vegetation as it was by taking the necessary time to properly fill all holes and re-root plants when possible.
- Remove or bury existing litter and all unwanted items from your search area, leaving it cleaner than you found it.
- As a representative of all bottle collectors and diggers, be thoughtful, considerate, and courteous at all times.

Rule No. 2:

Do not, under any circumstances, dig alone. Ignoring this rule is extremely dangerous. When digging an outhouse, my recommendation is to go with no fewer than three people, and be sure to tell someone exactly where you're going and how long you expect to be gone. Here are some tragic examples to stress the dangers of digging alone:

While this story isn't directly related to bottle digging, it is a good example of what can happen to anyone digging for bottles or other relics and artifacts. In April 2015, a fossil hunter was digging for shark teeth in Bakersfield, California, on an unstable hillside, on private property, and was buried from the neck down when a portion of the hillside collapsed. By the time help arrived, he was unable to be saved. It was noted by the authorities that this area was known to be composed of unstable sand, silt, and clay.

On Sept. 23, 2002, in Honolulu, Hawaii, a 55-year-old bottle collector was digging for bottles in a trench at the Waipahu Sugar Mill, which is a prized area because of the numerous plantations that were in the area. Without warning, the trench collapsed and he was buried under six feet of dirt and suffocated. Another tragedy happened in March 2003 in Ramona, California, when an avid bottle collector and digger, digging in a ravine soaked by several days of heavy rain, was crushed by concrete, stone, dirt, and a large boulder when the unstable ground collapsed.

In June 2005, a group of experienced bottle diggers were following the rules, as they always did, while digging in downtown Los Angeles at an old brewing company site when, without warning, a five-foot berm collapsed, pouring tons of earth and gravel over one of the club members. Firefighters tried desperately for 45 minutes to dig out the individual, but loose dirt continued to fall back on the digger. They couldn't get him out in time and he was slowly crushed to death.

These stories are a reminder that safety is the most important issue. Follow all rules and don't dig alone! Don't be discouraged if you don't find any bottles. If you unearth other objects such as coins, broken dishes, or bottle tops, continue to dig deeper and in a wider circle. If you still don't find any bottles, move to another spot. Always work from the edge to the center of the hole. Don't give up! Even the best have come home with empty bags and boxes but never without the memory of a good time. When you do find a bottle, stop digging and remove the surrounding dirt a little at a time with a small tool, brush, or spoon. Handle the bottle very carefully, since old bottles are very fragile.

Now that you know how to dig, what are you waiting for? Grab those tools, get those maps, and get started making the discoveries of a lifetime.

Bottle Diggers of New Orleans: 'The Crescent City Connection'

Rick Weiner of Allentown, Pennsylvania, who was featured in the "Digging for Bottles" section in the 7th edition, has not only been doing a lot of digging since he was 15, finding rare and scarce bottles, but also has been writing about his and others' digging adventures. In an article he wrote for the August 2014 edition of *Antique Bottle & Glass Collector* magazine, "The Crescent City Connection," he highlighted the adventures of two of his digging buddies, Charlie Cook and Terry Guidroz, who both reside in New Orleans. In fact, Rick considers Charlie his mentor. He helped Rick understand privy digging when he dug his first privy, and they still keep in touch on a regular basis. In order to enjoy the full experience of the digging adventures of Charlie and Terry, I recommend contacting John Pastor at *Antique Bottle & Glass Collector* for a copy of the magazine to read the entire article.

Terry Guidroz giving direction to his digging crew.

One of digging crew throwing out privy dirt.

New Orleans was known throughout the 18th century as The Crescent City because of the crescent-shaped turn in the Mississippi River.

After reading the article, I couldn't resist not featuring both of these guys in the 8th edition, and contacted Rick for permission to reference his article along with some photos. Just to add another twist to this fun story, I had featured Terry in the 3rd edition of my book in the "Digging for Bottles" section. He was also the poster boy for the front cover of the April 1999 edition of *Antique Bottle & Glass Collector*. As it worked out,

Introduction

because of Rick's article, Terry and I have had a bottle reconnection.

Rick's definition of Charlie and Terry is "happy-go-lucky and crazy. They love to dig just for the love of old bottles, with some odd behavior and craziness for good measure."

Since Charlie is 78 and Terry is a few years younger, occasional health issues have hampered their favorite hobby of privy digging, but not their passion for antique bottle collecting. Here are several photos of their digging adventures.

American Drug Store – New Orleans bottle, found during a privy dig.

Charlie Cook holding a freshly dug large cathedral bottle/jar.

Cleaned bottles from a privy dig.

More cleaned bottles from a privy dig.

Bottle Handling

While selling bottles and listening to buyers at various shows, I am inevitably asked questions about cleaning, handling, and storing old bottles. Some collectors believe cleaning a bottle diminishes its value and desirability. Leaving a bottle in its natural state can be special. Others prefer to remove as much dirt and residue as possible. The choice rests with the owner. The following information will help take care of your collection.

Bottle Cleaning

First, never attempt to clean a find in the field, since improper handling or cleaning may result in unwanted damage. In the excitement of the moment, it's easy to break the bottle or otherwise damage the embossing. With the exception of soda and ale bottles, glass bottles manufactured prior to 1875 usually have very thin walls. But even bottles with thicker walls should be handled carefully.

The first step is to remove as much loose dirt, sand, or other particles as possible with a small hand brush or a soft bristled toothbrush, followed by a quick warm water rinse. Then, using a warm water solution and bleach (stir the mixture first), soak the bottles for a number of days depending upon the amount of caked-on dirt. This should remove most of the excess grime. Also, adding a little vinegar to warm water will give an extra sparkle to the glass.

Other experienced collectors use cleaning mixtures such as straight ammonia, kerosene, Lime-Away, Mr. Clean, and chlorine Borax bleach. Do not use mixtures that are not recommended for cleaning glass, never mix cleaners, and do not clean with acids of any type. Mixing cleaners have been known to release toxic gases and poisonous vapors and fumes. A fellow bottle collector from Arizona has his own technique. He buys a special polish for rock-polishing and mixes it with warm water to form a compound. He then lightly rubs the bottle, continuing to use cool water on the surface. I have seen a number of his bottles and the finished results are fantastic.

After soaking, the bottles may be cleaned with a bottle brush, steel wool, an old toothbrush, any semi-stiff brush, Q-tips, or used dental picks.

At this point, you may want to soak the bottles again in lukewarm water to remove any trace of cleaning materials. Either let the bottles air-dry or dry them with a soft towel.

Introduction

If the bottle has a paper label, the work will become more difficult since soaking is not a cleaning option. I've used a Q-tip to clean and dry the residue around the paper label.

Never clean bottles in a dishwasher. While the hot water and detergent may produce a clean bottle, older bottles were not designed to withstand the extreme heat. As a result, the heat, combined with the shaking, could crack or even shatter fragile old bottles. Bottles with any type of a painted label may also be subjected to severe damage.

A better option is to consult a specialist who will clean your rare bottles with special tumbling, or cleaning machines. These machines work on the same principle as a rock tumbler with two parallel bars running horizontally acting as a "cradle" for the cleaning canisters. The machine cleaning process uses two types of oxides, one for polishing and one for cutting. The polishing oxides include aluminum, cerium and tin, which remove stains and give the glass a crystal clean and polished appearance, do not damage the embossing. The cutting oxides, such as silicon carbide, removes the etching and scratching. There are many collectors who are in the business of cleaning bottles, or you can purchase the machines, learn the process, and clean the bottles yourself. If you decide to use someone, always ask to see examples of his work and try to find someone who's been recommended by another collector.

Bottle Display

Now that you have clean, beautiful bottles, display them to their best advantage. My advice is to arrange your bottles in a cabinet rather than on wall shelving or randomly around the house. While the last two options are more decorative, they also leave the bottles more susceptible to damage. When choosing a cabinet, try to find one with glass sides that will provide more light and better viewing. As an added touch, lighting within the cabinet will set off your collection beautifully.

If you still desire a wall shelving arrangement, make sure the shelf is approximately 12" wide with a front lip for added protection. The lip can be made from quarter-round molding. After the bottle is placed in its spot, draw an outline around the base of the bottle and then drill four 1/4-inch holes just outside that outline for pegs. These pegs will provide further stability for the bottle. If you have picked up any other goodies from your digging like coins, tokens, railroad spikes, or gambling chips, scatter them around the bottles for a little Western flavor.

Bottle Protection

Because of earthquake activity, especially in California, bottle collectors across the country have taken steps to protect their valuable pieces.

Since most of us have our collections in some type of display cabinet, it's important to know how to best secure it. First, fasten the cabinet to the wall with brackets and bolts. If you are working with drywall and it's not possible to secure the cabinet to a stud, butterfly bolts will provide a tight hold. Always secure the cabinet at both the top and bottom for extra protection.

Next, lock or latch the cabinet doors. This will prevent the doors from flying open. If your cabinet has glass shelves, be sure not to overload them with too many bottles. In an earthquake, the glass shelving can break under the stress of excess weight.

Finally, it's important to secure the bottles to the shelves. A number of materials can be used, such as microcrystalline wax, beeswax, silicone adhesive, double-sided foam tape, or adhesive backed Velcro spots or strips. These materials are available at home improvement centers and hardware stores. One of the newest and most commonly used adhesives is called Quake Hold. This substance, available in wax, putty and gel, is similar to the wax product now used extensively by numerous museums to secure art, sculptures and various glass pieces. It is readily available at many home improvement stores and antiques shops.

Bottle Storage

The best method for storing bottles you've chosen not to display is to place them in empty liquor boxes with cardboard dividers, which prevent them from bumping into each other. For added protection, wrap individual bottles in paper prior to packing them in the boxes. As a general note, this method of storage is also a good idea when traveling to bottle club meetings, bottle shows, or antiques shows to display or sell your bottles.

Record Keeping

Last but not least, it's a good idea to keep records of your collection. Whether you use index cards or computer software, record where the bottle was found or purchased, including the dealer's name and price you paid. Many collectors keep records with the help of a photocopy machine. If the bottle has embossing or a label, put the bottle on a copy machine and copy it. Another method is to make a pencil sketch by applying white computer paper to the bottle and rubbing over the embossing with a No. 2 pencil. Then, record all the pertinent information on the back of the image and put it in a binder. When it comes to trading and selling, excellent record keeping will prove to be invaluable.

Old Bottles

Pre-1900

T he bottles in this section have been categorized by physical type and/or by the original contents of the bottle. For most categories, the trade names can be found in alphabetical order if they exist. Note that in the case of certain early bottles, such as flasks, a trade name does not appear on the bottle. These bottles have been listed by subject according to the embossing, label, or other identification on the bottle.

Since it is impossible to list every bottle available, I've provided a representative selection of bottles in various price ranges and categories, rather than listing only the rarest or most collectible pieces.

The pricing shown reflects the value of the particular bottle listed. Similar bottles could have higher or lower values than the bottles specifically listed in this book, but the listings that follow provide collectors an excellent starting point for determining a reasonable price range.

Ale & Gin

Since ale and gin bottles are similar and almost identical in style, it becomes difficult to determine what the bottle originally contained unless information is provided on the bottle itself. Ale bottles should not be confused with beer bottles, a common mistake due to the similarities in shape.

Ale was a more popular beverage at a time when available wines were not as palatable. Ale quickly became a favorite alternative since it was not expensive to make or buy. The bottles used by Colonial ale makers were made of pottery and imported from England. When searching out these bottles, keep

Group of four embossed miniature gin sample bottles, olive green and clear glass, 4" to 6-3/4", names as follows: small clear–H. Van Emden; large clear–Levert & Schudel; small green–E. Kinderlen; large green–JDKZ & John De Kuper & Son Rotterdam, 1855-1865, $100-150.

in mind that the oldest ones had a matte or unglazed surface. Unlike ale, gin doesn't have an ancient origin but it certainly does have a unique one.

In the 17th century, a Dutch physician named Francesco De La Bor prepared gin as a medical compound for the treatment of kidney disease, gout, and indigestion. While its effectiveness to purify the blood or cure anything was questionable, gin drinking became popular. It became so popular and profitable, in fact, that many chemists, along with physicians, decided to go into the gin-brewing business full time to meet the growing demand. Gin was cheap to make and even cheaper to buy, and soon became known as the working man's drink. During the 19th century, with increased imports of gin from the English and Dutch, and increased production in American, gin consumption in the still-growing United States increased at a steady rate.

Old Bottles

The design of the gin bottle, which has a squat body, facilitated the case packing and prevented shifting and possible damage in shipping. The first case bottles were octagonal with short necks and manufactured with straight sides that allowed four to twelve bottles to fit tightly into a wooden packing case. Designs that were introduced later featured longer necks.

Bottles with tapered collars are dated to the 19th century. The case bottle sizes vary in size from half-pints to multiple gallons. The early bottles were crudely made and have distinct pontil scars.

A.M. Bininger & Co. / No. 17 Broad St. – Old London Dock – Gin Yellow olive green, 9-1/2", smooth base, applied tapered collar top, American, 1865-1875.	$250-300	
A.M. Bininger & Co. / No. 17 Broad St. – Old London Dock – Gin (Small Crown on Shoulder) Yellow olive green, 9-3/4", smooth base, applied tapered collar top American, 1855-1870.	$350-400	
A.M. Bininger & Co. / No. 17 Broad St. – Old London Dock – Gin -75% Original Label Yellow olive green, 9-7/8", smooth base, applied tapered collar top, American, 1855-1870.	$300-350	
A.M. Bininger & Co. / No. 17 Broad St. – Old London Dock – Gin Dark amber, 10", smooth base, applied top, American, 1855-1870.	$300-350	
Anderson & Co / Home Brewed Ale / Albany, N.Y. Yellow with olive tone, 7-1/4", squat shape, smooth base, applied blob top, American, 1865-1875.	$500-700	

Very Old Gin – original label reads: Honey Suckle-Old Gin-J.J. Melchers Wz. Schiedam, yellow olive green, 10-1/2", applied top and handle, (Dutch for American Market), 1865-1875, $200-225.

Gin Cocktail – S.M & Co. – N.Y. (on applied seal), medium yellow amber, 10-1/8", open pontil, applied double collar top, 1855-1870, $600-700.

R.E. Messenger & Co. – London Cordial Gin, deep yellow olive amber, 9-7/8", iron pontil, applied double collar top, 1850-1860, $600-700.

Charles – London Cordial Gin, medium teal blue, 9-5/8", applied tapered collar top, 1865-1875, $400-450.

Old Bottles

Booth & Sedgwick's – London – Cordial Gin Emerald green, 9-7/8", iron pontil, applied tapered collar top, American, 1850-1860.	$900-$1,000	
Booth & Sedgwick's – London – Cordial Gin Dark teal, 9-7/8", graphite pontil, applied tapered collar top, American, 1850-1860.	$1,000-1,100	
Case Gin Bottle (Unembossed) Deep sapphire blue (shades from a darker color in the lower two-thirds to a lighter color in the upper one-third), 10-1/4", smooth base, tooled blob top, rare, American, 1875-1890.	$250-300	
Charles' – London – Cordial Gin Deep blue aqua/teal, 10", smooth base, applied tapered collar top, American, 1860-1875.	$150-200	
Cream Ale – A. Templeton / Louisville (Around Mug Base) Deep reddish amber, quart, 6-7/8", "L&W" on smooth base, applied sloping double collar top, American, 1870-1880.	$250-300	
Cream Ale – A. Templeton / Louisville (Around Mug Base) Amber, quart, 6-7/8" (large 5 pointed star) on smooth base, applied tapered double collar top, American, 1870-1875.	$400-500	
D. T. Sweeny – Philadelphia / XX /Porter & Ale Medium cobalt blue, 6-7/8", smooth base, applied tapered double collar top, American, 1855-1865.	$2,000-2,500	

Dr. Cronk Gibbons & Co / Superior Ale / Buffalo / N.Y. Deep emerald green, 6-5/8", squat shape, iron pontil, applied blob top, American, 1845-1869.	$500-600	
Gin Bottle Cobalt blue, 10-1/4", tapered body form, smooth base, tooled blob top, rare color, American, 1875-1890.	$325-350	
H.H.S. & Co. – Imperial Gin Orange amber, 9-5/8", tapered body shape, "L&W" on smooth base, applied top, rare, Lorenz & Wightman Glass Works, Pittsburg, PA, American, 1865-1875.	$250-300	
Herman Jansen / Schiedam / Holland (Applied Seal) Medium olive green, 10-3/8", smooth base, applied top, Dutch, 1875-1895.	$75-100	
J.C. Buffum / Pittsburgh – XXX / Porter Deep emerald green, 6-1/2", squat shape, smooth base, applied double collar top, American, 1860-1875.	$800-900	
J. H. Henkes Medium olive green, 11-5/8", smooth base, applied top, Dutch, 1875-1895.	$75-100	
J.T. Beueker's Schiedam Case Gin Dark forest green, 10-1/2", cross on smooth base, applied top, American, 1875-1890.	$100-150	
J. T. Daly Clubhouse Case Gin (With backward "S") Olive amber, 10-1/4", tapered shape, smooth base, applied top, American, 1875-1890.	$200-250	

Old Bottles

John Ryan / Phila. XX Porter & Ale Cobalt blue, 6-7/8", pontil scarred base, applied blob top, American, 1840-1860.	**$125-150**	
John Ryan / 1852 Augusta & Savannah GA / Philad. A XX Porter & Ale (on reverse) Cobalt blue, 6-7/8", smooth base, applied blob top, American, 1840-1860.	**$250-300**	
John Ryan / Philad. A XX/ 1859/ Porter & Ale Cobalt blue, 6-7/8", smooth base, applied top, American, 1850-1860.	**$100-150**	
London/Jockey-Club House/Gin (rider on a horse) Medium blue green, 9-1/4", smooth base, applied tapered collar top, American, 1860-1875.	**$900-1,000**	
London/Jockey-Club House/Gin (rider on a horse) Deep olive amber, 9-1/4", iron pontil, applied tapered collar top, rare color, American, 1855-1865.	**$900-1,000**	
London/Jockey – Club House/Gin Medium yellow amber, 9-1/4", smooth base, applied top, American, 1850-1860.	**$4,500-5,000**	
London/Jockey – Club House/Gin Almond straw yellow, 9-3/4", smooth base, applied tapered collar top, American, 1850-1860.	**$6,000-7,000**	

Ale & Gin

London/Jockey – Club House/Gin (rider on a horse) Emerald green, 9-3/4", iron pontil, applied tapered collar top, variant with the backward "Ns" in London, American, 1850-1860.	$2,200-2,300
London Royal Imperial Gin Cobalt blue, 9-3/4", smooth base, applied top, American, 1870-1880.	$600-700
M. Mc.Cormack – XXX / Porter Emerald green, 7", iron pontil, applied blob top, American, 1840-1860.	$450-500
Old Holland Gin – Greene & Gladding – 62 Cortland St/New York, New York Deep blue green, 8", smooth base, applied top, American, 1860-1875.	$400-500
Superior Old Centaur Gin – (Centaur)- L.M. & Co. New York –"LM & C" -99% Label (on applied shoulder seal) Deep olive green, 9-1/2", Case Bottle, smooth base, applied single collar top and seal.	$175-200
Van Denbergh & Co. (motif of a bell) Medium olive green, 10-3/8", smooth base, applied top, Dutch, 1875-1895.	$75-100
W.S.C./Club House Gin Yellow olive green, 9-1/4", tapered body form, smooth base, applied top, American, 1860-1870.	$100-150
W.S.C./Club House Gin Yellow olive green, 9-1/2", smooth base, applied ring top, American, 1860-1875.	$350-400

Barber

Starting in the mid-1860s and continuing to 1920, barbers in America used a wide variety of colorful and uniquely decorated bottles filled with various tonics such as hair oils, bay rum, rosewater, colognes, and scented shampoos. The mixture of these different types of tonics and colognes were usually accomplished by the barbers, who would then order and fill the containers from the various glass factories. The use of these unique and colorful pieces began when the Pure Food and Drug Act of 1906 restricted the use of alcohol based ingredients in unlabeled or refillable containers.

Early examples will have rough pontil scars, with numerous types depicting fancy pressed designs, paintings, and labels under glass. The bottles were usually fitted with a cork, metal, or porcelain-type closure. Since the value of barber bottles is dependent upon the painted or enameled lettering or decoration, it is important to note that when determining the value of a barber bottle, any type of wear such as faded decoration or color, faded lettering, or chipping will lower their value.

Barber bottle, medium cobalt blue, 8-1/4", pontil scarred base, tooled rolled lip, 1885-1925, $300-400.

Barber bottle, yellow green, 7-7/8", open pontil, sheared and tooled lip, 1885-1925, $150-200.

Barber Bottles (set of 2) Robin egg blue, 5", smooth base, tooled top, gold trim decoration, American, 1885-1920.	$100-125	
Barber Bottle Fiery opalescent cranberry, 7", stars and stripes pattern, polished pontil, tooled top, American, 1885-1920.	$150-200	
Barber Bottle Fiery opalescent cranberry, 7-1/8", Spanish lace pattern bell shape, polished pontil, rolled top, American, 1885-1920.	$200-225	
Barber Bottle Light turquoise blue, 7-1/4", rib pattern with multicolored enamel floral decoration, polished pontil, tooled top, American, 1885-1920.	$200-250	
Barber Bottles (set of 2) Medium amethyst, 7-1/2", enameled floral decoration, pontiled base, tooled top, American, 1885-1920.	$100-125	

Old Bottles

Barber Bottles (set of 2) - Bay Rum & Witch Hazel Opalescent milk glass, 8-1/2", multicolored trumpet flower and vine decoration, smooth base, applied top, American, 1890-1915.	$200-250	
Mahdeen For Dandruff / For External Use Only / The Mahdeen Company, Nachogdoches, Texas Clear glass, 8-1/4", white and blue enameled label, smooth base, ABM top, American, 1925-1935.	$150-200	
Barber Bottles (set of 2) Clear glass, 7 ", enameled dots with gold trim decoration, smooth base, rolled top, American, 1885-1925. Clear glass, 10", blue lupine flora decoration, smooth base, rolled top, American, 1885-1925.	$50-70 $50-70	
Barber Bottles (set of 2) Emerald green, 7-7/8", rib pattern, smooth base, rolled top, American, 1885-1925. Yellow olive, 6-3/4", rib pattern, pontil scarred base, tooled top, American, 1885-1925.	$50-75 $65-85	
Barber Bottles (set of 2) Turquoise blue, 7-3/4", rib pattern with white and orange enamel decoration, pontil scarred base, sheared and tooled top, American, 1885-1925. Metallic orange and pink, 7-3/4", rib pattern, smooth base, sheared and polished lip, American, 1885-1925.	$60-80 $70-90	

Barber Bottle Fiery opalescent cranberry red, 6-7/8", white coral decoration, polished pontiled base, tooled top, scarce pattern and form, American, 1885-1925.	**$300-400**
Barber Bottle Medium pink amethyst, 6-7/8", rib pattern, yellow/white/red floral decoration, open pontil, sheared and tooled top, American, 1885-1925.	**$175-250**
Barber Bottle Fiery opalescent turquoise blue, 6-7/8", bell shape, Spanish Lace Pattern, polished pontil, rolled top, American, 1885-1920.	**$200-250**
Barber Bottle Fiery opalescent turquoise blue, 7-1/8", white coral pattern, polished pontiled base, rolled top, American, 1885-1925.	**$250-350**

Barber Bottle	$250-350	
Clear glass, 7-1/8", coin spot pattern milk glass, polished pontiled base, rolled top, extremely rare, American, 1885-1925.		
Barber Bottle	**$200-300**	
Fiery opalescent milk glass, 7-1/2", colorful cherub decoration, pontil scarred base, sheared and tooled top, American, 1885-1925.		
Barber Bottle	**$200-250**	
Deep cobalt blue, 7-5/8", rib-pattern with white and orange enamel floral decoration, corset waist shape, pontil scarred base, rolled top, American, 1885-1920.		
Barber Bottle	**$200-250**	
Deep purple amethyst, 7-5/8", satin finish, rib-pattern with yellow and gold Art Nouveau-style floral decoration, pontil scarred base, rolled top, American, 1885-1920.		

Barber Bottle	$150-200	
Light apple green, 8-1/8", thumb spot pattern, white/yellow/orange enamel floral decoration, pontil scarred base, tooled top, American, 1885-1925.		

Barber Bottle	$150-250	
Opalescent turquoise blue, 8-1/4", square shape, white rib pattern swirled to right, smooth base, rolled top, American, 1885-1925.		

Barber Bottle	$300-400	
Medium cobalt blue, 8-1/4", white and orange floral design, pontil scarred base, tooled rolled top, American, 1885-1925.		

Barber Bottle	$200-250	
Fiery opalescent turquoise blue, 8-1/4", square shape, Spanish Lace Pattern, polished pontil, rolled top, American, 1885-1920.		

Barber Bottle Frosted clear glass, 8-1/4", blue and green enamel decoration and applied glass beads, pontil scarred base, rolled top, extremely rare, American, 1885-1920.	**$400-500**	
Barber Bottle Fiery opalescent cranberry red, 8-5/8", square shape, rib pattern to left, smooth base, rolled top, American, 1885-1925.	**$150-250**	
Barber Bottle Fiery opalescent robin egg blue, 8-5/8", white/green/maroon floral decoration, open pontil, rolled top, American, 1885-1925.	**$250-350**	
Barber Bottle Fiery opalescent turquoise blue, 9-1/4", white rib pattern, smooth base, rolled top, American, 1885-1925.	**$150-200**	

Beer

Attempting to find an American beer bottle made before the mid-19th century is a difficult task. Until then, most bottles used for beer and spirits were imported. The majority of these imported bottles were black glass pontiled bottles made in three-piece molds and rarely embossed. There are four types of early beer bottles:

1. **Porter**, which is the most common: 1820 to 1920

2. **Ale:** 1845 to 1850

3. **Early lager:** 1847 to 1850 - rare

4. **Late lager:** 1850 to 1860

In spite of the large amounts of beer consumed in America before 1860, beer bottles were very rare and all have pontiled bases. Most beer manufactured during this time was distributed and dispensed from wooden barrels, or kegs, and sold to local taverns and private bottlers. Collectors often ask why various breweries did not bottle the beer they manufactured. During the Civil War, the federal government placed a special tax, levied by the barrel, on all brewed beverages. This taxing system prevented the brewery from making the beer and bottling it in the same building. Selling the beer to taverns and private bottlers was much simpler than erecting

Boca (monogram B & B) Beer, amber, 11-1/2", quart, applied top, 1885-1900, $250-300.

Buffalo Brewing Co. – S.F. Agency, olive green, pint, applied double collar top, 1865-1875, $225-250.

another building for bottling. This entire process changed after 1890 when the federal government revised the law to allow breweries to bottle beer straight from the beer lines.

Along with the brewing processes, the federal government also revised guidelines for bottle cleanliness.

Old Bottles

The chart below reflects the age and rarity of beer bottles.

YEAR	RARE	SCARCE	SEMI-COMMON	COMMON
1860-1870	X			
1870-1880		X		
1880-1890			X	
1890-1930				X

Embossed bottles marked "Ale" or "Porter" were manufactured between 1850 and 1860. In the late 1860s, the breweries began to emboss their bottles with names and promotional messages. This practice continued into the 20th century. It is interesting to note that Pennsylvania breweries made most of the beer bottles from the second half of the 19th century. By 1890, beer was readily available in bottles around most of the country.

The first bottles used for beer in the United States were made of pottery, not glass. Glass did not become widely used until after the Civil War (1865). A wholesaler for Adolphus Busch named C. Conrad sold the original Budweiser beer from 1877 to 1890. The Budweiser name was a trademark of C. Conrad, but in 1891, it was sold to the Anheuser-Busch Brewing Association.

Before the 1870s, beer bottles were sealed with cork stoppers. Late in the 19th century, the lightning stopper was invented. It proved a convenient way of sealing and resealing blob top bottles. In 1891 corks were replaced with the crown cork closure invented by William Painter. This made use of a thin slice of cork within a tight-fitting metal cap. Once these were removed, they couldn't be used again.

Until the 1930s, beer came in green glass bottles. After Prohibition, brown glass came into use since it was thought to filter out damaging rays of the sun and preserve freshness.

Group of five Anheuser-Busch embossed beer bottles, blue aqua, 1880-1895 - $300-350.

Group of four Conrad & Co. Budweiser embossed beer bottles, blue aqua, 1st bottle 9-1/2", next three bottles 12-1/4", 1885-1895, $700-800.

A.G. Boehm – 78-82 Esses St. – Lawrence – Mass-Registered - This Bottle Not To Be Sold Orange amber, 9-3/8", smooth base, tooled blob top, American, 1885-1900.	$750-100	
A.G. Van Nostrano – Charlestown – Mass – Bunker Hill Lager (inside banner) – Bunker Hill – Breweries – Established 1821 – Registered Medium amber, 9-5/8", smooth base, tooled top, original lightning style closure, American, 1885-1900.	$100-125	
August Reinig – 2107 – Germantown –Ave – Philada. – This Bottle Not To Be Sold Yellow with olive tone, 9-1/2", smooth base (1A), tooled blob top, American, 1885-1900.	$75-100	
August Stoehr – Milwaukee-Lager-Mancheste, N.H. – This Bottle Not To Be Sold Medium yellow olive, 9", smooth base (No. 2), tooled top, original lightning style closure, American, 1885-1900.	$100-150	
Anheuser-Busch –Bottling Works – Los Angeles, Cal. Medium amber, half-pint, smooth base, tooled top, American, 1880-1890.	$800-900	
Anheuser-Busch – Liquid Bread – St. Louis USA Cobalt blue, 9-3/4", smooth base, applied top, original ceramic marked cap, intact paper label, rare, American, 1880-1900 (Morphy-1951).	$250-350	

Old Bottles

B & Co (monogram inside diamond) – A. Bierweiler & Co – Boston – Mass-Registered Medium golden yellow amber, 9-1/4", smooth mug base, tooled top, American.	$150-200	
B.B. Co. – This Bottle Not To Be Sold Clear, quart, smooth base, applied top, American, 1875-1885.	$75-100	
BayView – Brewing Co. – Seattle, Wash. Brilliant grass green, quart, smooth base, applied top, American, 1880-1890.	$300-400	
Boca (monogram B-B) Beer Medium amber, 11-1/2", smooth base, applied top, American, 1880-1890.	$250-300	

Buffalo BR'G Co. – Sacramento – Not To Be Sold Red amber, quart, smooth base, applied top, American, 1880-1890.	$75-100	
Chas Joly – No 9 – So Seventh St – Philadelphia – This Bottle Not To Be Sold Medium olive green, 9-1/2", smooth base, tooled top, American, 1885-1900.	$75-100	
Chas R. Puckhaber – 856-858 I. STR. – Fresno, CAL. Medium amber, quart, smooth base, crown top, American, 1920-1930.	$75-100	
Clapp (Porter Ale Beer) Red amber, smooth base, blob top, American, 1860-1870.	$250-300	

Clause Brothers – Birch Beer – Elizabeth N.J. – Bottle Not To Be Sold Medium yellow green (citron), 7-1/4", smooth base, Hutchinson Tooled top, American, 1890-1910.	$250-300	
Doering & Marstrand's Brewing Co. Vancover Medium yellow amber, quart, smooth base, applied top, American, 1880-1890.	$200-250	
Dr. Bates – Trade Mark – National Tonic Beer – Centennial 1876 - This Bottle Never Sold Red amber, 8-5/8", round-bottom shape, smooth base, applied top, original pull over wire closure, American, 1876.	$250-300	
Dr. Cronks – Beer Teal blue, 9-1/2", 12-sided, iron pontil, applied top, only known example in this color, American, 1845-1860.	$1,700-1,800	
Dr. Cronk's Sarsaparilla Beer Tan Stoneware, 10", 8-sided, smooth base (E.H. & C.J. Merrill Middlebury, Ohio) rolled top, American, 1840-1860.	$150-200	

Dr. Cronk's – R.MC.C Cobalt blue, 10", 12-sided, iron pontil, applied tapered collar top, American, 1850-1860.	$1,200-1,500	
Dr. J. Cornwall Brewin Co.- St. Louis, Missouri Brilliant medium amber, 7", smooth base, blob top, American, 1875-1890.	$400-450	
E & G – Doughty Millville Medium grass green, 6-3/4", smooth base, applied double collar top, American, 1860-1870.	$350-400	
E. Wagner – Trade W (inside cross) Mark – Manchester – N.H. – The Property Of E. Wagner – Not Sold Medium yellow with olive tone, 9-1/8", smooth base, tooled top, original lightning style closure, American, 1885-1900.	$150-200	
E. Wagner – Trade W (inside cross) Mark – Manchester – N.H. – The Property Of E. Wagner – Not Sold Medium yellow amber, 9-3/8", smooth base, tooled top, American, 1885-1900.	$150-200	
F. Jacob Jockers – 803-805 – Dickinson St – Phila, PA. – Registered – Contents 12-1/2 OZ. Medium cobalt blue, 9", smooth base, tooled top, original unmarked porcelain stopper and lighting style closure, few tall blob top beers made in cobalt blue glass, American, 1885-1900.	$250-300	
F. J. Kastner – FJK (monogram inside diamond) – Newark N.J. – This Bottle Not To Be Sold Medium yellow amber, 9-3/8", smooth base, tooled top, American, 1885-1900.	$150-200	

Fredericksburg Bottling Co.	$125-150	
Brilliant green, 9-1/4", pint, smooth base, applied top with original closure, American, 1880-1890.		

G. Rivera's – Pine. Apple. Beer – Patd Feb. 11, 1868	$250-300	
Aqua, 7-1/2", smooth base, applied blob top, original cork and wire closure, rare beer flavored by pine and apple, American, 1868-1880.		

G.W. Hoxsie's - Premium Beer	$250-300	
Blue green, 6-2/3", smooth base, applied tapered collar top, American, 1870-1885.		

Buffalo Bottling Works – S L O – Lager Beer, medium amber, quart, 1880-1985, $225-250.

Buffalo Br'G Co. – Sacramento – Not To Be Sold, red amber, quart, 1880-1895, $75-100.

Anheuser-Bush – Bottling Works – Los Angeles, medium amber, half-pint, 1885-1900, $800-900.

Assortment of five paper labeled beer bottles, two Old Nick (with contents), Cream City Brewery, Milwaukee – Pabst Sheboygan Aromatic Ginger Ale Beer – Pabst Breweries – Employees Beer – Milwaukee, Wisconsin – Jung's Pilsner Beer, 1920s-1930s, $50 ea.

Old Bottles

Geo. W. Hoxsie's – Premium Beer Dark olive amber, 7", smooth base, applied heavy collared top, Westford Glass Works, Westford, Connecticut, American, 1860-1873.	$350-400	
H. Clausen & Son – Brewing Co – 888-890-2nd Ave. – New York – Phoenix Bottling – This Bottle Not To Be Sold Medium olive green, 9-1/8", smooth base, tooled top, original lightning style closure, American, 1885-1900.	$100-125	
H. Koehler & Co. – Fidelio Beer – New York Deep amber, 8-5/8", smooth base, tooled top, original unmarked porcelain stopper and lightning style closure, American, 1885-1900.	$65-85	
H. B. Kilmer – New York – Philada-Porter & Ale Medium blue green, 6-1/2", iron pontil, applied top, scarce, American, 1840-1860.	$200-250	
Henry Weinhard – Export Beer - Portland, OR Medium amber, quart, smooth base (SF & PGW), tooled top, American, 1880-1890.	$150-200	

Hoosac Bottling Works – JLG (monogram) Hoosac Falls. N.Y. – This Bottle Not To Be Sold Medium amber, 9-1/8", smooth base, tooled top, American, 1885-1900.	**$75-100**	
I.F. Larson – S.F. Medium amber, quart, smooth base, applied top, American, 1880-1890.	**$75-100**	
J. Gahm – Trade (motif of mug) Mark – Boston – Mass- Milwaukee- Larger Beer Medium yellow amber, 9-3/8", smooth base, tooled top, original lighting style closure, American, 1885-1900.	**$65-85**	
J.C. Gibson – Millville N.J. – XX- Porter & Ale Medium blue green, 7", smooth base, applied double collar top, American, 1860-1870.	**$250-300**	
J. Corwell (in a slug plate)- Union Glass Works, Philada- Brown – Stout Sapphire blue, 6-3/4", squat shape, iron pontil, applied double collar top, American, 1840-1960.	**$1,000-1,100**	

Jacob Schuster – Danville PA (in a slug plate) – Brown – Stout Blue green, 7-1/4", smooth base, applied tapered collar top, American, 1855-1865.	$350-400	
Kensington – Brown Stout Emerald green, 6-7/8", squat shape, iron pontil, applied top, rare, Kensington District of Philadelphia, American, 1840-1860.	$200-250	
Kern County – Bakersfield CAL.- Bottling Works Medium amber, quart, smooth base, crown top, American, 1920-1930.	$50-75	
Lemp St. Louis – Lemp's Tally, Wm. J. Lemp Breweries – St. Louis, USA Dark amber, 12", smooth base, applied top, original intact label, American, 1880-1890.	$75-100	
Lemp St. Louis – Lemp's Buck, Wm. J. Lemp Breweries – St. Louis, USA Medium amber, 12", smooth base, applied top, original intact label, American, 1880-1890.	$75-100	
Lynch Bros – Plymouth, PA – This Bottle Not To Be Sold Medium citron green, 9-1/4", smooth base, tooled top, original lighting style closure, American, 1885-1900.	$200-250	

Milwaukee-Bottling Works – Tacoma- Wash. Aqua green, quart, smooth base (M), tooled top, American, 1880-1890.	$350-400	
National Bridge- White Beer – Brewery Light aqua, 9-1/2", smooth base, applied blob top, American, 1870-1885.	$1,300-1,400	
New England 'Stubby' Beer Dark grass green, 6-7/8", iron pontil, applied double collar top, blown in three-part mold, rare color, American, 1840-1860.	$100-150	
Peter Stumpf (eagle with a beer keg in its beak) -Trade Mark- Brewing Co. – Richmond VA – This Bottle Not To Be Sold Orange amber, 8-3/8", smooth base, applied blob top, American, 1880-1890.	$175-225	
Phila – Porter & Ale Medium emerald green, 6-3/4", iron pontil, applied tapered collar top, scarce, American, 1840-1860.	$175-225	
Phillips Bros. – Champion Bottling Works – Trade (motif of two boxers) Mark – Registered-Baltimore MD. U.S.A. – This Bottle is Registered – Not To Be Sold Amber, 9-1/8", smooth base, tooled top, American, 1885-1900.	$50-75	

Registered – The W.H. Cawley Co. – **Somerville – Dover – Flemington – N.J. –** **This Bottle Not To Be Sold** Light green, 9", smooth base (C), tooled top, original lighting style closure, American, 1885-1890.	$50-75	
Registered – Wagner and Matthes – **Lawrence, Mass. Registered** Dark amber, 9-1/4", smooth base, tooled top, American, 1885-1900.	$75-100	
Robert Portner-Brewing Co. – Trade – **Tivoli- Mark- Alexandria, VA – This Bottle** **Not To Be Sold** Yellow olive green, 9-3/8", smooth base, applied blob top, American, 1880-1895.	$150-200	
R. & W. S. – Excelsior – Beer Medium teal blue, 6-1/2", smooth base, applied top, American, 1865-1875.	$150-200	
Saltglaze Stoneware Beer – F. Sandkuhler Gray pottery, 7-1/8", smooth base, yellow mustard glaze blob top, American, 1870-1885.	$100-150	
Saltglaze Stoneware Beer – WC & J & G. **Wilson/Sarsaparilla Mead (impressed on** **shoulder)** Gray pottery, 9-3/4", cobalt blue wash across the impression, smooth base, blob top, American, 1855-1870.	$250-300	
Saltglaze Stoneware Beer – Dr. J. A. Brown Gray pottery, 9-3/4", smooth base, blob top, American, 1845-1850.	$75-100	
Saltglaze Stoneware Beer – Mattlingley's **Boston Beer** Gray pottery with brown shoulder coloration, 9-3/4", smooth base, blob top, American, 1855-1870.	$75-100	

Saltglaze Stoneware Beer – J. P. Plummer – 1853 Cream color body, 9-7/8", smooth base, cobalt blue blob top, light cobalt wash across the lettering, American, 1853-1860.	$75-100	
Saltglaze Stoneware Beer – Cole & Co. Gray brown pottery, 10", smooth base, blob top, Cole & Company bottled at various Baltimore locations from 1840-1870, American, 1855-1870.	$150-200	
Saltglaze Stoneware Beer – Butschky (impressed on shoulder) Gray pottery, 10-1/4", smooth base, blob top, Butschky was a brewer at 109 Eastern Avenue in Baltimore, American, 1840-1860.	$100-150	
Sierra Bottling Co. – Weiland's Best – Jamestown, CAL. Medium amber, quart, smooth base, tooled top, American, 1875-1890.	$600-700	

Bitters

Bitters bottles have long been a favorite of bottle collectors. Because of their uniqueness, they were saved in great numbers, giving the collector of today great opportunities to build a special and varied collection.

Bitters, which originated in England, were a type of medicine made from bitter tasting roots or herbs, giving the concoction its name. During the 18th century, bitters were added to water, ale, or spirits with the intent to cure all types of ailments. Because of the pretense that those mixtures had some medicinal value, bitters became popular in America since Colonists could import them from England without paying the liquor tax. While most bitters had low alcohol content, some brands ranged up as high as 120 proof, higher than most hard liquor available at the time. As physicians became convinced bitters had some type of healing value, the drink became socially acceptable, promoting use among people who normally weren't liquor drinkers.

The best known among the physicians who made their own bitters for patients was Dr. Jacob Hostetter. After his retirement in 1853, he gave permission to his son, David, to manufacture his "cure" commercially. Hostetter Bitters was known for its colorful, dramatic and extreme advertising. While Hostetter said it wouldn't cure everything, the list of ailments it claimed to alleviate with regular use covered most everything: indigestion, diarrhea, dysentery, chills and fever, liver ailments, and pains and weakness that came with old age (at that time, a euphemism for impotence). Despite these claims, David Hostetter died from kidney failure in 1888 that should have been cured by his own bitter formula.

One of the most sought after bitters bottles and perhaps the most unique is Drakes Plantation Bitters that first appeared in 1860 and recorded a patent in 1862. The Drakes Bitters resembles the shape of a log cabin and can be found in four-log and six-log variations with colors in various shades of amber, yellow, citron, puce, green and black. Another interesting characteristic of the Drake Bitters is the miscellaneous dots and marks including the "X" on the base of the bottles that are thought to be identification

Professor Geo. J. Byrne – New York – The Great Universal – Compound Stomach Bitters – Patented 1870, yellow amber, 10-3/4", applied top, 1870-1880, $3,500-4,000.

J. & C. Maguire Chemist & Druggists – St. Louis Mo., label reads: 'Maguire Chemists & Druggist, St.Louis,' cobalt blue, 7-3/4", tooled top, 1870-1880, $700-800.

Hartwig Kantorowicz – Posen – Hamburg – Germany, bright yellow green, case gin shape, 9-1/8", applied top, 1880-1895, $350-400.

marks of the various glass houses that manufactured the bottles.

Most of the bitters bottles, over 1,000 types, were manufactured between 1860 and 1905. The more unique shapes called "figurals" were in the likeness of cannons, drums, pigs, fish and ears of corn. In addition to these shapes, others were round, square, rectangular, barreled-shaped, gin=bottle shaped, twelve sided and flask shaped. The embossed varieties are also the most collectible, oldest and valuable.

The most common color was amber (pale golden yellow to dark amber brown), then aqua (light blue), and sometimes green or clear glass was used. The most rare and most collectible colors are dark blue, amethyst, milk glass and puce (a purplish brown).

A.M. S. 2- 1964- Constitution – Bitters – Seward & Bentley – Buffalo Yellow green, 9-1/2", smooth base, applied tapered collar top, rare color, American, 1865-1875.	$11,000-12,000	
Arabian Bitters – Lawrence & Weichselbaum – Savannah, GA Yellow amber, 9-1/2", smooth base, applied tapered collar top, American, 1870-1880.	$500-600	
Aromatic Orange – Stomach Bitters – Berry, Demoville & Co. – Nashville Medium amber, 9-1/8", smooth base (MCC), applied top, American, 1865-1875.	$1,700-1,800	
Baker's Orange Grove Bitters Yellow with olive tone, 9-1/2", smooth base, applied tapered collar top, American, 1865-1875.	$1,600-1,700	
Balstons Golden Bitters Yellow amber, 10", one of three bitter bottles produced in a triangular shape, smooth base, applied top, American, 1856-1865.	$4,000-5,000	
Blum Siegel & Bros. – New York – Wampoo Bitters Medium yellow green (citron), 10", smooth base, applied double collar top, rare, American, 1865-1875.	$1,200-1,300	
Boozer's – Liver & Kidney- Bitters – Oscar W. Olson – Danville, III Amber, 10-1/2", smooth base, tooled top, extremely rare, American, 1880-1890.	$1,500-1,600	

Boston – Boston – Hop Bitters (Inside an American Flag) – Hop – Bitters – Bitters Reddish amber, 9-5/8", semi-cabin shape, smooth base, applied tapered collar top, Australian, 1870-1880.	$1,300-1,400
Brady's Nerve Bitters Blue aqua, 9-1/4", smooth base, applied double collar top, extremely rare, American, 1865-1875.	$1,400-1,500
Brown's Catalina Medium amber, 10-7/8", figural Spanish cannon, smooth base, applied top, American, 1865-1875.	$350-400
Bryant's Stomach Bitters Olive green, 12-1/8", 8-sided ladies leg, pontil scarred base, applied double collar top, American, 1866-1865.	$2,000-2,200
C. Metzger's Bitters – Cleveland. O. Amber, 9", smooth base, applied tapered collar top, American, 1870-1885.	$1,300-1,400

Old Bottles

California Wine Bitters – From the Vineyards of (woman holding a wine glass)- Kohler & Frohling – Rennert, Prosch & Co. (label) Amber, 12-7/8", lady's leg shape, smooth base, applied top, American, 1880-1890.	**$500-600**	
Caspar Vetter's – Aromatic – German Bitters – 427 Poplar St. Philada Clear, 16-5/8", smooth base, tooled top, American, 1880-1895.	**$500-600**	
Castilian Bitters Yellow amber, 10", cannon figural, smooth base, applied top, scarce, American, 1865-1875.	**$900-1,000**	
Celebrated Crown Bitters – F. Chevalier & Co. – Sole Agents Medium amber, 8-3/4", smooth base, applied tapered collar top, rare, California, American, 1875-1890.	**$400-500**	
Curtis – Cordial – Calisaya – The Great Stomach Bitters – 1866 CCC 1900 Yellow amber with tint of olive, 11-5/8", smooth base, applied top, American, 1866-1875.	**$800-900**	

Dr. Anthony's – Angostura – Improved Bitters – Phila. PA. U.S.A. Golden yellow amber, 8-1/2", smooth base, tooled top, rare, American, 1885-1895.	$250-300	
Dr. Gilbert's Rock and Rye Stomach Bitters Medium teal blue, 7-5/8", smooth base, tooled top, American, 1875-1885.	$1,300-1,400	
Dr. Green's Poleish Bitters (around shoulder) Olive green, 10-7/8", iron pontil, applied double collar top, rare, American, 1845-1860.	$1,200-1,300	
Dr. J. W. James – India – Bitters Reddish amber, 9-1/8", smooth base, applied top, extremely rare, American, 1875-1885.	$800-900	
XX- Dr. Lovergood's Family Bitters Amber, 10-3/8", scarce cottage form, smooth base, applied top, American, 1865-1875.	$2,400-2,500	
Dr. H. Munholland – Chester Co. – Medicated Bitters Amber, 9", smooth base, applied top, American, 1875-1885	$500-600	

Dr. Med. Koch's – Universal – Magen Bitter Deep olive green, 8", smooth base, smooth top, German, 1860-1870.	$700-800	
Dr. R. F. Hibbard's – Wild Cherry – Bitters – C.N. Crittenton – Proprietors N.Y. Aqua, 8-3/8", smooth base, applied top, rare, American, 1855-1865.	$300-350	
Dr. S. Griggs. Detroit – Aromatic Bitters Medium golden amber, 10-3/4", smooth base, applied tapered double collar top, American, 1865-1875.	$1,800-1,900	
Dr. Sawens – Life – Invigorating Bitters – Utica N. Y. Yellow amber, 9-7/8", smooth base, applied tapered collar top, 80 percent original front and reverse labels, American, 1870-1880.	$250-300	
Dr. Stanley's South American Indian Bitters Medium amber, 9", smooth base, tooled top, American, 1880-1890.	$500-600	
Dr. Tompkins Vegetable Bitters Deep teal blue, 9", smooth base, tooled top, rare color, American, 1870-1880.	$900-1,000	

Dr. Walkinshaw's – Curative Bitters – Batavia N.Y. Yellow amber, 10-1/8", smooth base, applied tapered collar top, American, 1870-1880.	$600-700	
Dr. Washington's American Life Bitters Medium amber, 9-1/8", six-neck panels, smooth base, tooled top, rare, American, 1885-1895.	$1,700-1,900	
Dimmitt's – 50CTS. Bitters – Saint Louis Amber, 6-1/2", strap sided one-half pint flask, smooth base, applied top, rare, American, 1875-1885.	$500-600	
Drake's Plantation Bitters – Patented 1862 Yellow amber, 10", 5-Log Cabin, smooth base, applied top, American, 1862-1875.	$900-1,000	
Eagle – M. G. Landsberg-Chicago – 1776- American Shield- Bitters – 1876 Yellow amber, 11-1/8", smooth base (PAT), applied double collar top, American, 1876, made to commemorate 1876 Centennial.	$1,200-1,300	
Elias's Effectual Elixir Bitters- 1869 – E-E-E- (on two side panels) Clear, 8", smooth base, tooled top, extremely rare, American, 1870-1890.	$500-600	
F. Brown Boston Sarsaparilla & Tomato Bitters Aqua, 9-1/4", open pontil, applied top, American, 1840-1860.	$200-250	

Faith Whitcomb's Bitters – Faith Whitcomb's Agency – Boston, Mass. U.S.A. Aqua, smooth base, applied double collar top, 99% label, box, and contents, made for the Puzzoline Company, Boston, Mass, American, 1875-1885.	$150-200	
Foerster's Teutonic Bitters – Chicago Orange amber, 6-3/4", handled jug, iron pontil, applied ring top, extremely rare, American, 1855-1865.	$9,000-10,000	
G.M. Bayly & Pont Crescent Bitters – New Orleans LA. – Trade Mark (in a crescent moon), reverse side is identically embossed Amber, 9-7/8", smooth base (M.C. & Co.), applied top, American, 1865-1875.	$3,400-3,500	
G.W. Fraizer – California – Herb Bitters – Pittsburg, PA. Yellow amber, 9-1/2", semi-cabin, smooth base, applied top, American, 1865-1875.	$5,000-6,000	
Graves & Son – Tonic Bitters – Louisville, KY. Blue aqua, 10", semi-cabin shape, smooth base (5-pointed star), applied top, American, 1865-1875.	$1,300-1,400	
Hertrich's Gesundheits Bitter – Hans – Hertrich – Hof – Erfinder u. Alleih – Destillateur – Gesetzlich Geschutz (label reads: Hertrich's Health Bitters, for Medicinal Purposes.) Yellow green, 11-7/8", smooth base, tooled top, German, 1880-1910.	$400-600	
Highland Bitters and Scotch Tonic Yellow amber, 9-5/8", barrel shape, smooth base, applied top, scarce, American, 1865-1875.	$700-800	

J. M. Laroques (motif of a stomach and the appendix) Anti-Bilious Bitters- W.E. Thornton-Proprietor- Baltimore, Md. Amber, 10", smooth base, applied top, American, 1865-1875.	$2,200-2,300
J.T. Wiggins – PXUXRXE – Herb Bitters Amber, 9-3/4", smooth base, applied top, American, 1875-1885.	$900-1,000
Jone's Tonic Bitters Medium strawberry puce, 9-3/8", smooth base, applied tapered collar top, American, 1865-1875.	$2,800-3,000
Ko-HI – Bitters – Koehler & Hinrichs – St. Paul Medium amber, 9", smooth base, tooled top, American, 1890-1900.	$375-475
L. Goldheim Celebrate Swiss Wine – Stomach Bitters – No. 278 West Pratt St. – Bet. Sharp & Howard- Baltimore. MD. Deep amber, 9-3/4", smooth base, applied tapered double collar top, American, 1890-1910.	$1,800-1,900
Lippman's Great German Bitters – Savannah – Georgia Golden yellow amber, 9-3/4", smooth base, applied tapered collar top, American, 1875-1885.	$1,000-1,200
Mack's Orange Tonic Bitters Amber, 9-1/8", smooth base (Citrus Extracts Co.), tooled top, American, 1885-1895.	$150-200

Old Bottles

Maynard's – Star Bitters Amber, 8-7/8", smooth base, applied tapered collar top, American, 1870-1880.	$450-500	
Manitou (motif of an Indian head) Bitters Amber, 7-7/8", smooth base, tooled ring top, American, 1880-1890.	$600-700	
Mills' Bitters – A. M. Gilman – Sole Proprietor Yellow amber, 11-1/4", lady's leg shape, smooth base, applied ring top, American, 1875-1885.	$2,200-2,300	
Molton's Olorosa Bitters – Trade (Motif of Pineapple) Mark Deep blue aqua, 11-1/4", smooth base, applied top, American, 1865-1880.	$300-350	

Morning (Star) Bitters – Inceptum 5869 – Patented 5869 Yellow amber, 12-7/8", triangular shape, smooth base, tooled top, American, 1865-1870.	$700-800	
Newman's Golden Fruit Bitters Yellow with amber tone, 12-1/2", smooth base, applied top, American, 1875-1885.	$600-700	
Old Continental Bitters Medium amber, semi-cabin, smooth base, applied top, scarce, American, 1865-1875.	$400-450	
Pepsin Bitters – Francis Cropper & Co. – Chicago Clear, 11-1/4", smooth base, tooled double collar top, extremely rare, American, 1890-1910.	$2,000-2,100	
Purdy's Cottage Bitters Amber, 9-1/2", smooth base, applied double collar top, American, 1855-1865.	$1,500-1,700	

R. H. Baker's Russian Bitters Clear, 10-1/8", smooth base, tooled top, rare, American, 1880-1895.	$1,300-1,400	
Royal Flush Bitters (original label reads: Royal Flush- Kidney & Liver-Bitters - J.Quint Company – New Haven, Conn.) Amber, 12-1/4", smooth base, tooled top, extremely rare-only one of two or three known examples, American, 1895-1910.	$4,000-4,500	
Rosenheim's Bitters – The Great Western Remedy Medium amber, 10-1/8", smooth base, applied tapered double collar top, American, 1875-1890.	$300-350	
Rosswinkle's Crown Bitters Yellow amber, 9", smooth base, applied top, American, 1865-1875.	$1,800-1,900	
St. Drakes – 1860 – Plantation – X – Bitters- Patented 1862 Medium blue green, 10", 6-Log Cabin, smooth base, applied tapered collar top, rare and sought after color, American, 1862-1875.	$46,000	
St Drake's Plantation Bitters – Patented – 1869 Deep cherry puce, 10", 6-Log Cabin, smooth base, applied top with a hand-tooled pour spout, American, 1862-1875.	$200-250	

San Joaquin – Wine Bitters Reddish amber, 9 5/8", smooth base, applied double collar top, American, 1865-1875.	$2,000-2,200
Seaworth Bitters Co. – Cape May – New Jersey – U.S.A. Amber, 11-1/2", figural lighthouse, smooth base, tooled top, American, 1875-1885.	$1,500-1,600
Sharp's Mountain Herb Bitters Amber, 9-5/8", smooth base, applied top, American, 1875-1885.	$250-300
Simon's Prussian Vegetable Bitters Medium amber, 10-1/4", smooth base, applied tapered collar top, American, 1875-1885.	$600-700
Solomons' Strengthening & Invigorating Bitters – Savannah – Georgia Deep cobalt blue, 9-3/4", smooth base, applied top, American, 1865-1885.	$1,500-1,600
Suffolk Bitters – Philbrook & Tucker – Boston Yellow amber, 9-1/2" long, figural pig, smooth base, sheared and ground top, American, 1865-1875.	$600-700
Swan Bitters – McFarland Bros's – Meadville PA Amber, 9-1/2", smooth base, applied tapered collar top, American, 1870-1880.	$2,000-2,500

Old Bottles

Geo. C. Hubbel & Co. – Geo C. Hubbel & Co., blue aqua, 10-1/4", semi-cabin shape, applied top, 1865-1875, $150-200.

The California Remedy – Yerba Buena Bitters – S.F.CAL., (including box), medium amber, strapside flask, 9-3/4", tooled top, 1890-1900, $300-350.

Buhrer's Gentian Bitters, amber, 9-3/8", applied tapered collar top, 1860-1870, $1,300-1,400.

Holtzermanns –Patent – Stomach- Bitters, 100% Graphic Label, medium yellow amber, 4-roof log cabin, 9-7/8", tooled top, 1880-1900, $450-500.

Thads. Waterman – S – (Warsaw) – Stomach Bitters Medium amber, 10-7/8", 8-sided, smooth base, applied top, American, 1865-1875.	$500-600	
The- Fish Bitters – W.H. Ware – Patented 1866 Medium golden yellow amber, 11-3/8", smooth base, applied top, American, 1866-1875.	$250-300	
The Great English Tonic – Rothery's Appetizer – and Stomach Bitters Straw yellow, 8", smooth base, tooled top, extremely rare in amber, American, 1880-1895.	$800-900	
The Great Tonic-Dr. Caldwell's Herb Bitters Amber, 12-1/2", triangular shape, smooth base, applied double collar top, American, 1865-1875.	$200-250	
Tinkham's Golden Sherry Wine Bitters Clear glass decanter, 10-5/8", polished pontil, applied top and neck ring, pewter and cork dispenser, 97% multicolored painted label, American, 1850-1870.	$700-800	
Travellers-Bitters – (motif of Robert E. Lee with a cane) – 1834-1870 (on shoulder) Golden yellow amber, 10-3/8", smooth base, applied tapered collar top, extremely rare bottle and the first to be offered at auction in over five years, American, 1870-1875.	$10,000-11,000	

W & Co. – N.Y. Medium blue green, 8-1/2", pineapple figural, iron pontil, applied top, American, 1855-1870.	$5,000-6,000	
W. C. Bitters (on shoulder) – Brobst & Rentschler – Reading, PA Yellow amber, 10-1/2", figural barrel, smooth base, tooled top, scarce "wild cherry," American, 1885-1895.	$250-300	
W. L. Richardson's – Bitters – South-Reading Mass Blue aqua, 7", open pontil, applied top, American, 1840-1860.	$200-250	
Warner – German Hop – Bitters – 1880- Warner / Dr. C.D. Warner- Coldwater, Mich-1880 Medium amber, 7-3/4", semi-cabin, smooth base, tooled top, American, 1875-1885.	$600-700	
Weis Bros. – Knickerbocker – Stomach Bitters (on an applied seal) Orange amber, 12-1/8", ladies leg shape, smooth base, applied ring top and seal, American, 1865-1875.	$1,200-1,300	
Wheeler's Genuine Bitters Light apple green, 9-5/8", smooth base, applied tapered collar top, American, 1855-1865.	$250-300	

Black Glass

Whenever I see or handle black glass bottles at various shows or view displays, I immediately think of the shipwrecks of English whaling and cargo ships and Spanish Galleons lying of the bottom of the Atlantic, Pacific, and East-Indian oceans. The good news for the collectors is that not all of these ships went down, and the sailors and merchants who made dry land left behind plenty of black glass bottles. These bottles were actually the first glass containers with liquid contents shipped to America from Holland, England, Germany, Belgium, France, Italy, Spain and other European countries from the early 16th to the mid-19th centuries.

Until the mid-1800s, trade merchants believed that dark glass containers would provide a method of preserving their products for the long ship voyages and lengthy storage, resulting in an increased demand for black glass bottles. This demand caused the glasshouses to increase production and quickly produce an inexpensive type of black glass. By adding iron slag to the basic glass mixture of sand, soda and lime, they were able to produce the desired black glass. As the glass continued to be developed and improved, black glass proved to be durable and withstand more exposure to the natural elements as well as the shipping and handling process during the rough sea voyages and treacherous land trips. Another interesting fact is that not all black glass is actually black, but dark olive green. If you hold up a black glass bottle to good lighting, you will be able to observe the olive green tint.

The black glass bottles were manufactured by the free-blown method and therefore it's difficult to find any two bottles that are alike in shape. As the usage expanded, the bottles evolved into various shapes, forms, styles and sizes.

Shafts & Globes

The shaft and globe bottles made before 1630 were fragile and didn't last long during any type of travel, and not many of these bottles survived. It wasn't until the 1630s-1650s when the English glasshouses improved the development of their processes by burning coal instead of wood, and developed additional techniques to improve bottle making, resulting in a more durable and longer lasting bottle.

Old Bottles

Miniature Shaft & Globe Bottle Light blue green, 4", tubular open pontil, sheared top with an applied string lip, German, 1670-1690.	**$900-1,000**
Miniature Shaft & Globe Bottle Dark yellow olive green, 5-3/8", pontil scarred base, sheared top, applied string lip, English, 1660-1670.	**$5,000-6,000**
One-Half Size Shaft and Globe Wine Bottle Yellow olive green, 6-1/2", 1-3/4" base dia, pontil scarred base, sheared top, applied string lip, English, 1660-1670.	**$4,000-5,000**
Type II Shaft and Globe Wine Bottle Medium olive green, 6-3/4", 5-3/4" base dia, pontil scarred base, sheared and tooled mouth with applied string lip, English, 1670-1685.	**$1,500-2,500**
Magnum Shaft and Globe Wine Bottle Deep olive green, 7-1/2", 3-3/8" base dia, pontil scarred base, sheared top with an applied string lip, English, 1675-1680.	**$5,000-6,000**
Full Size Shaft and Globe Wine Bottle Yellow olive green, 8-7/8", 2-1/4" base dia, pontil scarred base, sheared top, applied string lip, English, 1660-1670.	**$8,000-9,000**
Full Size Shaft and Globe Wine Bottle Yellow olive green, 9-1/4", 2-1/4" base dia, pontil scarred base, sheared top, applied string lip, English, 1650-1660.	**$11,000-12,000**
Magnum Shaft and Globe Wine Bottle Deep yellow olive green, 10-1/2", 3-3/4" base dia, pontil scarred base, sheared top with applied string lip, English, 1650-1665.	**$8,000-9,000**

Seal Bottles

The process of attaching glass seals to the shoulder or bodies of wine bottles started in the mid-1600s in England. The method for this process was to apply the seal after the bottle was completed but not cooled (annealed). Then a glob of glass was taken from the furnace and fused to the still hot bottle. While the glob was still hot it was impressed with a stamp, similar to a stamp being impressed into sealing wax. These stamps would have the letters or design of the owners of the bottles. In some cases, the seals also included the date the bottle was manufactured or initially used which can be helpful for dating the bottles.

Jona-Mason-Boston (on applied seal), deep olive amber, 12-3/8", pontil scarred base, applied top, blown in a dip mold, 1780-1810, $800-1,200.

Sealed wine bottle – John Winn Jr. (on applied seal), olive green amber, cylinder, 8-7/8", pontil scarred base, applied collared top, blown in a dip mold, 1830-1840, $400-600.

Arm with Raised Scepter (on applied seal) Wine Bottle Deep olive green, 11-1/4", magnum size, pontil scarred base, sheared top with applied string lip, English, 1790-1810.	$500-600	
B.D. (in script on applied seal) Wine Bottle Emerald green, 10-3/4", cylinder shape, pontil scarred base, sheared and tooled top with applied ring lip, English, 1790-1920.	$250-300	
C.H.H. – Sillaton – 1789 (on applied seal) Wine Bottle Medium olive green, 9", 4-1/4" base dia, smooth base, deep kick-up, applied top, American, 1789.	$2,000-2,200	

Old Bottles

D. Sears (on applied seal with the number 8 inside a hexagon) Wine Bottle Medium olive green, 10-5/8", pontil scarred base (H. Rickett's & C. Glassworks-Bristol), patent embossed on shoulder, applied top, American, 1830-1850.	$150-200	
Dribur Water (on applied seal beneath a coat-of-arms) Spring Water Bottle Olive green, 10", 4" base dia, tubular open pontil, sheared lip and applied string lip, blown in a dip mold, German, 1730-1755.	$900-1,000	
E.H. – 1796 (on applied seal) Wine Bottle Medium olive green, 10-3/4", 3" base dia, pontil scarred base, sheared top with applied string lip, blown in a dip mold, English, 1796.	$500-600	
Class of 1846 – W (inside an embossed shield on an applied seal) Yellow olive green, 11-1/8", iron pontiled base, applied tapered double collar, American, 1846 top.	$800-900	
F. Seignouret & Co. (on applied seal with an American eagle and olive branch with arrows in its talons) - New Orleans – Wine Bottle Olive green, 11-3/4", smooth base with deep kick-up, rough sheared lip with applied string top, Seigouret was a veteran of the Battle of New Orleans and imported wine from France, American, 1850-1860.	$2,000-2,300	

Sealed wine bottle – Dry Williams & Humbert Sack (on applied seal), olive amber, 10-5/8", applied double collared top, blown in a 3-part mold, 1860-1880, $200-300.

Sealed wine bottle – Lupton (on applied seal), deep olive amber, cylinder, 11", applied collared top, blown in a 3-part mold, 1830-1850, $200-300.

I. Watson EFQR – Bilton Park (on applied seal), medium olive green, 8-7/8", pontil scarred base, sheared and tooled top with applied lip and seal, blown in a dip mold, 1780-1800, $500-600.

Saml – Etting (on applied seal), embossed on shoulder: H. Rickett Base, applied sloping collar top and seal, blown in a 3-part mold, 1835-1855, $300-400.

Sealed wine bottle – Revd. J.B. Melhuish (on applied seal), dark olive green, cylinder, 11", pontil scarred base, applied collar top, blown is a 3-part mold, 1820-1850, $200-300.

T.C. Pearsall (on applied seal), olive green, cylinder, 10-1/2", pontil scarred base, applied string lip, blown in a dip mold, 1760-1780, $600-800.

III To & b (ornament) – B III (on applied seal) – Sprits or Apothecary Bottle Medium olive green, 10-5/8", tubular open pontil, applied string lip, European, 1760-1790.	$300-350	
L.L. M. Smith – Wine Mercha. T – Baltimore (on applied seal)– Wine Bottle A label above the applied seal reads: Maderia – Lacock – Inpt 1802 Deep yellow olive green, 10-1/4", pontil scarred base, deep kick-up, applied top, American, 1800-1820.	$2,000-2,300	
LM (in script monogram on applied seal) Wine Bottle Deep olive amber, 11-1/8", 3-1/2"dia, pontil scarred base, applied double collar top, English, 1800-1820.	$175-190	
Joseph Wilson – 1839 (on applied seal) Wine Bottle Deep olive green, 9", pontil scarred base (H. Ricketts & Co. Glassworks Bristol), applied top, 'Patent' on shoulder, blown in a 3-part mold, English, 1839.	$800-900	
Manufacturer – De – Tabac – De – Natichitoches (on applied seal), (original label reads: Gedrundet 1811, Naticitoches (scene of a steamship with a town in the background) de la Manufacture De Tabac – Joseph Doms a Ratibor) Deep olive green, 9-1/2", smooth base, applied top, Natichitoches was established in 1714 and is Louisiana's oldest town, American, 1870-1880.	$900-1,000	
R.H.C. – 1815 (on applied seal) Wine Bottle Deep olive green, 10-5/8", pontil scarred base, applied double collar top, blown in a dip mold, Richard Hall Clarke (1750-1821) was the Justice of the Peace at Bridwell, Uffculme, Devon, England, English, 1815.	$700-800	

S. Lyne – 728 (on applied seal) Wine Bottle Medium olive green, 5-1/2", 5-1/4" base dia, pontil scarred base, applied lip, English, 1728.	**$4,000-4,500**	
TH (on applied seal) Wine Bottle Yellow olive green, 7-5/8", 5-3/4" base dia, pontil scarred base, applied string lip, English, 1725-1735.	**$2,500-3,000**	

Onion Squat Bottles

Squat wine bottles were manufactured in England from around 1600-1830, while the Dutch also made squat wine bottles during the 17th century. Some of the differences between the English and Dutch bottles:

- The Dutch version usually has a longer neck than the English model.
- English bottles have a non-existent base kick-up and a small pontil scar.
- Dutch bottles have a severe base kick-up and a large pontil scar.
- The Dutch bottleneck features a flat wraparound rim.
- English bottlenecks have an applied collar (laid-on ring).

Onion Shaped Wine Bottle Deep olive amber, 5-7/8", 4-3/4" base dia, pontil scarred base, sheared top, applied string lip, English, 1700-1715.	**$250-300**	
Onion Shaped Wine Bottle Dark olive green, 6-1/4", 3-7/8" dia, pontil scarred base, sheared top with applied ring lip, English, 1685-1695.	**$700-800**	

Onion Shaped Wine Bottle Deep yellow olive green, 6-7/8", 4-1/4" base dia, pontil scarred base, sheared top with an applied string lip, English, 1715-1725.	**$250-300**	
Wide Mouth Onion Shaped Bottle Deep olive green, 8-5/8", 4-3/4" base dia, pontil scarred base, sheared and tooled top with an applied string lip, Dutch, 1780-1800.	**$800-900**	
Mallet Shaped Wine Bottle Olive amber, 7-3/4", pontil scarred base, sheared top with applied string lip, English, 1680-1740.	**$150-200**	
Miniature Onion Shaped Utility Bottle Light blue green, 3-7/8", 2" base dia, pontil scarred base, deep kick-up, sheared top with applied string lip, German, 1700-1730.	**$500-600**	
Onion Shaped Wine or Storage Bottle Yellow olive green, 9-1/4", open pontil, sheared lip, applied top, Dutch, 1770-1790.	**$350-400**	

Mallet Bottles

As the demand from merchants increased for longer-term storage of wine, the onion squat bottles changed their shape around 1720 to be manufactured in a flatter shape resembling a mallet (tool). By the 1730s, the tapered shape started losing favor and the mallet bottles were manufactured with slight tapers, with narrower and deeper bodies with longer necks. By 1740 mallets were manufactured with longer necks, and by 1750 the neck length was becoming less than the body height.

Half–Size Mallet Wine Bottle Deep olive amber, 5-3/4", 3-1/8" base dia, pontil scarred base, sheared top with string lip, English, 1740-1750.	**$500-700**	
Mallet Wine Bottle Deep olive amber, 7-1/4", 5-3/8" base dia, pontil scarred base, sheared and tooled top with applied string lip, English, 1740-1750.	**$250-300**	
Mallet Wine Bottle Dark yellow amber, 8", 4-1/4" base dia, pontil scarred base, deep kick-up, sheared top, applied string lip, English, 1740-1750.	**$300-400**	
Mallet Wine Bottle Yellow olive green, 9-1/4", 4-1/8" base dia, tubular pontil, deep kick-up, sheared top with an applied string lip, Belgium, 1780-1810.	**$125-150**	

Old Bottles

Long-Neck Mallet Wine Bottle Medium blue green, 9-7/8", open pontil, deep pointed kick-up, sheared top with applied string lip, rare, German, 1760-1780.	$900-1,000	
Long-Neck Mallet Wine Bottle Deep green color, 10", pontil scarred base on deep kick-up, sheared and tooled lip, applied string lip, German, 1760-1780.	$350-400	

Cylindrical Bottles

The earliest shapes of cylinder bottles were introduced around 1760 with the now standard-wide body increasing in height and decreasing in width. In terms of storage and space, merchants were pleased with the thinner cylinder bottles rather than the mallet or squat-shaped bottles. By 1780 cylinder bottles were becoming more popular, and between 1820-1850, with the perfection of three-piece molds and other methods, the majority of wine bottles were being manufactured in the shape.

A.S. / C.R. (on applied seal) Deep olive amber, 10-3/8", pontil scarred base, applied top, blown in a dip mold, English, 1760-1780.	$150-200	
Air – No 1 (on applied seal) Medium olive green, 10", pontil scarred base, applied collared top, blown in a dip mold, English, 1790-1810.	$170-220	

Doneraile (eight -point star) House (on applied seal) Olive green, 11", pontil scarred base (H. Ricketts & Co. Glass Works Bristol), applied collared top, blown in a three-part mold, English, 1820-1850.	$250-350	
Eman –Coll (on applied seal) Deep olive amber, 11-1/2", pontil scarred base, applied collared top, blown in a three-piece mold, English, 1850-1860.	$150-200	
I.C. Hoffman (on applied seal) Medium olive green, 8-1/2", pontil scarred base, applied double collar top, blown in a dip mold, English, 1790-1810.	$200-250	
Lupton (on applied seal) Deep olive green, 11-1/8", pontil scarred base, applied collared top, blown in a dip mold, English, 1800-1820.	$250-300	
Trelaske (on applied seal) Deep olive green, 11", pontil scarred base, applied collared top, blown in a three-part mold, English, 1820-1830.	$200-300	

Utility and Other Bottles

Utility bottles are exactly what the name implies. These bottles were usually blown with a wide top or mouth and were used to store food supplies, snuff, ink, rum, gin, whiskey, or anything else that required a container for storage. These bottles, made by the thousands and often used and reused because of their durability, can be found in a wide variety of shapes and sizes.

Black Glass Wine Bottle Deep olive green, 7-5/8", 4" base dia, pontil scarred base, sheared top with applied string lip, blown in a dip mold, English, 1770-1780.	**$150-200**	
Utility or Apothecary Bottle Deep olive green, 9-3/4", pontil scarred base, applied double collar top, blown in a dip mold, English, 1790-1815.	**$150-200**	
Black Glass Decanter (set of 2) Deep olive green, 9-7/8", pontil scarred base, tooled flared out lips, portion of the remains of the original gold 'W. Port' and 'R.Port' inside, blown in a dip mold, English, 1790-1810.	**$350-400**	
Freeblown Miniature Globular Bottle Yellow olive green, 2-7/8", 1" base dia, pontil scarred base, applied ring top, Dutch, 1790-1810.	**$400-500**	
Lotharingen - Global Storage Bottle (Translates into Lorraine in Northern France) Medium olive green, 11", pontil scarred base, applied string lip, Dutch, 1750-1770.	**$500-600**	

Large Storage Bottle Dark olive amber, 17-1/4", smooth base, rough sheared lip with applied string, French or German, 1850-1870.	$125-150	
Wide Mouth Utility Jar Olive amber, 10-3/4", square shape pontil scarred base, sheared and tooled lip, Dutch or German, 1790-1820.	$450-500	
Wide Mouth Storage Jar Yellow olive green, 10-5/8", 4" base dia, pontil scarred base, tool flared out lip, blown in a dip mold, European, 1770-1810.	$125-150	
Wide Mouth Storage Jar Deep yellow amber, 11-3/4", 8-Sided Hexagonal shape, pontil scarred base, applied string lip, Dutch, 1780-1810.	$1,100-1,200	
Wine Bottle- Half-Size Bladder Shape Medium olive green, 5-3/4", pontil scarred base, sheared top with an applied string lip, scarce shape and rare size, Dutch or German, 1730-1770.	$800-900	
Wine Bottle – Octagonal Shape Yellow olive green, 8-3/4", 8-sided, pontil scarred base, sheared lip, applied string lip, English, 1735-1750.	$400-500	
Wine Bottle – Magnum Size Yellow olive amber, 11-1/4", 5" base dia, applied string lip, blown in a dip mold, English, 1740-1760.	$200-250	

Blown

Free-blown bottles, also called blown bottles, were made without molds and were shaped by the glassblower. It is difficult to determine age and the origin of these types of bottles since many were produced in Europe and America for a long period of time before records were kept.

Another type of blown bottle, the blown three-mold, was formed from a three-piece mold. These bottles were manufactured between 1820 to 1840 in Europe and the United States, and it is quite difficult to distinguish bottles from different sides of the Atlantic. Since blown three-mold and pressed three-mold are similar, it is important to know how to differentiate between the two types. With blown glass, the mold impression can be felt on the inside, while pressed glass impressions can only be felt on the outside. Most blown three-mold came in amethyst (purple), sapphire blue, and a variety of greens.

Another early type of blown bottles was based on the German half-post method, which was used in the late 1700s and early 1880s in Europe and in the United States at the Keene and Coventry Glass Works. This is a process where the initial gather of glass is dipped back again into the molten glass, coating it with the hot "metal." The second layer of glass does not totally cover the first gather of glass indicated by a heavy thick ridge on the upper shoulder of the bottle.

Free-Blown Bottles

Free-Blown Chestnut Shape Flask Light yellow olive green, 5-1/8", tubular open pontil, applied top, American, 1780-1810.	**$350-400**	
Free-Blown Chestnut Flask Medium yellow olive green, 5-1/2", tubular open pontil, applied top, American, 1790-1810.	**$350-400**	

Free-Blown Chestnut Flask Blue green, 5-1/2", tubular open pontil, applied string lip, American, 1785-1810.	$600-700	
Free-Blown Spirits Flask Light apple green, 5-3/4", pontil scarred base, sheared and tooled lip, American, 1780-1810.	$350-400	
Free-Blown Chestnut Shape Flask Light straw yellow with olive tone, 5-5/8", tubular open pontil, applied top, American, 1780-1810.	$350-400	
Pocket Flask Deep cobalt blue, 5-7/8", 18-rib pattern swirled to right, pontil scarred base, sheared and tooled lip, European, 1800-1820.	$500-700	
Free-Blown Chestnut Flask Medium olive green, 6-7/8", tubular open pontil, applied lip, American, 1785-1810.	$300-400	
Free-Blown Bladder or 'Kidney' Shape Wine Bottle Medium yellow olive green, 7", pontil scarred base, sheared mouth with applied string lip, Dutch or German, 1720-1760.	$700-800	
Free-Blown Chestnut Flask Medium olive green, 7", open pontil, applied lip, American, 1780-1810.	$350-400	
Free-Blown Decanter 'Rum' Deep cobalt blue, 7-1/2", polished pontil base, sheared and tooled lip, pewter and cork closure. possibly Bristol Glass Works, Bristol, England, English, 1820-1850.	$250-300	

Old Bottles

Free-Blown Flat Sided Chestnut Flask Yellow amber with olive tone, 7-3/4", tubular open pontil, outward rolled lip, American, 1780-1900.	$300-350	
Free-Blown Handled Decanter Deep purple amethyst, 8-1/2", pontil scarred base, applied handle, neck shoulder rings and eight vertical body rigarees, Dutch, 1720-1750.	$1,000	
Free-Blown Chestnut Flask Yellow amber, 8-1/2", pontil scarred base, sheared top with applied lip, American, 1790-1810.	$600-700	
Free-Blown Chestnut Flask Medium yellow olive, 8-1/2", tubular open pontil, outward rolled lip, American, 1785-1810.	$400-450	
Free-Blown Flattened Chestnut Shape Utility Bottle Yellow green, 8-1/2", rough pontil scarred base, sheared mouth with an applied top, American, 1800-1820.	$350-400	
Free-Blown Flattened Globular Bottle Medium emerald green, 8-1/8", tubular pontil, outward rolled lip, American, 1780-1800.	$800-900	
Free-Blow Ludlow Bottle Light apple green, 8-1/2", pontil scarred base, applied top American, 1780-1810.	$200-300	

Free-Blown Spa Water Bottle
Yellow olive green, 8-3/8", smooth base, sheared mouth
with applied cogwheel crimped string lip, this type
of bottle contained mineral water and was used by a
number of Belgium Spas such as Chevron, Niveze, and
Geronstere, Belgium, 1700-1750.

$250-300

Free-Blown Flattened Globular Bottle
Deep yellow 'old" amber, 8-3/4", tubular open pontil,
applied tapered collar mouth, American, 1790-1820.

$350-400

Free-Blown Storage Bottle
Yellow amber with olive tone, 9-1/4", pontil scarred base,
applied top, American or European, 1810-1830.

$300-400

Free-Blown Globular Bottle
Medium yellow green, 8-5/8", pontil scarred base,
sheared mouth with applied lip, American, 1790-1815.

$375-475

Free-Blown Ludlow Bottle
Light yellow olive, 9-1/4", pontil scarred base, applied
top, American, 1780-1810.

$200-300

Free-Blown Globular Tapered Shape Bottle
Deep olive amber, 10-3/4", pontil scarred base, applied
top, English, 1790-1820.

$500-600

**Free-Blown Globular Shape Apothecary
Bottle – TR: RHET. C**
Deep olive green, 12-1/2", pontil scarred base, wide
applied top, American, 1780-1840.

$700-800

Blown in German Half-Post Method

Miniature Pitkin Type Bottle Light blue green, 3-1/4", 2-rib pattern swirled to right, pontil scarred base, sheared and tooled lip, American, 1815-1830.	$1,500-1,600	
Pitkin Type Pocket Flask Medium olive green, 4-3/8", 22-vertical rib pattern, pontil scarred base, sheared and tooled lip, American, 1815-1835.	$600-700	
Pitkin Flask Light olive green, 5-1/8", 36-broken rib pattern to left, pontil scarred base, sheared and tooled lip, American, 1790-1810.	$600-700	
Pitkin Flask Straw yellow with olive tone, 5-1/4", 36-rib pattern swirled to left, pontil scarred base, sheared and tooled lip, American, 1790-1810.	$700-800	
Pitkin Flask Deep olive green, 5-1/2", 36-rib pattern swirled to left, pontil scarred base, sheared and tooled lip, American, 1790-1810.	$500-600	
Pitkin Flask Yellow olive, 5-3/8", 36-broken rib pattern swirled to right, open pontil, sheared and tooled lip, American 1780-1820.	$600-800	
Pitkin Flask Golden amber, 36-broken rib pattern swirled to left, open pontil, sheared and tooled lip, American, 1815-1835.	$300-350	

Pattern Molded Pitkin Flask Yellow amber, 6", 36-broken rib pattern swirled to the left, sheared and tooled lip, American, 1815-1835.	**$500-600**
Pitkin Flask Medium yellow green, 6-1/4", 32 broken rib pattern swirled to right, pontil scarred base, tooled top, American, 1780-1810.	**$600-800**
Pitkin Flask Straw yellow, 6-3/4", 36-broken rib pattern swirled to left, pontil scarred base, sheared and tooled lip, American, 1785-1820.	**$1,300-1,400**
Pitkin Flask Deep emerald green, 6-3/8", 30 broken rib pattern swirled to left, pontil scarred base, tooled top, American, 1780-1810.	**$250-300**
Pitkin Type Spirits Bottle Aqua, 7-3/8", 38-broken rib pattern, rectangular shape, tubular open pontil, tool flared out lip, Pitkin Glass Works – East Manchester, Connecticut, American, 1790-1820.	**$1,800-1,900**
Pitkin Flask Emerald green, 7-3/8", 36-broken rib pattern swirled to right, open pontil, sheared and tooled lip, Midwestern Glass House, American, 1815-1825.	**$400-450**
Pitkin Flask Yellow 'old' amber,7-1/2", 36-broken rib pattern, pontil scarred base, sheared and tooled lip, American, 1785-1820.	**$1,600-1,700**
Vertical Rib Pattern Pinched Spirits Bottle Deep cobalt blue, 8-5/8", 24-rib pattern, hand pinched in sides, tubular blowpipe pontil, tooled lip, German, 1800-1820.	**$400-500**

Blown Bottles

Blown Three-Piece Mold Decanter Cobalt blue, 5-3/8", pontil scarred base, tooled flared-out lip, original blown "tam" stopper, American, 1815-1835.	$450-500	
Blown Three-Piece Mold Toilet Water Bottle Cobalt blue, 5-1/2", pontil scarred base, tooled lip, original "Tam" stopper, American, 1815-1835.	$700-800	
Blown Three- Piece Mold Decanter Yellow amber, 7-1/8", open pontil, sheared and tooled lip, American, 1815-1835.	$350-400	
Blown Decanter Yellow 'old' amber, 7-3/8", 8-sided with each side having a molded diamond pattern, pontil scarred base, sheared mouth with an applied string lip, American, 1815-1830.	$1,900-2,000	
Blown Three- Piece Mold Decanter Yellow amber, 7-5/8", open pontil, sheared and tooled lip, American, 1815-1835.	$350-400	
Blown Globular Bottle Amber, 8-1/8", pontil scarred base, outward rolled lip American, 1810-1820.	$300-400	

Blown Three-Piece Mold Decanter Olive amber, quart, 9-1/4", pontil scarred base, sheared and tooled lip, Keene Glass Works, Keene, New Hampshire, American, 1815-1835	**$1,700-1,800**
Blown Three Piece Mold Decanter Medium olive green, 9-1/2", open pontil, sheared and tooled lip, American, 1815-1835.	**$1,000-1,200**
Blown Decanter Yellow amber, 10-5/8", pontil scarred base, applied top, collar impressed with 'Pat'd Oct. 13, 1863,' American, 1840-1860.	**$400-450**
Blown 'Ashburton' Pattern Decanter Turquoise blue, 10-3/8", polished pontil base, applied corset waist double collar mouth, American.	**$1,000-1,100**
Blown Decanter Blue green, 10-1/2", polished pontil, applied double collar mouth, extremely rare color, American, 1840-1860.	**$1,000-1,100**
Blown Three Piece Mold Decanter Clear, 11-1/2", pontil scarred base, tooled flared out lip, original glass stopper, American, 1815-1835.	**$700-800**
Blown Demijohn Type Storage Bottle Medium blue green, 17-1/4", pontil scarred base, applied top, American, 1850-1879.	**$350-400**

Cobalt Blue Medicine

One of the most sought after colors by bottle collectors is the brilliant cobalt blue. As discussed in the "Bottle Facts" chapter, colors natural to bottle glass production are brown, amber, olive green, and aqua. The true blue, green, and purple colors were produced by metallic oxides added to the glass batch. The blue was specifically produced by adding cobalt oxide to the basic glass batch. Since blue and other bright colors were expensive to produce and usually manufactured for specialty items, bottles with these colors are rare and highly sought after by most collectors.

Since cobalt blue bottles stood out among all other colors, many chemist, druggist, and pharmacist bottles were made with cobalt, along with elaborate monograms, pictures, and unique designs.

This chapter presents a cross-section of many cobalt blue medicine bottles manufactured prior to 1920 across the United States.

Reese Chemical Co.-
Original Label Reads:
"Prescription-1000-
External – Manganese
Dioxide Distilled Water-
A Prophylactic Against
Gonorrhoeal Infection
in the Anterior Uretha
– Not For Syphilis,"
medium cobalt blue,
6-1/4", original cover
over cork closure,
1890-1910, $75-95.

U.S.A. Dept.,
(in oval),
medium
sapphire blue,
7", applied top,
rare, 1860-
1870, $700-
1,000.

Allan's – AntiFat – Botanic Medicine Co. – Buffalo, N.Y. Medium cobalt blue, 7-5/8", smooth base, applied top, American, 1875-1886.	$400-450	
Alexander's Silameau Medium cobalt clue, 8-1/8", open pontil, applied top, American, 1840-1860.	$1,000-1,200	
Boswell & Warner's Colorific Deep cobalt blue, 5-5/8", smooth base, tooled top, American, 1880-1890.	$150-200	
C. Heimstreet & Co. – Troy, N.Y. Medium cobalt blue, 7-1/8", 8-sided, open pontil, applied double collar top, American, 1840-1855.	$250-350	
Dr. Chaussier's – Empress Medium cobalt blue, 7-5/8", smooth base, applied top, American, 1870-1880.	$500-600	
Dr. Ellel's – Liver Regulator – South Bend, Ind. Cobalt blue, 5-3/4", smooth base, tooled top, American, 1885-1910.	$200-250	
Dr. Wynkoop's – Katharismic Honduras – Sarsaparilla – New York Cobalt blue, 10-1/8", open pontil, applied tapered collar top, American, 1840-1860.	$4,000-4,300	

Old Bottles

E. Anthony – New York Medium cobalt blue, 6", open pontil, applied top, rare, American, 1840-1860.	$1,000-1,100	
Geo. W. Laird & Co. – Oleo-Chyle Medium cobalt blue, 10", smooth base, tooled top, American, 1875-1885.	$200-225	
Hale & Parshall – Peppermint Oil – Lyons, NY Cobalt blue, smooth base, applied top with pour spout, 99% label, American, 1885-1910.	$250-300	
J. & C. Maguire – Chemist and – Druggists – St. Louis, Mo. Medium blue, 7-1/2", smooth base, applied double collar top, scarce in cylinder shape, American, 1855-1865.	$400-500	
John H. Pope – Druggist – N. Orleans Medium cobalt blue, 5-3/4", pontil scarred base, applied tapered collar top, American, 1840-1860.	$800-900	
Keating & Babb – San Jose Cobalt blue, 6-1/4", smooth base, applied top, rare, American, 1880-1900.	$1,000-1,200	

Maximo M. Diaz – Druggist – Ybor City, Fla Cobalt blue, 5-1/8", smooth base (WT. & CO. U.S.A.), tooled top, American, 1890-1910.	$150-200	
Melvin & Badger – Apothecaries – Boston, Mass Cobalt blue, 6-3/8", irregular hexagon shape, smooth base (C.L.G. & Co. – Patent Appl'd for), tooled top, American, 1890-1915.	$200-250	
Mrs. Dr. Secor – Boston, Mass Cobalt blue, 9-1/2", smooth base, tooled lip, American, 1880-1895.	$300-400	
Newey's – Sanitary Lotion – Not to Be Taken Deep cobalt blue, 4-1/4", smooth base, tooled top, English, 1890-1910.	$200-250	
Prof. I. Huberts – Malvina Lotion – Toledo, Ohio Cobalt blue, 5", smooth base, tooled lip 98% label, American, 1880-1895.	$150-200	

Old Bottles

Pure – Cod Liver - Oil (motif of cod fish) – Reed-Carnrick & Andrus – Chemists – New York Deep cobalt blue, 9-3/4", smooth base, applied top, American, 1875-1885.	**$800-900**	
Sanford's Extract – Of – Hamamelis Witch Hazel (on indented panel) Cobalt blue, 10-3/8", cylinder shape, smooth base, tooled top, American, 1880-1895.	**$150-200**	
Sanford's – Radical Cure Cobalt blue, 7-1/2", smooth base (Potter Drug & Chem Corporation-Boston – Mass, USA), applied top, American, 1870-1880.	**$150-200**	
Sassafras (motif of eye above an eye cup) Eye Lotion – Sassafras – Eye Lotion, Co. – Mauch Chunk, PA Cobalt blue, 5-3/8", smooth base (T.C. W.Co,), tooled lip, American, 1890-1910.	**$150-200**	
T. Morris Perot & Co. – Druggist – Philda Medium cobalt blue, 4-3/4", open pontil, inward rolled lip, American, 1840-1860.	**$800-900**	
T. Morris Perot & Co. – Druggist – Philda Light cobalt blue, 5-1/4", open pontil, inward rolled lip, American, 1840-1860.	**$600-700**	
Tonisan – Tones The Nerves Cobalt blue, 9-3/4", smooth base, tooled lip, American, 1885-1895.	**$500-600**	

U.S.A. Hosp. Dept (lot of 2) Cobalt blue, 2-1/2", oval shape, smooth base, tooled top, American, 1860-1875.	$350-450	
U.S.A. Hosp. Dept. Cobalt blue, 4-7/8", oval shape, smooth base, tooled lip, American, 1860-1875.	$300-400	
U.S.A. Hosp. Dept. Cobalt blue, 9-1/8", smooth base, applied top, American, 1860-1870.	$375-475	
Wayne's – Diuretic Elixir – F.E. Suire & Co. – Cincinnati Medium cobalt blue, 7-1/4", smooth base, applied top, American, 1875-1885.	$250-300	
Wynkoop's & Co's – Tonic Mixture – New York – Warranted To Cure – Fever & Ague Medium cobalt blue, 6-3/8", open pontil, applied tapered collar top, American, 1840-1860.	$6,000-7,000	
Wynkoop's – Katharismic Honduras – Sarsaparilla – New York Medium cobalt blue, 10-1/4", rough snapped off tubular open pontil, applied tapered collar top, American, 1840-1860.	$7000-8000	

Cosmetic & Hair Restorer

This category includes those bottles that originally contained products to improve personal appearances including treatments for skin, teeth, and the scalp (hair and restoring agents). The more popular of these are the hair treatment bottles.

Hair bottles are popular as collector items due to their distinctive colors such as amethyst and various shades of blues. One of the more popular hair restorers was Mrs. S.A. Allen's World Hair Restorer. Susan A. Allen, the wife of a New York City dentist, started selling her hair restorer in 1854, according to the 1854 business directory. There are historic documents, however, that reflect she actually started selling her products around 1840. In 1862, Selah R. Van Duzer became the preparer and sole agent of the Allen hair products.

The main producer of American-made perfume bottles in the 18th century was Casper Wistar, whose clients included Martha Washington. Another major manufacturer of the 18th century was Henry William Stiegel. While most of Wistar's bottles were plain, Stiegel's were decorative and are more appealing to collectors.

In the 1840s, Solon Palmer started to manufacture and sell perfumes. By 1879, his products were being sold in drugstores around the country. Today, Palmer bottles are sought after for their brilliant emerald green color.

Ballards – No 1 – Hair Dye – New York Aqua, 3-3/4", open pontil, rolled lip, American, 1840-1860.	$50-75	
Cabiria – Hair Color – Restorer – Cabiria Co. New York Medium yellow green, 7-1/2", smooth base, tooled top, American, 1885-1895.	$100-125	
Chews – Hair Dye – No. 1 and Duesbury's –Dye Aqua, 3-5/8" and 4", open pontils, inward rolled and then flared out lips, American, 1840-1860.	$1,000-1,200	

Circassian – Hair – Restorative – Cincinnati Yellow amber, 7-3/8", smooth base, applied top, American, 1870-1880.	$200-250	
D. Mitchell's – Tonic for – The Hair – Rochester, N.Y. Clear, 6-3/8", open pontil, applied double collar top, American, 1840-1860.	$300-350	
Dr. Leons' – Electric – Hair Reneewer – Ziegler & Smith – Philada Pink amethyst, 7-3/8", smooth base, tooled top, scarce, American, 1870-1880.	$500-700	
Dr. Comstock's – Hair Dye Aqua, 5", open pontil, applied top, rare, American, 1840-1860.	$200-250	
Dr. D. Jayne's – American – Hair Dye – Philada Aqua, 4-3/4", cylinder shape, pontil scarred base, outward rolled top, American, 1840-1860.	$150-200	
Dr. F. Felix – Gourand's – Poudres –Subtitle – For Uprooting Hair – New York Clear with amethyst tint, 3-3/4", pontil scarred base, tooled flared out lip, extremely rare, American, 1835-1845.	$350-400	
Dr. Graham's – Tonic – Hair Balm – Rochester N.Y. Blue aqua, 4", smooth base, hand tooled flared lip, American, 1880-1900.	$1,000-1,500	

Dr. Tebbitts' – Physiological – Hair – Regenerator Light pink amethyst, 7-1/2", smooth base, applied double collar top, American, 1865-1875.	$1,300-1,400	
Dr. Tebbitts' – Physiological – Hair – Regenerator Light gasoline glass, 7-5/8", smooth base, applied double collar top, American, 1870-1880.	$900-1,000	
Dodge Brother – Melanine – Hair Tonic Deep pink amethyst, 7-1/2", smooth base, applied double collar top, American, 1865-1875.	$600-800	
E.S. Russell's – Castanaine – For The Hair – And Diseases Of The – Scalp and Skin – E.S. Russell – Nashua, N.H. Amber, 6-7/8", smooth base, tooled top, American, 1885-1890.	$150-175	
Fountain Of Youth – Hair Restorer – Trenton. N.J. Medium amber, 7-1/4", smooth base, tooled top, rare, American, 1880-1890.	$250-300	
Franklin's Eagle – Hair Restorer – Columbus, Ohio Medium amber, 8-1/4", smooth base (W.T. & Co. U.S.A.), tooled lip, scarce, American, 1885-1895.	$125-150	
George's – Hair Dye – No. 1 Aqua, 3-3/8", open pontil, inward rolled lip, rare, American, 1840-1860.	$100-150	

Halls's – Hair Renewer Teal blue, 7-1/4", smooth base, tooled top, correct stopper, American, 1890-1910.	$200-250	
Hover's – Hair Dye – Philada Aqua, 2-3/4", 6-sided, open pontil, rolled lip, American, 1840-1860.	$100-125	
Hurd's – Hair – Restorer Blue aqua, 7-3/4", oval shape, iron pontil, applied top, American, 1840-1860.	$200-225	
J.H. Sackett;s – Magic Coloris – J.H. Sackett, N.Y. (Label Reads: J.H. Sackett's Magic Coloris – Natural Brown or Black Deep cobalt blue, 6-1/4", smooth base, tooled top, American, 1890-1900.	$250-300	
Jerome's – Hair Color – Restorer Yellow olive, 6-1/4", open pontil, tooled flared out top, American, 1840-1860.	$1,000-1,200	
Jerome's – Hair Color – Restorer Vivid cobalt blue, 6-3/8", smooth base, flared top, American, 1860-1875.	$900-1,000	
Kalopean – Hair Dye – No. 1 Blue aqua, 3-1/2", open pontil, thin flared out lip, rare, American, 1840-1860.	$100-125	

Kickapoo – Sage – Hair Tonic and W.E. Hagan & Co., Troy N.Y. Cobalt blue and sapphire blue, 4-1/2" and 6-3/4", Hagan has 8-sides, smooth base, tooled and applied lips, Kickapoo Sage has original 'acorn' glass closure, American, 1875-1895.	$400-450	
Laird's – Bloom Of Youth – Or –Liquid Pearl – For The – Complexion & Skin – Broadway N.Y. Opalescent milk glass, 4-7/8", smooth base, tooled top, American, 1875-1900.	$600-700	
L. Miller's – Hair – Invigarator – N.Y. Aqua, 5-7/8", oval shape, open pontil, applied top, American, 1840-1860.	$150-200	
Lombard & Cundall – Springfield Mass – Excelsior – Hair Tonic Aqua, 6-1/2", open pontil, applied double collar top, American, 1840-1860.	$75-100	
Louden & Co's – Hair Tonic – Philada Clear, 5-3/8", open pontil, inward rolled lip, the Louden Medicine Company of Philadelphia produced a number of medicines, of which the Hair Tonic is among the rarest, American, 1840-1860.	$250-350	
Melanine – Hair Tonic – Dodge Brothers (Label Reads: Directions for Using the Melanine Hair Tonic) Pink amethyst, 7-1/4", smooth base, applied double collar top, American, 1865-1875.	$700-800	
Mrs. S.A. Allen's – World's Hair – Restorer – New York Dark pink amethyst, 7-1/4", smooth base, applied double collar top, American, 1865-1875.	$350-400	

Mrs. S.A. Allen's – World's Hair – Restorer – 255 Broome St. – New York Medium to deep pink amethyst, 7-1/4", smooth base, tooled top, American, 1865-1875.	$350-400	
Mrs. S.A. Allen's – World's Hair – Restorer – New York Yellow with amber tone, 7-1/4", smooth base, applied double collar top, American, 1865-1875.	$350-400	
Mrs. S.A. Allen's – World's Hair – Restorer – New York Medium amber, 7-1/4", smooth base (London on base), applied double collar top, scarce with London on base, American, 1865-1875.	$200-250	
Mrs. S.A. Allen's – World's Hair – Restorer – New York Apricot amber, 7-1/4", smooth base (London on base), tooled top, American, 1865-1875.	$200-250	
Oldridges – Balm – Of Columbia – For Restoring – Hair – Philadelphia Aqua, 5-1/8", open pontil, flared out top, American, 1840-1860.	$250-300	

Original Box for Mrs. S.A. Allen's World Hair Restorer – Box Reads: It Is Not A Dye – Mrs. S.A. Allen's – World – Hair – Restorer – An Unfailing Restorer And – Preserver Of the Hair and Sight Tan and green box, 9" wide and 7-1/2" high, top of box has the 255 Broome St., New York address, American, 1865-1875.	**$500-600**	
Nattan's – Crystal – Discovery (five-pointed star) – For The Hair Deep cobalt blue, 7-1/2", smooth base, tooled top, scarce hair bottle, American, 1875-1890.	**$350-400**	
Packard's – Regenerator – And – Reproducer – Of The Hair Aqua, 7", open pontil, applied top, extremely rare, American, 1840-1860.	**$300-350**	
Paul Westphal – Auxiliator – For- The Hair – New York (label under glass hair bottle) Clear, 8", gold, white, and blue label under glass reads, C.C. Rhodes, on the reverse side of the embossing, smooth base, tooled lip, American, 1885-1900.	**$350-400**	
Pearson & Co. – Circassian – Hair Rejuvenator – Brooklyn, N.Y. Deep amber, 6-3/4", smooth base, applied top, American, 1865-1875.	**$250-300**	
Prof. J.R. Tilton – The Great – Hair – Producer- The – Crown Of – Science – S.F. Cal Medium cobalt blue, 7", smooth base, applied top, one of only colored California Hair Bottles, American, 1970-1880.	**$500-600**	

Professor Wood – Hair Restorative – Depot – St. Louis, Mo – And New York Deep blue aqua, 9-1/8", iron pontil, applied double collar top, rare in this size, American, 1845-1860.	**$450-500**	
Riker's American Hair Restorer Orange amber, 6-3/4", smooth base, tooled top, American, 1875-1885.	**$75-100**	
Riker's American Hair Restorer Yellow amber, 7", oval shape, smooth base, tooled top, American, 1875-1885.	**$100-125**	
Shaker Hair Restorer Yellow amber, 7-7/8", smooth base, tooled double collar top, rare, American, 1880-1890.	**$200-250**	
W.C. Montgomery's – Hair – Restorer – Philada Medium pink topaz, 7-1/2", smooth base, applied double collar top, extremely rare, American, 1865-1875.	**$1,300-1,400**	
W.C. Montgomery's – Hair – Restorer – Philada Medium copper puce, 7-1/2", smooth base, applied double collar top, rare in this color, American, 1865-1875.	**$500-600**	
W.C. Montgomery's – Hair – Restorer – Philada Dark olive amber, 7-3/4", smooth base, applied double collar top, rare color, American, 1865-1875.	**$400-500**	

Crocks/ Stoneware

Although crocks are made of pottery rather than glass, many bottle collectors also have crock collections, since they have been found wherever bottles are buried. Crock containers were manufactured in America as early as 1641, and were used extensively in the sale of retail products during the 19th and early 20th centuries. Miniature stoneware jugs were often used for advertising, as were some stoneware canning jars. Store owners favored crocks since they kept beverages cooler and extended the shelf life of certain products. Crocks appeal to collectors because of their interesting shapes, painted and stenciled decorations, lustrous finishes, and folk art value. In addition, molded stoneware shouldn't be considered as an item produced in mass production since a great deal of detailed design and handwork had to be accomplished on each crock before it was completed.

In the late 1800s, the discovery of microbes in disease-causing bacteria prompted many medicine makers to seize a profitable if not unethical opportunity. An undocumented number of fraudulent cures were forced on gullible and unsuspecting customers. The most infamous of these so-called cures were produced and sold in pottery containers by William Radam. He was given a patent for his "Microbe Killer" in 1886, and remained in business until 1907 when the Pure Food and Drug Act ended his scheme. His "cure" was nothing more than watered down wine (wine comprised only 1 percent of the total contents).

With the invention of the automatic bottle machine in 1903, glass bottles became cheaper to make and hence more common. This contributed to the steady decline of production and the use of pottery crocks and containers.

Alex Thorn – Grocer – Plainfield, N.J. / Case's Pure Cider Vinegar-Clover Hill – Hunterdon Co. N.J. (impressed on front above base) Stoneware saltglazed 1-gallon cream advertising jug, 11", smooth base, handled, rare double advertising jug, one for the proprietor of the grocer and the other for maker of product it contained, American, 1890-1900.	$700-800	
American – Chalybeate-Spring – W.M. Clark – Danville JC, Maine (impressed on shoulder) Stoneware saltglazed 2-gallon jug, 14-3/8", smooth base, handled, hand whittled wooden stopper, rare, American, 1870-1890.	$175-200	
Bosworth – Hartford, Conn. 2' (impressed on shoulder) Stoneware saltglazed 2-gallon cream crock, 12-1/4", smooth base, doubles closed handles, American, 1870-1880.	$450-500	
Bowers – Three Thistles – Snuff Stoneware saltglazed jar, 14-1/2", smooth base, wooden lid, American, 1885-1910.	$200-250	
Bozo Radovich – 48 W. San Fernando St. – San Jose, Cal. Stoneware cream with black glaze , 7-1/4", smooth base (Macomb Pottery Co. Macomb, Ill), handled, American, 1890-1915.	$175-250	
Bullard & Scott – Cambridgeport, Mass – 3' (impressed on shoulder) Stoneware saltglazed gray crock, 10-1/2", smooth base, double closed handle, American, 1875-1895.	$200-250	

Burger & Lang – Rochester, N.Y. -2' **(impressed below the rim)** Stoneware saltglazed cream 2-gallon crock, 9", smooth base, double closed handles, American, 1875-1885.	$200-300	
C. Crolius – Manufacturer – New York **(impressed on shoulder)** Stoneware saltglazed 1-gallon gray ovoid jug, 11", smooth base, handled, American, 1825-1835.	$450-500	
Connolly & Palmer – New Brunswick, N.J. – **2' (impressed on shoulder)** Stoneware saltglazed 2-gallon gray butter crock, 6-1/8", smooth base, double closed ears, American, 1875-1895.	$350-400	
Cowden & Wilcox (impressed below the rim) **– '2' (impressed in the dome)** Stoneware saltglazed brown butter or cake crock, 5-1/4", smooth base, double closed handles, American, 1875-1890.	$400-450	
Easton & Stout (impressed on shoulder) Stoneware saltglazed 2-gallon gray ovoid crock, 9-3/4', smooth base, closed handles, American, 1825-1835.	$374-550	
Edmands & Co. – 3' (impressed on shoulder) Stoneware saltglazed 3-gallon cream crock, 10-5/8", smooth base, double closed handled, American, 1855-1875.	$250-300	
J. Clark & Co. – Troy (between two long **stemmed flowers)** Early ovid stoneware saltglazed gray brown jug, 13-3/8", handled, Troy was only in business for two years, American, 1826-1828.	$1,800-1,900	
J. M. Pruden – Eliz-Town-NJ – 2' (impressed **on shoulder)** Stoneware saltglazed cream crock, 12-1/4", smooth base, reverse is a '2' above a 'Viking Ship,' American, 1860-1880.	$500-700	

Description	Price	Image
Compliments of - John Keller & Co. – Fashion Saloon – Jerome, Ariz Stoneware cream with dark brown glaze advertising jug, 5-1/4", smooth base, handled, American, 1890-1915.	$800-900	
F.C. Bender & Son – Minersville – PA Stoneware saltglazed jug, 8-3/8", smooth base, cream color with cobalt blue lettering, handled, rare, American, 1880-1900.	$100-125	
J.A. Haines, & Co. – 153 & 155- Blackstone St. – Boston (impressed on shoulder) Stoneware saltglazed gray 2-gallon jug, 13-3/4", smooth base, open handle, American, 1880-1895.	$150-200	
J. F. Weiler – Allentown – PA. Stoneware saltglazed cream advertising whiskey jug, 13-5/8", smooth base, handled, American, 1890-1910.	$100-150	
John Burger – Rochester – 2' (impressed on shoulder) Stoneware saltglazed 2-gallon cream jug, 14", smooth base, handled, John Burger Pottery, Rochester, New York, American, 1865-1880.	$700-800	
Hunterdon County – Sweet Cider, Sold By – G.H. Hood – Jersey City (in script) Stoneware saltglazed 5-gallon jug, 18-1/8", smooth base, double open handles, American, 1885-1910.	$700-800	

Old Bottles

L Norton & Son – Bennington – 4' (impressed on shoulder) Ovoid Jug Stoneware saltglazed 4-gallon cream jug, 16-1/2", smooth base, handled, American, 1835-1845.	$300-400	
1844 1-Gallon Ovoid Crock Stoneware saltglazed gray 1-gallon ovoid crock, 7-7/8", smooth base, double closed handles, American, 1844.	$400-450	
Ovoid 2- Gallon Jug – 'T' and 'X' (on shoulder) Stoneware saltglazed gray jug, 14-3/4", smooth base, handled, American, 1845-1860.	$700-800	
Ovoid 3-Gallon Jug – '3' Stoneware saltglazed jug, 13-1/4", smooth base, handled, manufactured by Van Schoick & Dunn Pottery, Middletown Point, New Jersey, American, 1860-1885.	$250-300	
Ovoid 3-Gallon Crock Stoneware saltglazed gray crock, 9-1/4", smooth base, double closed handles, Warne & Letts, South Amboy, New Jersey, American, 1805-1815.	$600-900	
N. A. White & Son – Utica, N.Y. – '6' (Impressed below the rim) Stoneware saltglazed 6-gallon cream crock, 13", smooth base, double closed handles, American, 1880-1890.	$400-450	
N. Clark, Jr. Athens, N.Y. – Globe Works (Impressed on shoulder) Stoneware saltglazed 5-gallon cream jug, 18-1/2", smooth base, double open handles, American, 1845-1855.	$500-600	

N. Clark & Co. – Lyons – '3' Stoneware saltglazed 3-gallon ovoid gray jug, 17", smooth base, handled, American, 1835-1845.	$600-700	
Compliments of – Henry Hiller – Wholesale Liquors – 522 14th St. – Omaha, Neb. An Eye Opener – To Henry Hiller's – Fine Whiskies Stoneware mini advertising gray with dark brown glaze, 3-1/2", smooth base, handled, American, 1885-1910.	$375-475	
Nicolas & Boynton – Burlington, Vt. (impressed on shoulder) Stoneware saltglazed 1-gallon cream jug, 11-3/8", handled, American, 1880-1895.	$100-125	
Meyer Bros. – Paterson – N.J. Stoneware saltglazed 1-gallon advertising cream crock, 7-3/4", smooth base, double closed handle, Fulper Brothers Pottery, Flemington, New Jersey, American, 1890-1900.	$300-350	
'P V & S' (above a vine motif) – P. Vidvard & Son – Utica N.Y. (inside a floral wreath) Stoneware saltglazed 1-gallon cream jug, 10-3/8", smooth base, handled, rare, manufactured by Vidvard & Sheehan who made handled whiskey bottles, American, 1870-1875.	$900-1,000	
Sample – Fible + Crabb – Whiskey – Kansas City, Mo. Stoneware mini advertising jug, 3-1/8", smooth base, handled, American, 1885-1910.	$200-250	
Simon Sanders & Co. – Trinidad, Colo (on shoulder) Stoneware cream advertising jug, 8-1/4", smooth base, handled, American, 1880-1915.	$275-375	

Old Bottles

Stoneware Saltglazed Cuspidor Smooth base, 5-7/8", American, 1875-1885.	$400-500	
Stoneware Saltglazed Crock Gray, 9", smooth base, open handles, American, 1800-1820.	$500-600	
Stoneware Saltglazed Crock Gray, 12-2/3", smooth base, closed ears, American, 1850-1870.	$200-250	
Stoneware Saltglazed Ovoid Jug Cream, 14-3/4", smooth base, handled, American, 1835-1855.	$200-250	
Stoneware Saltglazed 4-Gallon Churn –'4' Brown, 16-1/8", smooth base, double closed handles, American, 1875-1885.	$400-600	
Smith & Day – Manufacturers, - Norwalk, Conn –'2' (impressed on shoulder) Stoneware saltglazed 2-gallon ovoid gray jug, 13-3/4", smooth base, handled, American, 1845-1855.	$250-300	
T. Wright & Son – Stoneware – Taunton, Mass –'3' (impressed below rim) Stoneware saltglazed 2- gallon gray crock, 9-1/4", smooth base, closed handles, American, 1870-1890.	$200-225	
T.O. Goodwin – Hartford –'2' (impressed on shoulder) Stoneware saltglazed brown 2-gallon ovoid jug, 13-1/2", smooth base, handled, American, 1825-1830.	$350-400	

The Little Brown Jug – Compliments of – The Temple Bar – The Harris Co. – San Francisco Stoneware cream advertising jug, 6-1/2", smooth base, cream color with brown glaze, handle, very rare, American, 1890-1910.	$150-200	
W. A. Macquoid & Co. – Pottery Works – Little 12th St. – New York (impressed below rim) Stoneware saltglazed 3- gallon cream crock, 10-1/4", smooth base, double closed handles, very rare, New York potters mark, American, 186-1875.	$500-600	
W.H. Harrison – Washington Ave & - Pacific St. – Brooklyn N.Y. (Impressed on shoulder) Stoneware saltglazed gray advertising jug, 7-7/8", smooth base, handled, American, 1880-1890.	$250-300	
W. Roberts, Binghamton, N.Y. –'2' (Impressed on shoulder) Stoneware saltglazed gray 2-gallon ovoid crock, 9-3/4", smooth base, double closed handles, American, 1860-1875.	$150-200	
Compliments of W.J. Smith – Cornhill, Tex Stoneware mini advertising jug, 3-1/2", cream with dark brown glaze, smooth base, handled, American, 1880-1910.	$400-450	
W T Spence, Dealer In Dry Goods Groceries & C – Centerville MD – P. Herrmann, 1gl (impressed on back) Stoneware saltglazed brown jar, 10-1/8, smooth base, American, 1880-1890.	$400-450	
Warren Bottling Co. – 291 Chamber St. – Phillipsburg- N.J. Stoneware saltglazed 1-gallon cream jug, 11", smooth base, handled, Fulper Brothers Pottery, Flemington, New Jersey, American, 1890-1900.	$400-500	

Figural Bottles

Figural bottles were produced in large numbers in the late 19th century and early 20th century. These whimsical bottles took on the shapes of animals, people, boots, and books, among other objects. They came in a wide variety of colors and sizes and were quite popular among the rich aristocrats of that time.

Whiskey nip figural revolver, amber, 8-1/2" l, ground lip, original metal screw-on cap, American, 1890-1910, $70-80.

Figural "man in the moon" decanter, straw yellow figural moon, original red and black paint, ground glass stopper, polished top, base is grass green with original metal connector and rack, American, 1890-1915, $500-600.

Alligator Milk glass, 10", pontil scarred base, sheared and tooled top, rare in milk glass, French, 1880-1910.	**$150-200**	
Arabian Sitting on a Hassock Reddish amber, 11-5/8", smooth base, applied top, rare color, American, 1875-1885.	**$150-200**	
Bather on Rocks Clear, 11-3/4", pontil scarred base (DEPOSE), tooled top, original ground glass stopper, French, 1880-1915.	**$50-75**	
Bearded Man Holding Bag and Broom Clear, 7-1/2", smooth base, sheared lip, American, 1890-1915.	**$50-100**	
Bear (applied face) Blue aqua, 8-1/4", smooth base, shared and tooled lip, possibly Russian, 1890-1900.	**$150-175**	
Bear Bottle – Label Reads: Bears Oil with 1 cent Tax Stamp and Contents Clear, 1-7/8" h, 3-3/4" l, smooth base (C. Knapp-Philada), American, 1890-1900.	**$1,500-1,700**	
Bird Cage Light teal blue with gold paint, 4-3/4", smooth base (Pat. Apl'd For), original glass lid, American, 1920-1935.	**$50-100**	
Bust of Sadi Carrot Clear, 11-1/2", D.D. Depose (embossed on back side of pedestal, pontil scarred base, tooled lip, French, 1890-1915.	**$100-125**	

Bust of Tsar and Tsarine (lot of 2) Clear, 12-1/4", smooth base, tooled tops, European, 1890-1920.	$200-300	
Cockatoo Black amethyst, 13-1/2", smooth base, sheared and ground lip, European, 1890-1810.	$100-250	
Chick Hatching From Egg - Easter Milk glass with original gold paint, 3-1/8", smooth base, egg was blown and twisted off at one end, American, 1880-1910.	$50-100	
Child in Rocking Chair Milk glass, 5-1/8", smooth base, sheared and ground lip, American, 1880-1910.	$350-400	
Child Sitting on a Barrel Clear, 4-7/8", smooth base (G & T), ground lip, American, 1890-1915.	$80-100	
Clam Shell Whisky Nip Cobalt blue, 5-1/4", sheared and ground lip, original screw on metal cap, American, 1890-1915.	$200-300	

Cluster of Grapes Clear, 5-3/4" long, smooth base, sheared and ground lip, American, 1885-1910.	$300-400	
Dog (free-blown figural) Green aqua, 5", pontil scarred front, original cork has a copper cone attached to the front that reads: Carl XV Sveriges Norr. G.O.V. Konung (around bust of man), Carl XV was the king of Sweden and Norway from 1859 until his death Sept. 18, 1872, Swedish, 1860-1873.	$350-450	
Duck on Nest Candy Container Clear glass with remnants of original yellow, red, and blue paint, 2-3/4", original metal screw on metal lid, American, 1915-1930.	$350-400	
Female Bather Clear, 17", bather being frosted, pontil scarred base (DEPOSE), original pineapple stopper, tooled top, French, 1885-1910.	$75-100	
Fox Reading a Book Clear, 4-5/8", smooth base (Pat. Apld For), ground lip with original screw-on cap, American, 1885-1910.	$40-60	

Frog Aqua, 7", smooth base, sheared and polished lip, European, 1890-1920.	$100-150	
Gordon's Hoof Ointment (horse hoof shape) Clear, 5-1/2", smooth base (Patented July 20th 1880), sheared and tooled lip, original screw-on zinc lid, American, 1880-1890.	$700-800	
Japanese Man – "J. P. G." on Forehead, "Trade Indestructible Mark" on collar, "Japanese-Gloss-Shake Me Well – Before Using" on long coat, "Sole Proprietors & Manufacturers – Baltimore, MD." around base. Teal green, 6-1/2", smooth base, sheared and ground lip, scarce size in rare color, American, 1890-1900.	$500-600	
Helmet Whisky Nip Red-ware with overall two tone glaze, 2-1/2", 'Helmet Rye' (impressed on brim), American, 1890-1910.	$150-200	
Liberty Bell – E. Hoyt & Co. – Celebrated – Perfumers – ESTB. 1868 – Sesqui Centennial – 1776-1926 Clear, 2-1/2", smooth base, tooled lip with original neck foil, American, 1926.	$250-350	

Madonna Bottles (lot of 2) Pale green and aqua, 9-1/2", pontil scarred bases, tooled tops, French, 1890-1910.	$200-300	
Man in Night Cap Holding a Mug Rockingham-type glaze, 8-3/4", smooth base (Manufacturer Wadtincote (impressed on base), English, 1860-1880.	$200-250	
Man Sitting on a Barrel Clear, 11-1/8", pontil scarred base ((DEPOSE), applied handle, tooled top, French, 1890-1920.	$150-200	
Milk Pail Straw yellow, 3-7/8", smooth base (Pat. Glass Pail, Boston Mass, June 24,84), ground lip, original tin collar, handle, and lid, American, 1884-1890.	$500-600	
Miniature Car Aqua, 2-7/8", 'Mirabel' (embossed on hood), smooth base, tooled top, European, 1900-1920.	$50-75	

Old Bottles

Oil Derrick Medicine Bottle (figural) – Bowens – Genuine- Crude Oil- Products (frame-work of oil derricks on three sides) Label Reads: Bowen Genuine Crude Oil Hair Gower, Liquid Velvet Clear with original contents, 6-1/2", smooth base, tooled top, original cork, American, 1880-1900	$150-200	
Oriental Man Holding a Large Bottle Clear, 10", pontil scarred base (DEPOSE), tooled top, original ground glass stopper, French, 1890-1920.	$100-125	
Pig (free-blown figural) Clear, 11-1/8", applied head, eyes, ears, feet, razor back, and lip, American, 1860-1880.	$200-300	
Powder Horn Candy Container Clear, 4-3/4", smooth base (Pat. Appld. For), ground lip with original screw on cap, American, 1890-1915.	$75-100	
Puss in Boot Candy Container Milk glass, 3", smooth base, American, 1915-1930.	$50-75	
Roasted Turkey Aqua, 4-3/4", smooth base, ground lip with original screw on cap, American, 1885-1910.	$200-300	

Shoe with Protruding Toe Frost clear glass, 5-1/2" long, smooth base, ground lip with original screw on cap, American, 1885-1910.	$150-200	
Slipper Bottle – Multi-Colored Label on top reads: Bears Oil Clear, 4 5/8" long, smooth base, tooled lip, American, 1890-1900.	$800-900	
Standing Soldier or Hunter Clear, 8-1/2", smooth base, sheared and ground lip, English, 1890-1920.	$75-100	
Standing Man Pondering Deep cobalt blue, 6-7/8", pontil scarred base, tooled lip, rare color, American, 1870-1880.	$350-400	
Turtle Bottle – Label on base reads: Fine Cologne (Walking Turtle)- This Style of bottle is – Original and is a – Trade Mark Amber body with black amber head, 4-3/4" long, tooled lip, rare with original glass head and label, American, 1890-1910.	$900-1,000	
Young Girl Sitting on a Basket Clear, 8-1/2", pontil scarred base, tooled top, American, 1885-1910.	$75-100	

Fire Grenades

Fire grenades are a highly prized item among bottle collectors and represent one of the first modern improvements in fire fighting. A fire grenade is a water-filled bottle about the size of a baseball. Its use was simple. It was designed to be thrown into a fire, where it would break and (hopefully) extinguishing the flames. The fire grenades worked best when the fire was noticed immediately.

The first American patent on a fire grenade was issued in 1863 to Alanson Crane of Fortress Monroe, Virginia. The best-known manufacturer of these specialized bottles, the Halden Fire Extinguisher Co., Chicago, was awarded a patent in August of 1871.

The grenades were manufactured in large numbers by companies with names as unique as the bottles themselves: Dash-Out, Diamond, Harkness Fire Destroyer, Hazelton's High Pressure Chemical Firekeg, Magic Fire, Y-Burn, Hayward Hand Grenade.

The fire grenade became obsolete with the invention of the fire extinguisher in 1905. Many of these grenades are considered rare and scarce and can still be found with the original closures, contents, and labels.

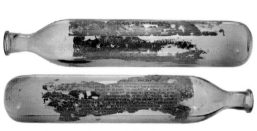

Spong & Cos. Hand Fire Extinguishing Tube & Grenade – London, bright yellow olive, 13-1/8", tooled lip, scarce, English, 1880-1900, $450-500.

Harkness Fire Destroyer, sapphire blue, 6-1/4", sheared and ground lip, 1875-1895, $300-350.

The following is an excerpt of a story in the June 7, 1885 issue of the *New York Times*, written about the Hayward Hand Grenade.

THE HAYWARD HAND GRENADE. HOW TO PREVENT FIRES – THE BEST FIRE EXTINGUISHER EVER INVENTED

Protection against fire is the duty of all, whether in a public or private capacity, but the great difficult has been to select the best means for the accomplishment of this aim. The very best yet invented, however, is that known as the Hayward Hand Grenade Fire Extinguisher, which is not only perfectly reliable, but simple and economical. It is not claimed by the company owning the patent, and whose office and salesrooms are at Nos 407 and 409 Broadway, New York City, that these grenades will extinguish large conflagrations, or take the place of steam for engines, but it has been practically demonstrated over and over again that no incipient fire can possibly develop itself further when they are use as directed The company guarantees everything claimed for these grenades, and no hotel, club, public building, private residence, steamboat, should be without a supply.

Manf'd By Fire Extinguisher M'F'G' Co. – Babcock – Hand Grenade – Non-Freezing – 325-331 S. Des Plaines St. Chicago Medium cobalt clue, 7-1/2", smooth base, rough sheared and ground top, original contents, American, 1880-1890.	$3,000-3,300	
Fire Grenade – C. & N-W. RY. (Chicago and Northwestern Railroad) Clear glass tube, 17-5/8", smooth base, rough sheared lip, original black shoulder and neck paint, two metal mounts, American, 1880-1900.	$100-150	
Fire Grenade – Grenade Securite – Extincteur (On raise center band) Yellow amber, 5-5/8", smooth base, sheared and ground top, French, 1880-1900.	$100-150	
Fire Grenade – Hayward's – Hand Fire – Grenade-S.F. Hayward-407-Broadway-New York – Patented - Aug – 8 -1871 Medium cobalt blue, 6", smooth base, sheared and ground lip, American, 1875-1900.	$250-300	

Fire Grenade – Hayward Hand Grenade Fire Extinguisher – New York (on shoulder) Cobalt blue, 6", smooth base (H), tooled top, original embossed red neck foil and contents, American, 1875-1900.	**$350-400**	
Fire Grenade – Hayward Hand Grenade Fire Extinguisher – New York (on shoulder) Clear glass, 6", smooth base (Design Pat'd), tooled top, American, 1875-1900.	**$150-200**	
Fire Grenade – Hayward Hand Grenade Fire Extinguisher – New York (on shoulder) Clear glass, 6", smooth base (Design Patd), tooled top, original embossed red neck foil and contents, American, 1875-1900.	**$125-175**	
Fire Grenade – S.F. Hayward -407-Broadway – N.Y.-Patented – Aug -8-1871-Hayward – Hand –Fire – Grenade- Embossed: Trade Mark – Hand with Hayward Hand Fire Grenade (inside a grenade) Turquoise blue, 6-1/8", smooth base (2), sheared and tooled top, American, 1875-1895.	**$100-150**	
Fire Grenade – Hayward's – Hand Fire – Grenade Patented –Aug -8-1871 - S.F. Hayward – 407- Broadway – New York Deep cobalt blue, 6-1/4", smooth base (3"), sheared and ground top, original contents, American, 1875-1895.	**$450-500**	
Fire Grenade – S.F. Hayward – 407-Broadway – N.Y. Patented –Aug -9-1871 Hayward's-Hand – Fire – Grenade: Original Label Reads: In case of fire throw or break The Grenade over the flames: Trade Mark (hand holding a grenade) 'Hayward Hand Fire Grenade (embossed on neck and mouth foil) Lime green, 6-3/8", smooth base (3") tooled top, American, 1875-1895.	**$350-400**	

Fire Grenade – S.F. Hayward -407-Broadway – N.Y.-Patented – Aug -8-1871- Hayward – Hand –Fire – Grenade- Embossed: Trade Mark – Hand with Hayward Hand Fire Grenade (inside a grenade) Foil Seal and Contents Light smoky amethyst, 6-3/8", smooth base (3), sheared and tooled top, rare color, American, 1875-1895.	$900-1,000	
Fire Grenade – S.F. Hayward -407-Broadway – N.Y.-Patented – Aug -8-1871-Hayward – Hand –Fire – Grenade- Embossed: Trade Mark – Hand with Hayward Hand Fire Grenade (inside a grenade) Foil Seal and Contents Light smoky aqua, 6-3/8", smooth base (3), sheared and tooled top, considered to the hardest Hayward grenade color to obtain, American, 1875-1895.	$900-1,000	
Fire Grenade – S.F. Hayward -407-Broadway – N.Y.-Patented – Aug -8-1871- Hayward – Hand –Fire – Grenade- Embossed: Trade Mark – Hand with Hayward Hand Fire Grenade (inside a grenade) Foil Seal and Contents Yellow olive, 6-3/8", smooth base (3), sheared and tooled top, American, 1875-1895.	$150-200	
Fire Grenade – Hayward Hand Grenade Fire Extinguisher – New York (on shoulder) Hayward's Hand Fire Grenade – Trade Mark (embossed on neck foil and partial contents) Pale aqua, 6-5/8", smooth base (Design Patd), tooled top, scarce middle size pleated style, American, 1875-1900.	$150-200	
Fire Grenade – HSN (Monogram on two Diamond panels) Clear glass, 7-1/8", smooth base, sheared and ground top, rare in clear glass, American, 1875-1900.	$350-400	
Fire Grenade – HSN (Monogram on two Diamond panels) Two Original Labels Golden yellow amber, 7-1/4", smooth base, rough sheared top, American, 1875-1900.	$150-200	

Old Bottles

Fire Grenade – HSN (monogram on two diamond panels) Two Original Labels Yellow with amber tone, 7-1/4", smooth base, rough sheared top, partial contents, wire neck hanger, American, 1875-1900.	$150-200	
Fire Grenade – (Unembossed Harkness Fire Destroyer) Deep cobalt blue, horizontal rib pattern with oval front labeled panel, 6-1/8", smooth base, sheared and ground lip, American, 1875-1900.	$200-250	
Fire Grenade – Imperial – D.R.P. – Hand Grenade – Fire Extinguisher Bright lime green, 6-1/2", smooth base, sheared and ground top, English, 1880-1900.	$100-125	
Fire Grenade – Magic – Fire – Extinguisher Co. Golden yellow amber, 6-3/8", smooth base, rough sheared lip, rare, American, 1875-1900.	$450-500	
Fire Grenade - M.P.R.R. (Missouri Pacific Railroad) Clear glass, 8-1/8", smooth base, ground lip, American, 1880-1900.	$1,400-1,500	

Fire Grenade – P.R.R. (in oval panel – Pennsylvania Railroad) Clear glass, overall horizontal rib pattern, 7", smooth base, tooled top, American, 1880-1900.	$1,500-1,600	
Fire Grenade – Perfection Hand Grenade (inside a horseshoe) – Pat'd –By – A. Jones – 1885 Amber, 7-1/2", fish scale pattern around the embossing, smooth base, sheared and tooled top, extremely rare, American, 1885-1900.	$2,000-2,300	
Fire Grenade – Sinclair (Original 'How to Use' neck label and contents) Deep cobalt blue, 7-1/4", smooth base (TOOT), tooled top, English, 1880-1900.	$400-500	
Fire Grenade – Star (inside a five-pointed star) – Harden Star Hand Grenade-Fire Extinguisher Clear glass, 6-1/2", smooth base, sheared and ground lip, English, 1880-1900.	$350-400	
Fire Grenade – The Kalamazoo – Automatic and – Hand Fire Extinguisher Patent Applied For Deep cobalt blue, 11-1/8", smooth base, sheared and tooled top, American, 1880-1900.	$300-350	

Old Bottles

Grenade L'urbaine, medium orange amber, 6-1/2", sheared and ground lip, 99% original label, French, 1875-1900, $200-250.

Flagg's Fire Extinguisher –Pat'd Aug 4th 1868, amber, 6-3/8", rough sheared lip, original seal and contents, rare, 1870-1890, $1,500-1,700.

Unembossed Fire Grenade Pink amethyst, 7", 16-rib pattern, smooth base, flared out ABM top, French or German, 1880-1900.	**$250-300**
Unembossed Fire Grenade Deep cobalt blue, 6-1/8", smooth base, sheared and ground top, original contents, Canadian, 1880-1900.	**$150-200**
Unembossed Fire Grenade – Overall Circle and Floral Pattern Pale aqua, 7", smooth base, applied top, original contents, French or German, 1880-1900.	**$400-600**
Un-embossed Fire Grenade Blue aqua, quart, 7-1/8", 16 vertical rib pattern, smooth base, applied top, original contents, French or German, 1880-1900.	**$400-600**

Haywards Hand Grenade Fire Extinguisher – New York (around shoulder), deep cobalt blue, 5-7/8", tooled lip, original contents, 1875-1895, $200-250.

Star (inside a 5-pointed star) – Harden Grenade Sprinkler, deep cobalt blue, tube shape, 17-1/4", tooled lip, scarce, 1875-1900, $900-1,000.

The Imperial Fire Extinguisher Co. Ltd. (inside an embossed 'belt') with an embossed crown in the center, medium cobalt blue, 6-1/2", rough sheared lip, extremely rare, 1885-1895, English, $2,500-3,000.

Systeme Labbe (diamond pattern in circle) – Grenade Extincteur (floral ornament in circle), L'Incombustibilite – Paris, orange amber, 5-1/2", French, 1880-1900, $150-200.

Star (inside a star inside a circle) Harden Hand Grenade-Fire Extinguisher, amber, quart, 8-1/8", 1880-1895, $900-1,000.

Flasks

Flasks have become a most popular and prized item among collectors due to the variety of decorative, historical, and pictorial depictions on many pieces. The outstanding colors have a major effect on the value of these pieces, more so than most other collectible bottles.

American flasks were first manufactured by the Pitkin Glasshouse in Connecticut around 1815, and quickly spread to other glass houses around the country. Early flasks were free-blown and represent some of the better craftsmanship with more intricate designs. By 1850, approximately 400 designs had been used. Black graphite pontil marks were left on the bottles because the pontils were coated with powdered iron allowing the flasks' bottoms to break away without damaging the glass. The flasks made between 1850 to 1870, however, had no such markings because of the widespread use of the newly invented snap-case.

Since flasks were intended to be refilled with whiskey or other spirits, more time and effort were expended in manufacturing than most other types of bottles. Flasks soon became a popular item for use with all types of causes and promotions. Mottoes frequently were embossed on flasks and included a number of patriotic sayings and slogans. George Washington's face commonly appeared on flasks, as did Andrew Jackson's and John Quincy Adams', the candidates for the presidential elections of 1824 and 1828. Events of the time were also portrayed on flasks.

One of the more controversial flasks was the Masonic flasks, which bore the order's emblem on one side and the American eagle on the other side. At first, the design drew strong opposition from the public, but the controversy soon passed, and Masonic flasks are now a specialty item for collectors.

Another highly collectible flask is the Pitkin-type named for Pitkin Glassworks, where it was exclusively manufactured. While Pitkin-type flasks and ink bottles are common, Pitkin bottles, jugs, and jars are rare. German Pitkin flasks are heavier and straight-ribbed, while the American patterns are swirled and broken-ribbed with unusual colors such as dark blue.

Because flasks were widely used for promoting various political and special interest agendas, they represent a major historical record of the people and events of those times.

Albany Glass Works – Bust of Washington – Albany – NY – Sailing Ship (GI-28) Medium sapphire blue, pint, open pontil, applied tapered collar top, American, 1835-1845.	$16,000-18,000	
American Eagle – Eagle With Serpent In Beak (GII-9) Clear glass, pint, pontil scarred base, sheared and tooled top, rare, referred to as the 'Snake of Corruption," American, 1835-1840.	$14,000-15,000	
(All Seeing Eye inside six-pointed star) – "A.D." (bent arm inside six-pointed star) "G R J A" Yellow olive amber, pint, open pontil, sheared top, American, 1835-1845.	$300-350	
"B.P & B" Scroll Flask Deep cobalt blue, half-pint, pontil scarred base, sheared and tooled top, rare in this shade of cobalt blue, American, 1840-1850.	$150-200	
Baltimore – Anchor – Glass Works – Sheaf Of Grain (GXIII-52) Medium cobalt blue, Calabash, open pontil, applied double collar top, rare color, American, 1855-1860.	$4,000-4,500	
Bininger's – Travelers – Guide – A. M. Bininiger & Co – No. 19 Broad St. N.Y. Medium amber, 6-3/4", Tear-Drop Flask, smooth base, applied double collar top, American, 1860-1865.	$400-500	
Banjo Player – Dancer (GXIII-8) Orange amber, half-pint, smooth base, applied double collar top, American, 1855-1865.	$450-500	
Benjamin Franklin – Bust of Franklin – Where Liberty Dwells – There is My Country – T.W. Dyott, M.D. – Bust of Dyott – Kensington Glass – Works – Philadelphia (GI-94) Light aqua, pint, open pontil, sheared and tooled top, American, 1825-1835.	$450-500	

Brachmann & Massard – 81 West Third St. – Cin. O Medium amber, 8", smooth base, applied tapered top, American, 1880-1900.	**$100-125**	
Christopher Columbus Holding a Globe – Columbus Clear glass, 6-1/4", pint, smooth base, sheared and ground top, original metal screw-on cap, made to commemorate the World's Colombian Exposition in Chicago in 1893, American, 1893.	**$400-450**	
Clasped Hands – Union – Eagle – A.R.S. (GIV-42) Light yellow green (citron), Calabash, open pontil, applied tapered collar top, scarce color, American, 1855-1865.	**$600-700**	
Columbia With Liberty Cap – Eagle – "B & W" (GI-121) Aqua, pint, tubular, open pontil, sheared and tooled top, Kensington Glass Works, Philadelphia, Penn, American, 1835-1845.	**$500-600**	
Concentric Ring Eagle (GII-76) Medium clear green, quart, pontil scarred base, sheared and tooled top, American, 1825-1835.	**$5,000-6,000**	

Corn For The World – (ear of corn) – Monument – Baltimore Teal blue, quart, 8-1/2", smooth base, applied double collar top, American, 1870-1875.	$5,000-6,000	
Cornucopia – Urn – Label Reads: Pale – Sherry Wine – For Medicinal Use – Thomas Hollis, Druggist – No.23 Union Street Boston (GIII-4) Olive amber, pint, open pontil, sheared and tooled top, American, 1825-1835.	$400-500	
Cornucopia – Urn Stoneware Flask (GIII-14) Brown and yellow mottled, half-pint , open pontil, sheared and tooled top, American, 1835-1845.	$500-600	
Corset Waist Scroll Flask (GIX-46) Blue aqua, quart, open pontil, sheared and tooled top, American, 1840-1850.	$600-700	
Eagle With Banner and Shield (GII-143) Medium green, quart calabash, iron pontil, applied tapered collar top, American, 1855-1865.	$300-400	
Eagle – Coffin & Hay – Stag – Hammonton (GII-50) Blue aqua, half-pint, open pontil, sheared and tooled top, scarce, American, 1825-1835.	$350-400	

Eagle – Continental – Indian Shooting A Bird – Cunninghams & Co. – Pittsburg, PA (GII-42) Olive yellow, quart, smooth base, applied ring top, Cunningham Glass Works, Pittsburg, Penn, American, 1855-1870.	$600-700	
Eagle – Eagle (GII-24) Medium sapphire blue, pint, open pontil, sheared top, Louisville Glass Works, Louisville, Kentucky, American, 1835-1845.	$3,500-4,000	
Eagle (inside oval) – Louisville – KY – Glass Works (inside oval) (GIII-36) Dark olive amber, half-pint, ribbed pattern, smooth base, crude finished applied top, rare in olive amber, American, 1850-1860.	$1,500-2,000	
Eagle (inside oval) – Louisville – KY – Glass Works (inside pointed frame) (GIII-36) Medium amber, pint, ribbed pattern, smooth base, crude finished applied top, extremely rare color, American, 1850-1860.	$5,000-6,000	
Eagle – Granite – Glass Co. – Eagle – Stoddard – N.H. (GII-81) Yellow amber, pint, tubular open pontil, sheared and tooled top, American, 1850-1860.	$350-400	
Eagle – New London – Anchor – Glass Works (GII-67) Medium blue green, half-pint, open pontil, sheared and tooled top, American, 1855-1865.	$400-500	
Easley's (Motif of Hand) "Saloon – Huntsville-Rough & (a man walking with a bottle in hand) "Ready – H. Easley's (GXIII-89) Aqua, 6-3/8", half-pint, smooth base, applied ring top, the "Rough & Ready" embossing appears on several earlier flask dating to 1830s, American, 1860-1870.	$6,000-7,000	

Edward Scanlan & Co. – Cincinnati – Ohio Amber, 5-3/4", tear drop flask, smooth base, applied double collar top, American, 1860-1870.	$700-800	
Elk Saloon – Harry Klasen Prop. – Tuolumne CAL. Clear glass, pint pumpkinseed flask, smooth base, tooled top, American, 1880-1910.	$900-1,000	
Fisher's Hotel – Ben Race Prop. – San Mateo, CAL. Clear glass, half-pint pumpkinseed flask, smooth base, tooled top, American, 1880-1905.	$600-700	
For Pike's Peak – Prospector – Hunter Shooting Stag (GXI-50) Blue aqua, pint, smooth base, applied ring top, American, 1865-1875.	$150-200	
For Pike's Peak – Prospector – Old Rye – Eagle – Pittsburg PA (GXI-8) Blue aqua, quart, red iron pontil, applied ring top, American, 1855-1870.	$200-250	
For Pike's Peak – Prospector – Eagle – Ceredo (GXI-34) Olive yellow, quart, smooth base, applied ring top, extremely rare color, American, 1860-1870.	$5,000-6,000	

Geo. W. Robinson – No 75 – Main St. W.VA. Blue aqua, quart, smooth base, applied top, American, 1875-1885.	$100-150	
Gilman Walker & Co. – 224 Front St. – S.F. Medium amber, half-pint – Union oval, smooth base, double rolled tolled collar, rare, American, 1878-1886.	$1,000-1,200	
Goudie & McKelvy – Pepper Tree Saloon – Agts. For Lewis Hunter – Rye – San Pedro, CAL Medium amber, half-pint coffin flask, smooth base, tooled top, American, 1905.	$1,500-1,600	
H. J. Schauffle – The Opera – Monterey CAL – Net Contents 5 Ounces Clear glass, 6", smooth base, tooled top, American, 1885-1900.	$200-225	

Hall's Luhrs & Co. – (monogram) – Sacramento Clear glass, half-pint pumpkinseed flask, smooth base, tooled top, American, 1882-1917.	$600-700	
Horseman – Hound (GXIII-18) Yellow amber, half pint, smooth base, applied double collar top, American, 1855-1870.	$300-350	
Hunter – Fisherman (GXIII-4) Golden yellow amber, Calabash, iron pontil, applied tapered collar top, American, 1855-1865.	$200-250	
Hunter – Fisherman (GXIII-4) Medium teal, Calabash, smooth base, applied tapered collar top, American, 1855-1865.	$600-700	
Jenny Lind – Bust Of Jenny Lind – Glass Work's – Glass Factory – S.Huffsey Medium blue green Calabash, open pontil, applied double collar top, American, 1850-1860.	$1,900-2,000	
Jesse Moore's – Old Bourbon – A. Walsh – Chinese Camp, CAL. (Label) Clear glass, half-pint pumpkinseed flask, smooth base, tooled top, American, 1800-1905.	$900-1,000	

Label Under Glass Whiskey Flask- Hanlen Bros. Wines & Liquors – Sole Distributors- 330 Market Street – Harrisburg, PA with U.S. on reverse side Clear glass, 5", smooth base, screw on cap is missing, American, 1895 1910.	$300-350	
Label Under Glass Whiskey Flask – Image of Pretty Girl Clear glass, 5-1/4", screw top cap, smooth base, American, 1895-1920.	$1,000-1,200	
Label Under Glass Whiskey Flask – Dancing Couple Clear glass 5-1/2", original screw top cap, smooth base, American, 1890-1910.	$350-400	
Label Under Glass Whiskey Flask – Whimsical Couple from the Revolutionary War Clear glass, 5-3/4", smooth base, original pewter cap, American, 1895-1925.	$500-600	
Label Under Glass Whiskey Flask – Young Woman in Hat Clear glass, 5-3/4", half pint, original screw top cap, American, 1895-1910.	$700-800	

Label Under Glass Whiskey Flask – **Young Woman With Fancy Hat and Dress** **Compliments of Henry Sadler – Salt Lake,** **Utah** Clear glass, 5-3/4", smooth base, original metal cap, American, 1860-1868.	$1,000-1,100	
LaFayette – Bust of LaFayette – T.S. – De Wit **Clinton – Bust of Clinton – Coventry (GI-80)** Medium yellow olive green, pint, open pontil, sheared and tooled top, American, 1825-1835.	$1,000-1,100	
Lilienthal & Co. – S.F. (Whiskey Flask) Medium amber, smooth base, double rolled collar top, American, 1885-1900.	$600-700	
M.F. Biern – Magnolia Hotel -469 South 8th **St. Phila (all inside an embossed wreath)** Amber, 7", tear-drop flask, smooth base, applied double collar top, original amber glass stopper with an embossed star on top, American, 1866-1875.	$900-1,000	
Masonic Arch – Eagle (GIV-8a) Note: **'Paschal Lamb' embossed in the lower left** **corner on the Masonic side** Clear glass with some amethyst, pint, pontil scarred base, sheared and tooled top rare variant, American, 1815-1825.	$2,000-2,500	
Masonic – Eagle (GIV-1) Medium to deep amethyst and deep cobalt blue at the top and near the bottom, half-pint, pontil scarred base, sheared and tooled top, American, 1822-1840.	$15,000- 16,000	

Old Bottles

Milk Glass Octopus Flask Milk glass, 5", possibly Poseidon on one side and a Liberty Eagle on the reverse side, with the date 1901 beneath the Eagle, original screw top cap, American, 1901.	$700-800	
Miller's Extra E. – Martin Old – Bourbon – Trade Mark Medium amber, smooth base, applied single rolled collar top, American, 1871-1879.	$400-500	
N.E. Yocum – Wines & Liquors - Arcata, CAL. Clear glass, pumpkinseed pint, smooth base, tooled top, American, 1906-1908.	$450-500	
Opera Saloon – Liquor Store – Arcata, CAL. – Net Contents 12 Ounces Clear glass, pumpkinseed pint, smooth base, tooled top, American, 1906-1908.	$600-700	

Phoenix – Old – Bourbon – Naber, Alfs, Brune- San Francisco – Sole Proprietors Medium amber, half-pint , smooth base, tooled top, American, 1880-1900.	$250-300	
Phoenix – Old – Bourbon – Naber, Alfs, Brune- San Francisco – Sole Proprietors Medium amber, pint , smooth base, tooled top, American, 1880-1900.	$400-450	
Prospector – Eagle (GXI-19) Blue aqua, half-pint, smooth base, applied tapered collared top, American, 1860-1870.	$200-225	
Rainer-Saloon – Bluegrass S. Hossli – Tuolumne, CAL. Clear glass, half-pint pumpkinseed flask, smooth base, tooled top, American, 1880-1900.	$800-900	
Roth & Co. – 214 & 216 – Pine St. – San Francisco Medium amber, pint, smooth base, double rolled collar top, ring mark on neck and applied top, American, 1880-1885.	$500-600	

Old Bottles

Sloop – Star Deep sapphire blue, half-pint, tubular open pontil, sheared and tooled top, extremely rare – one of only three known examples, Bridgeton Glass Works, Bridgeton, New Jersey, American, 1825-1840.	**$20,000-25,000**	
Sunburst Flask – "Keen – P & W" (GVIII-8) Yellow olive amber, pint, open pontil, sheared and tooled top, American, 1815-1825.	**$450-500**	
Sunburst Flask (GVIII-3) Yellow amber, pint, open pontil, sheared and tooled top, Coventry Glass Works, Coventry, Conn, American, 1815-1825.	**$1,800-2,000**	
Sunburst Flask (GVIII-16) Olive yellow, half-pint, pontil scarred base, sheared and tooled top, American, 1815-1835.	**$500-600**	
Sunburst Flask – Wide Mouth (GVIII-19) Deep blue aqua, 7-1/2", jar, pontil scarred base, sheared and tooled wide mouth, referred to as the "snuff jar" sunburst, six known examples, American, 1815-1825.	**$20,000-24,000**	
Henry Chapman & Co. –Sole – Agents – Montreal Yellow amber, 6", tear drop flask, smooth base, applied screw threaded top, original screw threaded stopper is embossed "Pat-1861," American, 1860-1870.	**$300-350**	
J.N. Kline & Co's – Aromatic Digestive Cordial (all inside an embossed wreath) Medium cobalt blue, tear drop flask, 5-3/8", smooth base, applied double collar top, American, 1860-1870.	**$450-500**	

Kossuth – Bust of Kossuth – Tree (GI-113) Olive yellow, quart calabash, pontil scarred base, applied top, American, 1855-1860.	$700-800	
Liberty – Eagle With Banner and Shield – Willington –Glass Co. – West Willington – Conn. (GII-64) Olive green, pint, smooth base, applied double collar top, Willington Glass Works, Willington, Connecticut, American, 1835-1845.	$450-500	
Warranted Flask Union Made – Original Label Reads: For The Signal Saloon (Picture of Woman On Front) – Whiskey – For The Signal Saloon- Los Angeles California - Label on Reverse depicts Woman Waving a Handkerchief Clear glass, pint, smooth base, tooled top, American, 1885-1905.	$200-250	
Wharton's – Whisky – 1850 – Chestnut Grove (all inside an embossed wreath) Amber, 5-1/2", tear drop flask, smooth base, applied double collar top, American, 1860-1870.	$400-450	
Scroll Flask Golden amber, half-pint, open pontil, sheared and tooled top, scarce, American, 1840-1860.	$250-300	

Scroll Flask Medium teal blue, pint, open pontil, sheared and tooled top, extremely rare color, American, 1840-1850.	**$1,000-1,200**
Scroll Flask Medium cobalt blue, pint, open pontil, sheared and tooled top, scarce, American, 1840-1855.	**$900-1,000**
Scroll Flask (GIX-3) Yellow amber, quart, open pontil, sheared and tooled top, American, 1840-1860.	**$200-250**
Scroll Flask Light blue green, quart, red iron pontil, applied ringed top, American, 1840-1860.	**$300-400**
S.F. Rose – Straight Goods from the Wood – Vallejo, Cal. Clear glass, half-pint pumpkinseed flask, smooth base, tooled top, American, 1880-1900.	**$600-700**

Summer Tree-Summer Tree (GX-18) Light blue green, quart, pontil scarred base, applied 'top hat' top, American, 1855-1865.	$500-600	
The Monte Carlo – Parker & Clifford – Bakersfield, CAL Clear glass, half-pint pumpkinseed flask, smooth base, tooled top, American, 1880-1900.	$600-700	
Traveler's (Star) Companion –Ravenna (Star) – Glass Co.(GXIV-2) Deep amber, pint, smooth base, applied double collar top, Ravenna Glass Works, Ravenna, Ohio, American, 1850-1860.	$700-800	
Unembossed Flask Yellow green, half-pint, smooth base, applied double collar top, American, 1870-1880.	$250-300	

Unembossed Pocket Whiskey Flask Medium amber, half-pint, smooth base, applied double collar top, American, 1860-1870.	$175-200	
Unembossed Pocket Whiskey Flask Yellow amber, half-pint, open pontil, sheared and tooled top, American, 1855-1865.	$175-200	
Union- Clasped Hands – FA & Co. – Cannon (GXII-40) Yellow with amber tone, pint, smooth base, applied ring top, American, 1855-1865	$2,800-3,000	
Washington – Bust of Washington – Jackson – Bust of Jackson (GI-31) Olive green, pint, open pontil, sheared and tooled top, American, 1825-1835.	$400-500	
Wheeling VA – Old Rye (GXV-25) Green aqua, pin, smooth base, applied ring top, American, 1850-1855.	$1,000-1,300	
W. Ihmsen's – Eagle – Glass – Agriculture – Sheaf And Farm Implements (GII-10) Light citron, pint, open pontil, sheared and tooled top, American, 1835-1845.	$900-1,000	

Food & Pickle

Food bottles are one of the largest and most diverse categories in the field of collectible bottles. They were made for the commercial sale of a wide variety of food products excluding beverages, except milk. Food bottles are an ideal specialty for the beginning collector since as a group they are so readily available. Many collectors are attracted to food bottles for their historical value. Nineteenth and early 20th century magazines and newspapers contained so many illustrated advertisements for food products that many collectors keep scrapbooks of ads as an aid to dating and pricing the bottles.

Lot of two Heinz pickle jars: 'Heinz Pystone Pickles' with original top and 'Heinz Mixed Pickles' with original stopper marked H.J. Heinz Co. Pittsburg, USA, 1885-1920, $425-430.

Before bottling, food could not to be transported long distances or kept for long periods of time on account of spoilage. Bottling revolutionized the food industry and began a new chapter in American business merchandising and distribution. With the glass bottle producers were able to use portion packaging, save labor and sell from long distances.

Suddenly local producers faced competition from great distances. As a result, many interesting bottles were created specifically to distinguish them from others. Green and clear Peppersauce bottles, for instance, were made in the shape of Gothic cathedrals with arches and windows (green and clear); mustard jars and chili sauce bottles with unique embossing; cooking oil bottles, which are tall and slim; and pickle bottles with large mouths.

The pickle bottle is one of the largest of the food bottles with a wide mouth and a

Old Bottles

square or cylindrical shape. While the pickle bottles were often unique in shape and design, its color was almost exclusively aqua although occasionally you will find a multi-colored piece. Since there are many variations of designs for these Gothic-looking pickle jars with many variations of colors, it's difficult to exactly identify what contents were in the bottles and the identification of the bottle manufacturer. While the oldest bottles may have used foil labels for identification purposes, paper labels and embossing provide additional identification. When looking through ghost town dumps and digging behind older pioneer homes, you are sure to find these food and pickle bottles in large numbers since pickles were a common and well-liked food, especially in the mining communities.

Two of the more common food bottles are Worcestershire sauce bottles distributed by Lea & Perrins and Heinz sauce bottles. Worcestershire sauce in the green bottle was in high demand during the 19th century and is quite common.

Henry J. Heinz began to introduce his various selections of sauces and food supplements in 1869 at Sharpsburg, Pennsylvania, when he founded Heinz Noble & Company with a friend, L. Clarence Noble, with the bottling of horseradish. The company went bankrupt in 1875 but in 1876 Heinz founded another company, F & J. Heinz, with his brother, John, and a cousin, Frederick. The company continued to grow, and in 1888 it was reorganized as the H. J. Heinz Company, with one of its first products being tomato ketchup in 1889. In 1896, the slogan "57 Varieties" was introduced and the rest is history.

| Berry or Food Jar
Yellow amber, 11-1/4", 10 shoulder and neck panels, smooth base, applied double collar top, American, 1860-1870. | $800-900 | |
| Berry or Food Jar
Deep blue aqua, 11-3/8", red iron pontil, applied top, American, 1850-1865. | $175-200 | |

Cathedral Peppersauce Medium teal green, 9", tubular open pontil, applied double collar top, American, 1845-1860.	$250-300	
Cathedral Pickle Jar – J. McCollick & Co. – New York (embossed) Blue aqua, 8-5/8", iron pontil, outward rolled top, rare embossed jar, American, 1850-1865.	$1,000-1,200	
Cathedral Pickle Jar Deep blue green, 9", smooth base, outward rolled lip, American, 1860-1875.	$1,900-2,000	
Cathedral Pickle Jar (five-pointed star) Aqua, 11-3/8", cross hatch pattern on two panels, smooth base, rolled top, American, 1860-1879.	$450-500	
Cathedral Pickle Jar – E.H.V.B. – N.Y. Medium blue green, 11-1/2", iron pontil, applied top, rare size, American, 1850-1860.	$100-150	

Old Bottles

Cathedral Pickle Jar Medium emerald green, 14", smooth base, outward rolled top, American, 1860-1870.	$700-800	
Cathedral Pickle – Original Label Reads: Bear Paws Homemade Pickles – Los Angeles, California Turquoise, 14", smooth base, original cork and metal closure, American, 1860-1870.	$1,000-1,100	
Cathedral Willington Pickle Jar Deep amber, 8-1/2", pontil scarred base, applied top, considered to be the sought after of all pickle jars, American, 1850-1860.	$1,000-1,100	
Cathedral Sauce Bottle – Original Metal Label is embossed: 'Super-Tomato-Ketchup – Prepared by – Danwood – Co – 28 North – Market St. – Boston Aqua, 10-5/8", open pontil, applied tapered collar top, American, 1840-1860.	$300-350	
Crown Celery Salt – Horton Cato & Co. – Detroit Golden yellow amber, 8-1/4", smooth base, ground top with metal screw cap, twisted Rib-pattern, American, 1890-1900.	$300-350	
Food Bottles (lot of 2): John W. Stout & Co.- X – New York Aqua, 8-1/2", iron pontil, applied tapered collar top, American, 1860-1875.	$100-125	
Curtice Brothers – CB (monogram) – Rochester, N.Y. Aqua, 8-1/2", smooth base, applied tapered collar top, American, 1860-1875.	$100-125	

Food Storage Bottle Red amber, 8", lobed corner panels segmented by a lobed rib, smooth base, crude laid on top, American, 1860-1870.	$900-1,000	
G.P. Sanborn & Son – Union (inside shield and sunburst) – Boston Pickles Medium amber, 5-1/8", smooth base, tooled top, American, 1890-1910.	$100-125	
Gerkins – From – Skilton, Foote & Co. - -Bunker Hill Pickles- Boston Mass, U.S.A (on paper label) Olive amber, 8-1/2", smooth base, ABM wide top, American, 1890-1910.	$200-250	
Glessen's – Union – Mustard – N.Y. (Eagle and Shield) Clambroth with a hint of blue, 5-1/8", mustard barrel, pontil scarred base, outward rolled top, period cork closure, American, 1850-1860.	$300-400	
Hale & Parshall – Label Reads: Hale & Parchall Growers and Manufacturers of First Premium Peppermint Oil, Lyons, Wayne Co. New York State U.S. America, etc. Medium sapphire blue, 10", smooth base, applied sloping double collar top, American, 1860-1870.	$100-125	
Knickerbocker Sauce (on shoulder) – WM. P. Cotter Blue aqua, 6-1/2", 8-sided, pontil scarred base, applied sloping double collar top, extremely rare, American, 1845-1855.	$350-400	

Lime Juice Bottle – J.Rose & Co. **(surrounded by vine bearing limes)** Deep amber, 12-1/8", smooth base (J.K. & S.-L), applied tapered double collar top, rare in amber American, 1875-1890.	$150-200	
Peppersauce – E.M. & Son Blue aqua, 6-5/8", pontil scarred base, applied top, American, 1840-1860.	$100-150	
Peppersauce – E.R.D. & Co. – Patd – FEB 17 – 1874 Yellow amber with aqua top, 8", horizontal rib pattern, smooth base (E.R. Durkee & Co – N.Y.), applied aquamarine double collar top, American, 1875-1885.	$900-1,000	
Peppersauce – Wells – Miller & Provost Medium sapphire blue, 8", open pontil, applied top, rare in this color, American, 1840-1860.	$2,000-2,500	
Peppersauce Medium emerald green, 8-3/8", smooth base, 8-sided, applied double collar top, American, 1860-1870.	$250-300	
Pickle Bottle- Label Reads: Shaker Society Home Made Ripe Cucumber Pickles Yellow olive, 7", smooth base, tooled top, American, 1875-1890.	$350-400	
Pickle Bottle – Label Reads: Puritan Brand Boston Packing Co. Medium amber, 13-5/8", smooth base, applied top, American, 1880-1890.	$250-300	

Pickle Jar Medium yellow amber, 8', lobbed panel shape, smooth base, applied top, American, 1860-1870.	$900-1,000	
Pickle Jar – H.S. (on one side at the base) Blue aqua, 9-1/2", iron pontil, applied top, rare, American, 1850-1865.	$350-400	
Pickle Jar – M.B. ESPY – Philada Blue aqua, 11-1/2", smooth base, applied top, American, 1865-1875.	$200-300	
Pickle Jar – R & F. Atmore Blue aqua, 11-1/2", open pontil, applied top, American, 1855-1865.	$600-700	
Pickle Jar with Draped Shoulder – Wells – Miller & Provost Blue aqua, 11-1/2", iron pontil, outward rolled top, American, 1845-1860.	$700-800	
Shriver's – Oyster – Ketchup – Baltimore Emerald green, 7-5/8", smooth base, applied tapered collar top, scarce in this color, American, 1855-1865.	$1,500-1,600	

Shaker Brand – E.D.Pettengill & Co – Portland – ME Citron, 5-3/8", smooth base, crude laid on top, rare, American, 1880-1890.	$900-1,000	
Siphon Kumysgen Bottle – For Preparing – Kumyss From – Kumysgen – Reed & Carnrick, N.Y. – Water Mark – Powder Mark Cobalt blue, 9-1/8", smooth base, tooled top, original metal closure and contents, 98% label, American, 1890-1900.	$200-225	
Skilton, Foote & Co's – Trade Mark (Motif of the Bunker Hill Monument) Bunker Hill Pickles Yellow green, 7-5/8", smooth base, applied top, American, 1875-1885.	$100-125	
Skilton, Foote & Co's – Trade Mark (motif of the Bunker Hill Monument) Bunker Hill Pickles Yellow amber, quart, smooth base, tooled top, American, 1875-1890.	$100-150	
Stoneware Jug – Label Reads: New England Tomato Relish – Skilton, Foote & Co. – Boston, Mass. U.S.A. Cream pottery with dark brown glaze, 6-3/4", smooth base, handled, American, 1890-1900.	$100-150	
Wendell &ESPY – Mince Meat – 152 So. Front Philada Blue aqua, 9", half-gallon, iron pontil, outward rolled top, American, 1845-1865.	$600-700	

Fruit Jars

Unlike food bottles, fruit jars were sold empty for use in home preservation of many different types of food. They were predominant in the 1800s when pre-packaged foods weren't available and home canning was the only option. Although fruit jars carry no advertising, they aren't necessarily common or plain since the bottle manufacturer's name is usually embossed in large lettering along with the patent date. The manufacturer whose advertising campaign gave fruit jars their name was Thomas W. Dyott, who was in the market early selling fruit jars by 1829.

For the first 50 years, the most common closure was a cork sealed with wax. In 1855, an inverted saucer-like lid was invented that could be inserted into the jar to provide an air tight seal. The Hero Glassworks invented the glass lid in 1856 and improved upon it in 1858 with a zinc lid invented by John Landis Mason, who also produced a wide variety

Atherholt, Fisher & Co. – Phila Aqua, quart, smooth base (2), applied top, hollow blow stopper (A.Kline Patent Oct 27, 63), original closure, American, 1862-1870.	$400-600	
Baltimore Glass Works Aqua, quart, smooth base, applied wide top for cork closure, American, 1855-1860.	$700-900	
Belle – Pat. Dec. 14th 1869 (on shoulder) Blue aqua, half-gallon, smooth base, ground lip, original domed lid, sheet metal band, wire closure, American, 1870-1880.	$2,000-2,100	

Old Bottles

of fruit jars that set the standard for canning jars across the country. Because the medical profession warned that zinc could be harmful, Hero Glassworks developed a glass lid for the Mason jar in 1868. Mason eventually transferred his patent rights to the Consolidated Fruit Jar Co., which let the patent expire.

In 1882, Henry William Putnam invented a type of fruit jar that utilized a glass lid and a metal clamp to the hold the lid in place. The "Lighting Jar" quickly became popular since there wasn't any metal contacting the food, and the metal clamps made the lids easier to seal and remove.

The Hazel-Atlas Glass Company soon followed with their own Atlas E-Z Seal, which was similar to the "Lighting Jar" except there was a raised lip to prevent the jar from cracking.

In 1886, William Charles Ball and his five brothers began to manufacture fruit jars and eventually began to distribute Mason jars. The Ball jars used a unique monogram name of the jar in gothic type letters in 1988 and continued until approximately 1892. Perfect Ball jars were manufactured in the thousands between 1910-1962 in blue and clear glass. In 1898 the use of a semi-automatic bottle machine increased the output of the Mason jar and the Ball jar, until the automatic machine was invented in 1903.

Fruit jars come in a wide variety of sizes and colors, but the most common are aqua and clear. The rarer jars were manufactured in various shades of blue, amber, black, milk glass, green and purple.

Bloeser Aqua, quart, smooth base, ground lip, glass lid and metal closure, American, 1886-1895.	$400-500	
Bloeser – Jar Aqua, half-gallon, smooth base, ground lip, embossed lid, wire, and metal clamp closure, American, 1887-1900.	$300-400	

Cunningham & Co. Pittsburg (on the base) Medium sapphire blue, quart, iron pontil, applied top for cork, American, 1850-1860.	$5,000-6,000	
Flaccus Bros. – Trade (Steers Head) Mark – Fruit Jar Medium green, pint, smooth base, sheared and ground lip, embossed clear glass screw on lid (To Remove Cap Press Down & Unscrew), American, 1890-1910.	$900-1000	
Franklin – R.W. King – 90 Jefferson Ave. – Detroit Mich – Fruit Jar Aqua, quart, smooth base, ground lip, embossed glass lid and screw band (Aug. 8th, 1865), American, 1865-1875.	$500-600	
Hamilton Glass – Works – 1 Quart Aqua, quart, smooth base, applied top, glass lid and iron yoke with thumbscrew (Hamilton-Glass Works), American, 1875-1885.	$300-400	
Hirsch Bro's & Co. – Fox (Fox head with Fish in mouth) Brand – Louisville, Ky & Pittsburgh, PA Opaque milk glass, pint, smooth base, rough sheared lip, embossed mild glass domed lid and screw on band (Hirsh Bro's & Co. – (fox head with fish in mouth) Fruit Products – Louisville, Ky & Pittsburgh, PA), American, 1890-1910.	$600-700	
Magic – Fruit Jar – WM. McCully & Co. – Pittsburg, PA. – Sole Proprietors – Patented – By – R.M. Dalby – June 6th 1866 Deep blue aqua, quart, smooth base (2), ground lip, American, 1866-1870.	$400-450	

Mason's – Patent – Nov. 30th – 1858 Aqua, quart, smooth base, squared shoulders, ground lip, original zinc screw on lid is impressed (Mason's Pat. 1857) with two brass 'wrench lugs,' American, 1858-1870.	**$1,800-2,000**	
Mason's – Patent – Nov. 30th – 1858 Medium yellow green (citron), quart, smooth base (3), ground lip, American, 1875-1895.	**$200-250**	
Mason's – CJFCO (monogram) Patent – Nov. 30th – 1858 Medium golden amber, quart, smooth base (1.66), ground lip, American, 1875-1895.	**$400-500**	
Mason's – CJFCO (monogram) Patent – Nov. 30th – 1858 Yellow amber, quart, smooth base (D140), ground lip, American, 1875-1895.	**$450-500**	
Mason's – (Hero Cross) Patent – Nov. 30th – 1858 Golden amber, quart, smooth base (Pat Nov – 755-67-68), ground lip, American, 1875-1895.	**$400-500**	
Patented – Oct. 19. 1858 (on glass lid) Light to medium blue green, quart, smooth base, ground lip, original matching color embossed lid, American, 1858-1870.	**$250-300**	
Pet Aqua, quart, smooth base, applied top, embossed glass lid and brass sprint wire clamp (Patented Aug 3 1869, T.G. Otterson), American, 1869-1875.	**$150-120**	

Petal Jar Medium cobalt blue, 8", 10 fluted panels around the shoulder and neck, smooth base, applied top, rare color, American, 1860-1865.	$1,800-2,000	
Petal Jar Deep emerald green, 8-3/8", 10 fluted panels around the shoulder and neck, red iron pontil, applied top, American, 1850-1865.	$1,300-1,500	
Petal Jar Deep olive green, 10-1/4", half-gallon, 10 fluted panels around the shoulder and neck, red iron pontil, applied top, American, 1850-1865.	$1,500-1,600	
Preserving House- Max Ams – New York Aqua, pint, smooth base (Glass Mfg. Co, - Cohansey – Philada.), ground lip, embossed dated lid and closure, American, 1870-1885.	$200-225	
Put On Rubber Before Filling – Mrs. S.T. Dorer's – Star & Crescent (star and moon monogram) Self Sealing Jar Aqua, quart, smooth base, ground lip, correct zinc with milk glass insert, American, 1896-1900.	$350-400	
Queensland – (Letter 'Q' inside a Pineapple) – Fruit Jar Green aqua, quart, smooth base, ground lip, glass lid and lighting style wire closure, Australian, 1890-1900.	$250-350	
R. Authur's Patent – Jan. 2nd 1855 – Arthur, Burnam & Gilroy – 10th & Geo. STS. – Philadelphia Blue aqua, quart, smooth base, ground lip with pressed down wax seal ring, American, 1855-1860.	$100-150	

Old Bottles

The – Doolittle – Self Sealer Aqua, pint, smooth base (GJCO (Monogram), ABM lip, embossed glass lid with wire and ear closure (Patented January 1900), American, 1905-1910.	$300-400	
The Howe - Jar –Scranton – PA Aqua, pint, smooth base (2), ground lip, embossed glass lid and original wire bail, American, 1885-1895.	$150-250	
The King – Pat Nov 2, 1869 Aqua, quart, smooth base (2), ground lip, glass lid and iron yoke clamp, American, 1869-1875.	$250-350	
Safety Yellow amber, pint, smooth base, rough sheared and ground lip, glass lid and wire closure, American, 1890-1895.	$150-200	
Safety Amber, quart, smooth base, rough sheared and ground lip, glass lid and wire closure, American, 1890-1895.	$150-200	
Standard (In an arch) – W. McC & Co. Medium cobalt blue, quart, smooth base (X), applied top with wax seal ring, original embossed metal lid (W. McCully & Co. – Glass – Pittsburg), American.	$350-400	

Joshua Wright (fancy ornament) Philada, aqua, half-gallon, barrel shape, iron pontil, rolled lip, 1845-1865, $550-600.

BEE, aqua, quart, ground top, original cast iron screw-on band is embossed 'E. Boorse Patd. Nov 16, 1869,' glass lid, extremely rare, 1870-1875, $5,500-6,000.

Mason's – Patent – Nov. 30th – 1858, golden yellow amber, quart, ground lip, zinc screw-on lid with milk glass insert, 1875-1895, $450-500.

The – Automatic – Sealer, aqua, pint, smooth base (Clayton Bottle – Works-1- Clayton, N.J.), original embossed domed glass lid (Patd. Sept. 15, 1885), sheet metal band and wire closure, 1885-1895, $1,000-1,300.

S – Mason's- Patent – Nov. 30th – 1858, teal blue, half-gallon, smooth base (B9), 1875-1895, $350-400.

Early canning jar, medium sapphire blue, quart, red iron pontil, applied top, utilized a cork closure, extremely rare color, 1850-1860, $250-300.

The –Alton –Bail Here Clear glass, quart, smooth base (Pat'd April 1900 Dec. 1901), smooth lip, original tin lip and wire, American, 1900-1910.	$200-250	
The - Automatic – Sealer Aqua, half-gallon, smooth base (Clayton Bottle – Works -1 – Clayton, N.J.), ground lip, embossed domed glass lid and coiled spring wire enclosure (Patd Sept. 15, 1885), American, 1885-1895.	$300-350	
The Canton – Electric – Fruit Jar Medium cobalt blue, quart, smooth base, sheared and ground lip, clear glass high finned closure is embossed, American, 1887-1895.	$4,000-3,000	
The J.O. Schimmel – Pres'g Co. – Phila Aqua, pint, smooth base (Glass Mfg. Co. – Cohansey – Philada), ground lip, embossed dated lid and wire closure, American, 1880-1890.	$300-350	
The Ladies Favorite (Woman in full dress holding a jar) – WM. L. Haller – Carlisle – PA Blue aqua, quart, smooth base, applied top, original two piece iron disk and wing nut (J.D. Willoughby Patented January 4, 1859), American, 1860-1870.	$150-200	
The Leader Yellow amber, quart, smooth base (26), ground lip, original embossed lid (Pat.D June 28,1892) and wire clamp, American, 1892-1900.	$150-200	
The Magic (five-pointed star) – Fruit Jar Aqua, quart, smooth base (4), ground lip, original embossed lid and metal cam clamp (Clamp Pat. March 30th), American, 1885-1895.	$250-300	
The – Van Vliet – Jar – Of 1881 Aqua, quart, smooth base(4), ground lip, original embossed lid (Pat May 3D 1881), original wired and cast iron yoke with thumbscrew closure, American, 1881-1885.	$700-800	

Trade (stag head) Mark – E.C. Flaccus Co. Yellow with amber tone, pint, smooth base, rough sheared lip, correct 'starburst' embossed milk glass insert and screw on band, American, 1890-1910.	**$500-600**	
Trade (stag head) Mark – E.C. Flaccus Co. Opaque milk glass, pint, smooth base, rough sheared lip, correct 'starburst' embossed milk glass insert and screw on band, American, 1890-1910.	**$200-250**	
Trade Mark – Lighting Olive yellow, quart, smooth base (Putnam -17), ground lip, embossed dated matching color lid and lighting style closure, American, 1885-1895.	**$150-200**	
Trade Mark – Lighting Yellow with amber tone, quart, smooth base (Putnam 404), ground lip, original glass dated lid and lighting style closure, American, 1885-1895.	**$150-200**	
Wax Seal Fruit Jar (unmarked) Medium cobalt blue, half-gallon, smooth base, applied wax seal ring, original tin lid, American, 1870-1880.	**$3,500-4,000**	
Whitmore's – Patent – Rochester – NY Aqua, quart, smooth base, ground lip, embossed double finned lid, original wire bail, American, 1868-1875.	**$200-250**	

Ginger Beer

The origins of ginger beer can be traced back to England in the mid-1700s. There was, however, an earlier type of ginger beer produced by Mead & Metheglin dating to the early 1600s in Colonial America. Metheglin was more of a naturally carbonated, yeast-fermented honey tasting beverage, often including ginger, cloves and mace, which proved to be a popular drink in the colonies. The difference was that while ginger beer included the yeast for fermentation, it was also sweetened with honey, cane sugar or molasses. Additional ingredients included whole Jamaica ginger root and fresh lemons. After brewing, the ginger beer was stored in stoneware bottles and corked to maintain a natural effervescence. When the carbonation process was introduced in 1899, an essence of extract was used to achieve the right taste. But the old English brew masters observed that naturally fermented ginger beer still produced the best flavor. Until the mid-1800s, a number of ginger beers contained large amounts of alcohol content, some as much as 11 percent.

Ginger beer eventually was introduced to the United States and Canada around 1790, with England shipping large amounts to both countries during the 1800s. England was able to continue this huge export since its stoneware bottles were of a better quality based on a process developed in 1835 called "improved Bristol glaze." After brewing, the bottles were corked and wired to maintain the initial pressure, which maintained the

"Moerlein's – Old – Jug Lager," 10-1/2" and "Moeerlein's – Old – Jug Lager," 8-1/2", Cincinnati, Ohio, 1885-1905, $25 ea.

alcohol and carbon dioxide in solution, improving preservation and shelf life.

The early stoneware bottle was used extensively from 1790 until 1880 to 1890, when industrialization and new manufacturing techniques introduced a new gray stone bottle. These new bottles were used from approximately 1885 to 1920 and were stamped with various logos and designs to attract the interest of the buyer.

The popularity of ginger beer in the United States came to an end in 1920 with the advent of Prohibition. In England and Canada, ginger beer peaked around 1935. During the late 1940s, the manufacturing of ginger beer containing alcohol ended when the popularity of grain beer took hold. At this point, the use of stoneware bottles also became less popular. At one point there were 300 ginger beer breweries in the United States, 1,000 in Canada, and 3,000 in England. While the breweries have disappeared, today's collectors still enjoy finding many varieties of bottles in colors of green, red, blue, tan and purple, along with unique slogans and logos.

While this chapter presents a good cross-section of ginger beer bottles from the United States and Canada, I recommend collectors check out two books co-authored by Scott Wallace and Phil Culhane, both specialists in the field of Canadian glass and stoneware ginger beers: *Transfer Printed Ginger Beers of Canada* and *Primitive Stoneware Bottles of Canada*. Scott Wallace also conducts a number of auctions throughout the year and can be contacted at www.mapleleafauctions.com.

A.C. Feaver – Ginger Beer- Inglewood Cream pottery with light brown glazed neck shoulder, New Zealand, 1890-1910.	$900-950	**Brewed – Ginger Beer – C. Kickley** Clear body with light tan on neck and shoulder, lighting stopper, Guelph, ON, 1885-1895.	$35-40
Black Bear Brand – Olde Fashioned – Ginger (Black Bear) Beer – Meikle Bros. & Co. Ltd. Cream body with medium tan on neck and shoulder, smooth base, blob top with marked and matching stopper Vancouver, BC, 1880-1890.	$3,500-4,000	**C. L. Innes – Genuine Brewed – Ginger Beer – Auckland & Hamilton** Cream pottery and light brown glazed neck and shoulder, New Zealand, 1890-1910.	$35-45

Old Bottles

Chris Morley – Ginger Beer – Victoria, BC Cream body (90%) with medium tan on neck and shoulder, smooth base, blob top with marked stopper, rare variant, Victoria, BC, 1880-1895.	$2,800-2,900
Colonial Bottling Works – Ginger Beer – Simcoe Canada Cream body with tan neck and shoulder, smooth base, crown top, scarce, Simcoe, Canada, 1900-1920.	$200-250
Dolan Bros. – Stone Ginger Beer – 1916 – 348 Brussels St. – St. John NB Ivory body with dark blue on neck and shoulder, blue transfer, quart, smooth base, St. John, NB, 1916.	$75-100
Drink – Giering's – Ginger Beer (Display Bottle) Dark top and cream half, 21-3/4", smooth base, crown top, American, 1910-1920.	$100-125
Enterprise Bottling Co. – King Ginger Beer – Fredericton, NB – 1914 Ivory body with light tan on neck and shoulder, smooth base, Fredericton, NB, 1885-1915.	$150-200
Gilberd's – Ginger Beer Cream pottery with light brown glazed neck and shoulder, New Zealand, 1880-1900.	$1,400-1,500
Grumman's Bottling Works – G – So. Norwalk, Conn. – Registered – 24 ozs Cream body, 10", smooth base, American, 1880-1900.	$40-50
H. Martin – Stone Ginger Beer – Gisborne Cream pottery with light brown glazed neck and shoulder, New Zealand, 1890-1910.	$300-325
Home Brewed – Maker – D.J.Berry – Ginger Beer – Auckland Cream pottery with light brown glaze on shoulder and neck, Auckland, NZ, 1890-1910.	$200-225
Itheel Walter – Brewed Ginger Beer – Port Hope, Ont. Cream body, light tan on neck and shoulder, smooth base, lighting stopper, Port Hope, ON. 1880-1895.	$50-75
Ginger Shandy – J. M. McLaughlin – Limited – Toronto and Edmonton Ivory body with blue transfer and fancy decoration, smooth base, crown top, Toronto, ON, 1915-1930.	$200-300
Givans & Sons – Ginger Beer – Moncton, N.B. Cream body with medium tan on neck and shoulder, smooth base, Moncton, NB, 1885-1895.	$900-1,000
J.S. Rupp – Port Jervis – N.Y. Cream glaze, 8-1/8", smooth base, original lighting style stopper, 'The Robinson Merrill Co. Akron, Ohio' is stamped on the side at the base, rare, American, 1890-1910.	$100-150

John Dixon – Old Time – Ginger Beer – Halifax, N.S. – Barnett & Foster Light cream body with light tan neck and shoulder, smooth base, crown top, Halifax, NB, 1900-1925.	$150-175	**M.V. McCoy. – English – Brewed – Ginger – Beer – Watertown, N.Y.** Cream body with light brown glazed mouth, 6-5/8", smooth base, American, 1900-1910.	$45-55
Dobson & Caldicutt – Kamloops, B.C. Cream body with medium tan on neck and shoulder, crown top, one of BC's rarest ginger beers, Kamloops, BC, 1915-1930.	$850-900	**Napoleon's – Celebrated – Buffalo Ginger Beer – N. Sarault** Cream body with tan neck and shoulder, smooth base, crown top, Ottawa, ON, 1915-1925.	$100-150
Laurie's –Ginger Beer – Perth Solid cream, Eastern Ontario, Brantford Potteries, rare, Perth, ON, 1875-1885.	$1,000-1,200	**Nelson Soda – Stone Ginger Beer – Factory** Cream body with medium tan on neck and shoulder, smooth base, cross marked internal threads stopper, Nelson, BC, 1885-1895.	$1,800-2,000
M. Bourke – Ginger (Monogram) Beer – Brockville Cream body with dark brown on neck and shoulder, smooth base, Brockville, ON, 1880-1895.	$75-100	**Old Fashioned –Ginger Beer – Thomas Lewis – Wellington, Wanganui & Petone** Cream pottery with light brown glazed neck and shoulder, New Zealand, 1890-1910.	$45-55

Five ginger beer bottles: plain, "Chapman Bros. – Limited RYE," "Nash & McAllister – Stone – Ginger Beer – Sydney, C.B.," "Townsend's – Stone Brewed Ginger Beer – Salford," and plain; Canadian 1880-1920, $7 ea.

Old Bottles

Orange Crush of Truro Limited – Old English – Ginger Beer –In Stone – Truro Nova, Scotia Light cream body with medium tan on neck and shoulder, crown top, smooth base, Truro, NB, 1900-1930.	$50-75
Pacific Dry – Stone Ginger Beer Light cream body with light tan on neck and shoulder, smooth base, crown top, rare, Vancouver, BC, 1930s.	$300-400
Reed Bros – Stone Ginger Beer – Dundas Road – Guelph Cream body with tan neck and shoulder, smooth base, lightning stopper, Guelph, ON, 1888-1895.	$500-600
Royal Export – S.V. Horne – Kingston – Brewed Ginger Beer Cream body with tan neck and shoulder, smooth base, rare, Kingston, ON, 1880-1895.	$300-400
Ross Brothers – Trade – R. & B. – Mark – London, Ont. (CDN Ginger Beer) Light color on body with dark brown on neck and shoulder, smooth base, original lighting stopper (bail is rusted), scarce, London, ON, 1888-1895.	$500-600
Simons – Ginger Beer – Whangaret Cream pottery with light brown glazed neck and shoulder, New Zealand, 1880-1895.	$700-750
Smith Bros – Home Brewed- Ginger Beer – Whangaret Cream pottery with light brown glazed neck and shoulder, New Zealand, 1890-1910.	$550-600
T. Taylor – Strathroy Cream with tan on neck and shoulder, smooth base, lighting stopper, Strathroy, rare.	$400-500
Tho (Thomas) Robertson – O.T.G.B. – St. Catharines Cream body with light tan on neck and shoulder, smooth base, blob top, scarce, St. Catharines, ON, 1880-1895.	$50-75
Thrope & Co, Ltd. – British Columbia – Made From- English Ginger Beer – Best Jamaica Ginger – Thrope & Co. Ltd. – British Columbia Cream body with tan on neck and shoulder, quart, smooth base, blob top with marked and matching stopper, Victoria, BC, 1880-1895.	$400-500
Voakes & Co. – Ginger Beer – Windsor, Ont. Cream body with tan neck and shoulder, smooth base, scarce, Windsor, ON, 1880-1900.	$200-300
W. A. Cole – Stone Ginger Beer – Whangaret Cream pottery with light brown glazed neck and shoulder, New Zealand, 1880-1900.	$150-200
Wm. B. Daley – Ginger Beer – St. John. N.B. Ivory body with tan on neck and shoulder, smooth base, blob top, St. John, NB, 1875-1890.	$200-300

"Felix J. Quinn – Ginger Beer Manufr – Halifax N.S."; "G. & C. Moore – Stone Ginger Beer"; "Kings's Old Country Limited – King's Old Country Stone Ginger Beer, Winnipeg, Manitoba"; "Ye Old Country – Stone – Ginger Beer – Vancouver, B.C. 10 oz," Canadian, 1886-1930, $20 ea.

"John Milne – Brewed – Ginger Beer – Stonehaven"; "Sussex Mineral Springs Ld. – Old English Ginger Beer – Sussex New Brunswick"; "Gurd's Stone – Ginger Beer – The Perfect Drink," Canadian, 1880-1910, $20 ea.

Hawaiian

This chapter wouldn't have happened without a lot of help. I need to thank Mike Leong and Mel Tanka of the Hawaiian Bottle Club for providing the pricing details and background information; Mike's son, Brennan, for his great photography work; and Brandon Lee, also a Hawaiian Bottle Club member, for providing the history of Hawaiian bottling companies and bottle dating. I would also like to thank the Hawaiian Bottle Club and other members who contributed because this chapter wouldn't have been possible without their assistance.

Hawaiian History of the Islands

Macfarlane & Co. – Honolulu H.I. – beer, medium amber, applied top, scarce circa early 1880s: quart, 11-1/2", $600-700; pint, 9-1/2", $500-600.

The history, culture, and beauty of the Hawaiian Islands are intertwined with the history of the many varieties of bottles from all of them. While Hawaii, sometimes referred to as "The Aloha State," didn't become a U.S. state until 1959, its history and culture began centuries earlier, when a 1,600-mile-long fissure on the floor of the Pacific Ocean produced the Hawaiian Ridge.

Along the top of this ridge were individual protrusions of domes that over time formed the Hawaiian Islands: Hawaii (The Big Island), Maui, Oahu, Kauai, Molokai, and Lanai. Approximately 1,500 years ago, Polynesians from the South

Pacific found the Hawaiian Islands. About 500 years later, settlers from Tahiti arrived and initiated a ruling king for each island. Social classes emerged, and the Hawaiian culture began to form.

Captain James Cook founded Oahu and Kauai on Jan. 18, 1778. He named Hawaii the Sandwich Islands in honor of the Earl of Sandwich, but he met his demise in a battle with natives on Feb. 13, 1779. In 1810, King Kamehameha I unified the Hawaiian Islands under a single rule and soon promoted trade with Europe and the United States. Hawaiian rule continued until 1893, but Western influence continued to grow, and American colonists overthrew the Hawaiian kingdom on Jan. 17, 1893. In 1898, Hawaii officially became a territory of the United States.

Bottling Companies, Manufacturers, and Dating of Bottles

The timeline of Hawaii's history directly relates to the extensive importing of bottles dating back to 1851, when German merchant Ulrich Alting imported the first known Hawaiian embossed soda bottles. As the need intensified to satisfy the numerous ships arriving in Honolulu carrying whalers, sailors, English visitors, and settlers, the need to satisfy their thirst also increased. In addition to the Alting imports, C. L. Richards & Co. began importing embossed whiskey bottles around 1878, and Geo. C. McLean started importing blob top blown sodas around 1885.

The continued influx of visitors and new inhabitants eventually led to the establishment of Hawaii's first bottling companies in the early 1880s, and when Hawaii became a territory of the United States in 1898, many more bottling companies came into existence.

While the islands have produced a variety of bottles, the most common and numerous were the soda bottles that have become the highlight of most Hawaiian bottle collections. As an example, when pineapple companies became the main economy of Hawaii, each island had its own sugar and pineapple company with its own company store. During the late 1880s into the early 1900s, there were more than 44 different soda companies that manufactured Hutchinson, crown top, and over 270 variations of BIMALS (bottles hand blown into a mold) soda bottles. These many variations rank right at the top of the majority of Hawaiian bottle collections.

During the most productive years, Hawaii's four largest and most populated islands,

Old Bottles

Oahu, Kauai, Maui, and the Big Island, shared these 44 bottling companies, with 25 of them located on Oahu. Besides the manufacturing of soda, products also included whiskey, gin, beer, medicines, and milk.

Sailors and whalers who drank their whiskey in Hawaii prior to 1898 drank from bottles – manufactured for Hawaiian companies – that were embossed H.I. (Hawaiian Islands) or in some cases S.I. (Sandwich Islands), which can be found on whiskey bottles dating to the late 1850s. After Hawaii became a U.S. Territory in 1898, the abbreviation H.T. (Hawaiian Territory) or T.H. (Territory of Hawaii) appeared on the bottles and was carried through statehood in 1959. The use of the initials H.I. and H.T. continued on Hawaiian BIMALS and machine-made bottles well into the 1920s and early 1930s.

Beer Bottles, Oahu

HONOLULU BREWING CO / HONOLULU, H.T. Pale green aqua, 11-3/4", 1 pint 9 oz, smooth base (315), tooled top, 1908-1911.	$20-25	**HONOLULU BREWING & MALTING CO. LTD** Pale green aqua, 11-3/4", 1 pint 9 oz, smooth base (317), tooled crown top, 1911-1917.	$10-15
HONOLULU BREWING CO. / HONOLULU, H.T. Pale green aqua, 11-3/4", 1 pint 9 oz, smooth base (317), tooled top, (Note: Different plate – larger letters and words higher up on bottle), 1908-1911.	$20-25	**HONOLULU B. & M. Co., LTD** Pale green aqua, 9-1/2", 12 oz, smooth base, tooled crown top, 1911-1917.	$10-15
HONOLULU BREWING CO / HONOLULU, H.T. (no period after CO) Pale green aqua, 11-3/4", 1 pint 9 oz, smooth base (317), tooled crown, 1911.	$600-700	**MACFARLANE & CO. / HONOLULU H I** Medium amber, 11-1/2", l pint 8 oz, smooth base (M G Co on round seal), applied top, 1880-1885.	$275-350
		MACFARLANE & CO. / HONOLULU H I Medium amber, 9-1/2", 12 oz, smooth base (M G Co 5), applied top, 1880-1885.	$275-350

226 • Antique Trader Bottles

Kona Kanning Ko. – K.K.K. – Kealakekua,
Kona, - Hawaii, T.H., stoneware crock with
wording stenciled in black, off white, lid
marking reads: The Weir Pat. March 1st 92 No
4 April 146h 1901, circa 1915, $300-400.

Gonsalves & Co., Ltd,
medium green aqua, 8-1/4",
gin, tooled top, rare, circa
1910, $800-1,000.

Gin Bottles

GONSALVES & CO. LTD Clear, 8-1/4", smooth base, tooled top, 1910.	**$300-400**
LOVEJOY & CO. / HONOLULU, T.H. Clear, 8-1/4", smooth base, tooled top, 1908.	**$175-225**
HOFFSCHLAEGER CO. LTD. / HONOLULU Clear, 8-1/2", smooth base, tooled top, 1905-1915.	**$75-100**
HOFFSCHLAEGER CO. LTD. / HONOLULU Clear, 8-1/2", slanting letters due to slumping of hot glass after molding, smooth base, tooled top, 1905-1915.	**$100-150**
HOFFSCHLAEGER CO. LTD. / HONOLULU Clear, 10-1/4", smooth base, tooled top, 1905-1915.	**$150-185**
MACFARLANE & CO. / HONOLULU Clear, 11-1/4", smooth base, applied top, 1885.	**$2,500-3,000**
MAUI WINE & LIQUOR CO. / WAILUKU, MAUI, T.H. Clear, 8-1/4", smooth base, tooled top, 1908.	**$400-500**
SERRARO LIQUOR CO. LTD / HILO, T.H. Clear, 8-1/4", small letters, 'S' in SERRARO is 3/8" high), smooth base, tooled top, 1910.	**$400-500**
SERRAO LIQUOR CO. LTD / HILO, T.H. Clear, 10", smooth base, tooled top, 1912.	**$1,300-1,500**
T. SUMIDA / HONOLULU, T.H. Clear, 8-1/4", smooth base, tooled top, 1910.	**$175-200**
W.C. PEACOCK & CO. LTD. / HONOLULU, T.H. Medium blue aqua, 8-1/2", smooth base, tooled top, 1910.	**$350-400**
W.C. PEACOCK & CO. LTD. / HONOLULU, T.H. Medium blue aqua, 8-1/2", smooth base, tooled top (wider mouth top), 1914.	**$500-600**

Medicine Bottles, Oahu

A. McWayne – Druggist – Honolulu H.I. Clear, 1-1/8" x 2-7/8", oval shape with flat panel, smooth base, tooled flanged top, 1880.	**$125-150**
A. McWayne – Druggist – Honolulu H.I. Clear, 2" x 4-7/8", oval shape with flat panel, smooth base, tooled flanged top, 1880.	**$150-200**

A. McWayne – Druggist – Honolulu H.I. Clear, 3-1/4" x 8-1/4", oval shape with flat panel, smooth base, tooled flanged top, 1880.	$700-800
K.A (K. Akahoshi Drug Store) Amber, 1" x 2" cylindrical, smooth base (K.A. embossed on base only), tooled top for cork stopper, 1910.	$10
K.A - Made In Japan (with embossed fan) Amber, 1" x 2-1/4" cylindrical, smooth base, tooled top for cork stopper, 1920.	$10-15
K.A (K. Akahoshi Drug Store) Amber, 1" x 2" cylindrical, smooth base (K.A. MADE IN JAPAN with Japanese fan embossed on base only), tooled top for cork stopper, 1915.	$10 -15
BENSON, SMITH & CO, / HONOLULU, H. I. Clear, 2-1/8" x 5-7/8", rectangular form, smooth base (W.T. 7 CO. B U.S.A. PAT. DEC 11 1894), flanged tooled top for cork stopper, 1894-1899.	$75-100
BENSON, SMITH & CO, / HONOLULU Clear, 3-1/2" x 7-5/8", oval shaped Nursing bottle, measuring scale embossed on back, smooth base (W.T & CO. A U.S.A. PAT. FEB. 24. 1891), flanged tooled top, 1891-1900.	$1,000-1,500
BENSON, SMITH & COL, LTD. / REXALL DRUG STORE/ HONOLULU, HAWAII Clear, 1-1/2" x 4-1/2", rectangular form, smooth base (BLUE RIBBON), flanged tooled top, 1911.	$75-100
BENSON, SMITH & CO / HONOLULU Medium green aqua, 1-7/8" x 5-1/2", rectangular with sunken front and side panels, angular front corners and flat back, smooth base, flanged tooled top, 1891-early 1900.	$250-300
DR.O.S. CUMMINGS / HONOLULU, H.I. Clear, 5/8" x 2", square form, smooth base, flanged tooled top, 1880.	$50-75
HOBRON DRUG CO. / HONOLULU Clear, 3-1/4" x 6-1/4", oval shape nursing bottle with 8 oz measuring scale embossed on the back, smooth base (W.T. & CO. P U.S.A. PAT FEB. 24. 1891), flanged tooled top, 1892.	$1,500-1,800
HOBRON DRUG CO. / HONOLULU Clear, 2-1/8" x 5-3/8", rectangular form, smooth base (W.T. & CO. P U.S.A. PAT JAN 5 1892), flanged tooled top, 1892.	$75-100
HOLLISTER & CO / HONOLULU Clear, 1-3/4" x 2-1/8", square form, smooth base (W.T. & Co U.S.A.), flanged tooled top, 1880.	$75-100
HOLLISTER & CO. /DRUGGIST / HONOLULU, H.I. Clear, 1-3/4" x 4", rectangular with flat front and back with sunken side panels, smooth base, flanged tooled top, 1880s or early 1890s.	$125-175

HOLLISTER & CO. / DRUGGISTS / HONOLULU, H.I. Clear, 4-1/8" x 9-3/4", oval form, smooth base (W.T. & CO. F), flanged tooled top, 1881.	**$250-350**
HOLLISTER DRUG CO. LTD. / HONOLULU Clear, 2-1/4" x 5-1/2", round form, smooth base (W.T. & CO. PAT. JAN. 22 78 G U.S.A.), flanged tooled top, 1890.	**$75-100**

ISHII DRUG STORE / MADE IN JAPAN (in Japanese) Clear, 1-1/4" x 2-5/8", rectangular form, smooth base, ground lip top, 1905-1910.	**$10-15**
THE NEWMAN DRUG CO. / HONOLULU, H. I. Clear, 1-3/4" x 4-3/8", rectangular shape with flat front, sides and back, rounded corners, smooth base (W.T.& Co. E U.S.A. Pat Jan, 5 1892), tooled flanged top, 1903.	**$150-200**

Hawaii

HILO DRUG CO. / LIMITED / HILO, HAWAII Clear, 1-7/8" x 5-7/8", square with round corners, smooth base, flanged tooled top, 1905.	**$75-125**
HILO DRUG CO. / "THAT BUSY CORNER" / HILO, HAWAII Clear, 2-1/8" x 5-3/4",oval with flat front panel, smooth base (W.T. & CO. 1 U.S.A) flanged tooled top, 1911.	**$100-150**
T.M. (inside a diamond) – T. MACHIDA DRUG STORE Amber, 1-3/4" x 2-3/8", flattened oval form, smooth base, flanged tooled top, 1910-1915.	**$20-25**

THE OWL DRUG CO. LTD – HILO, H.T. (embossed on base) Medium green aqua, 2" x 5-1/8", smooth base, tooled flanged top, cylindrical, 1901.	**$40-50**
THE OWL DRUG CO. LTD – HILO, H.T. (embossed on base) Medium green aqua, 2-7/8" x 7-1/4", smooth base, tooled flanged top, cylindrical, 1901.	**$200-300**
THE OWL DRUG CO. LTD – HILO, H.T. (embossed on base) Medium green aqua, 3-1/2" x 10", smooth base, tooled flanged top, cylindrical, 1901.	**$800-900**

Milk Bottles

AHUIMANU (WITH PERIOD) / PAT. SEPT 17 89 / TO BE WASHED AND RETURNED Clear, 6-1/2", pint, smooth base, tooled top, 1904.	$1,200-1,800	HONOLULU DAIRYMEN'S ASSOCIATION, LTD. Clear, 6-3/4", 1 pint, bowling pin shape, smooth base, tooled top, 1906.	$1,000-1,500
AHUIMANU (WITH PERIOD) / PAT. SEPT 17 89 Clear, 5-3/8", half -pint, smooth base, tooled top, 1904.	$1,200-1,800	HONOLULU DAIRYMEN'S ASSOCIATION, LT./ TO BE WASHED AND RETURNED / NOT TO BE BOUGHT OR SOLD Clear, 6-5/8",1 pint, smooth base, tooled top, 1908.	$1,000-1,500

Siphon (Seltzer) Bottles, Footed Siphons

ARTIC SODA WORKS / HONOLULU, T.H. Clear, 11-3/4", 36 oz, stencil etched, smooth base, 1900-1905.	$175-250	ESCELSIOR / SODA WATER CO. LTD / HILO, H.I. Clear, 11-1/4", 25 oz, stencil etched, smooth base, early 1900s.	$200-300
CONSOLIDATED SODA WATER WORKS CO. LD. / HONOLULU, T.H. Clear, 11-3/4", 34 oz, stencil etched, smooth base, 1906.	$225-300	EWA PLANTATION CO. / EWA, HAWAII Clear, 11-1/4", 27 oz, stencil etched, smooth base (MADE IN AUSTRIA-Two headed eagle), 1905.	$400-500
DRAGON SODA WORKS / HONOLULU, TH. Clear, 11-3/4", 36 oz, stencil etched, smooth base (Registered Trade-Mark (King's Crown) MADE IN AUSTRIA), 1910.	$400-500	FOUNTAIN MINERAL AND SODA WORKS / HONOLULU H I / R R (Robert Rycroft) Clear, 11-1/4", 27 oz, stencil etched, smooth base, 1905.	$400-500
ENTERPRISE SODA WORKS Clear, 12", 35 oz, stencil etched, smooth base, 1905.	$200-300	HAWAIIAN SODA WORKS / H / HONOLULU. T.H. Clear, 11-3/4", 38 oz, stencil etched, smooth base, 1904.	$375-475
ESCELSIOR / SODA /WORKS Clear, 11", 27 oz, stencil etched, smooth base (Matthews Apparatus Co. New York; Man Slaying a Bear), early 1900s.	$400-500	HAMAKUA SODA WORKS Clear, 11", 26 oz, stencil etched, smooth base, 1910.	$275-475

Old Bottles

HAWI / ICE WORKS / KOHALA, HAWAII Clear, 12", 42 oz, stencil etched, smooth base (Registered Trade-Mark (A King's Crown) Made in Austria), 1910.	**$400-500**
LIHUE ICE CO. / LIHUE, KAUAL Clear, 10-3/4", 26 oz, stencil etched, smooth base.	**$300-400**
MAUI SODA WORKS Clear, 11", 27 oz, stencil etched, smooth base, 1905.	**$150-175**

NORTH HILO SODA WORKS Clear, 11", 27 oz, stencil etched, smooth base, 1910.	**$400-500**
PACIFIC / SODA WORKS / HILO HAWAII Clear, 11-1/4", 26 oz, stencil etched, smooth base, 1910.	**$300-400**
WAIMEA SODA & ICE WORKS Clear, 11-3/4", 35 oz, copper wheel etched, smooth base, 1900.	**$375-450**

Plain Siphons

HONOLULU SODA WATER Co. LTD. / HONOLULU, T.H. Blue, 11-3/4", 35 oz, stencil etched, smooth base (MADE IN CZECHO-SLOVAKIA-Impressed light bulb with number 4 inside), smooth base, 1915.	**$300-425**

KAUAI SODA WORKS LTED. / KAUAI Clear, 11-1/2", 37 oz, stencil etched, smooth base (Made in Germany (inside a circle), 1915.	**$275-300**

Paneled Siphons

LIBERTY BOTTLING WORKS / L.B.W. / Wahiawa, T.H. Emerald green, 12-1/4", ten-sided, 35 oz, stencil etched, smooth base (MADE IN CZECHOSLOVAKIA), 1925.	**$700-800**

PACIFIC SYPHON / PACIFIC SODA WORKS CO. LTD. / HILO Emerald green, 13-1/4", twelve-sided, 35 oz, stencil etched, smooth base (MADE IN CZECHOSLOVAKIA), 1925-1930.	**$650-750**
WAIALUA SODA WORKS / WAIALUA, OAHU, T.H. Emerald green, 12-1/2", twelve-sided, 28 oz, stencil etched, smooth base (MADE IN CZECHOSLOVAKIA), 1928-1935.	**$350-475**

Soda Bottles, Oahu

AIEA SODA WORKS CO. / H.T Pale green aqua, 7-1/4", smooth base (W), tooled Hutchinson top, 1903.	$1,200-1,500	**THIS BOTTLE IS THE PROPERTY / OF THE CONSOLIDATED WATER WORKS CO.LD. / HONOLULU, T.H. / THIS BOTTLE NOT TO BE SOLD/ REGISTERED** Clear, 8-3/4", semi-round smooth base, embossed oval area is sunken by slug plate, tooled crown top, 1908.	$1,200-1,700
AIEA SODA WORKS CO. / H.T Pale green aqua, 8-1/4", smooth base (W), tooled crown top, 1902.	$1,500-1,700		
ARTIC SODA WATER WORKS/ HONOLULU H.I./ H. SITTENFELD & CO. PROPS Pale green aqua, 7-3/4", smooth semi-round base, tooled Hutchinson top, 1895-1900.	$1,000-1,500	**CRYSTAL SODA WORKS / HONOLULU H.I.** Aqua, 8", round base (Trade Mark J.A. P.), applied Hutchinson top, 1883.	$60-75
		DRAGON SODA WORKS Medium blue aqua, 7-3/4", smooth base (D), tooled Hutchinson top, 1909.	$300-400
THIS BOTTLE IS THE PROPERTY OF / ARTIC SODA WATER WORKS / HONOLULU T.H. / REGISTERED Yellow straw, 7-3/4", smooth base (A.S.W.) tooled Hutchinson top, 1909.	$1,200-1,500	**DRAGON SODA WATER CO. / HONOLULU** Pale green aqua, 7-3/4", smooth base (D), tooled Hutchinson top, 1910.	$75-100
ARTIC SODA WORKS / HONOLULU Medium blue-green aqua, 7-3/4", smooth semi-round base, tooled Hutchinson top, 1905.	$300-400	**ENTERPRISE SODA WORKS / HONOLULU H.I.** Clear, 7-1/2", smooth base, tooled Hutchinson top, 1899.	$300-400
CONSOLIDATED SODA WORKS CO Medium blue green aqua, 8-3/4", smooth base (C.S. W.W. CO.), tooled crown top, 1898.	$600-700	**E P CO. / EWA** Pale green aqua, 7-1/2", smooth base (EP CO) (no periods after E and P), tooled Hutchinson top, 1903.	$150-175
CONSOLIDATED SODA WATER WORKS CO / LIMITED / HONOLULU H.I. Medium blue green aqua, 8-3/4", smooth base (C.S. W.W. CO.), tooled crown top, 1900-1910.	$30-40	**E.P. CO. /EWA** Pale green aqua, 7-1/2", smooth base (E.P. CO -1-1/2" wide/smaller E.P. CO.,PCGW, PCGW (backward 3) 8), tooled Hutchinson top, 1905.	$65-175

Old Bottles

EWA BOTTLING WORKS Medium blue aqua, 7-3/4", smooth base, tooled Hutchinson top, 1902.	$50-60
FIRST INFANTRY EXCHANGE / SCHOFIELD BARRACKS / T.H. Pale green aqua, 7-3/4", semi-round smooth base (P.C.G. W.), tooled crown top, 1915.	$125-175
FOUNTAIN MINERAL AND SODA WORKS / HONOLULU H-I – R-R / THIS BOTTLE NOT SOLD Clear glass, 9-1/4", longer neck, smooth base 9 (semi-round), tooled lightning stopper, 1904.	$350-450
FOUNTAIN MINERAL AND SODA WORKS/ HONOLULU-H-I Clear, 8-3/4", semi-round smooth base, tooled lightning top, 1901.	$200-300
HANA ICE CO. Blue aqua, 7-1/4", smooth base, tooled Hutchinson top, 1900.	$600-900
HAWAIIAN SODA WORKS / HONOLULU / BOTTLES NOT SOLD / RILEY MNFG CO/ LONDON S.W Medium green aqua, 7", semi-round smooth base (RILYE'S PATENT LONDON), inside screw with applied top and hard rubber stopper, 1898.	$150-200

HAWAIIAN SODA WORKS / HONOLULU, H.I. Clear, 8", flat panel front and back, smooth base (H), tooled Hutchinson top, 1899.	$1,400-1,800
HAWAIIAN SODA WORKS / HONOLULU, H.I. Dark amber, 7-1/2", smooth base (H), tooled Hutchinson top, 1899.	$2,500-4,500
HAWAIIAN SODA WORKS / HONOLULU, T.H. Medium amber, 7-3/4", smooth base (H), tooled Hutchinson top, 1909.	$800-1,200
H & H HONOLULU Aqua, 7-1/4", smooth base, applied blob-top, 1869.	$1,700-2,500
HOLLISTER & Co. / HONOLULU, H.I. Medium blue aqua, 7-1/4", tapered shoulders and long neck, smooth base (dot in center), applied Hutchinson top, 1883.	$75-100
HOLLISTER & CO. / HONOLULU Sapphire aqua, 7-3/4", smooth base, blob top, 1885.	$400-425
HOLLISTER & CO. / HONOLULU Aqua, 7-3/4", smooth base, applied top.	$250-275

1875

HOLISTER & CO / HONOLULU H.I. /BARNETT & FOSTER MAKERS/ LONDON'N THE NIAGAARA BOTTLE / RD 65443 (around base rim) Pale green aqua, 8-3/4", semi-round smooth base, Codd marble stopper.	$250-350

234 · Antique Trader Bottles

1893

HONOLULU SODA WATER CO. LTD / T.H. Pale green aqua, 7-3/4", smooth base (Maltese Cross), tooled Hutchinson top, 1910.	$75-100
K.I. SODA WORKS / HONOLULU, T.H. Pale green aqua, 7-3/4", flat panels front and back, smooth base (K), tooled Hutchinson top, 1908.	$375-425
K.I. SODA WORKS / HONOLULU Pale green aqua, 7-3/4", smooth base (K), tooled Hutchinson top, 1909.	$300-400
OAHU SODA WORKS / H.I. Aqua, 7-1/4", smooth base, tooled Hutchinson top, 1900.	$150-200
OAHU SODA WORKS / AIEA, OAHU / BOTTLE NOT SOLD Pale green aqua, 9", semi-round smooth base (O), tooled crown top, 1913.	$100-125
PACIFIC SODA WORKS CO. Ltd. / HONOLULU T.H Pale green aqua, 8-1/2", smooth base (P), tooled crown top, 1916.	$90-115
POST EXCHANGE– 1st INF. – SCHOFIELD BKS. Pale green aqua, 7-3/4", smooth base (semi-round), tooled crown top, 1914.	$1,500-2,000

RYCROFT-ARTIC SODA CO. Ltd./HONOLULU/ T.H. / RYCROFT'S OLD FASHIONED GINGER BEER/ NET CONTENTS 9 FLUID OZ. Chocolate brown top, cream colored bottom, 7", smooth base, stoneware crown top, 1917.	$250-350
STAR SODA WATER WORKS/ HONOLULU T.H. Aqua, 7-3/4", semi-round smooth base, tooled Hutchinson top, 1900.	$75-100
SUNRISE SODA WATER WORKS / HONOLULU Pale green aqua, 7-3/4", smooth base (S), tooled Hutchinson top, 1911.	$75-100
TAHITI LEMONADE WORKS CO / HONOLULU H.I. Aqua, 7-1/4", smooth base, tooled lightning top, 1890.	$175-200
WAIALUA SODA WORKS Medium blue aqua, 8-3/4", smooth base, tooled lightning top, 1902.	$150-175
WAIALUA SODA WORKS LTD. / BOTTLE IS NOT SOLD Pale gray green aqua, 8-3/4", smooth base (Waialua), tooled crown top, 1913.	$25-30

Old Bottles

Fountain Mineral and Soda Works – monogram depicting Hawaiian girl standing in fountain, Honolulu, R*R, clear, 11-1/4", footed siphon, rare, circa 1905, $400-500.

Hoffschlaeger Co. Ltd. – Monogram – Honolulu, dark amber, whiskey, 11", tooled top, circa early 1900s, $500-600.

Hawaii

BAY CITY SODA WORKS / HILO Medium blue aqua, 7-3/4", smooth base, tooled Hutchinson top, 1903.	$200-300
BAY CITY SODA WORKS / KAU T.H. Medium green aqua, 7-3/4", smooth base (B), tooled Hutchinson top, 1910.	$450-600
EXCELSIOR SODA WORKS / HILO Aqua, 7-3/4", smooth base, tooled Hutchinson top, 1895-1899.	$40-60
EXCELSIOR SODA WORKS CO. LTD / REGISTERED Dark green aqua, 9", smooth base (E), tooled crown top, 1901.	$500-700
HAMAKUA SODA WORKS Aqua, 8", smooth base (H), tooled Hutchinson top, used at Kukuihaele from 1897-1905.	$50-75
HAMAKUA SODA WORKS Pale green aqua, 7-3/4", ten-sided smooth base (H), tooled Hutchinson top, 1910.	$200-300
HAWI ICE WORKS Clear glass, 8-3/4", smooth base, tooled crown top, 1912.	$700-1,000
W.A.HARDY & CO. / HILO H.I. Dark blue aqua, 7", smooth base, tooled Hutchinson top, 1897.	$300-400
HAWAII SODA WORKS CO. Aqua, 8", smooth base, tooled Hutchinson top, 1900-1910.	$75-100
HAWAII SODA WORKS CO. / KOHALA Aqua, 8-3/4", smooth base (347 H), tooled crown top, 1906.	$250-375
HIGH TEST SODA WORKS / HILO Aqua, 7-3/4", smooth base (PCGW), tooled Hutchinson top, 1905.	$200-300
HILO SODA WORKS CO. / HILO H.I. Aqua, 7", smooth base, tooled Hutchinson top, 1890-1895.	$150-200
A.W. HOBSON / HILO Pale green aqua, 8", smooth base, tooled Hutchinson top, 1896.	$900-1,200
KONA BOTTLING WORKS CO. LTD. Aqua, 8-3/4", smooth base, tooled crown top, 1902.	$15-25
KURTISTOWN SODA WATER CO. Medium green aqua, 6-3/4", smooth base (K), tooled Hutchinson top, 1913.	$250-400
N. HILO SODA WORKS (A.W. HOBSON/HILO removed and recut as N. HILO SODA WORKS) Medium blue aqua, 8", smooth base, tooled Hutchinson top, 1897.	$75-100
PACIFIC SODA WORKS Pale green aqua, 6-3/4", smooth base, tooled Hutchinson top, 1896.	$1,000-1,200
PACIFIC SODA WORKS Pale green aqua, 7-3/4", smooth base (X), tooled Hutchinson top, 1908.	$50-60
UNION SODA WORKS / HILO H.I. Medium blue aqua, 7-3/4", smooth base, tooled Hutchinson top, 1900.	$70-80

Old Bottles

W.C. Peacock & Co. Ltd. – Honolulu T.H., gin, medium green aqua, 8-1/2", double collar tooled top, rare, circa 1910-1914, $800-900.

W.C. Peacock & Co. Ltd. – Honolulu, clear, pocket whiskey pint flask, 8-1/4", tooled top, circa 1914, $1,100-1,300.

W.A. Hardy & Co. – Hilo H.I., strong blue aqua, soda, 7", tooled Hutchison top, rare, circa 1897, $900-1,000.

Hollister & Co. – Honolulu, smoky amethyst mid-bottle and straw yellow toward the bottom, soda, 8", tooled Hutchinson top, rare, circa 1907, $1,500-1,600.

Hawaii – Soda Works Co., – aqua, tooled
Hutchinson top and tooled crown top tooled
Hutchinson top: 8", 1900-1910, $100-125; tooled
crown top: 8-3/4", 1906, $250-375.

Lovejoy & Co. –
Monogram – Honolulu
T.H., medium amber,
whiskey, tooled top, 11",
circa 1908, $150-200.

Old Bottles

Maui

HYGEIA SODA WORKS / KAHULUI, H.T. Medium green aqua, 7-3/4", smooth base (star), tooled Hutchinson top, 1906.	**$60-90**
LAHINA ICE WORKS ("A" Missing in LAHINA) Medium blue aqua, 7-3/4", smooth base, tooled Hutchinson top, 1901.	**$800-1,200**
LAHAINA ICE WORKS / MAUI T.H. Dark blue aqua, 7-1/4", smooth base, tooled Hutchinson top, 1904.	**$75-125**
LAHAINA ICE COM. LTD / LAHAINA MAUI Pale green aqua, 7-1/2", smooth base (323 H), tooled Hutchinson top, 1908.	**$60-90**

LAHAINA ICE CO. LTD. / LAHAINA MAUI / NET CONTENTS 10 OZ Pale blue aqua, 8-3/4", smooth base (PCGW 38), tooled crown top, 1913.	**$45-60**
MAUI SODA WORKS Medium green aqua, 8", round base (G&M – Initials of the first owners-Gibbens & Macauley), applied Hutchinson top, 1884.	**$1,200-1,600**
MAUI SODA WORKS Medium blue aqua, 8", round base (GHF – Initials of the second owner-Gilbert H. French), tooled Hutchinson top, 1888.	**$1,200-1,600**
MAUI SODA WORKS Medium blue aqua, 8" round base (W– Initials of the third owner-Ralph A. Wadsworth), tooled Hutchinson top, 1894.	**$600-800**

Kauai

HANAPEPE SODA WORKS Pale green aqua, 7-3/4", smooth base, tooled Hutchinson top, 1901.	**$600-800**
HANAPEPE SODA WORKS / HANAPEPE KAUAI Medium green aqua, 7-1/4", semi-round smooth base (H.S.W.), tooled Hutchinson top, 1905.	**$400-600**
KAUAI SODA WORKS Aqua. 7-1/4", smooth base, tooled Hutchinson top, 1900.	**$100-150**

KAUAI SODA WORKS Medium green aqua. 7-3/4", smooth base (K), tooled Hutchinson top, 1904.	**$100-150**
KAUAI SODA WORKS Medium green aqua, 8-3/4", smooth base (K), tooled crown top, 1904.	**$300-350**
LIHUE ICE CO. Aqua, 7-1/4", smooth base, tooled Hutchinson top, 1898.	**$75-100**

LIHUE ICE CO. Medium green aqua, 8-1/2", smooth base (L over P.C. G. W.), tooled crown top, 1904.	$600-800
LIHUE ICE CO. / KAUAI T.H. Aqua, 8-1/4", smooth base (IPGCO-2454 above IPGCO Diamond), tooled crown top, 1912.	$25-35

WAIMEA SODA & ICE WORKS Dark blue aqua, 7-1/4", smooth base, tooled Hutchinson top, 1899.	$150-175
WAIMEA WATER COMPANY LTD. Medium blue aqua, 7-3/4", smooth base (100 B), tooled Hutchinson top, 1908.	$75-100

Whiskeys, Oahu

CJ. McCARTHY / HONOLULU, T.H. (Pocket Flask) Clear, 6-1/2", smooth base (1242), tooled screw top, 1907.	$1,200-1,500
HOFFSCHLAEGER CO. LTD. (HCOLTD Monogram) / HONOLULU Dark amber, 11", concave base with ring encircling recessed center with convex bulge, tooled top, 1900-1910.	$175-200
IMPORTED BY C.C. RICHARDS & CO. / HONOLULU S.I. Olive green, 11-1/4", shallow concave bowl base, applied top, (note: Hawaiian Islands earliest embossed liquor bottle – S.I. stands for Sandwich Islands), 1858.	$3,000-5,000
LOVEJOY & CO. (L & CO Monogram) / HONOLULU T.H. Medium amber, 11", base has recessed cone with small flat plateau, tooled top, 1908.	$175-200
MACFARLANE & CO. (M & CO Monogram) / HONOLULU Light amber, 11-3/4", beveled edge inside base rim and shallow round concave center, applied top, 1880-1885.	$275-350

MACFARLANE & CO. (M & CO Monogram) / HONOLULU (Malt Whiskey) Medium amber, 9-5/8", base is slight recessed wide plateau, short neck, tooled top, 1888-1905.	$5,000-7,000
W.C. PEACOCK & CO. / HONOLULU, H.I. / WINE & LIQUOR MERCHANTS (WCP & CO Monogram) Dark red amber, 11-1/4", flat edge inside base rim and center is recessed plateau, applied top, 1887-1893.	$300-350
W.C. PEACOCK & CO. / HONOLULU, H.I. / WINE & LIQUOR MERCHANTS (WCP & CO Monogram) Medium orange amber, 11", flat edge inside base rim and center is recessed plateau, tooled top, 1900-1910.	$125-175
W.C. PEACOCK & CO. LTD. / HONOLULU/ FULL PINT (pint flask) Clear, 8-1/4", smooth base (109), tooled top, 1914.	$500-600

Hawaiian ACL (applied color label) Soda Pop Bottles

Coca-Cola / Trade Mark Registered / Min. Contents 6FL OZS (reverse the same) Greenish aqua, 7-3/4", Hobbleskirt shape, smooth base (Kaunkakai / T.H.), ABM lip. Territory of Hawaii 1951-1958 (Note: Prior to 1898, bottles were marked S.I (Sandwich Islands or H.I (Hawaiian Islands). After 1898 when Hawaii became a U.S. territory, the abbreviation H.T.(Hawaiian Territory) or T.H. (Territory Hawaii) was used until Hawaii entered statehood in 1959. The 'Min. Contents 6 FL OZS' designation was used from 1951-1958.	$150-175
Diamond Head – Honolulu, HI -1958 – Depiction of 'diamond head' and ocean in a diamond Clear glass, green and white, 7 oz.	$10-15
Hamakua – Paauilo, HI – 1940 – Depiction of hula dancer, grass shack, and palm trees Clear glass, white, 12 oz.	$25-40

Maui – No-Ka-Oi – 1966- Depiction of Island of Maui with volcano, mountains, and fish Clear glass, red and white, 7 oz.	$10-15
Pacific – Honolulu, HI – 1953 –Depiction of surfer and girl on the beach Clear glass, green and white, 6-1/2 oz.	$65-90
Pahoa Soda Works – Pahoa, HI – 1949 – Depiction of Palm Trees Clear glass, white, 6-1/2 oz.	$25-40
Smile – Honolulu, HI – 1968 – Depiction of an orange with a smiling face Clear glass, red and white, 7 oz.	$10-15
Sparkle Springs Soda Works, HI -1938 – Depiction of a man drinking from a shell by a stream Green glass, white, 7 oz.	$10-15
Star Soda – Wailuku, Maui – 1956 – Depiction of lady in star holding soda) Clear glass, blue and white, 7 oz.	$15-20

Hawaiian Bottles –
Realized Prices from Recent Auctions

Crystal – Soda Works – Honolulu. H.I. Medium blue aqua, 6-3/4:, smooth base (Trade Mark J.A.P.) tooled top, late 1880s, American Bottle Auction, January 19, 2014.	$90	
Crystal – Soda Works – Honolulu HI. Medium blue aqua, 8", round bottom, tooled blob-style top, 1890, American Bottle Auction, April 29, 2012.	$375	
Hawaiian – Soda Works – Honolulu –Bottles Not Sold –Riley MNFG Co. / London/ S.W. Medium green aqua, 7", smooth base (Riley's Patent London), applied top with original hard rubber screw-in top, 1898, American Bottle Auction, January 19, 2014.	$450	
Hawaiian – Soda Works – Honolulu H.I. Dark amber, 7-1/4",smooth base (H), tooled top, Hutchison, 1899, American Bottle Auction, March 3, 2013.	$1,500	

Holister - & Co. – Honolulu Medium blue aqua, 7", smooth base, applied blob-style top, mid-1880s, American Bottle Auction, March 3, 2013.	$300	
Lovejoy & Co. (L &CO monogram) Honolulu T.H. Medium amber, 11", smooth base, tooled top, 1908, American Bottle Auction, March 3, 2013.	$250	
Tahiti / Lemonade / Works Company / Honolulu. H.I. / "ACME Patent / Rylands Valve / 4 / Sole Maker / Dan Rylands / Barnsley / Trade Mark Rd" (on both shoulders) Pale green aqua, 8-1/2", smooth base, applied top with codd marble stopper, 1892, American Bottle Auction, January 19, 2014.	$375	
W.C. Peacock & Co. / Honolulu, H.I. / Wine & Liquor Merchants (WCP & Co Monogram) Medium orange amber, 11", smooth base, applied top, early 1900s, American Bottle Auction, January 19, 2014.	$300	

Glenn Takase – Hilo, Hawaii, standing next to a small portion of his Hawaiian bottle collection, from the top: top row- whiskeys/ 2nd row- gins / 3rd row - blob top sodas / 4th row – lightning stopper and marble soda bottles / bottom row – applied painted label (acl) soda pop bottles.

Selection of various shades of cobalt blue, aqua, amber, and green Japanese and Chinese medicine, beers, whiskey, and apothecary and herb bottles, owned by George Hedemann, Kona, Hawaii.

Hutchinson

Charles A. Hutchinson developed the Hutchinson bottle in the late 1870s. Interestingly, the stopper, not the bottle itself, differentiated the design from others. The stopper, which Hutchinson patented in 1879, was intended as an improvement over cork stoppers, which eventually shrank and allowed the air to seep into the bottle. It didn't take long for the newly developed stopper to catch the attention of bottlers and consumers. Soon, cork and other types of closures lost their appeal as Hutchinson's internal, less expensive stopper rose to become the industry standard for the North American bottling industry.

The new stopper consisted of a rubber disc that was held between two metal plates attached to a spring stem. The stem was shaped like a figure eight, with the upper loop larger than the lower to prevent the stem from falling into the bottle. The lower loop could pass through the bottle's neck and push down the disc to permit the filling or pouring of it contents. A refilled bottle was sealed by pulling the disc up to the bottles shoulder, where it made a tight fit. When opened, the spring made a popping sound. Thus, the story goes that the Hutchinson bottle had the honor of originating the phrase "pop bottle," which is how soda came to be known as "pop." Whether the story is true is probably another story, but it sure sounds good.

Hutchinson stopped producing bottles in 1912, when warnings about metal poisoning were issued. As collectibles, Hutchinson bottles rank high on the curiosity and price scales, but pricing varies quite sharply by geographical location, compared to the relatively stable prices of most other bottles.

Hutchinson bottles carry abbreviations of which the following three are the most common:

- TBNTBS – This bottle not to be sold
- TBMBR –This bottle must be returned
- TBINS – This bottle is not sold

Bonanza Bottling Co. – Dawson N.W.T Aqua, 7-3/4", smooth base, Northwest Territory, American, 1885-1900.	**$800-900**	
C. Andrae – Port Huron – Mich – C. & Co. 2 Medium cobalt blue, 6-5/8", smooth base, American, 1885-1900.	**$150-200**	
Central – Bottling Works – Detroit, Mich – **This Bottle Is Never Sold – C. & Co. Lim No. 5** Medium cobalt blue, 7", smooth base (J.J.G.), American, 1885-1900.	**$150-200**	
Claussen Bottling Works – Charleston – S.C. Yellow amber, 6-5/8", smooth base, extremely rare, South Carolina, American, 1885-1900	**$300-350**	
Comanche Bottling- Works – Comanche, I.T. Aqua, 6-3/4", smooth base, tooled top, the town of Comanche is located in Southwest Oklahoma and until 1907 was considered Indian territory, American, 1900-1907.	**$400-500**	

Crown – Bottling Mfg. Co. – (embossed crown)- Ardmore, I.T. Aqua, 6-1/8", smooth base (S), Idaho Territory, American, 1885-1900.	$450-500	
C. W. Rider – Watertown – N.Y. Deep teal blue, 6-3/4", smooth base, rare color and only one of two known examples, American, 1890-1900.	$800-1,200	
Distilled – Soda Water Co. – of – Alaska – S.B. & C. Co. Green aqua, 7-1/2", 10 panels on side at base, smooth base, a rare Hutchinson Soda from the Territory of Alaska prior to statehood, American, 1885-1900.	$800-1,000	
E. Ottenville – Nashville – Tenn – MCC Medium cobalt blue, 6-5/8", smooth base, American, 1885-1900.	$150-200	
Eureka – California (embossed eagle) Soda Water Co. –S.F. Light amethyst, 6-3/4", smooth base, American, 1885-1900.	$600-700	

Geo. Disbro - & Co. – Chicago Cobalt blue, 7-5/8", smooth base (D), 10 panels on side at base, American, 1885-1900.	**$350-400**	
Geo. Schmuck's – Ginger Ale – Cleveland, O – C. & Co. Lim Yellow amber, 7-3/4", 12-sided, smooth base, American, 1885-1900.	**$250-300**	
Geo. Schmuck's – Ginger Ale – Cleveland, O – C. & Co. Lim Orange amber, 8", 12-sided, smooth base, American, 1885-1900.	**$250-300**	
G. Norris & Co. – City – Bottling Works – Detroit, Mich – C&Co Lim Medium cobalt blue, 6-3/4", smooth base, American, 1885-1890.	**$100-125**	
Guyette & Company – Registered – Detroit, Mich. – This Bottle Is Never Sold-C &Co. Lim No. 5 Medium cobalt blue, 6-7/8", smooth base (G), American, 1885-1900.	**$150-200**	
H.W. Buffum & Co. – Pittsburg – Penna – A. & D.H.C. Light cobalt blue, 6-1/2", smooth base (H), American, 1870-1880.	**$500-600**	
H.L. Wigert – Burlington – Iowa – This Bottle – To Be Returned Medium cobalt blue, 6-3/4", smooth base, rare colored hutch, American, 1885-1900.	**$200-300**	
Hayes Bros – Trade Mark – NB – Registered – Chicago, Il – MCC Cobalt blue, 7-3/8", smooth base, 10-panels on side at base, American, 1885-1900.	**$150-200**	

H.O. Krueger – Grand Forks – Oak. Blue aqua, 7-1/4", smooth base (WIS.GLASS CO. MLW), American, 1885-1900.	$350-400	
J. G. Bolton – Lemont – Ills – A.&D.H.C. Medium cobalt blue, 6-7/8", smooth base, American, 1885-1900.	$200-350	
J.H. Fett & Son – Reading – PA. – F&S Yellow amber, 6-5/8", smooth base (F&S), possibly only known example in this color, American, 1885-1895.	$2,000-2,500	
Jacob Schmidt – Pottsville, PA. Medium olive green, 6-3/4", smooth base, rare coal region colored Hutchinson, American, 1890-1900.	$350-450	
J. E. Esposito – 812 & 814 – J. Koca Nola – Washington Ave – Philada Yellow amber, 7-3/4", smooth base (JE), American, 1885-1900.	$1,000-1,200	

Trade Mark – Jal (inside a diamond) – Registered – J.A. Lomax – 14 16 & 18-Charles Place – Chicago – This Bottle Must Be Returned Deep cobalt blue, 6-3/4", smooth base (J.L.), American, 1885-1900.	$100-125	
J. Weilersbacher – Pittsburg, PA. – Trade (W inside a sunburst) Mark – Registered – D.C.C. 149 Yellow amber, 7-5/8', four front panels with rounded back, smooth base, American, 1885-1900.	$300-400	
James Ray – Savannah – Geo. – Ginger Ale Deep cobalt blue, 7-3/4", smooth base, American, 1885-1900.	$300-450	
Lascheid – Pittsburg – Pa – L (Inside a Wreath) – Registered – St. Clair – Carbonating – Est Amber, 8", four front panels and a round back, smooth base (ST), American, 1885-1900.	$250-300	
Leland Ice & - Cold Storage Co. – Leland, Miss. Light blue aqua, 7-1/4", smooth base, back base (Not To Be Sold), American, 1885-1890.	$100-150	
Lohrberg Bros's – Bed Bud – Ill. Light to medium apple green, 6-3/4", smooth base, American, 1885-1900.	$400-500	
Mel. Aro (Around Shoulder) – Eclipse Carbonating Company (inside a horseshoe) – ECCO (Monogram) – St. Louis – 2 ½ Cents Deposit – Required For Return – Of This Bottle Deep amber, 6-1/2", smooth base (ECCO), American 1885-1900.	$100-125	

Moriarty & Carroll – Registered – Waterbury, Conn. Deep amber, 7-3/8", 10-panels on side as base, smooth base, American, 1885-1900.	**$350-400**	
Muskogee – Bottling Works- Muskogee, I.T. Aqua, 6-1/4", smooth base (S), reverse base (N.B.B.G. CO 630), Idaho Territory, American, 1885-1900.	**$350-400**	
Norwich Bottling – Works – Norwich – N.Y. Amber, 6-3/8", smooth base, American, 1885-1900.	**$250-300**	
P.G. Stephan – Buffalo, N.Y. Deep teal, 7", 8-sided, smooth base (S), American, 1885-1900.	**$150-200**	
P.J. Serwazi – Manayunk – PA. Medium olive green, 7-5/8", smooth base (S), original loop wire closure, American, 1890-1900.	**$350-450**	
Pearson Bros. – Bodie Deep aqua, 7-1/4", smooth base, gravitating stopper style, Bodie, California, American, 1882-1891.	**$2,800-3,000**	

Pensacola – Bottling Works – Penssacola, FLA Deep teal, 6-3/4", 8-sided, smooth base, American, 1885-1900.	$100-125	
Richmond Soda Works – R.W.W. – Point Richmond Blue aqua, 7", smooth base, American, 1902-1915.	$400-450	
Somps & Herve – San – Francisco, CAL. Aqua, 7-1/4", smooth mug base, American, 1885-1900.	$200-250	
Standard – Bottling Works – Minneapolis – Minn. Deep amber, 6-3/4", smooth base (HR), American, 1890-1900.	$250-300	
Standard – Bottling Works – Minneapolis – Minn. –SABCO Deep amber, 6-7/8", smooth base (HR), American, 1890-1900.	$250-300	

Old Bottles

Star Bottling – Works – Amadarko. D.T. – T & M Light amethyst, 6-7/8", smooth base, back base (I.G. CO. 433), Oklahoma Territory, American, 1890-1905.	$800-900	
Steam Bottling Works – (anchor) Registered – Shawnee O.T. Aqua, 6-3/4", smooth base, reverse back base (A.G.W.), American, 1890-1905.	$600-700	
Sullivan Bros – Providence, R.I. (80% Label Reads: Mirror Lake, Bottling Works, Sarsaparilla, Soda, Purity Guaranteed Aqua, 6-3/4", smooth base (C/25), most difficult state to obtain a Hutchinson Soda, American, 1885-1890.	$1,600-1,800	
The Boley Mfg. Co. – Bottles & Demijohns – 414 West 14th St. – N.Y. Registered Medium yellow green (citron), 6-7/8", smooth base, American, 1885-1890.	$400-450	

T. Burkhardt – Braddock, PA Yellow amber, 6-3/4", smooth base, American, 1885-1900.	$400-450	
The City – Bottling – Works – Louisville – Seltzer Water Cobalt blue, 6-5/8", smooth base (MK), American, 1885-1900.	$800-1,200	
Ukiah Soda Works – Ukiah – CAL. Aqua, 7", smooth based, American, 1885-1900.	$100-125	

Ink Bottles

Ink bottles are unique because of their centuries-old history, which provides collectors today with a wider variety of designs and shapes than any other group of bottles. People often ask why a product as cheap to produce as ink was sold in such decorative bottles. While other bottles were disposed of or returned after use, ink bottles were usually displayed openly on desks in dens, libraries, and studies. It's safe to assume that even into the late 1880s people who bought ink bottles considered the design of the bottle as well as the quality of its contents.

Blown three-mold geometric ink, yellow amber, 1-1/2", tubular open pontil, tooled disk mouth, 1815-1835, $175-200.

S.O. Dunbar – Taunton, aqua, 2-3/8", eight-sided, open pontil, inward rolled lip, 1840-1860, $200-250.

Prior to the 18th century, most ink was sold in brass or copper containers. The rich would then refill their gold and silver inkwells from these storage containers. Ink that was sold in glass and pottery bottles in England in the 1700s had no brand name identification, and, at best, would have a label identifying the ink and/or the manufacturer.

In 1792, the first patent for the commercial production of ink was issued in England, 24 years before the first American patent that was issued in 1816. Molded ink bottles began to appear in America around 1815-1816 and the blown three-mold variety came into use during the late 1840s. The most common shaped ink bottle, the umbrella, is a multi-sided conical form which can be found with both pontiled and smooth bases. One of the more collectible ink bottles is the teakettle, identified by the neck, which extends upward at an angle from the base.

As the fountain pen grew in popularity between 1885-1890, ink bottles gradually grew less decorative and became just another plain bottle.

Albert's – Writing Fluid – Pitts – PA. Aqua, 2-5/8", tubular open pontil, inward rolled lip, American, 1840-1860.	$400-450	
Cone Ink – G & R'S – American – Writing Fluid Blue aqua, 2", open pontil, inward rolled lip, American, 1840-1860.	$300-350	
Cone Ink – G & R'S – American – Writing Fluid Aqua, 2-1/2", open pontil, inward rolled lip, American, 1840-1860.	$500-600	
Cone Ink – Hibbert – Pittsburg Aqua, oversized cone, open pontil, inward rolled lip, extremely rare, American, 1840-1860.	$1,000-1,300	
Draped pattern cone ink Medium sapphire blue, 2-1/8", open pontil, applied lip, rare shape and color, American, 1840-1860.	$1,900-2,000	
Cone Ink – Cooke's – Carmine Ink Pale aqua, 2-3/8", open pontil, sheared and inward rolled top, rare embossed ink, American, 1840-1860.	$500-600	
Cone ink Yellow amber, 2-3/8", open pontil, sheared and tooled top, possibly Stoddard Glass Works, American, 1840-1860.	$150-200	
Cone Ink Medium sapphire blue, 2-1/2", open pontil, inward rolled top, rare in this color, American, 1840-1860.	$1,500-1,700	
Cottage Ink – original label reads: Kirtland's – Jet Black – Cottage Ink Aqua, 2-5/8", smooth base (Patd Mar 14, 1871), applied top, Kirkland Ink Co., American, 1875-1895.	$500-600	
Cottage Ink – NE – Plus – Ultra – Fluid Blue aqua, 2-1/2", smooth base, rough sheared top, American, 1875-1895.	$500-600	
Cottage Ink – S.I. – Comp. Opaque milk glass, 2-3/4", smooth base, tooled top, Senate Ink Co., American, 1875-1895.	$800-900	

Davids & Black – New York (around shoulder) Medium blue green, 6-1/4", cylinder, tubular open pontil, applied top, American, 1840-1860.	$200-300	
De Halsey – Patente Olive yellow, 2-7/8", open pontil, tooled top, American, 1840-1860.	$500-700	
Domed ink Yellow amber with olive tone, 2", open pontil, sheared and tooled top, possibly Coventry Glass Works, American, 1825-1845.	$1,000-1,100	
Farley's – Ink Yellow "old" amber, 1-3/4", eight-sided, tubular open pontil, American, 1850-1860.	$400-450	
Farley's – Ink Yellow amber, 3-5/8", eight-sided, open pontil, thin flared out lip, pristine, American, 1840-1860.	$1,800-2,000	
George Ohr Pottery cabin inkwell Motted olive green glaze, 3", smooth base (G.E. Ohr – Biloxi), American, 1880-1900.	$6,000-7,000	
Gross & Robinson's – American – Writing Fluid Blue aqua, 4-3/4", open pontil, applied top, rare inks, American, 1840-1860.	$500-600	
Gross & Robinson's – American – Writing Fluid Blue aqua, 7-1/8", iron pontil, applied top, rare, American, 1840-1860.	$600-700	
Hand-blown cut glass inkwell Canary yellow, 1-3/4" x 3-1/4" x 2-3/4" h, cut glass inkwell, American, 1880-1900.	$150-200	
Harrison's – Columbian – Ink Cobalt blue, 4-3/4", open pontil, applied top, American, 1840-1860.	$800-900	

Harrison's – Columbian – Ink –Patent Aqua, 7-3/8", Master Ink , 12-sided, open pontil, applied top, American, 1840-1860.	$300-350	
Hover – Phila Medium olive green, 5-1/8", cylinder, open pontil, tooled flared out lip, American, 1840-1860.	$450-500	
Igloo ink Black amethyst, 2", smooth base, sheared and ground lip, American, 1875-1890.	$700-800	
Igloo ink Medium blue green, 2-1/4", smooth base, sheared and ground lip, scarce color, American, 1875-1890.	$180-200	
J.E. – Petermans – Ink – Philada Aqua, 3-5/8", 12-sided, open pontil, thin flared-out lip, extremely rare, American, 1840-1860.	$800-900	
J.J. Bulter's Fluid – Inks Cinct. O. (around shoulder) Blue aqua, 9-3/4", master ink, smooth base, applied top and hand crimped pour spout, blown in three-part mold, J.J. Butler Co., master inks are rare, American, 1855-1865.	$200-300	
Jones – No. 1 Aqua, 2-7/8", vertical rib pattern on all sides, open pontil, tooled flared out lip, rare, American, 1840-1860.	$250-300	
Jones – Empire – Ink – N.Y. Emerald green, 5-7/8", 12-sided, iron pontil, applied top, rare, American, 1840-1860.	$5,000-6,000	
Kirtland's – Writing Fluid – Poland – Ohio Aqua, 2-1/2", tubular open pontil, outward lip, American, 1840-1860.	$500-600	

Log cabin ink Clear glass, 2-1/2", log cabin shape, smooth base, tooled top, ink bottle mold patented on April 15, 1884 by Emil Herchner, Millville, N.J., American, 1885-1890.	**$1,000-1,200**	
Log cabin ink Clear glass, 3-1/4", log cabin shape, smooth base, sheared and ground top, American, 1875-1890.	**$1,500-1,800**	
Semi-cabin form – Zieblein - St. Louis Blue aqua, 2-5/8", open pontil, inward rolled lip, American, 1840-1860.	**$500-600**	
Sided master ink Deep grass green, 4-1/2", eight sided, smooth base, tooled lip, American, 1880-1895.	**$150-200**	
Sided master ink Cobalt blue, 6-1/8", eight sided, pontil scarred base, tooled top with hand crimped pour spout, American, 1845-1865.	**$600-700**	
Master ink Deep pink amethyst, 10", smooth base, applied top with hand crimped pour spout, blown in three-part mold, American, 1860-1875.	**$300-350**	
Miniature – loaf of bread-shaped ink Black glass with swirls of whitish color, 2-1/8" x 2-3/8" x 1-3/4", eight sided, pontil scarred base, sheared and tooled lip, rare, French, 1840-1860.	**$400-500**	
Miniature teakettle ink Medium deep green, 1-1/8", eight sided, cut and polished, polished pontil and lip, original brass neck ring and hinged lid, rare, American, 1875-1890.	**$250-300**	
Multisided ink – JW –P-E-N-N-E-L-L Blue aqua, 1-7/8", eight sided, smooth base, tooled top, rare with embossing on all eight panels, American, 1880-1890.	**$150-200**	
Teakettle ink Medium cobalt blue, 2-1/4", barrel shape, smooth base, rough sheared and ground lip, American, 1875-1895.	**$650-750**	

Teakettle ink Green semi-opaque, 2-3/8", smooth base, ground and polished top, American, 1880-1895.	**$325-350**	
Beehive-shaped teakettle ink Cobalt blue, 2-3/8", smooth base, rough sheared top, original neck ring and hinged cap, scarce in this color and shape, American, 1875-1895.	**$4,000-5,000**	
Cut glass teakettle ink Cobalt blue, 2-5/8", eight-sided with ornate brass filigree on all sides, top and pour spout, polished pontil base, sheared and polished top, 12 ruby-type jewels, six located on top of ink, European or Middle East, 1880-1910.	**$500-600**	
Umbrella ink Deep yellow olive amber, 2 3/8", eight-sided, open pontil, sheared and tooled lip, American, 1840-1860.	**$350-400**	
Umbrella ink Deep olive green, 2-3/8", 16-sided, tubular open pontil, sheared and tooled lip, American, 1845-1860.	**$400-450**	
Umbrella ink Medium blue green, 2-5/8", eight-sided, open pontil, inward rolled lip, American, 1850-1860.	**$450-500**	
Umbrella ink Reddish amber, 2-1/2", eight-sided, open pontil, sheared and tooled lip, Stoddard Glass Works, New Hampshire, American, 1845-1860.	**$150-200**	
Umbrella ink – Davis & Miller D.M. Aqua, 2-1/2", open pontil, inward rolled lip, rare with a different design, American, 1840-1860.	**$350-400**	
Umbrella ink – M & P – New York Light blue green, 2-1/2", eight-sided, open pontil, inward rolled lip, rare embossed ink, American, 1840-1860.	**$400-500**	

Medicine

The medicine bottle group includes all pieces specifically made to hold patented medicines. Bitters and cure bottles, however, are excluded from this category because the healing powers of these mixtures were questionable.

A patent medicine was one whose formula was registered with the U.S. Patent office, which opened in 1790. Not all medicines were patented, since the procedure required the manufacturer to reveal the medicine's contents. After the passage of the Pure Food and Drug

Dr. Convers Invigorating Cordial, deep blue aqua, 6-1/8", oval shape, open pontil, applied tapered collar top, 1840-1860, $125-150.

Jacobs & Brown – Hamilton O., deep blue aqua, 5-3/4", open pontil, applied tapered collar top, 1840-1860, $150-200.

Act of 1907, most of these patent medicine companies went out of business after they were required to list the ingredients of the contents on the bottle, and consumers learned that most medicines consisted of liquor diluted with water and an occasional pinch of opiates, strychnine, and arsenic. I have spent many enjoyable hours reading the labels on these bottles and wondering how anyone would survive after taking the recommended doses.

One of the oldest and most collectible medicine bottles was manufactured in England from 1723 and 1900 – the embossed Turlington "Balsam of Life" bottle. The first embossed U.S. medicine bottle dates from around 1810. When searching out these bottles, always be on the lookout for embossing and original boxes.

Embossed "Shaker" or "Indian" medicine bottles are collectible and valuable. Most embossed medicines made before 1840 are clear and aqua; the embossed greens, ambers, and various shades of blues, specifically the darker cobalt blues, are much more collectible and valuable.

A B L Myers. AM – Rock Rose – New Haven Deep blue green, 9-7/8", iron pontil, applied blob top, American, 1845-1860.	$500-600	
Addison Hill's – Buffalo, N.Y. Yellow olive amber, 9-1/4", open pontil, applied double collar top, rare, American, 1845-1860.	$1,500-1,600	
American – Medicinal – Oil – Burkeville, KY. Aqua, 6-1/4", open pontil, applied top, rare, American, 1840-1860.	$600-700	
Arabian Oil – New York Blue aqua, 5-1/2", open pontil, applied tapered collar top, rare, American, 1840-1860.	$325-350	
Beekman's – Pulmonic – Syrup – New-York Olive green, 7-1/4", eight-sided, pontil scarred base, applied tapered double collar top, American, 1840-1860.	$5,000-5,500	
Blood Elixir Or – German Sanative Blue aqua, 7-1/2", tubular open pontil, applied top, extremely rare, American, 1840-1860.	$500-600	
Burrington's – Vegetable Croup Syrup – **Providence, R.I.** Aqua, 5-1/2", cylinder, open pontil, inward rolled lip, American, 1840-1860.	$200-250	
C. Brinkerhoff's – Health Restorative – Price **$1.00 – New York** Deep yellow olive green, 7-1/8", pontil scarred base, applied tapered collar top, American, 1840-1860.	$900-1,000	

C. R. – Canandaigo – N.Y. – Ring Bone & Spaven – Liniment Blue aqua, 6-1/8", open pontil, applied tapered collar top, American, 1840-1860.	$1,000-1,200	
Carter's – Spanish – Mixture – 98% original label reads: Carter's Spanish Mixture, Bennett & Beers, Druggist, General Agents and Proprietors, No. 125 Main Street, Richmond, VA Yellow olive green, 8-1/4", open pontil, applied top, American, 1840-1860.	$600-700	
Chamberlain's – Immediate – Relief – A.N. Chamberlain – Elkhart – Ind. Aqua, 4-7/8", cylinder, open pontil, inward rolled lip, American, 1845-1860.	$100-125	
Chapman's – Genuine – No. 4 Salem St. Boston Olive amber, 8", pontil scarred base, applied top, American, 1840-1860.	$1,000-1,200	
Compound – Extract – Of – Hops & Boneset Blue aqua, 6", pontil scarred base (part of reversed numbers embossed on base), inward rolled lip, American, 1840-1860.	$200-250	
Dr. Browder's – Compound Syrup – Of Indian Turnip Aqua, 7", open pontil, applied tapered collar top, American, 1840-1869.	$200-225	
Dr. D. Jayne's – Life Preservative – Philda. A Aqua, 5-1/2", tubular open pontil, flared out lip, rarest of all Dr. Jayne's collectible bottles, American, 1835-1860.	$1,300-1,400	

The Dr. D. M. Bye – Combination Oil Cure Co. – 316 N. Illinois St. Indianapolis, Ind. – The Originator Copyrighted Clear glass, 7-5/8", smooth base, tooled lip, American, 1890-1900.	$200-250	
Dr. R. R. Hopkins – Fever & Ague – Tonic Drops Blue aqua, 6-1/8", open pontil, applied tapered collar top, American, 1840-1860.	$1,300-1,400	
Dr. E.J. Cox – New Orleans Light to medium green, 7-1/4", tubular open pontil, applied top, American, 1840-1860.	$400-450	
Dr. H. C. Porter & Son – Druggist – Towanda, PA -16 oz Medium amber, 8-1/4", smooth base (Pat. June 17,88-S.B.), American, 1885-1895.	$200-225	
Dr. H.W. Jackson – Druggist – Vegetable – Home Syrup (upside-down "M" in "Home") Yellow amber, 4-1/2", cylinder, open pontil, applied top, rare, American, 1840-1860.	$1,000-1,300	
Dr. Hersey's – Worm Syrup Aqua, 5-1/2", open pontil, inward rolled lip, American, 1840-1860.	$350-400	
(Motif of medicine man standing by table full of medicines while holding one in his hand) Trade Mark – J.A. Burgoon's System – Renovater Aqua, 8-1/8", smooth base, tooled double collar top, American, 1880-1890.	$180-225	

Rowand & Walton's – Panacea – Philada., pale aqua, 6-3/8", open pontil, applied tapered collar top, very rare, 1840-1860, $500-600.

M. Lewis – Mother's Friend – Louisville, KY., deep blue aqua, 9-1/8", iron pontil, applied top, extremely rare, 1845-1860, $600-700.

Monk's – Old Bourbon – Whiskey For – Medicinal Purposes – Wilson, Fairbank & Co. – Sole Agents, olive green, 8", iron pontil, applied tapered collar, 1850-1860, $1,300-1,500.

Dr. Foord's Pectoral Syrup – New York, aqua, 5-3/8", open pontil, applied and tooled top, 1840-1860, $75-100.

Dr. Davis's – Depurative – Phila., medium blue green, 9-3/4", iron pontil, applied top, 1845-1860, $1,200-1,400.

Dr. J. Clawson Kelley's – Antiseptic Detergent – New-York Blue aqua, 9-1/4", pontil scarred base, applied tapered collar top, rare, American, 1840-1860.	$450-500	
Dr. J. W. Poland (in arched indented panel) Deep yellow amber, 7-7/8", applied top, American, 1855-1865.	$350-400	
Dr. Jackson's – Pile – Embrocation – Phil. A Aqua, 3-7/8", wide mouth, open pontil, then flared-out lip, American, 1840-1860.	$800-900	
Dr. Larookah's – Indian – Vegetable – Pulmonic Syrup Deep emerald green, 8-3/4", smooth base, applied tapered collar top, American, 1860-1875.	$200-250	
Dr. Mitchel's - Ipecac Syrup – Terry, N.Y. Aqua, 4-3/4", open pontil, tooled flared-out lip, American, 1840-1860.	$200-225	
Delmonico's – Syrup Pectoral – New York Aqua, 7-1/8", tubular open pontil, applied top, rare, American, 1840-1860.	$600-700	
Dr. Rall – Liniment Aqua, 4-1/4", tubular open pontil, inward rolled lip, extremely rare, American, 1840-1860.	$300-350	

Dr. Rose's – Antidispeptic – Vermifuge – Philada Pale green aqua, 5-1/2", open pontil, applied tapered collar top, American, 1840-1860.	$250-300	
Dr. Swett's – Panacea – Exeter, N.H. Medium amber, 8-1/4", pontil scarred base, applied double collar top, rare, American, 1840-1860.	$4,000-4,300	
Dr. Van Baum's – Rheumatic – Lotion – And Magic – Pain – Extractor Blue aqua, 6-1/8", open pontil, applied top, American, 1840-1860.	$400-500	
Dr. W. J. Haas's – Expectorant – Schuylkill Haven – PA Aqua, 5-3/8", open pontil, tooled flared-out lip, scarce, American, 1840-1860.	$150-175	
Dr. W. N. Handy – Easton, N. Y. Deep olive green, 12-sided, smooth base, applied top, rare, American, 1855-1865.	$2,500-3,000	
Dr. William Clark – 514 Washington St. – Boston Aqua, 9-3/4", open pontil, applied tapered collar top, American, 1840-1860.	$250-350	
Doc. T. Fowler's – Anti – Epicholic – Canton, N.Y. Aqua, 6", tubular open pontil, applied top, American, 1840-1860.	$150-200	

Drs. D. Fahrney & Son – Preparation For – Cleansing The Blood – Boonsboro, M.D. Yellow amber, 9-1/2", smooth base, applied top, American, 1870-1880.	**$350-400**	
Dexter's – Syrup Blue aqua, 9-1/2", iron ponil, applied tapered collar top, rare, American, 1840-1860.	**$1,500-1,600**	
Dunbar & Co's – Wormwood – Cordial – Boston Medium emerald green, 9-5/8", smooth base, applied tapered collar top, American, 1855-1870.	**$500-600**	
Freiot's Renovator Aqua, 9-3/4", iron pontil, applied tapered collar top, rare, American, 1840-1860.	**$900-1,000**	
(Five stars) G. Watts – Baltimore – (five stars) – Aromatic – Salts Pink amethyst jar, 2", smooth base, sheared and ground and polished lip, American, 1865-1880.	**$400-450**	
Glenn – Bear – Oil Aqua, 2-7/8", tubular open pontil, thin tooled flared-out lip, extremely rare, L.W. Glenn & Co. located at 168 Chestnut St. in Philadelphia, American, 1835-1860.	**$300-350**	
Hampton – V. Tincture – Mortimer – & Mowbray – Balto Light copper topaz, 6-3/8", tubular open pontil, applied top, American, 1840-1860.	**$1,300-1,400**	

Hart's – Carminative – Philad. A Aqua, 3-5/8", six-sided, iron pontil, inward rolled lip, American, 1840-1869.	$500-600	
Henshaw Ward & Co. – Druggist – Boston Deep apple green, 8-3/4", cylinder, open pontil, applied tapered double collar top, American, 1840-1860.	$700-800	
Howard's – Vegetable – Cancer and – Canker Syrup Reddish amber, 7-1/4", smooth base, applied top, American, 1855-1865.	$450-500	
Hyatt's – Infallible – Life Balsam – N.Y. Rich emerald green, 10", iron pontil, applied double collar top, American, 1845-1860.	$1,000-1,100	
Covert's – Balm of Life Deep olive green, 5-7/8", open pontil, applied tapered collar top, American, 1840-1860.	$1,900-2,000	
Indian – Clemens Tonic – (standing Indian) Prepared By – Geo. W. House Blue aqua, 7-1/8", tubular open pontil, applied top, rare, American, 1840-1860.	$600-700	
Indian – Specific – For Coughs – Prepared By Dr. C Freeman Pale aqua, 6", tubular open pontil, applied top, American, 1840-1860.	$150-200	
J. A. Limcricks – Great Master – of Pain – Rodney, Miss. Aqua, 6-1/4", open pontil, applied tapered collar top, extremely rare, American, 1840-1860.	$1,300-1,500	

J.C. Wadleigh – Bears Oil Aqua, 4-1/4", open pontil, applied tapered collar top, extremely rare, American, 1835-1860.	$1,000-1,100	
J. L. Leavitt – Boston Deep olive green, 8-1/2", iron pontil, applied top, blown in three-part mold, American, 1845-1860.	$200-225	
J. M. Henry & Sons – Vermont – Liniment – Waterbury, VT Blue aqua, 5-1/4", open pontil, applied top, scarce, American, 1840-1860.	$150-200	
J. S. Gregory – Chemist Aqua, 4-3/4", open pontil, inward rolled lip, earliest of J.S. Gregory bottles, American, 1845-1855.	$300-325	
Jones' American – Cholagogue – Barnes & Park – 304 Broadway, N.Y. Aqua, 7", open pontil, applied double collar top, original contents, American, 1840-1860.	$700-800	
Lee & Osgood – 127 Main St. – Norwich Conn. Aqua, 8-7/8", open pontil, applied top, American, 1840-1860.	$250-300	
Liquid – Opodeldoc Medium yellow olive amber, 4-1/2", cylinder, open pontil, tooled flared-out lip, extremely rare, American, 1840-1860.	$800-900	

Old Bottles

Louden & Co's – Female Elixir – Philad. A Aqua, 4", open pointil, thin flared-out lip, rare, American, 1840-1860.	**$900-1,000**	
Mackenzie's – Tonic – Febrifuge Blue aqua, 6-3/8", iron pontil, applied top, American, 1840-1860.	**$500-600**	
MFF (monogram) – Mykramtz – Columbus – O. – 95% label on back panel reads: I Quart Bemzpte (handwritten) and "The" Kauffmn-Lattimer Co. – Manufacturing Chemist – Columbus, O. Bright yellow green, 11", smooth base (C.L.G.Co.), American, 1890-1910.	**$900-1,000**	
Mrs. M. Cox's – Indian – Vegetable – Decoction – Balto Aqua, 8-1/4", open pontil, applied tapered collar top, scarce "Indian" medicine bottle, American, 1840-1860.	**$700-800**	
M. Wood – Portland – ME. Yellow amber, 7-1/4", pontil scarred base, applied tapered collar top, American, 1840-1860.	**$2,000-2,200**	
Nuttall's – Syriacum – Confirmed – Consumption Blue aqua, 6-1/4", open pontil, applied top, extremely rare, American, 1840-1860.	**$600-700**	
O'Neill's – Genuine – Anti- Rheumatic – Decoction Aqua, 7-1/2", open pontil, applied top, extremely rare, American, 1840-1860.	**$1,600-1,700**	

Orange Tonica – Risley & Co. N.Y. Yellow amber, 10-1/4", smooth base, tooled lip, American, 1890-1895.	$100-125	
Phelps's – Arcanum – Worcester – Mass. Olive amber, 8-1/2", rough pontil scarred base, applied tapered double collar top, American, 1840-1860.	$3,000-3,300	
Pike & Osgood – Boston Mass – Alternative Syrup Deep amber, 8-5/8", pontil scarred base, applied tapered collar top, rare New England medicine bottle, American, 1840-1860.	$5,000-6,000	
Preston's – Veg Purifying – Catholicon Aqua, 9-5/8", oval shape, tubular open pontil, applied tapered collar top, American, 1840-1860.	$500-600	
Queru's – Cod Liver Oil – Jelly Aqua, 5-1/2", open pontil, outward rolled lip, American, 1840-1860.	$125-150	
Rev. T. Hill's – Vegetable Remedy Aqua, 4-3/4", oval shape, open pontil, inward rolled lip, American, 1840-1860.	$350-400	
Rexford's – Chamomile – Cordial – Ogdensburg, N.Y. Medium blue green, 9-3/4", iron pontil, applied tapered collar top, American, 1840-1860.	$6,000-7,000	

Old Bottles

Sargent & Co – American – Canchalagogue – New York Aqua, 9-7/8", open pontil, applied double collar top, American, 1840-1860.	$1,900-2,000	
Seaver's – Joint $ - Nerve – Liniment Medium yellow amber, 4", open pontil, flared out lip, American, 1840-1860.	$700-800	
No. 1 – Shaker Syrup – Canterbury, N.H. Aqua, 7-1/2", open pontil, applied tapered collar top, American, 1840-1860.	$100-125	
Skinner – Vosburgh – & Dalee's – Reumatic Mixture Aqua, 7", open pontil, applied double collar top, American, 1840-1860.	$600-700	
Smith's – Green Mountain – Renovator – East Georgia VT Yellow amber, 7-1/8", pontil scarred base, applied double collar top, American, 1840-1860.	$2,000-2,300	
Taylors – Indian – Ointment Aqua, 3-3/8", six-sided, open pontil, inward rolled lip, rare, American, 1840-1860.	$300-350	
True – Daffy's – Elixir – See That – The Words – Dicey & Co. – No. 10 Bow – Church – Yard – London Light olive green, 5", pontil scarred base, applied top, most popular of English pontil period medicines, English, 1825-1840.	$2,000-2,200	
Waters – Pulmonica – Troy, N.Y. Clear glass, 5", open pontil, applied top, extremely rare, American, 1840-1860.	$800-900	

Wells – German – Liniment – St. Louis Mo. Blue aqua, 6" cylinder, open pontil, applied tapered top, American, 1840-1860.	**$150-200**
Westlake's – Vegetable – Ointment – Lima, N.Y. Cornflower blue, 3", tubular open pontil, inward rolled lip, scarce, American, 1840-1860.	**$100-150**
Winans – Bear – Oil Blue aqua, 2-7/8", tubular open pontil, inward rolled lip, N. & I. Winans Druggist located in Cincinnati, Ohio, American, 1835-1860.	**$900-1,000**
Winans – Relief – Liniment Blue aqua, 4-1/4", tubular open pontil, inward rolled lip, American, 1840-1860.	**$250-300**
WM. S. Dunham – Manufacturer – New York Light to medium green, 10", open pontil, applied top, American, 1840-1860.	**$300-350**
Zollickoffer's – Anti Rheumatic – Cordial – Philad. A Medium amber, 6-1/2", smooth base, tooled lip, American, 1879-1880.	**$400-500**

Milk

The first patent date for a milk bottle was issued to the "Jefferson Co. Milk Assn." in January 1875. The bottle featured a tin top with a spring clamping device. The first known standard-shaped milk bottle (pre-1930) was patented in March 1880 and was manufactured by the Warren Glass Works of Cumberland, Maryland.

In 1884, A.V. Whiteman patented a jar with a dome-type tin cap to be used with the patented Thatcher and Barnhart fastening device for a glass lid. No trace exists of a patent for the bottle itself, however. Among collectors today, the Thatcher milk bottle is one of the most prized. There are several variations on the original. Very early bottles were embossed with a picture of a Quaker farmer milking his cow while seated on a stool. "Absolutely Pure Milk" is stamped into the glass on the bottle's shoulder.

An important development in the design of the milk bottle was the patent issued to H.P. and S.L. Barnhart in September 17, 1889, for their methods of capping and sealing. Their invention involved the construction of a bottle mouth that received and retained a wafer disc or cap. It was eventually termed the milk bottle cap and revolutionized the milk bottling industry.

Between 1900-1920, not many new bottles were designed or had patents issued. With the introduction of the Owens Semi-Automatic and Automatic Bottle machines, milk bottles became mass produced. Between 1921 and 1945, the greatest number of milk bottles were manufactured and used. After 1945, square milk bottles and paper cartons became common.

Recently, there has been a renewed interest in collecting milk bottles. Two types of milk bottles are especially collectible. The first is the "Baby Top" bottle, which features an embossed baby's face on the upper part of the bottle's neck. The second is the "Cop-the-Cream," which displayed a police officer's head and cap embossed into the neck. The "Baby Top" design was invented by Mike Pecora Sr. in 1936, of Pecora's Dairy in Drums, Pennsylvania. Pecora's Dairy used quart, pint, and half-pint round bottles with pryo printing. Fifteen years after the original baby face was introduced, a "twin face" Baby Top was made with two faces, back to back, on opposite sides of the bottle. The Baby Top and Cop-the-Cream, as well as Tin Tops, are very rare and valuable.

The color mentioned in the following bottle descriptions is the color of the lettering on the bottle.

Magic Milk, green, $10; Monence, Monence, Ill., purple, $10; Crane Dairy, orange, $10; J & J Dairy, Atlantic City, N.J., red, $10; Sunflower, red, $20.

Diamond Dairy/ IV. Ketcham (inside diamond), clear glass, quart, American 1900-1915, $40-50; Property Of The N.Y. Condensed Milk Co., clear glass, quart, American 1900-1915, $40-50; two pints, This Bottle To Be Washed And Returned – Not To Be Bought Or Sold, American 1900-1915, $34-45.

Sweet's Dairy – Fredonia, N.Y., orange, $150.

Four A.G. Smalley & Co. milk bottles – half-pint, pint, quart, and half-gallon, patent April 5, 1898, Boston, Mass., American 1900-1910, $400-425 (total).

Cop the Cream

Alameda Dairy – Alameda, CA Orange quart.	$100		Muhienberg Dairy – Reading, PA Red quart.	$100
Belmont Dairy – Warren, OH Red quart.	$100		Orchard Farm Dairy – The Milk Of Perfection – Orchard Farm – Dallas, PA Red.	$85
Cop The Cream – Bentley's Dairy – Fall River, Mass. Red.	$200		Silver Hill Dairy – Portland, OR Red quart.	$100
Diamond Rock Creamery – Troy, NY Red quart.	$100		West End Dairy – Jeanette, PA Red quart.	$100
Frozen Gold Safe Milk – Sheboygan, WI Black half-pint.	$150		Yearick's Dairy – Mill Hall, PA Red.	$100
Greenleaf Dairy -Petersburg, VA Green.	$85			

Cream Tops

Bellview Farm – Himrod, NY Orange.	$30		Chelsea Farm – Vineland, N.J. Orange.	$30
Burroghs Brothers – Walnut Grove Farm – Knightsen, Calif – Milk & Cream Red.	$65		Cloverleaf Dairy – Stockton, CA Orange.	$65
C.A. Dorr Dairy – Watertown, N.Y. Red.	$50		Damascus Milk – Cream Top Milk – Portland, Ore. Red.	$60
			Gage's Dairy – Ilion, NY Orange.	$30

Geo. Thomas – Brattelboro, VT Orange.	$30
Gnagey's Dairy – Meyersdale, PA Orange.	$30
Hileman Dairy – Altoona, PA Orange.	$30
Hoak's Dairy – Harrisburg, PA Brown.	$20
Hudson Valley – Jacksonville, IL Red.	$50

Maple Tree Dairy – Fall River, MA Orange.	$50
Marshall Dairy – Ithaca, NY Orange.	$20
Miller Reed Dairy – Shippensburg, PA Orange.	$30
Mt. Ararat Farm – Port Deposit, MD Orange.	$30
St. Lawrence Dairy – Reading, PA Red.	$30
Sprague's Dairy – It Whips – Joilet – Lockport Ill. Red.	$90

Pints

A. R. Perley's – Richford, VT Red.	$10
Alba Dairy – Boulder, CO Orange.	$15
Bentley & Son Farm Dairy – Fairbanks, AK Green.	$50
Bryncoed Farm – Harrisburg, PA Blue.	$161

Chestnut Farms/ Chevy Chase Dairy – Washington, DC Red.	$20
Frank H. Rohrer Dairy – Strasburg, PA Red.	$125
H.W. Parthmore Dairy – Highspire, PA Clear glass, embossed.	$92
Hertzler's Dairy – Elizabethtown, PA Brown.	$161

Old Bottles

J. H. Shetter Dairy – Campbelltown, PA Clear glass, embossed, extremely rare – only one known.	$748
March's Deer Park Creamery – Port Jervis, NY Red.	$20
North Nile Dairy – St. Thomas, ND Red.	$35
North Utica Dairy – Utica, NY Red.	$15
Old Dominion Creamery – Orville, WA Orange.	$12

Pleasant View Dairy – B.Z. Miller Clear glass, embossed.	$150
Sanitary Milk Co. – Curtwensville, PA Pyro logo of Mickey Mouse.	$374
Spickler's Dairy – Elizabethtown, PA Orange.	$115
Willow Lane Farm Dairy – Lancaster, PA Clear glass, embossed.	$195
Winchester Creamery – Winchester, VA Red.	$12

Half Pints

Bennett's Dairy – Paris, AZ Orange.	$50
Buttercup Dairy – Alturas, CA Orange.	$35
C.E. Grime's Dairy – Fredericksberg, PA Red, half-pint cream top.	$161
Cadillac Dairy – Cadillac, MI Black.	$25
Hauck Dairy Farm- Harrisburg, PA Clear glass, embossed.	$138

Highs Dairy – Baltimore, MD Red.	$30
Hoopers Dairy – Jamestown, NY Red.	$25
J.K.Stauffer – Mount Joy, PA Clear glass, embossed.	$115
Katahoin Creamery – Caribou & Ft. Fairfield, ME Green.	$15
Kenolie Dairy – Newfane, VT Red.	$30

Linton & Linton – Dairy Products Red.	$50	**Ravenswood Milk, McCook, NE** Black.	$50
Log Cabin Farms Dairy – Lititz, PA Clear glass, embossed, rare.	$127	**Red Cannon Dairy – Cannon City, CO** Red.	$20
Mac Kenzie – Guernsey Milk – Acre Wide Farm – Keene, N.H. Red.	$35	**Reiss Dairy – Sikeston, MO** Red.	$15
Mission Dairy – Phoenix, AZ Red.	$25	**Scott Key Dairy – Frederick, MD** Black.	$30
Missouri Pacific Lines Red.	$45	**Superior Dairy – Frederick, MD** Red.	$30
Mountain Valley Dairy – Manheim, PA Clear glass, embossed.	$230	**Thomas Dairy – Auburn, CA** Black.	$50
		Wilson Dairy, Wilson, AZ Red.	$50
Palmer's Dairy – Middlebury, VT Black.	$50	**Witchwood Farm – Springhouse, PA** Red.	$50

Quarts

Anchorage Dairy – Anchorage, AK Red, rare.	$150	**Bram City Dairy – W. C. Butler – Bessemer, AL** Green.	$100
Avon Mills Dairy – Sylacauga, AL Red, semi-rare.	$70	**Burbiano Dairy – Santa Barbara, CA** Red.	$70
Bluebird Dairy Co. – Riverside, CA Green and blue.	$90	**C.M. Cooley Dairy – Mount Joy, PA** Clear glass, embossed.	$185

Old Bottles

Clover Dairy – Torrington, CT Green.	$30
Clover Dairy – Seal of Quallty – Chlppewa Falls, Wisconsin Orange.	$80
Cloverleaf Dairy – Progress, PA Red and black.	$70
Comstock Farm Dairy – Pueblo, CO Black.	$50
Cramer & Aument Dairy – McGovernville, PA Clear glass, embossed.	$161
Creamer's Dairy – Fairbanks, AK Black and red, rare.	$200
It's The Cream – Curly's Dairy – Phone 8783 – Salem, Ore. Green and red.	$85
Douglaston Manor Farm (Flying Goose) Pulaski, NY Black.	$100
East End Dairy – large "E" on reverse side – decoration on neck – circa 1934 (made to contain eggnog) Bright emerald green, embossed, extremely rare.	$3,740
Fred H. Rabe & Sons – Dairy Products – Elmhurst, IL Red and yellow.	$110

Fry's Sanitary Dairy – Milford, DE Red.	$50
Green Valley Farms – Tucson, AZ Green.	$250
J. B. Bayshore Dairy – Annville, PA Clear glass, embossed, rare.	$375
Joe Rosser & Sons Dairy – Dairy Farm – Bessemer, AL Blue, semi-rare.	$70
John B. Henry Dairy – Rohrerstown, PA Clear glass, embossed.	$195
Kennedy Dairy, Huntington, W. VA Red.	$80
Kilgore's Dairy – Redmond, Oregon Green.	$95
Kruft Jersey Dairy – Phoenix, Arizona Red and orange.	$150
Lindsey Dairy Products – Safford, AZ Black lettering on red background.	$50
Missouri Pacific Lines Railroad Clear glass, embossed.	$69
Pendergast Bros. Dairy – Tuscon, AZ Red.	$50

Pocahontas Dairy – Pocahontas, AR Black.	$80		**Standard Dairy Co. – Wallace, Idaho** Red.	$150
Serra Oaks Dairy – Sacramento, CA Red.	$70		**W.A. W. Dairy Farm – Elizabethtown, PA** Clear glass, embossed on top.	$115
			W. H. Wolf Dairy – Royalton, PA- Circa 1914 Clear glass, embossed, rare.	$460

Half Gallon

Borden's – Saguaro Cactus – Phoenix, Arizona Orange.	$60

Gallon

Borden's Red.	$35		**Olson Dairies – Butler, PA** Black.	$25
Capital Dairies – IL Red.	$50		**Sutherland Dairy – Aliquippa, PA** Red.	$25
Farmers Co-op – Connellsville, PA Orange.	$25		**The Dells of Wisconsin, WI** Red.	$50
Furer's Milk – PA Orange.	$50		**United Dairy Co. – Ambridge, PA** Black.	$25
Harmony Dairy Red.	$25		**Valentine's – Smithton & West Newton, PA** Red.	$25
I.X.L. Creamery Inc. – Pasteurized Dairy Products – Friedens, PA Red.	$25		**Walker's Creamery – Warren, PA** Red.	$25

Coffee Creamers

Brookfield Dairy – **Westfield. CT** Orange.	$25		**Richards Dairy –** **Newark, DE** Orange.	$35
Greenhill Golden **Guernsey – Greenhill, DE** Orange.	$50		**Silverside Dairy –** **Wilmington, DE** Orange.	$35
Johnson's Dairy - **Cooperstown, N.Y.** Black.	$35		**Silver Hill – Milford, DE** Red.	$35
Mayfair Diner – **Waterford, CT** Green.	$30		**Twin Cedar Dairy –** **McClare, PA** Red.	$40
N. Mex Milk Prods. Inc. – **Belen, NM** Red.	$35		**Young's Dairy – Twin** **Falls, Idaho** Red.	$30
Pompell Restaurant – **New Castle, DE** Black.	$35			

Miscellaneous

Absolutely – Pure Milk (man milking cow) **The Milk Protector – To Be Used Only As** **Designated – Milk – & – Cream – Jar** Clear glass, quart, smooth base (embossed: Thatcher Mfg. Co – Potsdam, N.Y.), tooled lip, original metal clamp, American, 1890-1910.	$350-400	
Big Elm – Dairy – Company – One Quart – **Liquid – Registered** Bright yellow green, 9-1/8", quart, smooth base, ABM lip with cap seat, American, 20th century.	$150-200	

One Quart – Liquid – Brighton – Place Dairy – Rochester, N.Y. Bright yellow green, quart, smooth base (38), ABM lip with cap seat, American, 20th century.	$250-300	
Two bottles, Chicago Sterilized – Milk Co. – Chicago, Ill. – Chicago-Sterilized Milk – Company Pale aqua, 8" and 12-1/4", smooth bases (S.B.&G), tooled blob tops, original lighting style-wire closures, American, 1890-1900.	$200-250	
Milk For Infants – From – Dr. Brush's Farm – This Bottle – To Be Washed – and Returned Amber, 7-1/8", pint, smooth base (GI), tooled lip, original metal cap and wire closure, American, 1910-1920.	$400-450	

Mineral Water

The drinking of water from mineral springs was popular for a full century with the peak period falling between 1860 and 1900. Consequently, most collectible bottles were produced during these years. While the earliest bottles have a pontil mark, the majority of them have a smooth base. The sources of these natural waters came from various springs that were high in carbonates (alkaline), sulfurous compounds, various salts, and often carbonated naturally.

The waters were also thought to possess medical and therapeutic qualities and benefits. Spring water was also another popular name often used for natural or unaltered mineral water.

Although the shapes and sizes of mineral bottles are not very creative, the lettering and design, both embossed and on paper, are bold and interesting. Mineral bottles can range in size from seven inches up to 14 inches. Most were cork-stopped, manufactured in a variety of colors, and embossed with the name of the glasshouse manufacturer. In order to withstand the strong gaseous pressures of the contents and the severe high-pressure bottling process, most bottles produced were manufactured with heavy, thick glass and were reused as often as possible.

Star Spring Co. (five-pointed star) Saratoga, yellow amber, pint, applied top, 1865-1875, $100-125.

Haskins Spring Co. – H. – Shutesbury-Mass – H.S.CO., emerald green, pint, applied top, 1865-1875, $1,500-1,600.

A.W. Knapp's – Soda or Mineral – Waters – New York – R – Improved – Patent Medium emerald green, 6-7/8", iron pontil, applied tapered collar top, American, 1840-1860.	$400-450	
A.W. Rapp's – Improved – Patent – Mineral Water – Soda Waters (backwards "S") – R – New York Rich blue green, 7-1/8", scarred base, applied tapered collar top, American, 1840-1860.	$500-600	
Barton & Davis's – Patent – Mineral – Waters Blue green, 7-3/8", iron pontil on unusual pointed kick-up, applied top American, 1845-1855.	$2,300-2,500	
C.A. Reiners & Co. – 723 – Turk ST. – S.F. – Improved – Trade Mark (motif of man in the moon and stars) Mineral Water Light blue green, 7-1/2", smooth base, applied top, American, 1875-1882.	$275-375	
Campbell Mineral Spring Co. – C – Burlington Aqua, quart, smooth base, applied tapered collar top, American, 1865-1875.	$900-1,000	
Champion Spouting Spring Co. – Saratoga – Springs N.Y. – Saratoga Mineral – C – Springs – S Co. S – Limited Blue aqua, quart, smooth base, applied tapered collar top, American, 1865-1875.	$2,000-2,500	
Congress Hall – Mineral Water Blue aqua, pint, smooth base, applied top, extremely rare, American, 1865-1875.	$2,500-3,000	

Covert – Morristown – N.J. – Superior Mineral – Water Cobalt blue, 7", mug base panels, iron pontil applied top, American, 1840-1860.	$400-450	
Dr. C.L. Whitney's – Patent Soda & – Mineral Water – N.Y. Medium blue green, 7-3/4", iron pontil, applied tapered collar top, extremely rare, American, 1840-1860.	$400-500	
Davenport & Cos. – Mineral & Soda – Waters – D.G. & K – Patent Deep blue green, 6-7/8", pontil scarred base, applied top, American, 1830-1840.	$600-700	
Dyottville Glass Works – Philada – A.W. Rapp – New York – Mineral Water – R – This Bottle – Is Never Sold Aqua, 7-1/8", iron pontil, applied blob top, American, 1840-1860.	$500-600	
F. Gleason – Sarsaparilla & Lemon – Mineral Water- Rochester Cobalt blue, 7-1/2", 10-sided, iron pontil, applied top, American, 1840-1860.	$400-500	
Fithian's – Mineral Water – Bridgeton – N.J. – This Bottle – Is Never Sold Medium blue green, 7-1/2", iron pontil, applied top, American, 1840-1860.	$800-900	
Franklin Spring – Mineral Water – Ballston Spa – Saratoga, Co. –N.Y. Yellow olive green, pint, smooth base, applied top, American, 1865-1875.	$900-1,000	

Geo. Schoch & Co – Mineral – Waters – Philada- Union Glass Works Medium cobalt blue, 7-5/8", eight-sided, iron pontil, applied top, extremely rare, American, 1840-1860.	$1,800-2,000	
Geyser Spring – Saratoga Springs – New York – Avery. N. Lord – 66 Broad St. – Utica. N.Y. Blue aqua, quart, smooth base (A&DHC), applied top, American, 1865-1875.	$200-225	
Gleason - & Cole – Pittsbg – Mineral Water Deep cobalt blue, 7-3/4", 10-sided, iron pontil, applied top, American, 1840-1860.	$250-300	
Gleason – & Cole – Pittsbg – Mineral Water Yellow olive, 7-3/4", 10-sided, iron pontil, applied sloping collar top, American, 1840-1860.	$500-600	
Hamilton (in slug plate) – & Church – Excelsior Mineral Water – Brooklyn Medium blue green, 7-1/8", iron pontil, applied top, American, 1840-1860.	$700-800	
Heiss' – Superior – Soda Or – Mineral – Water – H Medium sapphire blue, 7-5/8", 10-sided, iron pontil, applied top, American, 1840-1860.	$450-500	
Hulshizer & Co. (in slug plate) – Premium – Mineral – Water Emerald green, 7-3/4", eight-sided, iron pontil, applied blob top, scarce, American, 1840-1860.	$400-500	
Hulshizer & Co. (in slug plate) – Premium – Mineral – Water Emerald green, 7-3/4", eight-sided, iron pontil, applied blob top, scarce, American, 1840-1860.	$500-700	

Old Bottles

Improved – Mineral Water Deep teal, 7-1/4", iron pontil, applied blob top, American, 1840-1860.	$700-800	
J. & H. Casper (in arched slug plate) – Mineral Water – Lancaster, PA Medium blue green, 7-1/2", iron pontil, applied top, American, 1840-1860.	$100-125	
J.H.V. – Premium – Soda or Mineral – Water – Troy Sapphire blue, 7-1/8", 10-sided, iron pontil, applied blob top, rare, American, 1840-1860.	$500-600	
J. Dowall (in slug plate) – Union Glass Works Phila – Superior – Mineral Water Deep cobalt blue, 7-1/2", mug base, iron pontil, applied blob top, extremely rare, American, 1850-1860.	$2,800-3,000	
J. Lamppin's – Mineral Water – Utica – Utica Bottling – Establishment Medium cobalt blue, 7", iron pontil, applied blob top, rare, American, 1840-1860.	$350-400	
J. & W. Coles – Superior – Soda & - Mineral Water – Staten Island Medium cobalt blue, 7-3/8", iron pontil, applied blob top, American, 1840-1860.	$350-400	
John Boardman – New York – Mineral Waters Light sapphire blue, 7-1/8", eight-sided, iron pontil applied top, American, 1840-1860.	$800-900	
John Shrink's – Superior – Mineral Water – Cleveland – This Bottle – To Be Returned Medium sapphire blue, 7-3/8", iron pontil, applied tapered collar top, American, 1840-1860.	$700-800	
Napa (five-pointed star) Wood's (five-pointed star) Natural – Mineral Water – T.W.F.A.G.T. Deep cobalt blue, 7-1/4", smooth base, applied blob top, American, 1870-1880.	$500-600	

Napa – Soda –Natural – Mineral Water – T.A.W. Medium green, 7-1/4", smooth base, applied top, scarce, American, 1861-1862.	$200-250	
M.A.Rue – Cranbury – N.J. (in slug plate) – Mineral – Waters Medium emerald green, 7-1/4", iron pontil, applied top, American, 1840-1860.	$350-400	
M.T. Crawford – Springfield (in slug plate) – Union Glass Works Phil.A Superior – Mineral-Water Deep cobalt blue, 7-1/2", paneled "mug" base, iron pontil, applied blob top, American, 1840-1860.	$250-300	
Poland – Water – Poland Mineral Spring Water (monogram) H. Riker & Son's Proprietor Clear glass, 11-3/4", pontil scarred base, applied top, 95% multicolored paint, American, 1855-1865.	$900-1,000	
Powell & Dr. Burns – Mineral Water – Burlington – N.J. Emerald green, 7-1/4", eight-sided, iron pontil, applied sloping collar top, rare, American, 1840-1860.	$1,800-2,000	
R.C. Worthendyke – Agent – Superior – Mineral Water – XX Cobalt blue, 7-1/4", eight-sided, iron pontil, applied top, scarce, American, 1840-1860.	$800-900	
Round Lake – Mineral – Water – Saratoga, Co. Yellow amber, pint, smooth base, applied top, American, 1865-1875.	$2,500-3,000	
Round Lake – Mineral – Water – Saratoga, Co. Orange amber, quart, smooth base, applied double collar top, extremely rare, American, 1865-1875.	$5,000-6,000	

Old Bottles

S. Keys – Burlington – N.J. (in slug plate) – Union Glass Works Philad. – Superior – Mineral Water Cobalt blue, 7-1/8", mug base, iron pontil, applied blob top, American, 1845-1860.	$500-600	
S.Smith – Knickerbocker – Mineral & Soda Waters – New York Aqua, 6-3/4", iron pontil, applied top, American, 1840-1860.	$800-900	
S.Smith – Knickerbocker – Mineral & Soda Waters – New York Medium emerald green, 7", iron pontil, applied tapered collar top, American, 1840-1860.	$900-1,000	
S. Wiestling – H – Union Glass Works Phila – Superior – Mineral Water Medium cobalt blue, 7-1/2", mug base, iron pontil, applied top, American, 1840-1860.	$400-500	
St. Regis – Water – Massena Springs Medium teal blue, pint, smooth base, applied top, American, 1865-1875.	$200-225	
Seitz & Bro. – Easton, PA. – Premium – Mineral – Water Medium sapphire blue, 7-1/8", eight-sided, iron pontil applied blob top, American, 1840-1860.	$350-400	
Sharon – Sulphur – Water – John H. Gardner & Son – Sharon Springs – N.Y. Medium blue green, pint, smooth base, applied top, American, 1865-1875.	$400-425	

Smith's – Mineral - & Soda Water – New York –S Blue green, 7-5/8", iron pontil, applied top, American, 1835-1850.	$500-600	
Superior – Mineral Water – Union Glass Works Emerald green, 7-5/8", mug base, iron pontil, applied top, American, 1840-1860.	$450-500	
Suydam & Dubois – N.Y. –Union Glass Works Philada – Superior Mineral Water Medium cobalt blue, 7-1/2", mug base, iron pontil, applied tapered collar top, extremely rare, American, 1840-1860.	$2,000-2,200	
Syracuse Springs – Excelsior Deep reddish amber, quart, smooth base, applied top, American, 1865-1975.	$700-800	
Syracuse Springs – D – Excelsior – A.J. Delatour – New York Yellow amber, pint, smooth base, applied top, rare, American, 1865-1875.	$375-500	
Tarr, Smith. & Clark – Boston – Mineral Water Medium green, 7-1/4", iron pontil, applied blob top, American, 1840-1860.	$275-375	

Twitchell – T – Philada – Superior – T – Mineral Water Teal blue, 7-1/8", iron pontil, applied "top hat" top, American, 1840-1860.	**$100-125**	
Utica Bottling – A.L. Edic. – Establishment – Superior – Mineral Waters Light green, 7", iron pontil, applied blob top, American, 1840-1860.	**$400-600**	
W. Eagle's – Superior – Soda & Mineral – Waters W.E. – N. York Medium green, 6-3/4", iron pontil, applied blob top, American, 1840-1860.	**$300-350**	
W. Eagle's – Superior – Soda & Mineral – Waters W.E. – N. York Medium teal blue, 7", iron pontil, applied tapered collar top, American, 1840-1860.	**$250-300**	
W. Eagle's – Superior – Soda & Mineral – Waters W.E. – N. York Deep emerald green, 7-1/2", iron pontil, applied tapered collar top, extremely rare, American, 1840-1860.	**$500-600**	
WM. A. Carpenter's – Mineral Water – Hudson –N.Y. Medium green, 7", eight-sided, iron pontil, applied top, American, 1845-1860.	**$400-450**	
W.M. Fraser - & Co. – Soda Or Mineral – Waters – New York – Improved – F-Patent Medium emerald green, 6-3/4", iron pontil, applied tapered collar top, extremely rare, American, 1840-1860.	**$900-1,000**	

W.M. Fraser - & Co. – Soda Or Mineral – Waters – New York – Improved – F-Patent Deep emerald green, 7", iron pontil, applied tapered collar top, extremely rare, American, 1840-1860.	$450-500	
WM P. Davis & Co – Excelsior – Mineral Water – Brooklyn Emerald green, 7-1/4 ", eight-sided, iron pontil, applied blob top, American, 1940-1860.	$1,300-1,500	
WM P. Davis & Co – Excelsior – Mineral Water – Brooklyn Light aqua, 7-1/2", eight-sided, iron pontil, applied blob top, American, 1940-1860.	$800-900	
WM. W. Lappeus – Premium – Soda Or – Mineral – Waters – Albany Deep cobalt blue, 7-1/4", 10-sided, iron pontil, applied blob top, American, 1840-1860.	$350-400	
Washington – Lithia Well – Mineral Water – Balston Spa – N.Y. Aqua, pint, 7-7/8", smooth base, applied top, American, 1865-1875.	$150-200	
Washington – Lithia Well – Mineral Water – Balston Spa – N.Y. Aqua, pint, 7-3/4", smooth base, applied top, rare, American, 1865-1875.	$600-700	
Weddle's – Mineral Water – West – Chester Medium blue green, 7-1/2", iron pontil, applied tapered collar top, American, 1840-1860.	$400-450	
Wood's – Napa – Soda-Natural – Mineral Water – T.A.W. Cobalt blue, 7-3/4", smooth base, applied top, American, 1868-1873.	$200-250	

Patriotic

At the beginning of World War II, the bottling industry, specifically milk bottling manufacturers, began a patriotic campaign that had never been experienced in American history. World War II resulted in some of the most unique and collectible bottles with war slogans depicting tanks, soldiers, fighter planes, "V" for victory signs, and slogans about Pear Harbor. While some bottles, especially milk bottles, were colorful and had detailed graphics, many displayed simple slogans such as "Buy War Savings Bonds – Keep it Up" and "Buy Bonds and Stamps" on the wings of bombers and fighter planes.

The applied color label (ACL) soda pop bottle was conceived in the 1930s when Prohibition forced brewing companies to sell soda pop. During World War II, soda pop bottlers throughout the United States created labels that will forever preserve unique patriotic moments and figures in American history, such as American flags, the Statue of Liberty, "V" symbol, fighter planes, fighter pilots, soldiers, and stars and stripes. Bottles with images of Uncle Sam and the American flag are the most popular.

Other groups of bottles such as historical flasks, figurals, and Jim Beam bottles have depicted patriotic figures, embossed images, and paintings of important patriotic milestones in the history of America. In fact, there are 25 different types of flasks representing the flag as a symbol of patriotism, a rallying cry for battle, and the re-establishment of the Union following the Civil War.

War Bonds For Victory –
(depiction of Uncle Sam drinking
milk) – Milk For Strength – Athens
Co-Operative Creamery, Athens,
GA, $100-125.

Milk Bottles, War Slogans

Cream Tops

Buy War Bonds – Walnut Grove Dairy – Alton, IL Red.	$75	**It Whips – Food For Victory – Careful Wartime Meal Planning- Will Help Us Win** Orange.	$75
It Whips – America Has A Job To Do! (depiction of pilot with "V" for victory sign) – Shamrock Dairy – Tucson, AZ Orange.	$75	**Uncle Sam Prescribes Milk – (depiction of Uncle Sam shaking hands with soldier)** Black and orange, rare.	$100

Half Pints

America – Speed Victory – Aldren's Dairy Red.	$25	**Help Relieve The Bottle Shortage (Korean War bottle dated 1953) – Woodson Dairy, Red Hill, PA** Orange.	$25
Buy Bonds For Victory – Dairylea Black.	$35		
For Victory – Buy War Bonds – To Keep Your Freedom – D.R.D.A – Denver, CO Orange.	$75	**They Guard Your Home (depiction of soldier, sailor, marine) We Guard Your Health – On Base – Covington, OH** Orange.	$35

Old Bottles

Quarts

Buy More War Bonds Today (depiction of Statue of Liberty) – Haskels Dairy, Augusta, GA Green.	$50
City Dairy – Salisbury, MD (front) – There Is No Substitute For Liberty (depiction of Statue of Liberty) – There Is No Substitute For Milk (back) Green.	$100
Conserve – For Victory – Buy War Bonds and Stamps – Clarksburg Dairy, Clarksburg, WV Red.	$85
America At War – Our Home Front Support Our Fighting Front (depiction of factory worker) – Tuschlag Bros, Greenville, PA Green, semi-rare.	$150
Buy War Bonds and Stamps – J. F. McAdams & Bros., Cheasea, MA (depiction of tank)–Rare Red and blue.	$250
Buy War Bonds – Everybody – Every Payday Red and blue, semi-rare.	$150
Drink – Augusta Dairies – Augusta, GA (front) – God Bless America-Augusta (depiction of Statue of Liberty) Dairies – Land Of The Free (back) Orange.	$90
Erving Denver – Frink – The Best – Milk (front) –Keep American Strong – depiction of young girl in front of eagle – Drink More Milk (back) Red.	$100
For Freedom – Buy War Bonds (depiction of eagle) For Health Red, rare.	$100
For Safety Buy War Bonds (depiction of Minuteman) Brown, semi rare.	$150
For Victory – Buy – United States Savings Bonds and Stamps – Frear Dairy, Dover, DE Brown.	$70
Keep 'Em Flying (Depiction of Fighter Plane) Buy War Bonds and Stamps Blue.	$100

Keep Them Rolling (depiction of tanks and airplanes) Buy Bonds and Stamps – Haskell's Dairy, Augusta, GA Green, semi-rare.	$250	**Store Bottle – Clovis Quality Dairy (in circle) – Behymer – Minnewawa – Clovis, CAL. (front) – American Is A Great Place To Live – (depiction of Statue of Liberty in front of United States) – Let's Keep It That Way** Red.	$90
Let's Go! – U.S.A. (depiction of Uncle Sam marching behind soldier, sailor, marine) Green, extremely rare.	$450		
Nob Hill Milk – IXL – It Is Good – Colo. Springs, Cold (front) – For Victory – Buy – United States Savings Bonds and Stamps (back) Black.	$110	**Sunburst – Grade – Milk – Pasteurized – Registered – Union Dairy Company – Union City, Tenn. (front) – Food Fight Too – Use It Wisely – Plan All Meals For Victory (back)** Orange.	$100
Remember Pearl Harbor ('V" for victory sign) Be Prepared – Hi Grade Dairy, Harrington, DE Red, rare.	$250	**The Navy – Our Protector (depiction of navy destroyer)** Red, rare.	$250
Shrum's Dairy - Phone 63 – Jeanette, PA (front) – (depiction of eagle) National-Defense – Starts With – Good Health – Build America's Future – Drink More Milk (back) Green.	$115	**Unity – Freedom – Equality (depiction of eagle and American flag)** Red, rare.	$125
		Work (depiction of fighting soldier) For Victory Brown, rare.	$150

America (eagle) – First – Last – Always, Everson's, Fort Plain, NY, $75-100.

Back Their Attack – Buy More War Bonds (depiction of soldiers fighting) – Brink Milk for Health, Cloverleaf Diary, Springfield, MO, $150-200.

God Bless America – (depiction of Statue of Liberty inside wreath), Agusta Dairies, Augusta, GA, $75-100.

The United States is a Sound Investment (Statue of Liberty) – Buy War Bonds and Stamps, Diamond Rock Creamery, Troy, NY, $200-250.

For Our Defense – Pursuit Plane – 350 M.P.H. One Man (depiction of fighter plane) – Milk Defender of Health, Valley Dairy, Cochranton, PA, $150-200.

Make America Strong (depiction of young girl in front of eagle) – Drink More Milk, Frink Milk, Denver, CO, $50-75.

Figurals

Bust of Washington – "Washington – Patd April 11, 1876" Clear glass, 4-1/4", rough sheared and ground base, missing lid, token giveaway at the American Centennial held in Philadelphia in 1876, American, 1876.	$250-300	
Uncle Sam Hat Milk glass, 2-1/2", red and blue paint, smooth base, tooled rim, original tin insert and cardboard closure (Republican nominees, Wm. H. Taft, President, and James S. Sherman, Vice President), (made for 1908 presidential campaign), American, 1908.	$500-600	
Statue Of Liberty Opaque milk glass base, original brass Statue of Liberty stopper, 9-1/4", smooth base, ground lip, American, 1892-1900.	$250-300	
Statue Of Liberty Milk glass base, 15-3/8", original cast metal Statue of Liberty, smooth base, ground lip, American, 1885-1895.	$500-600	
Liberty Bell – E. Hoyt & Co. – Celebrated – Perfumers – ESTB. 1868 – Sesqui Centennial – 1776-1926 Clear glass, 2-1/2", smooth base, tooled lip with original neck foil, rare sesquicentennial item, American, 1926.	$250-350	
Liberty Bell – Proclaim Liberty – Throughout The Land – Unto All The Inhabitants – There Of LevXXVX – Phila. – MDCCLIII Amber, 5-1/8", bell shape, smooth base, sheared and ground lip, original metal screw-on cap, American, 1885-1900.	$150-175	
Liberty Bell – Proclaim Liberty Throughout – All The Land – 1776 – Exposition – 1876 - Patnd Nov 17, 1874 –By – S.C. Upham Phila Clear glass, 6" (including stopper), smooth base, tooled lip with original stopper and contents, American, 1876.	$200-225	

Flasks/Bottles/Pottery Jugs

Doulton pottery whiskey jug stamped on base: "Dewars White Label Whisky" Rd. No 504,944-Royal Doulton England Multicolored glazings of red, white, and blue over raised decoration of Uncle Sam smoking long-stemmed pipe, 7-3/8", English, 1907-1910.	$250-300	
Eagle – Eagle Olive amber, pint, pontil scarred base, sheared lip, American, 1825-1935.	$450-475	
Eagle on Flag – Morning Glory Deep blue aqua, pint, open pontil, sheared and tooled lip, American, 1835-1845.	$700-800	
Label under glass back bar bottle – ginger (depiction of American flags, eagle with shield, and Liberty Bell) Clear glass, 10-3/4", smooth base (E. Packham, Jr / Patented / July 13th 1897 / Baltimore, MD), tooled top, rare, American, 1897-1910.	$4,000-4,300	
Union / clasped hands – eagle with banner and shield Amber, half-pint, smooth base, applied top, American, 1855-1870.	$200-225	
Label under glass military whiskey flask – 33rd National Encampment G.A.R. 1899 – Philadelphia, PA – Compliments of J.A. Brennan, US, embossed on reverse side with eagle on flag and two unfurling American flags Clear glass, 4-1/2", canteen-type flask, smooth base, original metal screw-on cap, American, 1899.	$900-1,000	
Label under glass whiskey flask – (depiction of American soldier and sailor shaking hands with embossed eagle on reverse) Clear glass, 5-7/8", pocket flask, smooth base, sheared and ground lip, original metal screw-on cap and shot glass, American, 1898-1900, commemorative flask from the Spanish American War, which lasted only 10 weeks.	$1,000-1,100.	

Jim Beam Bottles

D-Day 1984 Depiction of combat boot stepping onto three D-Day assault beaches: Gold, Omaha, and Utah.	**$18-22**
Marine Corps 1975 – "Once a Marine-Always a Marine" – monument at Iwo Jima (on reverse side) Replica of canteen.	**$40-45**
Marine "Devil Dog" 1979 Replica of the Marine mascot, the bulldog, wearing World War I helmet.	**$40-45**

Short Timer 1975 Replica of combat helmet on combat boots.	**$25-30**
Statue of Liberty 1975 Depiction of Statue of Liberty with "Give me your tired…" on reverse.	**$20-25**
101st Airborne 1977 – "101st Airborne Division – Screaming Eagles" Replica of flying eagle on white base.	**$10-15**

Soda Bottles

Aircraft Beverages – Stanford, CT. – 1958 Clear glass, red and white, 26 oz., depiction of four-propeller cargo plane.	**$36**
Dunn's – Sedalia, MO – 1954 Clear glass, red, white and green, 10 oz., depiction of Statue of Liberty in front of clouds.	**$22**
Pure Club Seltzer Water – Washington, PA – 1948 Clear glass, red, white and blue, 28 oz., depiction of George Washington on shield of red stripes.	**$46**

Victory Cola –Pacoima, CA. – 1940-1945 Green glass, white, 12 oz., eagle on shield above the Stars and Stripes.	**$175**
Victory Root Beer – Pacoima, CA – 1947 Clear glass, red and white, 10 oz., depiction of Stars and Stripes banner.	**$65**
Victory Root Beer – Pacoima, CA – 1947 Clear glass, black and white, 10 oz., depiction of Stars and Stripes banner.	**$65**

Uncle Sam Beverages – Houston, TX – 1947 Clear glass, red and yellow, 7 oz., depiction of Uncle Sam surrounded by stars.	$75

Yankee Doodle Old Fashioned Root Beer – Los Angeles, CA – 1940-1945 Clear glass, red and white, 10 oz., depiction of Minuteman with fife.	$20

Miscellaneous

Fraternal shaving mug – F.O.E (Fraternal Order of Eagles) – American eagle above two flags – A.A. Gloninger Porcelain mug, 4", smooth base (Koken Barber Supply Co.), American, 1885-1925.	$175-200

Patriotic shaving mug made for "Pietro" Porcelain mug, 3-7/8", smooth base, depiction of American and Italian flags separated by eagle, American, 1885-1925.	$50-75

Occupational shaving mug made for H.C. Major, Company H, depicting Union Soldier with rifle Porcelain mug, 3-5/8", smooth base (T & V France), rare mug made for veteran of Civil War, American, 1890-1925.	$1,900-2,000

Early Times – Bicentennial Limited Editions – vintage whiskey commemorative decanter Porcelain cream-colored decanter, "1886 – (eagle with American flag) – 1976," American Revolution bicentennial – large colored portrait of signing of Declaration of Independence – red stars "Nevada" red stars, American, 1976.	$25-35

Pattern-Molded

A pattern-molded bottle is one that is blown into a ribbed or pattern mold. This group includes globular and chestnut flasks. One of these, the Stiegel bottle, manufactured during the late 18th century, is considered very rare and valuable. The two types of Stiegel bottles manufactured at the Stiegel Glass Factory are the Diamond Daisy and Hexagon designs.

Since pattern-molded bottles are among the more valuable and rare pieces, collectors need to familiarize themselves with the types, sizes, colors, and various manufacturers of these bottles.

Midwestern globular bottle, deep blue aqua, 7-3/8", 24 rib-pattern swirled to right, pontil scarred base, outward rolled lip, 1815-1835, $350-400.	Club bottle, blue aqua, 7-7/8", 24 rib-pattern swirled to right, pontil scarred base, outward rolled lip, 1810-1825, $125-150.	Midwestern globular bottle, deep blue aqua, 7-7/8", 24 vertical rib-pattern swirled to right, 1815-1835, $200-225.	Midwestern chestnut flask, clear glass, 5-1/8", pontil scarred base, sheared and tooled lip, pontil scarred base, sheared and tooled top, 1820-1835, $1,000-1,300.

Chestnut flask Deep cobalt blue, 3-5/8", 20 rib-pattern swirled to right, pontil scarred base, sheared and tooled lip, American, 1815-1835.	**$200-225**	
Pattern-molded pocket flask Cobalt blue, 3-7/8", 16 broken-rib pattern swirled to right, pontil scarred base, sheared and tooled flared out lip, German, 1815-1830.	**$200-250**	
Pattern-molded chestnut flask Light yellow green, 4-1/2", 24 vertical-rib pattern, pontil scarred base, sheared and tooled lip, American, 1815-1835.	**$350-400**	
Midwestern chestnut flask Light golden yellow amber, 4-1/2", 24 vertical rib pattern, pontil scarred base, sheared lip, American, 1915-1835.	**$350-400**	
Midwestern chestnut flask Medium yellow amber, 4-1/2", 24 vertical-rib pattern, pontil scarred base, sheared lip, American, 1915-1835.	**$450-500**	
Rib-pattern chestnut flask Medium yellow amber, 5", 24 rib-pattern swirled to left, pontil scarred base, sheared and tooled lip, American, 1815-1835.	**$250-300**	

Old Bottles

Midwestern chestnut flask Blue aqua, 5", 24 vertical-rib pattern, pontil scarred base, sheared lip, American, 1815-1835.	**$75-100**
Pattern-molded chestnut flask Medium amber, 5", 24 vertical-rib pattern, pontil scarred base, sheared and tooled lip, American, 1815-1835.	**$200-250**
Pattern-molded chestnut flask Yellow amber with olive tone, 5-1/8", 24 rib-pattern swirled to left, pontil scarred base, sheared and tooled lip, American, 1815-1830.	**$300-450**
Pattern-molded chestnut flask Yellow amber, 5-3/8", 10-diamond pattern, pontil scarred base, sheared and tooled lip, American, 1825-1835.	**$600-700**
Pattern-molded chestnut flask Amber, 5-1/4", 24 vertical rib-pattern, pontil scarred base, sheared and tooled lip, American, 1815-1830.	**$200-275**

Pattern-molded chestnut flask Deep amber, 5-1/2", 24 vertical-rib pattern, pontil scarred base, sheared and tooled lip, American, 1815-1835.	$300-350	
Pattern-molded handled chestnut flask Medium green, 5-1/2", 24 vertical-rib pattern, pontil scarred base, applied top and unusual rat-tail handle, American, 1820-1835.	$450-500	
Pattern-molded chestnut flask Citron, 5-3/8", 20 rib-pattern with slight twist to left, pontil scarred base, sheared and tooled lip, American, 1815-1825.	$350-400	
Pattern-molded 10-diamond chestnut flask Yellow with amber tone, 5-3/8", pontil scarred base, sheared lip, American, 1815-1830.	$600-800	
Pattern-molded pocket flask Light blue green, 5-7/8", 16 alternating rows of flutes and diamonds, pontil scarred base, sheared and tooled lip, American, 1810-1820.	$200-250	
Pattern-molded chestnut flask Pink amethyst, 5-7/8", 18 vertical-rib pattern, pontil scarred base, sheared and tooled lip, American, 1815-1835.	$600-700	

Midwestern chestnut flask Green aqua, 6", 16 rib-pattern to left, pontil scarred base, sheared and tooled lip, American, 1820-1835.	**$250-300**
Pattern-molded pocket flask Medium pink amethyst, 6-1/4", pontil scarred base, 18 rib-pattern, sheared and tooled lip, Germany, 1795-1820.	**$400-600**
Pattern-molded pocket flask Clear glass with amethyst tint, 6-1/4", pontil scarred base, sheared and tooled lip, American, 1800-1810.	**$250-350**
Midwestern chestnut flask Green aqua, 6-3/8", 18 rib-pattern to left, pontil scarred base, tooled and sheared lip, American, 1815-1835.	**$100-125**
Pattern-molded chestnut form flask Yellow olive with amber tone, 6-5/8", 16 broken rib-pattern, pontil scarred base, applied top, American, 1820-1835.	**$300-350**

Pattern-molded pocket flask Light apple green, 6-3/4", 24 rib-pattern twisted to left, open pontil, sheared and tooled lip, American, 1800-1815.	$150-200	
Chestnut form pocket flask Deep cobalt blue, 6-3/4", 18 vertical rib-pattern, open pontil, sheared and tooled lip, American, 1815-1830.	$500-600	
Midwestern globular bottle Deep blue aqua, 7-1/8", 24 vertical rib-pattern, pontil scarred base, rolled lip, American, 1815-1835.	$350-400	
Midwestern globular bottle Medium apple green, 7-5/8", 24 rib-pattern swirled to left, pontil scarred base, outward rolled lip, American, 1815-1835.	$1,000-1,300	
Midwestern club bottle Green aqua, 7-5/8", 16 vertical rib-pattern, pontil scarred base, applied lip, American, 1815-1835.	$250-300	
Midwestern globular bottle Deep amber, 7-5/8", 24 rib-pattern swirled to left, pontil scared base, outward rolled lip, American, 1815-1835.	$150-175	

Old Bottles

Globular bottle Deep amber, 7-5/8", 24 rib-pattern swirled to left, pontil scarred base, outward rolled lip, American, 1820-1835.	**$700-800**
Midwestern globular bottle Yellow with olive tone, 7-1/2", 24 rib-pattern swirled to right, pontil scarred base, folded lip, American, 1815-1835.	**$900-1,000**
Midwestern Globular bottle Medium amber, 7-1/2", 24 rib-pattern swirled to right, pontil scarred base, outward rolled lip, American, 1815-1835.	**$550-650**
Pattern-molded Flask Smoky clear glass, 7-1/2", 20-ogival pattern, pontil scarred base, sheared and tooled lip, American, 1815-1835.	**$150-200**
Pattern-molded "beehive" club bottle Blue aqua, 7-3/4", 24 rib-pattern swirled to right, open pontil, applied top, American, 1815-1830.	**$150-200**
Globular bottle Medium amber shading to yellow amber in center, 8", 24 rib-pattern swirled to left, pontil scarred base, outward rolled lip, American, 1820-1835.	**$600-700**

Pattern-molded "beehive" club bottle Aqua, 8", 16 broken rib-pattern swirled to right, open pontil, outward rolled lip, American, 1815-1830.	**$200-250**	
Pattern-molded handled whiskey Yellow amber, 8-1/4", blown in 26 rib-pattern then flattened, ribs swirl to right, open pontil, applied ringed mouth and handle, American, 1840-1855.	**$500-600**	
Midwestern club bottle Pale aqua, 8-1/4", 24 broken rib-pattern swirled to right, pontil scarred base, applied top, American, 1815-1835.	**$100-125**	
Pattern-molded globular bottle Blue aqua, 8-1/4", 24 rib-pattern swirled to right, pontil scarred base, outward rolled lip, American, 1815-1830.	**$300-400**	
Pattern-molded globular bottle Amber, 8-1/2", 24 rib-pattern swirled to left, pontil scarred base, outward rolled lip, American, 1815-1830.	**$500-600**	

Pattern-molded handled whiskey Red amber with puce, 8-1/2", blown in 26 rib-pattern mold and then flattened, open pontil, applied ringed mouth and handle, American, 1845-1855.	**$450-500**	
Midwestern flattened globular Deep blue aqua, 9", 25 rib-pattern swirled to right, pontil scarred base, applied top, American, 1815-1835.	**$150-200**	
Pattern-molded spirits "pinched" flask Cobalt blue, 9-1/2", 24 rib-pattern swirled to left, pontil scarred base, sheared and tooled lip, blown in German half-post method, German, 1790-1830.	**$600-700**	
Pillar mold-pattern decanter Deep cobalt blue, 10", eight rib-pattern, polished pontil scarred base, applied double collar top and shoulder band, very rare, American, 1835-1860.	**$1,900-2,000**	
Pillar mold-pattern decanter Medium pink amethyst, 10-5/8", eight rib-pattern, pontil scarred base, applied double collar top and shoulder band, very rare, American, 1835-1860.	**$1,500-1,700**	
Pattern-molded sauce or oil bottle Green aqua, 12-1/4", 16 rib-pattern swirled to left, smooth base, deep kick-up, applied top, American, 1850-1865.	**$150-200**	
Large pattern-molded storage bottle Clear glass with smoky green, 17", 22 vertical rib-pattern, pontil scarred base, sheared and tooled lip, American or European, 1825-1850.	**$250-300**	

Perfume & Cologne

Collectors look for two types of perfume bottles – decorative and commercial. Decorative bottles include any bottles sold empty and meant to be filled with your choice of scent. Commercial bottles are sold filled with scent and usually have the label of a perfume company. Since there are thousands of different perfume bottles, most collectors specialize in a subcategory.

Arrowhead-shape scent bottle, deep cobalt blue with large fleur-de-lis on both sides, 2-1/8", pontil scarred base, sheared and tooled top, extremely rare, 1840-1860, $500-600.

Popular specialties with collectors of decorative perfume bottles include: ancient Roman or Egyptian bottles; cut-glass bottles with or without gold or sterling silver trim or overlay; bottles by famous glassmakers such as Moser, Steuben, Webb, Lalique, Galle, Daum, Baccarat, and Saint Louis; figural porcelain bottles from the 18th and 19th centuries or from Germany between 1920 to 1930; perfume lamps (with wells to fill with scent); perfume burners; laydown and double-ended scent bottles; atomizer bottles; pressed or molded early American glass bottles; matched dresser sets of bottles; or hand-cut Czechoslovakian bottles from the early 20th century.

Among collectors of commercial perfumes, there are favorite specialty collections including color of glass; bottles by a single parfumer (Guerlain, Caron, or Prince Matchabelli); bottles by famous fashion designers (Worth, Paul Poiret, Chanel, Dior, Schiaparelli, or Jean Patou); bottles by a particular glassmaker or designer (Lalique, Baccarat, Viard, or Depinoix); giant factice bottles (store display bottles not filled

Old Bottles

with genuine fragrance); little compacts holding solid (cream) perfume, which are often figural; tester bottles (small bottles with long glass daubers); and figural, novelty, and miniature perfumes (usually replicas of regular bottles given as free samples at perfume counters).

For the novice perfume bottle collector, it may surprise you to learn that the record price for a perfume bottle at auction was over $200,000, and those little sample bottles that were given free at perfume counters in the 1960s can now bring as much as $300 or $400. It may also surprise you that those miniature bottles are more popular with European collectors than their full-size counterparts, and bottles by American perfume companies are more desirable to European collectors than to Americans, and vice-versa. Also, most collectors of commercial perfume bottles will buy empty examples, but those still sealed with the original perfume carry a premium, and the original packaging can raise the price by as much as 500%! The rubber bulbs on atomizer bottles dry out over time, but the lack of one or the presence of a modern replacement does not really affect the price.

Collecting perfume bottles is one of those hobbies that can begin with little or no investment. Just ask your friend who wears Shalimar to save her next empty bottle for you. But beware. Investment-quality perfume bottles can be pricey. The rules for value are the same as for any other kind of glass – rarity, condition, age, and quality of the glass.

There are, however, some special considerations when collecting perfume bottles:

1. You do not have an investment-quality bottle (one that will appreciate in value over time) unless the bottle has its original stopper and label (if it's commercial).

2. It is a high-quality glass bottle (not a lower end eau de cologne or eau de toilette bottle) and there is no corrosion on any metal part.

3. With commercial perfume bottles, prior to the introduction of those little plastic liners on the dowel end of a stopper in 1963, all stoppers had to be individually ground to match the neck of their specific bottle. Bottles without those liners are preferred to those that have them.

4. Special note on perfume bottle values: All dates given are for the introduction of the scent (if applicable), not for the issue of the particular bottle.

I want to thank Penny Dolnick, who provided the background and pricing

Scent bottle, cobalt blue, 2-1/2", "Sunburst and Diamond" pattern, pontil scarred base, sheared and tooled lip, 1840-1860, $250-300.

Seahorse scent bottle, cobalt blue body with clear glass coggle wheel-applied rigaree, 2-1/4", sheared and tooled lip, 1815-1830, $150-200.

information, and the International Perfume Bottle Association, whose mission is to provide information and education about all aspects of perfume and scent bottles, and promote fellowship among its members. Penny's credentials speak for themselves as a past president of IPBA, author of the *Penny Bank Commercial Perfume Bottle Price Guide*, 8th edition, the *Penny Bank Miniature Perfume Bottle Price Guide*, 3rd edition, and the *Penny Bank Solid Perfume Bottle Price Guide*, 4th edition. Penny, who can be contacted at alpen@att.net, is willing to help fellow collectors identify and date bottles, but not conduct actual appraisals.

The IPBA is an organization of 1,000 perfume bottle collectors in several countries. Its main objective is to foster education and comradeship for collectors through its quarterly full-color magazine, regional chapters, and annual convention. If interested in obtaining further information on future conventions or membership, the organization's website is www.perfumebottles.org.

In addition, every year the IPBA convention hosts the Ken Leach Perfume Bottle Auction, featuring approximately 400 perfume bottles and related items. A full-color hard-bound catalog of the auction is available by contacting Ken Leach at ken@perfumebottlesauction.com. Ken also provided some great photographs for this 8th edition's "Perfume & Cologne" chapter.

Decorative Perfume Bottles

German ceramic crown top of Dutch boy holding flowers c1920, 4.2".	$85-105		Volupte atomizer enameled with Art Deco motifs Unsigned, 9.3", c1930s.	$600
German ceramic crown top of seated Kewpie doll c1930s, 2.9".	$79-95		Devilbiss perfume lamp enameled with dancing girls Metal cap and base, 7.5", c1930s.	$500
Baccarat signed atomizer for Marcel Franck c1930s, 3.75".	$90		Austrian square metal filigree over glass with glass jewels c1920s, 2.1".	$80-90
Ruby cut glass with sterling neck and elaborate stopper French, 3.8", c1855.	$459		Czechoslovakian pale blue cut glass with matching keyhole stopper 5", c1920s.	$155-225
English ruby glass double ended scent with sterling mounts Signed, 4.5", c1905.	$220		Birmingham engraved sterling laydown with glass liner Hinged cover, 4.5", 1885.	$270
Elsa Peretti for Tiffany 18k gold necklace Pouch, box 3.6", c1990s.	$2,700		Ingrid Czech lapis lazuli glass atomizer cut with roses Label, 5.0", c1920s.	$350-500
R. Lalique "Myosotis #3" Green stain, nude stopper, signed, 9.0", c1928.	$4,350		Moser amber with gold frieze of female warriors Signed, 6", c1920s.	$200
R. Lalique "Sirenes" perfume burner Blue stain, nude figures, signed, 7", c1920.	$3,100		Hoffman clear with amber lady and cherub stopper Many jewels, signed, 6.8", c1920s.	$155-180
Limoges enameled with lady Enameled overcap, inner stopper, 2.5", c19th century.	$670		Czechoslovakian clear with pale blue nude figure dauber Blue jewels, unsigned, 5.7", c1920s.	$6,200
French rock crystal with 19k gold neck and flip top Leather case, 6.5", c1875.	$320-450			

Shuco mohair monkey figure with perfume tube inside c1930s, 5".	$175	**Fenton blue opalescent Coin Dot pattern atomizer for DeVilbiss** 4", c1940s.	$45
American molded paperweight bottle with bird stopper Unsigned, 5.3", c1940s.	$25-35	**Steuben blue aurene atomizer** Acorn finial, for DeVilbiss, 9.5", c1930s.	$650
American clear bottle with elaborate silver overlay Ball stopper, 5.1", c1930s.	$140	**Cambridge pink footed urn** Stopper with long dauber, label, 4.75", c1940s.	$90
American pressed glass footed urn with large sunflower stopper c1940s, 10.5".	$45-55	**L.C. Tiffany blue Favrile footed urn** Signed, 6", 1930s.	$525
Alvin clear boule bottle with elaborate sterling overlay Signed, 6.5", c1930s.	$160-185	**Czechoslovakian Irice import iligree cap with dauber** Blue glass cat dangle, 2.75", c1920s.	$130
Kosta faceted bottle and stopper Signed V Lindstand, 3.5", c1950.	$40-60	**Bavaria Combo perfume/ powder lady fig in court dress** Long dauber, 9.0", c1930s.	$90-122
Galle atomizer Yellow with maroon berry and leaf overlay, cameo signed, 7.36", c1910.	$1,450-1,700	**Wedgwood teardrop shape** Slate blue Jasper with draped lady fig, 4.5", 18th century.	$410
Daum Nancy peach with amber leaf and flower overlay Cameo signed, 6.5", c1915.	$1,100	**DeVilbiss perfume lamp** White with black nude silhouette figures, 7.5".	$275-308
Baccarat two dolphins bottle Ball stopper, signed, 6", c1925.	$200	**Bavaria green crowntop lion figure** 2.5", c1930s.	$140
Austrian square metal filigree over glass with glass jewels 21", c1920.	$110	**Lalique Clairfontaine MIB oversized floral spray stopper** 4.75".	$256
		R. Lalique travel atomizer Deep impressed flowers, blue stain, 4", c1920s.	$625

Old Bottles

Lalique "Deux Fleurs" two flowers bottle Signed Lalique, 3.75", c1950s to present.	$80-145
Lalique "Clairefontain" with lily of the valley stopper Signed Lalique, box 5", c1960s to present.	$190-235
Lilmoges white ceramic with hand-painted flowers 6.5", c1960s.	$25-35
English porcelain mottled tan "bird's-egg" with sterling cap Marks CF FS, 2.5", c1885.	$300
English double-end cobalt bottle Unmarked silver caps, 5.5", c1850-1890.	$175
Fostoria USA black glass combo perfume/powder Clear stp, 7.25", 1920s-1940s.	$85-100
Baccarat Rose tiente (Amberina) swirl pattern bottle and stopper 6.5".	$90-125
Orient & Flume USA teardrop shape Clear with red bird, signed, c1980s, 7.5".	$180
S. Mordan London sterling over glass purse bottle with engraved decorations Signed, dated 1890, 2.1".	$250
Czechoslovakian dark red lithyalin (stone-like) with raised red nude Attributed to H. Hoffman, 3.8", c1920s.	$2,425
Bohemia cranberry cut to clear three-tier cologne Gilt flowers, 7", c1850-1890.	$100-225
French purse bottle with woven reed covering and 18k cap 2.25", c1830s.	$200
Czechoslovakian set of three cut glass bottles with pale green stripes and tray Marked Czech, 2.5".	$375-450
Sabino, France opalescent with raised draped women c1890s, 6".	$85-140
Sabino, France opalescent with embossed nude women c1920s, 6.25".	$105-125
S. Lundberg Signed, clear studio glass bottle with internal flowers, 7.5", c1985.	$170
Webb, England red cone shape Silver hallmarked cap, hand-painted gold flowers, 3.87", c1890.	$325
Shuco, Germany mohair bunny with perfume vial inside, 5".	$525
Shuco, Germany mohair bear Gold fur with perfume vial inside, 5".	$235
Shuco, Germany black mohair Felix the Cat with perfume vial inside, 5".	$1,095

Commercial Perfume Bottles

Elizabeth Arden It's You MIB Baccarat white figural hand in dome c1938, 6.5".	$3,850		**Corday Tzigane R Lalique tiered bottle and stopper** Label, 5.5", c1940.	$200-246
Babs Creations Forever Yours heart in composition hands with dome c1940, 3.5".	$115		**Coty Ambre antique R Lalique with gray-stained maidens** c1913, 6.0".	$1,250
Bourjois Evening in Paris, cobalt with fan stopper Banner label, 4.5", c1928.	$150		**Coty L'Origan MIB Baccarat** Flat rectangle, sepia stained moth stopper, 3.25", c1903.	$300
Bourjois Evening in Paris, cobalt bullet-shape laydown Good label, tassel, 3.5", c1928.	$15-25		**D'Albert Ecusson Urn with gold label** Box, 3.87", c1952.	$50
Hattie Carnegie Carnegie blue clear head and shoulders bottle Label, 3.25", c1944.	$85-100		**Jean Desprez Votre Main Sevres porcelain hand with applied flowers** 3.2", c1939.	$1,250-1,550
Caron Nuit de Noel MIB black glass Gold label, faux shagreen box with tassel, 4.36", c1922.	$150-175		**Dior Diorissimo urn with gilt bronze flowers stopper** Box, 9", c1956.	$1,900
Chanel Chanel #5 Glass giant factice (store display) 10.5", c1921.	$350-450		**D'Orsay Toujours Fidele Baccarat** Pillow shape with bulldog stopper, box, 3.5", c1912.	$500
Mary Chess Souvenir d'un Soir MIB replica of Plaza Hotel fountain c1956, 3.62".	$1,150		**Dior Poison, snake bracelet** MIB with funnel, c1980s.	$170
Colgate Cha Ming glass stopper Flower label, box 3", c1917.	$35		**Duchess of Paris Queenly Moments Queen Victoria bottle on wood base** c1938, 3.5".	$25-40

Faberge woodhue oversize upright logo stopper c1940, 3.5".	$35	**Lancome Envoi** Upright stopper, box, some contents, 2.87", c1958.	$185
Forvil Relief R Lalique round bottle with swirl pattern No label, signed, 6.87", c1920.	$450	**Lanvin Arpege MIB black boule with gold logo** Gold raspberry stopper, 3.5", c1927.	$145-195
Dorothy Gray Savoir Faire bottle with enameled mask Gold stopper, 4", c1947.	$410	**Lanin Arpage** MIB, black boule with gold logo, gold raspberry stopper, 4.75", c1935.	$90-135
Jacques Griffe Griffonage square bottle Flat top glass stopper, box, 2.25", c1949.	$45-55	**Guy Laroche Fidji** Indented bottle, glass stopper, full, c1966.	$100
Guerlain Shalimar Baccarat signed classic winged bottle Blue stopper, 5.5", c1921.	$100-125	**Lucien Lelong Indiscret draped bottle** Glass bow stopper, label, 4.75", c1935.	$55-75
Guerlain Shalimar, classic winged bottle Mint in two boxes, blue stopper with plastic liner, 4", c1970.	$175-190	**Prince Matchabelli Added Attraction MIB red crown** Velvet case, 2.12", c1956.	$245-280
Houbigant Parfum Ideal Baccarat Faceted stopper, gold label, box, 4.2", c1900	$52	**Molinrd Habanita** MIB flat rectangle bottle with upright stopper, 4.5", c1920.	$495
Isabey Bleu de Chine Viard Gray stain with enameled flowers, 5.75", c1926.	$1,275	**Molinard Xmas Bells MIB black glass figural bell** Gold lettering, 4.25, c1926.	$625
Andrew Jergens Ben Hur rounded bottle Frosted stopper, black label, 5.25", c1904.	$25	**Solon Palmer Gardenglo Simple bottle** Glass ball stopper, label, 4.75", c.1913.	$20
Lander Gardenia dime store bottle with orange plastic tiara stopper 4.75", c1947.	$10-16	**Raphael Replique MIB R logo stopper** Red seal, 3.25", c1944.	$50-60

Nina Ricci L'Air du Temps MIB Lalique Double dove stopper, 4.5", c1948	$225	**Nina Ricci Coeur Joie** Empty open heart signed Lalique, 4".	$66-130
Elsa Schiaparelli Shocking Torso with flowers Tape measure, dome, 4", c1936.	$110-215	**Lanvin Arpege black boule with logo** Gold raspberry stopper, empty, 3.5".	$55-85
Elsa Schiaparelli Sleeping Candle bottle, glass flame stopper, label, 4.12", c1938.	$135	**T Jones Gai Paris frosted with gray stain** Molded labels (rare), 3.75",c1912.	$3,416
Tre Jur Suivez Moi Lady figure bottle with long dauber 2.5", c1925.	$115-240	**Gabilla Mimosa MIB** Flat stopper with name, black floral label, 3.25".	$125-150
Vigny Golliwogg MIB black face stopper with seal fur hair 3.5", c1919.	$350	**Prince Matchabelli Royal Gardenia white enameled crown** Cross stopper, 3.75".	$590-625
Vigny Golliwogg, black face stopper with seal fur hair Good label, empty, c1919.	$95-145	**Jay Thorpe Jaytho signed R Lalique all over tulips** No label, 4".	$730
Worth Dans la Nuit R Lalique matt blue boule Name on stopper, 5.75", c1920.	$600	**Milart Naughty 90s female torso wearing corset under dome** Full, 5.6".	$200
Ybry Femme de Paris Baccarat green opaque with enameled overcap 2.25", c1925.	$675	**Elsa Schiaparelli Zut figural lower female torso** 3.62".	$158-255
Guerlain set of four MIB ribbed purse bottles with horse hangtags 3.25".	$300-335	**Guerlain Bouquet des Faunes Lalique bottle with four faces** 4".	$183-375
Nina Ricci Coeur Joie MIB Open heart signed Lalique, 4".	$275	**D'Orsay Roses signed R Lalique** Figural stopper, 3.875".	$2,036-2,555
		Dior J'Appartiens a Miss Dior figural Bichon Frise dog 7".	$3,385-5,779

Old Bottles

Grossmith Phul Nana good graphics label Upright disc stopper, 4.5".	$87-101	**Lancome Kypre bottle with raised nudes** Box, 3.5".	$44
Vantine Gardenia Buddha bottle In wooden case, 3.5".	$200-267	**Weil Secret of Venus Zibilene waisted bath oil bottle** Full, 3".	$176-245
Worth Dans la Nuit Lalique signed matt blue factice (dummy) name stopper 11"..	$787-990	**Woodworth Fiancee flat rectangle bottle** Sepia stained stopper, 2.5".	$85
Lancome Cuir MIB star-shaped bottle 4.75".	$450-668	**Isabey Amber de Carthage clear and frosted with leaves** Gray stain, 3".	$225-330
Jean Patou Joy MIB Baccarat signed "pleated" bottle 2.5".	$145-190	**Dorothy Gray Flutter heart-shaped bottle on Bakelite base** Full, 3".	$175-212
Renoir Chi Chi figural heart bottle with bakelite "arrow" stopper 2".	$45-72	**By name Caravane ridged bottle and fan-shaped stopper** 4".	$55

Miniature Perfume Bottles

Elizabeth Arden Blue Grass blown bottle with blue horse figure inside, box, 2.2", c1934.	$925-1,060	**Bourjois Evening in Paris cobalt mini** In peach Bakelite shell, 2", c1928.	$175
Elizabeth Arden Blue Grass c1969.	$45	**Bourjois Evening in Paris cobalt mini** In green Bakelite shell, 2", c1928.	$400
Artfield Creations Baby Grand Piano Mini in metal piano presentation, 1.34", c1940.	$124	**Bourjois on the Wind peach label and cap** 1.5", c1930.	$15

Hattie Carnegie A Go Go square mini In hat box, 1.36", c1969.	$45
Caron Nuit de Noel tester Black cap and label, full, 1.75", c1922.	$35
Ciro Chevalier de la Nuit frosted figural knight Black head, 2.36", c1923.	$250-300
Colgate Caprice worn label Twisted screw cap, 2", c1893.	$12
Corday Toujours Moi shield-shape label Pink plastic cap, 1.75", c1923.	$17
Coty A'Suma Boule with embossed flowers No label, 1.5", c1934.	$65
Jean Desprez Sheherazade MIB Tall spire stopper, 3", c1960s.	$240
Dior Diorama round laydown "pebble" Black label, 1", c1950.	$70
Dior Miss Dior round laydown "pebble" White label, 1", c1953.	$30
D'Orsay Intoxication draped bottle Gold label, gold pouch, 1.62", c1942.	$10
Evyan Great Lady laydown heart bottle Full, 2.25", c1958.	$12
Max Factor Hypnotique Sophisti-Cat Mini with black cat in dome, 1.75", c1958.	$19-25
Guerlain Chamade green plastic pagoda cap 1.25", c1969.	$185
Guerlain L'Heure Bleu tester Black cap with dauber, horse label, 2.25", c1912.	$65-80
Guerlain Mitsouko replica mini Glass stopper, full, 1.5", c1919.	$20
Guerlain Nahema Blue plastic cap, MIB, 1.5", c1979.	$16-28
Guerlain Parure Green plastic pagoda cap, 1.25", c1969.	$212
Richard Hudnut Le Debut Bleu MIB Blue with gold raspberry stopper, 1.25", c1927.	$148
Richard Hudnut Le Debut Noir MIB Black with gold raspberry stopper, 1.25", c1927.	$235
Karoff Buckarettes set of two cowboy and cowgirl with wooden heads 1.87", c1940.	$55-79
Lanvin Arpege tiny black boule with logo 1.2", c1927.	$400-425
Lanvin Arpege, tester Black cap with long dauber, 3", c1927.	$45
Estee Lauder Cinnabar Faux red carved cinnabar necklace, 2.12", c 1976.	$26-42

Old Bottles

Le Galion Sortilege tiny mini with ship cap and gold label 1.25", c1937.	$20
Lucien Lelong Passionment tiny mini with pearl cap, label 1.12", c1940.	$15
Germain Monteil Laughter blown bottle Blue threaded stopper, full, 1.5", c1941.	$25
Raphael Replique MIB Lalique acorn in plastic case 2", c1944.	$120-144
Revillon Detchma MIB urn shape Metal cap, 2.25", c1955.	$15
Nina Ricci set of three Sunburst Leaf and heart minis in box, 1.25-1.5", c1952.	$440
Nina Ricci L'Air du Temps Double dove stopper, mint in plastic dome, 1.5", c1970.	$18-25
Rochas Femme Round laydown "pebble" Gold label, 1.5", c1945.	$35
Elsa Schiaparelli Shocking set of three torsos in jack-in-box with flowers 1.36", c1936.	$920
Rose Valois Canotier figural mini wearing hat in plastic case 2.3", c1950.	$175

Weil Cobra MIB ball stopper Worn box, 1.5", c1941.	$25
Weil Secret of Venus (antilope) waisted bottle Blue cap, full, 1.36", c1942.	$45
Elsa Schiaparelli Snuff torso shape Brown S label, 1.75".	$26
Ybry Devinez opaque orange Label, worn overcap, 2".	$695-723
Saville Mischief MIB Black mini in white plastic tophat, 2".	$115
Saville Mischief MIB Black mini in black plastic tophat, 2".	$65-80
Prince Matchabelli Beloved blue crown Screw cap, velvet case, 1.62".	$30-45
Germaine Monteil Nostalgia jug with open handles 1.75".	$63
Lucien Lelong Indiscret pearl cap Good label, clamshell case, 1.12".	$55-90
Nina Ricci Fille d'Eve Flat apple with embossed leaf in basket, 2.25".	$375-490
Nina Ricci Fille d'Eve Flat apple with embossed leaf, 2.25".	$125-155
Guerlain Vol de Nuit clear lyre-shape eau de toilette with box 2.75".	$75-90

Corday Quand MIB Black bottle and glass stopper, 1.75".	$125-180
Coty set of two MIB frosted waves stoppers in wooden shoes Worn box, 1.25".	$90-115
Lilli Dache Dachelle simple bottle Full, 1.25".	$10
D'Orsay Fleur de France flat round bottle Glass stopper, leather case, 1.62".	$55

Helena Rubenstein Heaven Sent figural angel Label, 2.36".	$20-38
Jean Patou set of three bumpy bottles Glass stoppers, hangtags, worn box, 2.12".	$105-155
Bourjois Evening in Paris Cobalt in figural marble arch, box, 2".	$355-470
Elizabeth Arden My Love Glass bottle in brass & aluminum snowman, 2".	$185
Marquay Set of 6 metal caps Good labels, brocade pouches, box, 1.5".	$51-110

Miscellaneous Perfume/ Cologne Bottles

Blown paneled cologne bottles (two) Deep cobalt blue and medium pink amethyst, 4-5/8", 12-sided with sloped shoulders, smooth and pontiled scarred base, inward and outward rolled lips, American, 1850-1870.	$200-250	
Blown paneled cologne bottle Medium cobalt blue with white flecks, 7-1/4", 12-sided, smooth base, tooled top, part original label, American, 1850-1870.	$150-200	

Old Bottles

Cologne bottle Medium cobalt blue, 7-3/8", 12-sided, smooth base, outward rolled lip, Sandwich Glass Works, Sandwich, Mass., American, 1850-1870.	**$100-125**	
Cologne bottle "Thumbprint and Herringbone" pattern Cobalt blue, 9-1/8", smooth base, sheared and rough finished tooled lip, American, 1850-1870.	**$400-450**	
Concentric ring scent bottle Deep cobalt blue, 2-1/8", pontil scarred base, sheared and tooled top, possibly Keene, New Hampshire, or Coventry, Conn., Glass Works, American, 1825-1845.	**$500-600**	
Cut overlay cologne bottle Clear glass with cut cobalt blue overlay, 5-1/2", cut rayed star on base, tooled and polished top, original cut glass stopper, Sandwich Glass Works, Sandwich, Mass., American, 1845-1865.	**$600-700**	
Cut overlay cologne bottle Clear glass with cut cobalt blue overlay, 8", polished pontil, tooled and polished top, original cut glass stopper, Sandwich Glass Works, Sandwich, Mass., American, 1845-1865.	**$700-800**	

Fancy cologne bottle "Floral and Scroll" pattern Sapphire blue, 3-7/8", open pontil, sheared and tooled lip, American, 1830-1855.	$1,000-1,300	
Fancy cologne bottle "Knight Standing Inside a Gothic Arch" Cobalt blue, 4-1/8", open pontil, thin flared-out lip, American, 1840-1860.	$1,400-1,500	
Fancy cologne bottle "Diamond and Acanthus" Medium cobalt blue, 5-3/4", open pontil, sheared and tooled lip, American, 1840-1860.	$900-1,000	
Fancy cologne bottle (oversized) Deep cobalt blue, 9-1/2", pontil scarred base, tooled flared-out lip, embossed wreath and Roman-style columns, American, 1840-1860.	$1,000-1,200	
Fancy scent bottle Medium cobalt blue shading to deep purple cobalt near base, slender shape with diamond daisy and waffle pattern, 3-5/8", smooth base, ground and polished lip, original metal screw-on cap, rare, American, 1855-1870.	$200-300	
Sandwich-type cologne bottle Deep teal green, 4-5/8", eight-sided hourglass shape, smooth base, tooled lip, Boston and Sandwich Glass Works, Sandwich, Mass., American, 1855-1870.	$600-700	

Sandwich-type cologne bottle Medium to deep purple amethyst, 5-5/8", eight-sided hourglass shape, smooth base, inward rolled lip, Boston and Sandwich Glass Works, Sandwich, Mass., American, 1855-1870.	$400-450	
Sandwich-type cologne bottle Deep lavender blue, 5-7/8", eight-sided hourglass shape, smooth base, tooled lip, Boston and Sandwich Glass Works, Sandwich, Mass., American, 1855-1870.	$400-450	
Sandwich-type cologne bottle Brilliant cobalt blue, 7", eight-sided hourglass shape, pontil scarred base, inward rolled lip, scarce in this large size, Boston and Sandwich Glass Works, Sandwich, Mass., American, 1855-1875.	$900-1,000	
Scent bottle Clear glass body with two cobalt blue bands of applied rigaree, 3", pontil scarred base, sheared and tooled lip, American, 1820-1850.	$200-250	
Stiegel-type scent bottle| Deep cobalt blue, 2-1/16", 22 vertical rib-pattern, pontil scarred base, tooled top, extremely rare form, American, 1815-1835.	$250-375	

Stiegel-type scent bottle Deep amethyst, 2-5/8", tight rib pattern to right, pontil scarred base, tooled top, scarce color in rare small size, American, 1815-1835.	$350-400	
Stiegel-type scent bottle Deep cobalt blue, tight rib pattern to right, pontil scarred base, tooled top, American, 1815-1835.	$250-300	
Sunburst scent bottle Deep cobalt blue, 2-1/2", flattened elliptical shape, pontil scarred base, sheared and tooled top, rare, American, 1825-1845.	$900-1,000	
Seahorse scent bottle Cobalt blue, 2", applied clear glass rigaree, pontil scarred base, tooled top, American, 1820-1840.	$350-400	
Seahorse scent bottle Cobalt blue, 2-1/2", rib-pattern body, applied clear glass rigaree, pontil scarred base, tooled top, American, 1820-1840.	$350-400	
Tall "Beaded Flute" pattern cologne bottle Cobalt blue, 10-1/4", smooth base, tooled top, American, 1850-1869.	$600-700	

Poison

By the very nature of their contents, poison bottles form a unique category for collecting. While most people assume that poison bottles are plain, most are very decorative, making them easy to identify their toxic contents.

In 1853, the American Pharmaceutical Association recommended that laws be passed requiring identification of all poison bottles. In 1872, the American Medical Association recommended that poison bottles be identified with a rough surface on one side and the word "poison" on the other. But as often happened during that era, the passing of these laws was difficult and the manufacturers were left to do whatever they wanted. Because a standard wasn't established, a varied group of bottle shapes, sizes, and patterns were manufactured, including skull and crossbones, or skulls, leg bones, and coffins.

These bottles were manufactured with quilted or ribbed surfaces and diamond/lattice-type patterns for identification by touch. Colorless bottles are very rare since most poison bottles were produced in dark shades of blues and browns, another identification aid. When collecting these bottles, caution must be exercised since it is not uncommon to find a poison bottle with its original contents. If the bottle has the original glass stopper, the value and demand for the bottle will greatly increase.

Poison – Pat. Appld. For, cobalt blue, 2-7/8", figural skull, smooth base (Pat. June 26th 1891), tooled top, smallest of three skulls, American, 1891-1900, $500-600

Poison – F.A. – Thompson - & Co., amber, 3-1/8", coffin shape, smooth base, tooled top, scarce, American, 1890-1910, $1,000-1,200

Diamond and quilt poison bottle, label reads: Dispensary Tablets – Atropine – Sulfate – 1-2 Grain – Poison Cobalt blue, 2-1/2", smooth base, tooled top, smallest size of 12-bottle set, American, 1890-1910.	$60-75	
Diamond and quilt poison bottle Dark moss green, 4-1/2", smooth base, tooled top, scarce color, American, 1890-1910.	$600-700	
Diamond pattern poison – 99% label reads: Solution Formaldehyde Poison Caution – Baker's Pharmacy – Eugene, Oregon Cobalt blue, 9", smooth base, tooled top, original "Poison" embossed stopper, American, 1890-1910.	$300-350	
Diamond pattern poison Cobalt blue, 11-1/4", half-gallon, smooth base, tooled top, original "Poison" embossed stopper, scarce size, American, 1890-1910.	$500-600	
Diamond and quilt pattern poison Deep cobalt blue, 13", gallon, smooth base (U.S.P.H.S.), tooled wide lip, gallon size is most difficult to find, American, 1890-1910.	$2,000-2,500	
Diamond quilted poison bottles (two) Cobalt blue, 9" and 5-1/2", smooth bases, tooled tops, 5-1/2" bottle with original "Poison" embossed stopper, American, 1890-1910. Note: The 9" poison is more difficult to find than 11-1/2" bottle.	$275-300	
Diamond quilted poison bottle Cobalt blue, 11-1/2", half gallon, smooth base, tooled top, missing stopper, American, 1890-1910.	$300-325	

Bowman's Drug Stores – Poison, cobalt blue, 7-1/2", original label, American, 1890-1920, $550-600.

Labeled three-sided poison bottle, cobalt blue, 5-1/4', tooled top, American, 1890-1910, $125-150.

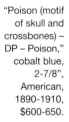

"Poison (motif of skull and crossbones) – DP – Poison," cobalt blue, 2-7/8", American, 1890-1910, $600-650.

"Poison (motif of star above and below skull and crossbones) Poison," yellow amber, 4-5/8", American, 1890-1910, $300-350.

Doctor Oreste – Sinanide's – Medicinal – Preparation – Orestorin Deep cobalt blue, 4-5/8", smooth base, tooled top, original ground glass stopper, American, 1890-1910.	$250-300
Doctor Oreste – Sinanide's – Medicinal – Preparation – Orestorin Milk glass, 4-1/2", smooth base, tooled top, original ground glass stopper, American, 1890-1910.	$350-400
For – External-Use-Only-Prescription – Reese Chem. Co. – 1000 – External-Use 4 Times Daily – Mfg. By – Reese Chem. Co. – Cleveland – O. Deep cobalt blue, 5-1/2", smooth base, ABM top, American, 1915-1925.	$100-125
Giftlache – (skull and crossbones) and a Poison – (skull and crossbones) Gift (skull and crossbones) – Veleno Medium emerald green, 6-1/4", smooth bases, tooled and ABM lip, German, 1890-1930.	$100-125
Giftlache – (skull and crossbones) and a Poison – (skull and crossbones) Gift (skull and crossbones) – Veleno Medium emerald green, 8-1/4", smooth bases, tooled and ABM lip, German, 1890-1930.	$100-125

Not To Be Taken – Trade Aegis Mark – Po. No. 448773 Cobalt blue, 4-5/8", coffin shape, smooth base, tooled top, manufactured by Alfred Mignots of London and referred to as "Aegis Coffin," considered to be one of the rarest of all poison bottles, American, 1890-1910.	$9,000-10,000
Not To Be Taken – 99% original label reads: Whats Home Without a Clean Bed, Mexican Brank Insect Fluid Compound, (woman in bedroom using the product) Mexican Roach Food Co., Buffalo, N.Y., Under the Insecticide Act of 1910, Serial No. 269, etc. Cobalt blue, 5-1/2", hexagon shape, smooth base (4), tooled top, Canadian, 1900-1915.	$150-200
Poison jar – "Poison" Medium yellow amber, 3-1/2", smooth base, ABM lip, original screw cap, rare, European, 1925-1935.	$50-75
Poison flask Medium sapphire blue, 4-1/4", overall hobnail pattern, pontil scarred base, sheared lip, extremely rare color and small size, American, 1845-1860.	$1,200-1,400
Poison flask Ice blue, 4-5/8", hobnail pattern, pontil scarred base, tooled top, German, 1890-1915.	$150-200

Poison (on neck) – Electric Balm – G.M. Rhoades – Grand Rapids – Mich Clear glass, 6-5/8", smooth base, tooled top, American, 1885-1895.	$150-200
Poison – Bowman's – Drug Stores – Poison-original back panel label reads: Denatured Alcohol, Poison, Bowman Drug Co., Oakland Cobalt blue, 7-1/2", irregular hexagon shape, smooth base (G.L.G. & Co. – Applied Appl'd For), tooled top, rare to find in this size, American, 1890-1910.	$1,000-1,200
Columbian Pharmacy, Inc. – 461 State St. Perth Amboy, N.J. Medium yellow green, 5", irregular hexagon shape, smooth base (C.L.G.Co. Patent Appl'd For), tooled top, extremely rare, possibly one of only two known examples, American, 1890-1915.	$3,500-4,000
F. E. Bailey & Co. – Lowell, Mass Cobalt blue, 5", smooth base (C.L.G.Co. Patent Appl'd For) tooled top, American, 1890-1915.	$900-1,000
Gray & Pearse – Druggist – Poison – Take Care – Cheyenne – Wyo. Cobalt blue, 3-5/8", smooth base (W.T. & Co.) tooled top, extremely rare Western poison, American, 1890-1915.	$6,500-7,000
(Skull and crossbones) – Poison – Tinct – Iodine Deep cobalt blue, 2-1/8", smooth base, tooled top, American, 1890-1910.	$100-125
Poison (skull and crossbones) Golden amber, 2-3/4", smooth base (P.D. & Co.), tooled top, American, 1890-1910.	$100-125
Poison Yellow amber, 3", triangular shape, smooth base (J.T.M. & Co.), tooled top, American, 1890-1910.	$150-200
Poison Light cobalt blue, 3-1/2", coffin shape, smooth base, tooled top, American, 1890-1910.	$100-125
Poison – 100% label on reverse side reads: The Norwich Pharmacal Co, Norwich, New York, etc. Dark cobalt blue, 3-1/2", coffin shape, smooth base, tooled top, American, 1890-1910.	$100-125
Poison – 100% label on reverse side reads: The Norwich Pharmacal Co, Norwich, New York, etc. Amber, 3-1/2", coffin shape, smooth base, tooled top, rare in amber, American, 1890-1910.	$300-350
Poison Cobalt blue, 3-5/8", octagonal shape, smooth base, rough sheared unfinished lip, unusual bulged-out neck that is part of mold, American, 1890-1910.	$100-125

Poison – motif of star above and below skull and crossbones) Poison Yellow amber, 4-3/4", smooth base (S &D), tooled top, scarce, American, 1890-1910.	**$450-500**
Poison Medium amber, 4-7/8", smooth base, tooled top, scarce, American, 1890-1910.	**$200-225**
Poison Medium reddish puce, 5-1/8", triangular shape, 98% original label, tooled top, scarce in this color, American, 1890-1910.	**$500-600**
Poison Amber, 8-3/8", hexagon shape, smooth base (E.B, & Co. LO – 5000), tooled top, English, 1900-1920.	**$200-300**
Poison – 95% original label reads: Germicidal Tablets, etc. Cobalt blue, 3-1/8", smooth base (Davis & Geck – Monogram – Brooklyn, N.Y.), tooled top, American, 1890-1915.	**$1,000-1,300**
(Skull and crossbones) Gift Medium green, 6-1/4", smooth base, tooled top, German, 1890-1920.	**$100-125**
(Skull and crossbones) Poison – Jacobs – Bichloride – Tablets (skull and crossbones) Poison Medium amber, 2-1/4", eight-sided, smooth base, tooled top, rare poison from Atlanta, Georgia, American, 1890-1915.	**$1,300-1,400**

(Skull and crossbones) Poison – Jacobs – Bichloride – Tablets (skull and crossbones) Poison Amber, 3-3/8" eight-sided, smooth base, tooled top, difficult to find in this larger size, American, 1890-1915.	**$2,000-2,500**
Poison – Poison – 97% Original Label Reads: Poison – Diamond – Antiseptics – For External Use Only – Eli Lilly and Company, Indianapolis, U.S.A. Amber 10-1/2", smooth base, tooled top, American, 1890-1910.	**$100-125**

Three poison "The Owl Drug Co." bottles, cobalt blue, 4", 5-3/4", and 6-5/8", American, 1915-1920, $250-275.

Pair of poison bottles, emerald green, 5-1/2", American, 1890-1920, $140-160.

Poison (graduating scale) – O.K. Is Absolutely Sure – "Special" Is King Of All Pale aqua, 11", smooth base, tooled top, American, 1885-1900.	$200-250	
Poison – Poison – Sharpe & Dohme (on base) Amber, 3", smooth base, tooled top, American, 1890-1910.	$75-100	
Poison – Poison Yellow moss green, 7-7/8", square shape, smooth base (CIO), tooled top, horizontal ribs, extremely rare, American, 1890-1910.	$2,500-3,000	
Poison – Poison Medium amber, 8-1/4", smooth base, tooled top, American, 1890-1910.	$100-125	
Rat – Poison Clear glass, 2-3/8", smooth base, tooled top, American, 1890-1920.	$50-75	
Super – Pittsburg Medium cobalt blue, 3-3/8", multi-sided, smooth base, tooled top, American, 1862-1863. Bottle was owned by Charles H. Super during 1862-1863 in Pittsburgh. Due to color and rib pattern, it is considered to be a poison bottle.	$350-400	
The Paine Drug Co – Rochester N.Y. Bright grass green, 7-3/4", irregular hexagon shape, smooth base (C,G.G. & CO. – Patent Appl'd For), tooled lip, difficult to find in this larger size, American, 18901-1910.	$600-700	
Wide Mouth Poison Bottle Cobalt blue, 5-3/8", smooth base (U.S.P.H.S.) tooled top, American, 1890-1910.	$200-250	

Pot Lids (Ceramic)

At various bottle shows and club meetings, more than one collector has asked me, "When are you going to give pot lid collectors some love and add a chapter to your book?" I got the message and the time has come.

I'm sure many bottle collectors have walked past a sales table with pot lids for sale, not realizing their connection to bottle collecting. I should know because I was one of those collectors. All avid bottle collectors are aware of the impact of advertising and go-with (or sales giveaway) items associated with the manufacturer of bottles and their contents, items made by druggists, chemists, and medical companies. It's not difficult to understand the connection between pot lids produced by these same companies and their impact on bottle collecting.

For example, I've always been a collector of Nevada bottles and associated items (meaning "anything"). Druggist and chemist A.M. Cole, who was a dealer in drugs and other medical preparations, was also a major contributor to the history of Virginia City, Nevada, from 1861 to 1908, where his business operated at various locations on C Street. He had an ability to combine ingredients in such a way that his prescriptions usually brought about good results, with 10 variants of different bottles and medicines. But in addition to his medicines, one of his other best-sellers was a cold cream with an ornate pot lid that read: "Unequaled – Cold Cream – for softening beautifying & Preserving the Skin – Made By – A.M. Cole – 88 South C Street – Virginia Nevada." This pot lid was recently auctioned for $1,000.

Another example pertains to H.P. Wakelee, who was also a druggist, chemist, and dealer in the medical business. He started doing business in San Francisco in 1850. His company imported goods from Europe and had agents in London, England, and Paris. In addition to his "Wakelee Cameline," which was produced in a cobalt blue bottle, he also produced a "citrate of magnesia" in a cobalt blue bottle. But just like A.M. Cole, some of his other best-sellers were his potted creams: "H.P. Wakelee Druggist – Cold Cream – San Francisco" (recently sold for $299), "H.P. Wakelee Druggist – Burdells – Tooth – Powder – San Francisco" (recently sold for $399), and a "H.P. Wakelee Druggist – Odonto – San Francisco" (estimated value of $299).

The manufacturing of pot lids began in Liverpool, England, mainly from 1840-1910. One of the early manufacturers, Felix Edward Pratt, recognized the commercial use using new printing technology to decorate lids of containers to help promote products. After 1840, his firm, F.& R. Pratt of Fenton in Straffordshire, became one of the leading manufacturers of multicolored transfer-printed pot lids, with related wares.

In general, these covers were for small ceramic or pottery containers used to store a variety of different products such as cold cream, toothpaste, cosmetics, meats, sauces, fish paste, and bear's grease. While bear's grease wasn't always considered the most decorative or attractive lid, it is considered to be one of the most desirable by collectors. Bear's grease was popular in England in the 17th century, used to promote hair growth, but in fact was actually just another early form of perfumed hair grease.

While most pot lids are circular in shape, square, rectangular, and oval examples have been found. They also come in various sizes, from the small sample size of less than a half-inch in diameter to 10 inches for the economy size. The earliest pot lids (pre-1860) were handmade and most have flat tops. Following the introduction of machine production during the 1860s, lids were molded and tops became domed.

Since pot lids originated in England, English lids number in the thousands, whereas American lids number only in the hundreds. There are a number of locations in the United States where pot lids can be found, the most popular being near San Francisco, New York, and Philadelphia.

If you are interested in learning more about pot lid collecting, there are a number of great references: *The Price Guide to Black and White Pot Lids* by Ronald Dale, 1987; *Collecting Australian Pot Lids* by Robert Keil, 1981; *American Pot Lids* by Barbara and Sonny Jackson, 1987; *Millers: Bottle & Pot Lids* by Alan Blakeman, 2002; *Pot-Lids & Other Coloured Printed Staffordshire Wares* by V. Mortimer and Geoffrey Gorden, 2003 and 2007; *Price Guide to Pot Lids* by Abraham Bell, 1991; and *Trash to Treasure*, George D. Dean, 1998, www.deantiques.com.

Note: All descriptions here are for pot lids only, unless indicated otherwise.

Amadine – for the Cure and Prevention – of – Chapped Hands – Directions, etc. – Bazin Succor to E. Roussel No. 144 Chestnut St. Philadelphia White pottery, black transfer, 3" dia., American, 1840-1860.	$250-300	
Atkinson's – Rose – Cold Cream – 24 – Old Bond Street – London – Price Is Cream pottery, black transfer, 2-3/8" dia., English, 1860-1879.	$45-55	
Bazin's Ambrosial – Shaving Cream – Premium Perfumer (in banner held by eagle's beak) – X. Bazin Philadelphia White pottery, purple transfer, 3-1/4" dia., American, 1845-1860.	$400-450	
Bazin's Unrivaled Premium Shaving Cream, X. Bazin Perfumer Philadelphia Cream-color lid and pot, red transfer, 3" dia., smooth base ("Nine Highest Premiums Awarded, Also a Prize-Medal at the World's Fair to X. Bazin Philadelphia"), American (Pennsylvania).	$150-200	
Bedford's – Sweet Honeysuckle – Tooth Paste – Laden with the Scent of Flowers – and Breath of Odorous Spring White pottery, sepia transfer with overall floral design, 2-3/4" dia., English, 1855-1865.	$120-125	
Cherry – Tooth Paste (fruit and leaves) A Standard Tooth – Paste of Great-Repute – and of Exceptional Perfume (scroll and border) White pottery, reddish transfer, 2-1/2", English, 1865-1880.	$50-75	
Chlorine Detergent & Orris Dentifrice – Royce & Esterly – For – Cleansing & Preserving – the – Teeth – Prepared by – C. Helmstreet Troy. N.Y. White pottery, dark brown transfer, 3" dia., American, 1840-1860.	$450-600	

Old Bottles

Compound Extract – of – Caopaiba – Cubebs – and Iron – Prepared Only by – C.E. Monell, Chemist, New York White pottery, black transfer, 2-7/8" dia., original pot, American (New York), 1845-1860.	**$150-200**	
"Cremed" Amade – For – Shaving – directions, etc. Boots – Cash Chemist Cream pottery, black transfer, 3-1/2" dia., English, 1865-1875.	**$65-75**	
Crosse & Blackwell's by Appointment – Anchovy – Paste – A Tea-Table Delicacy (two men off-loading boat at dock) Crosse & Blackwell, Ltd. – London Cream pottery, sepia color transfer, 3-3/8", English, 1865-1875.	**$75-85**	
Dr. E.J. Coxe's – Extract – Of – Copaiva – Sarsaparilla – And – Cubebs. – The Remedy – Dose, One Large Pill - 4 to 6 Times a Day – New Orleans Cream-color lid and pot, black transfer, 3-1/4" dia., American (Louisiana), 1845-1855.	**$400-500**	
Eugene Roussel – Odontine – or – Rose Tooth Paste - Prepared by – Eugene Roussel – Philadelphia. – 114 Chestnut St. Philada. White glazed pottery with black transfer, square shape, 2-3/4" dia., American (Pennsylvania), 1845-1860.	**$350-400**	
Fragrant Cherry Tooth Paste – H.C. Baildon & Son – Scott's Monument – Princes, St. Edinburgh Cream pottery, black transfer, faded gold border, 3-1/2" dia., Scottish, 1865-1875.	**$150-200**	
General Depot in Philada. – Purified – Charcoal – Tooth Paste – A – New Dentifrice – Prepared by – Jules Hauel – Perfumer and Chemist – Premiums – Awarded – 120 Chestnut Street White pottery, black transfer, square shape, 2-7/8" x 2-7/8", American, 1840-1860.	**$300-400**	
Genuine Beef Marrow – Pomatum – (standing steer) – Eugene Roussel – 114 Chestnut Street – Philadelphia Cream lid and pot, black transfer, 3" dia., American (Pennsylvania).	**$450-500**	

H.P & W.C. Taylor's New Size Saponaceous Shaving 2oz Compound, Seven Highest Premium Awarded at the World's Fair 1851 Cream-color lid and pot, black transfer, 3-1/2" dia., American (Philadelphia).	$100-125	
H.P. Wakelee Druggist – Cold – Cream – San Francisco Cream-color lid and blue and olive background colors, gold band and black lettering, 3-1/8" dia., American (San Francisco).	$200-250	
Hazard, Hazard & Co. Cucumber Cream, 1150 Broadway, New York, Chemist, N.Y. City & Newport R.I. White pottery, black transfer, 2-7/8" dia., American, 1845-1860.	$150-200	
Highly Perfumed Bear's Grease For Beautifying and Strengthening the Hair – Prepared by X. Bazin (two standing bears) – 114 Chestnut St. Philadelphia Cream-color lid and pot, black transfer, 2-3/4" dia., American (Pennsylvania), 1845-1860.	$450-500	
Hocklin's – Cherry – Tooth – Paste (on scroll with fruit border) White pottery, black transfer, 2-3/4" dia., English, 1865-1875.	$45-55	
Improved – Cold Cream – of Roses – Prepared and Sold by – Eugene Rimmel – Perfumer – 96, Strand – 180 Regent S.- 64. Cheapside – London Cream pottery, blue transfer, 2-3/4" dia., English, 1845-1860.	$50-75	
Invented by the Proprietors – 1833- The – Original Unrivalled – Saponaceous Compound – for Shaving – by – Glenn & Co. Phila White pottery, black transfer, 3-3/4" dia., American (Philadelphia), 1845-1855.	$350-400	

Jules Hauel Perfumer, 120 Chestnut St Philadelphia, Premium Ambrosial Cream, Premiums Awarded by the Franklin Institute of Penn'a' White porcelain with purple transfer, 3" dia., original base ("Jules Hauel Perfumer, No 120 Chestnut Street Philadelphia"), American (Pennsylvania), 1845-1860.	$450-500	
Jules Hauel – Saponaceous – Shaving – Compound – 120 Chestnut St. – Philadelphia Red transfer, 4-1/4" dia., original pot with "Jules Hauel Perfumer, No 120 Chestnut Street Philadelphia" on side, American (Pennsylvania), 1845-1860.	$150-175	
Massey's Elder Flower & Cucumber Cream For Softening the Skin, Caswell Massey & Co. New York & Newport, R.I. Cream-color lid, red transfer, square shape, 1/2" x 2-5/8", 2-1/2", American, 1850-1865.	$200-275	
Perfumers H.P. & W.C. Taylor Philadelphia – (classic scene of Gen. Washington crossing the Delaware River) – "Washington Crossing the Delaware" White glazed pottery with detailed multicolored transfer, 5-1/8" dia., original pot, American (Pennsylvania), 1875-1878. In 1991, A. Ball chose this pot lid for the cover of his book, *The Price Guide to Pot Lids*.	$2,500-3,000	
Perfumers H.P. & W.C. Taylor Philadelphia – (classic scene of Gen. Washington crossing the Delaware River) – "Washington Crossing the Delaware" White glazed pottery with purple transfer, 3-1/2" dia., original pot, American (Pennsylvania), 1845-1860. In 1991, A. Ball chose this pot lid for the cover of his book, *The Price Guide to Pot Lids*.	$3,000-4,000	

Purified Charcoal Tooth Paste – Prepared by X. Brazin Perfumer, Philada Cream-color lid, black transfer, rectangular shape, 3-3/4" dia., American (Pennsylvania), 1850-1865.	$125-150	
Purified Charcoal Tooth Paste – For Cleansing the Teeth – and Gums, and Purifying the Breath – Prepared by – X. Bazin – Successor to – E. Roussel – 114 Chestnut Street Philadelphia White glazed pottery, black transfer, 2-3/8" dia., rectangular shape, American, 1840-1860.	$125-150	
Rose Vegetable Tooth Paste, Prepared by Jules Hauel, Perfumer, No. 120 Chestnut Street, Philadelphia, for the preservation of the Teeth and Gums White pottery, red transfer, 2-3/4" dia., American, 1845-1860.	$275-375	
Roussel's Unrivaled Premium Shaving Cream, X. Bazin, 114 Chestnut St. Philadelphia Cream-color lid and pot, red transfer, 3-1/4" dia., smooth base ("Gold Medals Awarded – E. Roussel Perfumer – 114 Chestnut St. Philada"), American (Pennsylvania).	$150-200	
Russian Bear's Grease (walking bear with banner) – Genuine As Imported - Nicely Scented White pottery, black transfer, 3" dia., English, 1850-1870.	$200-250	
Savage's Celebrated – Peruvian Balm (basket of roses) – For Restoring The Hair – 105 High St. Guildford Cream pottery, black transfer, 2-7/8" dia., English, 1845-1865.	$50-75	

Superior Purified – Bear's Grease – Manufactured by – T.H. Peters – Late of the Firm of – Jules Hauel & Co. – 182 Chestnut St. Philadelphia White pottery, black transfer, 3" dia., on side of pot "T.H. Peters & Co. Theo. JH. Vetterlein, Theo. H. Peters No 182 Chestnut St. Philadelphia," American, 1840-1860.	$500-600	
Superior – Shaving Cream – Manufactured – of the purest Ingredients – by – Glenn & Co. Phila. Cream pottery, black transfer, 3-1/2" dia., rare, American (Pennsylvania), 1850-1865.	$300-350	
Taylor's Saponaceous Compound – (man shaving while looking at mirror) Manufacture by H.P. & C.R. Taylor, Philadelphia Blue transfer, 3-7/8" dia., original unmarked pot, normally found in black, scarce with blue transfer, American (Pennsylvania), 1845-1860.	$500-600	
Taylor's Saponaceous Compound – (man shaving while looking at mirror) Manufacture by H.P. & C.R. Taylor, Philadelphia – Business Established in 1820 White glazed pottery with purple transfer, 3-3/4" dia., original unmarked pot, rare variant where man is missing his sideburns, American (Pennsylvania), 1845-1860.	$650-700	
The – Egyptian Salve – For the Cure of All Kinds of Sores, Wounds, Ulcers, Abscesses, Burns, Scalds, etc. Price 2s/9d – Prepared Only by – Reade Brothers & Co. Ld. – Wolverhampton Cream pottery, black transfer, 3-1/4" dia., English, 1865-1875.	$80-100	
Trouchet's – Corn Cure – Safe (lighthouse) Reliable – Trade Mark Cream pottery, red transfer, 2-1/8" dia., English, 1860-1870.	$65-75	

Vertiable Roelle de Boeuf (standing cow), L.T. Piver, 10 Bouleve de Strasbourg, Paris White pottery, blue transfer, 2-3/4" dia., French, 1845-1865.	$200-250	
Williams' Swiss Violet Shaving Cream, Prepared by The J.B. Williams Co., Manufacturing Chemists, Glastonbury, Conn. Proprietors of Genuine Yankee Shaving Soap White pottery, multicolored transfer, 3-5/8" dia., American, 1875-1885.	$275-375	
Woods – Is – Dandruff – Pomade – To be rubbed into the roots of – The Hair – Every Alternate Morning – Proprietor – W. Woods – Chemist – Bedford Street Plymouth Cream pottery, black transfer, 3-1/2" dia., English, 1875-1885.	$55-65	
World's Fair – Premium Perfumery – Purified – Charcoal Tooth Paste – A New Dentifrice Prepared by – Jules Hauel – Philadelphia White pottery, black transfer, 2-3/8" dia., rectangular shape, one of few American pot lids with color in transfer, extremely rare, American, 1845-1860.	$750-800	
Worsley's Saponaceous Shaving Compound Philadelphia – (Independence Hall, Philadelphia) Cream-color lid and pot, black transfer, 4-1/8" dia., American (Pennsylvania), 1950-1860.	$150-200	
Yarmouth Bloater Past – Prepared with Selected Fish – Trade (fishing boat) Mark – The Yarmouth Fishing Boat – Blanchflower – Manufacturer – Great Yarmouth – Sole Proprietor of the Celebrated Masonic Sauce Cream pottery, black transfer, 3-3/4" dia., English, 1860-1870.	$100-125	

Sarsaparilla

Sarsaparilla was advertised as a "cure-all" elixir, which actually makes these bottles a subset of the "cures" or "bitters" category. In the 17th century, sarsaparilla was touted as a blood purifier and later as a cure for the dreaded disease of syphilis. The drink became popular in the United States in the 1820s as a cure-all for a number of different ailments but soon was recognized as nothing more than "snake oil" with ornate and descriptive bottle labels sold at medicine shows.

One of the most popular brands among collectors is Doctor Townsend, which was advertised as "the most extraordinary medicine in the world." The bottles are usually aqua or green, with blues or dark colors considered much rarer.

A.H. Bull – Extract Of – Sarsaparilla – Hartford Conn., deep blue aqua, 6-7/8", American, 1840-1860, $200-225.

Sands Sarsaparilla, aqua green, 8", applied top, American, 1885-1895, $100-125.

Log Cabin – Sarsaparilla – Rochester, N.Y., medium amber, 9", American, 1887-1895, $100-125.

A. H. Bull – Extract Of – Sarsaparilla - Hartford Conn. Aqua, 6-7/8", tubular open pontil, applied double collar top, American, 1840-1860.	$150-200	
A. Rodemann – Compound Sarsaparilla – Elizabeth, N.J. Aqua, 9-3/8", smooth base, tooled top, American, 1885-1895.	$250-300	
Baldwin's – Sarasaparilla – West Stockbridge – Mass. Pale aqua, 9", smooth base, tooled top, American, 1885-1895.	$150-200	
Bixby's Sarasaparilla – Bixby's Drug Store – Santa Cruz, CAL. Aqua, 8-7/8", smooth base, tooled top, American, 1880-1890.	$150-200	
Bristol's – Extract of – Sarsaparilla – Buffalo Blue aqua, 5-5/8", pontil scarred base, applied sloping collar top, American, 1840-1860.	$250-350	

Old Bottles

Bristol's – Genuine – Sarsaparilla – New York Blue aqua, 10", iron pontil, sloping collar top, American, 1840-1860.	**$375-475**	
Buffum's – Sarsaparilla - & Lemon – Mineral Water – Pittsburg Light ice blue, 7-3/4", 10-sided, iron pontil, applied sloping collar top, American, 1840-1860.	**$375-475**	
Buffum's – Sarsaparilla - & Lemon – Mineral Water – Pittsburg Deep cobalt blue, 7-1/8", 10-sided, iron pontil, applied sloping collar top, American, 1840-1860.	**$500-700**	
Bush's – Smilax – Sarsaparilla Aqua, 9-7/8", open pontil, applied top, American, 1840-1860.	**$400-600**	
Carrol's – Soda & Sarsaparilla Depot – 272 Washington - & - 133 &35 Miel St Newburgh N.Y. Aquamarine, 7-3/8", smooth base, applied blob top, extremely rare, American, 1855-1870.	**$300-400**	

Charles Joly – Philadelphia – Jamaica Sarsaparilla Medium yellow amber with olive tone, 9-5/8", smooth base, applied top, rare, American, 1875-1890.	**$125-175**	
Dr. B. W. Hair – Sarsaparilla Ice blue, 9-5/8", open pontil, applied sloping collar top, American, 1840-1860.	**$200-250**	
Dr. Cooper's – Sarsaparilla – Woodard, Clarke & Co. – Portland, Ore Aqua, 10-1/4", smooth base, tooled top, American, 1885-1895.	**$150-200**	
Dr. Cumming's – Compound Extract – Sarsaparilla and Dock – Portland, ME. Blue aqua, 7-1/8", pontil scarred base, tooled flared-out lip, rare with a lot of whittle marks, American, 1840-1860.	**$250-350**	
Dr. Dennison's – Sarsaparilla Aqua, 7-5/8", oval shape, open pontil, applied tapered top, American, 1840-1860.	**$450-500**	

Old Bottles

Dr. E.R. Palmers – Compound Extract – Of Sarsaparilla – & Wild Cherry – Auburn. N.Y. Blue aqua, 9-3/8", smooth base, applied double collar top, American, 1855-1865.	$700-800	
Dr. Guysott's – Compound Extract – Of Yellow Dock – & Sarsaparilla Deep emerald green, 9-3/8", smooth base, applied tapered collar top, American, 1855-1860.	$6,500-7,000	
Dr. Guysott's – Compound Extract – Of Yellow Dock – & Sarsaparilla Blue aqua, 9-3/4", pontil scarred base, applied tapered collar top, American, 1855-1860.	$150-200	
Dr. Ira Baker's – Honduras – Sarsaparilla Light apple green, 10-1/8", smooth base, tooled lip, American, 1885-1895.	$125-175	
Dr. James – Sarsaparilla – J.W. James & Co. Aqua, 9-1/4", smooth base, tooled top, American, 1885-1895.	$150-200	
Dr. King's – Sarsaparilla Blue aqua, 9-3/8", smooth base, tooled top, rare, American, 1885-1895.	$200-125	
Dr. Myer's Vegetable – Extract – Sarsaparilla – Wild Cherry – Dandelion – Buffalo. N.Y. Blue aqua, 9-3/4", graphite pontil, applied tapered collar top, American, 1840-1860.	$900-1,000	
Dr. Signorett's Comp Ext. – Sarsaparilla – A.B. Stewart, Seattle Aqua, 8-3/4", smooth base, tooled top, American, 1880-1890.	$125-150	

Dr. Townsend's – Sarsaparilla – Albany – N.Y. Deep blue green, 9", iron pontil, applied wide top on short neck, American, 1840-1860.	$800-900	
Dr. Wester's – Sarssaparilla – Ithaca Blue aqua, 6-1/2", pontil scarred base, applied sloping collar top, extremely rare—only a few known examples, American, 1840-1860.	$400-600	
Dr. Wilcox's (backwards "s") – Compound Extract –Of – Sarsaparilla Blue green with teal tint, 9-1/2", iron pontil, applied top, American, 1840-1860.	$4,000-4,300	
Dr. Woodworth's – Sarsaparilla – Birmingham, CT. – 99% label reads: Dr. M. Woodworth's Compound Sarsaparilla, Birmingham, Ct. 1852 and signed by M. Woodworth Blue aqua, 10-14", big rough open pontil, applied tapered collar top, American, 1840-1860.	$3,000-3,500	
Emerson's Sarsaparilla – 3-Bottles Guaranteed To Cure – 3 – Kansas City, MO., original label reads: Emerson's Compound Extract of Sarsaparilla Co. Kansas City, Mo. Clear glass, 8-1/4", smooth base, tooled top, American, 1885-1895.	$100-125	
Fry's Sarsaparilla – Salem, Oregon Pale aqua, 9-1/2", smooth base, tooled top, American, 1885-1895.	$100-125	

Old Bottles

George's – Sarsaparilla – Comstock & BR – NY Blue aqua, 9-3/8", iron pontil, applied target collar top, American, 1840-1860.	$1,400-1,500	
Gilbert's – Sarsaparilla – Bitters – N.A. Gilbert & Co. – Enosburgh Falls VT Medium yellow amber, 8-3/4", eight-sided with rounded label panel, smooth base, tooled top, scarce, American, 1880-1890.	$500-800	
Grant's Sarsaparilla – Fremont, NEB Aqua, 9-1/2", smooth base, tooled double collar top, American, 1885-1895.	$175-225	
Hall's – Sarsaparilla – Shepardson & Gates – Proprietors. S.F. Ice blue, 9-1/4", smooth base, applied sloping collar top, American, 1875-1890.	$150-200	
Hartman's – Sarsaparilla Deep blue aqua, 8-5/8", smooth base, tooled top, American, 1885-1895.	$100-125	
Lacours Bitters – Sarsaparihere Medium amber, 9-1/8", column shape, smooth base, applied top, American, 1865-1875.	$500-800	
Morison's – Comp'd Syrup Of – Sarsaparilla Medium amber, 9-3/4", smooth base, applied sloping collar top, rare, American, 1885-1895.	$150-200	

Old Dr. – J. Townsends – Sarsaparilla – New York Cornflower blue, 9-3/8", iron pontil, applied tapered collar top, rare and unusual color, American, 1840-1860.	$700-800	
Purley Vegetable – Preparation. – Beckwith's – Sarsaparilla Quisia – & Wild Cherry Bitters Blue aqua, 9-1/4", smooth base, applied double collar top, rare sarsaparilla bitter, American, 1855-1865.	$600-900	
Putman & Walker's – Ruby – Sarsaparilla Pale aqua, 9-1/4", smooth base (W.T.& Co. U.S.A.), tooled top, American, 1880-1895.	$200-250	
Sand's Sarsaparilla – Genuine – New York Medium aqua, 9-3/4", graphite pontil, applied tapered collar top, American, 1855-1875.	$150-200	
Scotch – Sarsaparilla Blue aqua, 7-5/8", smooth base, tooled top, American, 1885-1895.	$100-150	
The G.E.M. – Sarsaparilla – Geo. E. Mariner – La Crosse, Wis. Aqua, 9", smooth base (W.T. & Co. – U.S.A.), tooled top, American, 1885-1895.	$100-125	

The Hondura Co's – Compound Extract – Sarsaparilla – Abrams & Carrol – Sole Agents – S.F. Blue aqua, 9-5/8", smooth base, tooled top, extremely rare, American, 1885-1895.	$300-400	
Turner's – Sarsaparilla – Buffalo N.Y. Blue aqua, 12-1/8", smooth base, applied sloping collar top, rare size, American, 1855-1865.	$800-1,200	
Warner's – Log Cabin – Sarsaparilla – Rochester, N.Y. Medium amber, 9", smooth base (Pat Sept 6-87), 98% original label, contents, and box, applied top, American, 1887-1895.	$500-600	
Wynkoopo's – Katharismic Hondura – Sarsaparilla – New York Medium cobalt blue, 10-1/4", rough snapped-off tubular open pontil, applied tapered collar top, American, 1840-1860.	$7,500-8,000	

Snuff

Snuff was a powered form of tobacco mixed with salt, various scents, and flavors such as cinnamon and nutmeg. Inhaling snuff was much more fashionable than smoking or chewing tobacco. It was yet another substance touted as a cure-all for ailments like sinus problems, headaches, and numerous other problems.

Most snuff bottles from the 18th and early 19th centuries were embossed dark brown or black glass with straight sides. They were either square or rectangular in shape, with beveled edges and narrow bodies with wide mouths. In the latter part of the 19th century, the bottles were colorless or aqua and rectangular or cylindrical, with occasional embossing and possibly labels.

Snuff bottle, medium yellow olive, 7-3/4", smooth base,tooled top, European, 1850-1870, $200-225.

Old Bottles

Snuff bottle, medium olive green, 6-1/8", pontil scarred base, rolled lip, European, 1780-1810, $200-250.

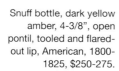

Snuff bottle, dark yellow amber, 4-3/8", open pontil, tooled and flared-out lip, American, 1800-1825, $250-275.

Bonn's – Pure – Scotch – Snuff Yellow topaz, 4", open pontil, sheared and tooled flared-out lip, rare, American, 1845-1860.	$3,000-3,500	
E. Waters – Troy N.Y. Deep yellow amber, 5-5/8", pontil scarred base, applied top, Elisha Waters opened his business at River and Second Street in Troy, New York, American, 1840-1860.	$3,000-4,000	
J.J. Mapes – No. 61 Front St. Yellow "old" amber shading from lighter upper one-third to darker lower two-thirds, 4-1/2", tubular open pontil, tooled flared out lip, rare, American, 1835-1850.	$2,000-2,100	
J.J. Mapes – No. 61 Front St. – N – York Yellow "old" amber, 4-3/8", open pontil, sheared and tooled lip, rare, American, 1835-1850.	$2,800-3,000	
J.J. Mapes – No. 61 Front St. – N – York Yellow amber with hint of olive, 6-1/4", open pontil, sheared and tooled lip, scarce in larger size, American, 1840-1860.	$1,500-2,000	
Snuff bottle Yellow olive amber, 4", eight-sided, open pontil, tooled flared out lip, rare form, American, 1790-1820.	$700-800	
Snuff jar Yellow amber, 4", square form, pen pontil, tooled flared out lip, American, 1840-1860.	$200-250	
Snuff bottle Medium emerald green, 4-1/8", pontil scarred base, tooled top, American, 1790-1830.	$400-500	
Snuff bottle Yellow amber with olive tone, 4-1/8", rectangular with beveled corner panels, open pontil, tooled flared out lip, American, 1799-1820.	$450-500	

Blown snuff jar – 96% label reads: Best Virgin Scotch Snuff, Manufactured by Sweetser Brothers, Boston, Mass. Etc. Medium olive emerald green, 4-1/4", open pontiled scarred base (F), tooled flared-out lip, American, 1825-1835.	**$600-700**	
Snuff bottle Dark amber, 4-1/4", square form, big open pontil, tooled flared out lip, American, 1790-1820.	**$300-400**	
Snuff jar Medium olive yellow, 4-3/8", open pontil, sheared and tooled top, rare in this light color, American, 1800-1820.	**$350-400**	
Snuff jar Yellow "old" amber, 4-5/8", tubular open pontil, sheared and tooled lip, blown in dip mold, American, 1790-1820.	**$150-200**	
Snuff bottle Deep amber, 4-5/8", open pontil, tooled flared-out lip, blown in dip mold, American, 1800-1820.	**$100-150**	
Blown snuff jar Olive yellow, 4-3/4", tooled flared lip, blown in dip mold, scarce color, American, 1780-1820.	**$300-400**	
Snuff jars (two) Yellow olive, 4-7/8", open pontil, tooled flared out lips, blown in dip mold, American, 1810-1830.	**$200-250**	
Snuff jar Yellow amber, 5", rectangular with side beveled corner panels, pontil scarred base, tooled flared out lip, American, 1790-1820.	**$400-500**	
Snuff jar Medium olive green, 5", tubular open pontil, sheared and tooled flared out lip, blown in dip mold, scarce in this size, American, 1790-1830,	**$300-350**	

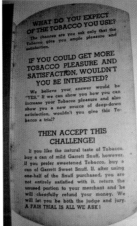

W.E. Garrett & Sons
– Scotch Snuff –
Information / Purchase
Information Pamphlet,
1880-1900, American,
$35-40.

Snuff bottle Medium olive green, 5", squared form with beveled corner panels, 5", open pontil, tooled flared out lip, rare in larger size, American, 1790-1820.	$500-600	
Snuff bottle Olive green, 5-1/4", rectangular form, pontil scarred base, sheared and tooled lip, blown in dip mold, American, 1790-1810.	$300-350	
Snuff jar Olive amber, 5-3/4", square with rounded corner panels, pontil scarred base, tooled flared out lip, American, 1790-1820.	$500-550	
Snuff jar Yellow "old" amber, 5-7/8", tubular open pontil, tooled flared out lip, American, 1800-1820.	$300-350	
Large wide-mouth snuff bottle Dark olive green, 7-1/2", rectangular with wide corner panels, smooth base, tooled wide mouth, German, 1860-1880.	$100-150	
Black glass snuff bottle Bright medium yellow olive, 7-3/4", smooth base, tooled top, unique large size, European, 1850-1870.	$200-300	

Soda

After years of selling, buying, and trading, I have come to believe that soda bottles supports one of the largest collector groups in the United States. Even collectors who don't normally seek out soda bottles always seem to have a few for sale on (or under) their tables.

Soda is basically artificially flavored or unflavored carbonated water. In 1772, an Englishman named Joseph Priestley succeeded in defining the process of carbonation. Small quantities of unflavored soda were sold by Professor Benjamin Silliman in 1806. By 1810, New York druggists were selling homemade seltzer as cure-all for stomach problems with flavors being added to the solution in the mid-1830s. By 1881, flavoring was a standard additive to these seltzers.

Because of pressure caused by carbonation, bottle manufacturers had to use a much stronger type of bottle, which eventually led to the heavy-walled blob-type soda bottle. Some of the more common closures were the Hutchinson-type wire stoppers, lighting stoppers, and cod stoppers.

Soda bottles generally aren't unique in design because the manufacturers had to produce them as cheaply as possible to keep up with demand. The only way to distinguish among bottles is by the lettering, logos, embossing, or labels (not very common).

Comstock, Gove, & Co., teal blue, 7-1/8", ten-pin shape, applied blob top, 1855-1865, $200-250.

Steinke & Kornahrens – Soda Water – Return This Bottle, Charleston S.C., deep olive amber, 8-3/8", eight-sided, iron pontil, applied top, 1840-1860, $2,500-3,000.

Alden's – Extract Of – Coffee Light blue green, 6", iron pontil, applied top with hand-crimped pour spout, American, 1840-1860.	$500-550	
American Desiccating Co – Of – New York Medium amber, 7-1/4", smooth base, applied tapered double collar top, extremely rare, American, 1860-1865.	$2,400-2,500	
A. Richards – Reading (in slug plate) Union Glass Works – Philad.A Medium sapphire blue, 7", iron pontil, applied double collar top, extremely rare, American, 1840-1860.	$1,800-2,000	
A.P. Smith – Charleston – S.C. Deep cobalt blue, 7-5/8", iron pontil, applied tapered collar top, American, 1840-1860.	$400-450	
A.R. Cox – Norristown Blue green, 7", iron pontil, applied double collar top, American, 1840-1860.	$150-200	

Old Bottles

Bostick's – Soda Water – New York Light to medium emerald green, 6-5/8", pontil scarred base, applied tapered collar top, extremely rare, American, 1835-1845.	$1,500-1,700	
Boyd – Balt. Deep olive green, 8-3/4", ten-pin shape, smooth base, applied tapered collar top, American, 1855-1865.	$1,500-2,000	
Brown & Co (inside indented panel with chamfered corners) Cobalt blue, 7-1/2", smooth base, applied blob top, American, 1855-1865.	$400-450	
C. & K. – Eagle Works – SAC. City Medium cobalt blue with deeper cobalt striations throughout bottle, 7-1/4", smooth base, applied top, American, 1858-1866.	$400-500	
C. Cleminshaw – Troy N.Y. – C Blue aqua, 6-5/8", overall vertical rib pattern, smooth base, applied double collar top, American, 1855-1865.	$100-125	
Carpenter – & Cobb – Knickerbocker – Soda Water – Saratoga – Springs Medium teal blue, 7-3/8", 10-sided, iron pontil, applied blob top, American, 1840-1860.	$1,400-1,500	

Craven (in slug plate) – Union Glass Works – Phila Medium blue green, 7-1/2", iron pontil, applied blob top, American, 1840-1860.	$400-500	
Crystal Palace – Premium – Soda Water – W. Eagle – New York (motif of Crystal Palace) – Union Glass Works – Phila Medium blue green, 7-1/4", iron pontil, applied top, American, 1853-1856. The Crystal Palace was constructed for the Exhibition of the Industry of All Nations Exposition held in Manhattan, New York, in 1853. President Franklin Pierce spoke at its dedication on July 14, 1853. It was destroyed by fire in 1856.	$800-900	
Crystal Palace – Premium – Soda Water – W. Eagle – New York (motif of Crystal Palace) – Union Glass Works – Phila Aqua, 7-1/4", smooth base, applied top, American, 1853-1856. The Crystal Palace was constructed for the Exhibition of the Industry of All Nations Exposition held in Manhattan, New York, in 1853. President Franklin Pierce spoke at its dedication on July 14, 1853. It was destroyed by fire in 1856.	$1,600-1,800	
D & T – Knickerbocker – S. P. Deep blue aqua, 7-1/2", pontil scarred base, applied blob top, American, 1840-1860.	$125-150	
D.L. Ormsby – New York – Union Glass Works Phila Blue aqua, 7-3/8", iron pontil, applied top, American, 1840-1860.	$300-350	
Egg Soda – Trade Mark – Simes – 20th & Spruce St. Aqua, 9-1/8", round bottom, smooth base, applied tapered collar top, American, 1855-1865.	$700-800	

E. N. Ladley – German – Town Deep cobalt blue, 7", iron pontil, applied double collar top, extremely rare, American, 1840-1860.	$3,500-4,000	
E.W. Reynal – Troy, N.Y. Medium cobalt blue, 7-1/4", smooth base, applied top, extremely rare, American, 1860-1870.	$600-700	
F.C. Kuentzler – Pottsville Light to medium blue green, 7", iron pontil, applied blob top, scarce, American, 1845-1860.	$200-250	
F. Gleason – Rochester – N.Y. Light cobalt blue, 7-1/2", iron pontil, applied blob top, American, 1840-1860.	$400-500	
F. Nusbaum (in slug plate) – Weissport Medium teal blue, 7-1/4", iron pontil, applied blob top, American, 1840-1860.	$800-900	
G.A. Cook & Bro – Philipsburg – N.J. (in slug plate) Medium emerald green, 7-1/2", iron pontil, applied top, American, 1840-1860.	$400-500	

G.A. Kohl – Lambertville – K (in script) Medium topaz, 7-3/8", smooth base, applied double collar top, extremely rare–one of only two or three known examples, American, 1855-1865.	$4,500-5,000	
G. H. Armstrong – 327th Sh. St. Emerald green, 7-1/8", pontil scarred base, applied double collar top, extremely rare, American, 1840-1860.	$1,500-1,600	
G. Gent – New – York Pale aqua, 7", iron pontil, applied blob top, American, 1840-1860.	$150-200	
Gannt - & - Hoffman – Gloucester – N.J. Emerald green, 7-1/4", iron pontil, applied top, rare, American, 1840-1860.	$1,500-1,600	
Gardner - & Brown Yellow green, 8-3/4", round bottom, smooth base, applied tapered collar top, American, 1850-1865.	$900-1,000	

Old Bottles

Geo Burrill (on shoulder) Deep yellow amber, 7", iron pontil, applied double collar top, American, 1845-1860.	**$150-200**	
Geo. Eagle (diagonal rib pattern) Medium blue green, 7", iron pontil, applied tapered collar top, American, 1840-1860.	**$1,000-1,300**	
H.H.P. Medium sapphire blue, 9-3/4", 10-sided, smooth base, applied tapered collar top, American, 1855-1865.	**$2,000-2,200**	
H. Nash & Co. – Root Beer – Cincinnati Medium cobalt blue, 8-3/4", 12-sided, iron pontil, applied top, American, 1850-1860.	**$1,000-1,200**	
Heiss – Philda – H (in script) – Union Glass Works – Philada Medium cobalt blue, 7-1/2", iron pontil, applied top, American, 1840-1860.	**$300-350**	
Hopkins – Milwaukee Deep cobalt blue, 7-1/8", iron pontil, applied top, rare, American, 1845-1860.	**$500-600**	

Howell & Smith – Buffalo Medium cobalt blue, 7-1/2", iron pontil, applied "tophat" top, American, 1840-1860.	$500-600	
Hyatt & Co. – Patent – Jan 5th 1869 – New York – Codd Liver – Oil – Soda Water Yellow amber, 5-3/4", quarter pint, smooth base, applied top, American, 1870-1875.	$900-1,000	
Ira. Harvey – Prov. R.I. – H – This Bottle – Is Never Sold Cobalt blue, 7-1/8", iron pontil, applied tapered collar top, American, 1840-1860.	$600-700	
J. A. Dearborn - & Co. – New York – Soda Water Deep cobalt blue, 7-3/8", iron pontil, applied top, American, 1840-1860.	$250-300	
J. H. Harris – Soda Water – New Haven – Conn. Medium sapphire blue, 7-1/2", eight-sided, iron pontil, applied top, American, 1840-1860.	$400-450	
J.T. Brown – Chemist – Boston – Double – Soda – Water Blue green, 8-3/8", round bottom, pontil scarred base, applied tapered collar top, American, 1855-1865.	$1,000-1,200	
J.Harvey & Co. – 65 1/2 Canal St. – Providence, R. I. Deep red amber, 7-3/4", smooth base, applied blob top, American, 1860-1865.	$450-500	

J. Lake – Schenectady, N.Y. Cobalt blue, 7-5/8", ten-pin shape, iron pontil, applied blob top, scarce, American, 1840-1860.	$375-500	
J. Monier & Co – CL-FR-NA Light to medium green aqua, 7-3/8", iron pontil, applied top, rare, American, 1856-1858.	$1,000-1,200	
J. Rother Medium green, 8-3/4", round bottom, smooth base, applied tapered top, extremely rare, American, 1840-1860	$3,000-3,300	
J. Thompson – Salem N.J. Medium yellow green, 7-1/8", smooth base, applied double collar top, American, 1860-1870.	$200-250	
John Cable – 1848 – J.C. Light to medium blue green, 7-1/8", iron pontil, applied tapered collar top, American, 1840-1860.	$400-500	
John J. Staff – New York Medium orange amber, 7-5/8", smooth base, applied double tapered collar top, unusual long neck, American, 1855-1858.	$900-1,000	

John N. Torlotting Deep cobalt blue, 7-3/8", smooth base, applied top, American, 1855-1865.	**$150-200**	
Keys – Burlngton – N.J. Medium blue green, 6-7/8", iron pontl, applied top, American, 1840-1860.	**$300-375**	
Knicker – Bocker – Soda – Water – 18 S.S. 52" (two slightly indented circular panels on "Knicker" embossing) Deep Prussian blue, 10-sided, iron pontil, applied blob top, American, 1840-1860.	**$700-800**	
L. Fisher – Philada. A Cobalt blue, 7-1/2", iron pontil, applied tapered collar top, American, 1840-1860.	**$600-700**	
L. Snider – Wheeling Blue aqua, 7-1/4", iron pontil, applied blob top, American, 1840-1860.	**$200-250**	

Luke Beard Medium green, 9-1/4", ten-pin shape, smooth base, applied top, American, 1850-1865.	$150-200	
Mc. Ewin – San Francisco Blue aqua, 7-1/8", 10-sided, smooth base, applied top, American, 1863-1870.	$200-250	
M.R. – Sacramento Deep cobalt blue, 7-3/8", iron pontil, applied top, rare, American, 1851-1863.	$1,300-1,400	
M. Monju & Co. – Mobile Medium blue green, 7-3/8", iron pontil, applied blob top, rare, American, 1840-1860.	$500-600	
M. Richardson Aqua, 10", cylinder, smooth base, applied tapered collar top, American, 1855-1865.	$450-500	
McKay & Clark – No 130 – Franklin St. – Balt. Medium blue green, 8-5/8", ten-pin shape, iron pontil, applied blob top, rare, American, 1840-1860.	$1,500-1,600	
Millville Glass Works Sapphire blue, 7-1/8", iron pontil, applied top, American, 1845-1860.	$400-450	

Owen Casey – Eagle Soda – Works – Sac City (two bottles) Sapphire blue and deep blue aqua, 7-3/8", smooth bases, applied blob tops, American, 1865-1875.	$300-350	
P. Babb – Balto (in slug plate) Teal blue, 7-3/8", squat shape, iron pontil, applied top, American, 1840-1860.	$175-200	
P. Babb – Balto (in slug plate) Emerald green, 7-1/2", squat shape, iron pontil, applied top, American, 1840-1860.	$150-200	
R. C. & T. – New York Medium cobalt blue, 7-1/4", iron pontil, applied tapered collar top, American, 1840-1860.	$350-400	
R. & H. – Sutton Medium cobalt blue, 7-1/4", iron pontil, applied blob top, American, 1845-1860.	$300-350	
S. Smith – Auburn. N.Y. – 1856 – KR. S – Water Medium sapphire blue, 7-3/8", 10-sided, iron pontil, applied blob top, American, 1840-1860.	$700-800	

Old Bottles

S. Smith – Schenectady, N.Y. Medium cobalt blue, 7-1/2", iron pontil, applied tapered collar top, American, 1840-1860.	$500-600	
San Francisco – Glass Works Blue aqua, 7-1/4", smooth base, applied top, American, 1870-1876.	$75-100	
Southwick - & G.O. Tupper – New York – Adna – H Cobalt blue, 7-1/2", 10-sided, iron pontil, applied tapered collar top, American, 1840-1860.	$500-600	
Southwick - & G.O. Tupper – New York Medium teal blue green, 7-5/8", 10-sided, iron pontil, applied tapered collar top, American, 1840-1860.	$200-250	
T.H. Paul – Glassboro – N.J. Medium blue green, 7-1/2", iron pontil, applied double collar top, American, 1840-1860.	$450-500	
Taylor & Co. – Soda Waters – San Francisco Medium sapphire blue, 6-3/4", iron pontil, applied blob top, American, 1840-1860.	$400-500	
Taylor – Never – Surrenders (in slug plate) – Union Glass Works – Phild. A. Light to medium cobalt blue, 7-3/8", pontil scarred base, applied top, American, 1848-1850.	$900-1,000	

Thomas. McCloskey – Mantuaville (in slug plate) Medium blue green, 7-3/8", smooth base, applied double collar top, American, 1855-1865.	$300-350	
W. H. Burt – San Francisco Deep green, 7-1/2", iron pontil, applied top, American, 1852-1860.	$400-450	
W. Eagle – Vestry, Varick – Canal Sts. – Prem. M.- Soda Water – Union Glass Works- Phila. Teal blue, 7-5/8", iron pontil, applied blob top, American, 1840-1860.	$400-500	
W. Feice & Son – Pittsfield – Mass. Sapphire blue, 7-3/8", smooth base, applied blob top, American, 1865-1875.	$150-200	
W. Ryer – R – Union Glass Works – Philada Light cobalt blue, 7-1/2", iron pontil, applied tapered collar top, American, 1840-1860.	$500-600	
Washington Spring Co. (Bust of Washington)- Ballston Spa – N.Y. Deep emerald green, pint, smooth base, applied double sloping top, American, 1865-1875.	$1,500-1,700	

Soda Fountain Syrup Dispensers

When was the last time anyone remembers hanging out at the local corner drugstore, sitting down at the soda fountain counter, and ordering an ice cream soda or a root beer float, where the syrup was squirted into the glass from a decorative ceramic dispenser? Sounds good, doesn't it? Unless you entered that drugstore 75 or maybe even 100 years ago, you didn't have the fun of enjoying that experience.

U.S. pharmacists first began selling all types of fountain drinks for a number of various physical ailments, from the common cold to lung diseases, during the late 1850s. In fact, the majority of these early drink mixes consisted of various drugs such as codeine, alcohol, and cocaine mixed with water. Pharmacists soon realized that by mixing different fruit extracts, along with sugar and carbonated water, they could produce a drink that everyone would buy.

Following the early successes of Coke and Pepsi with their flavored drinks in the late 1880s and 1890s, other new soft drink companies began to produce additional soda flavors and sold their syrup bases to drugstores. As the competition heated up and soda syrup began to be mass-produced, it didn't take long for pharmacists to figure out that having a soda fountain in their drugstore might make more money than selling drugs.

As a gimmick to sell the syrups, the companies actually gave away the dispensers as free advertising if the drugstore owner continued to purchase large supplies of soda syrup. This wasn't difficult since soda fountains became popular during the 1920s, with the help of Prohibition.

The active use of a small number of drugstore soda fountains, with their unique and ornate dispensers, continued into the 1950s. But with the arrival of modern technology and the onslaught of fast food chains, drugstore soda fountains were closed down and became a thing of the past.

It should be noted that while all dispensers are decorative and unique in their own style, the ceramic dispenser demands the highest prices at auctions.

Ward's Lemon Crush, 13-1/2", American, 1900-1930, $1,210.

Always Drink – Cherry Smash – Our Nation's Beverage, 13-1/2", American, 1900-1940, $1,840.

Grape Crush syrup dispenser, amethyst glass, 15", American, 1900-1930, $1,150.

Drink – Mo-Pep – syrup dispenser, 13-3/4", American, 1900-1930, $690.

Beats All – 5cents – Root Beer White ceramic ball shape with original ball pump and red lettering, American, 1900-1935.	$3,500-4,000		**Buckeye – Root Beer (The Cleveland Fruit Juice Co. – Cleveland, Ohio)** Black ceramic with white lettering, 14", American, 1920-1940.	$700-800
Bowey's – Old Style – Root Beer White ceramic barrel shape with red lettering, old ball plunger pump, American, 1915-1930.	$2,000-2,500		**Cherryallen – Allens – Red Tame – Cherry** Glass ball with advertising or front and back, 21-1/2", marble base, American, 1920-1935.	$500-600
Buckeye – Root 5cents Beer (centaurs dancing) Ceramic urn shape, 16", old pump with RB reset button, American, 1915-1935.	$2,500-3,000		**Citro – The Thirst Quencher – 5cents** White ceramic barrel shape with blue lettering on yellow background, 15", old plunger pump, American, 1910-1930.	$900-1,000

Old Bottles

Christo – Ginger Ale – 5cents Drink 5cents Plunger pump marked "raspberry," white with red lettering, American, 1910-1935.	$1,400-1,500	
Douglas – Root Beer White ceramic barrel-shape dispenser, original plunger pump with cap marked "Root Beer," gold lettering, American, 1920-1940.	$1,000-2,000	
Drink Hires – 5cents – Hires Root Beer barrel syrup dispenser Plunger pump with top cap with embossed Hires logo, American, 1920-1940.	$450-500	
Drink – Fowler's – Root Beer – 5 – The Best White ceramic ball shape, 13-1/2", advertising on front and back, old pump with strawberry button, American, 1900-1925.	$900-1,000	
Drink –Ginger Mint – Julep (Property of Anderson Drug Co. – Baltimore) (stamped on bottom) White ceramic barrel shape, 14-1/2", gold background with light brown letters, American, 1900-1925.	$700-800	
Drink – Grape – Juice Light purple ceramic ball shape, 14", old-style plunger insert with lemon button insert, American, 1915-1935.	$2,000-2,200	
Drink – Ver-ba – Safe – Sane – 5cents White ceramic urn shape, 15", old-style plunger insert with lemon button insert, American, 1900-1930.	$1,800-2,000	

Douglas – Root Beer White ceramic barrel shape with light brown lettering, 15", plunge-style pump, American, 1915-1940.	**$800-900**	
5cents – Drink – S& M- Root Beer – 5cents Plunger pump with top cap marked "Root Beer," American, 1930-1940.	**$700-800**	
5cents Drink 5cents – Massey's – Root Beer – Refreshing Plunger pump marked "Root Beer" on top cap, American, 1900-1925.	**$1,200-1,500**	
Drink – Grapefruitola – 5cents Grapefruit shape with original marked plunger pump, top cap in embossed with "Grapefruitola," ceramic with yellow background and red lettering, extremely rare, American, 1913.	**$65,000-66,000**	
Drink – Grape – Julep Grape-color ceramic, old ball plunger pump, gold bands on porcelain stand, rare, American, 1900-1930.	**$11,000-12,000**	
Drink – Red Keg – Refreshing Plunger pump cap marked "Nectar," red barrel with white lettering, American, 1910-1925.	**$2,000-2,500**	

Old Bottles

Drink – Howell's – Orange-Julep Shape of orange, 13-1/2", orange color ceramic, old ball plunger pump, gold bands on porcelain stand, American, 1900-1935.	$7,000-7,500	
Getz Blend (large B) Root Beer White ceramic with original old ball plunger pump, blue background with gold lettering, gold trim, American, 1900-1940.	$4,000-5,000	
Jersey Crème – The Perfect Drink White ceramic urn shape, 15", original pump with Jersey crème button insert, American, 1905-1930.	$1,400-1,500	
Liberty – Root Beer – Try a Stein – It's Fine – Richardson – Corp – Rochester, N.Y. White ceramic ball shape, 15-1/2", blue, red, and black lettering, American, 1900-1930.	$2,500-3,000	
Magnus – Root Beer Barrel shape with white ceramic, 16", blue background and gold lettering, gold bands, American, 1925-1940.	$2,500-3,000	
Montelaise – Cheriola – The Invigorating Beverage White porcelain with red and gold lettering, 14-1/2", original plunger pump, extremely rare, American, 1900-1930.	$46,000-47,000	
Or-Lem – Fresh Fruit Frosted glass syrup dispenser, original plaster or chalk-like mounting secures dispenser to it, original metal base, original plunger pump, graphics incised into glass, orange and lemon in background with green and orange lettering, American, 1920-1930.	$600-700	
Pokagon (on front) – Orange (on back) Indian decal on front and orange decal on back, 14-1/2", white ceramic ball shape with red lettering and red designs, old plunger-style pump with correct orange button insert, rare, American, 1920-1940.	$6,000-7,000	

Ward's – Orange – Crush Oversized shape, 13", orange sitting on base with decorative flowers, unmarked ball pump, date "1919" embossed on dispenser, American, 1919-1930.	$3,500-4,000	
Schuster's – Root Beer Red wood-type barrel with plunger pump, middle of barrel is white, brown lettering, American, 1910-1930.	$500-550	
Triple – XXX – Ginger Ale – "It Satisfies" White dispenser, 14-1/2", barrel shape, red, black, and orange lettering, American, 1905-1925.	$400-500	
Zipp's (depiction of waiter) Root Beer White ceramic with blue lettering, 15", old plunger pump with root beer insert, great art work, American, 1915-1935.	$1,800-2,000	
Zipps's Root Beer Iron, metal, and porcelain with red paint, extremely rare, American, 1900.	$800-900	

Target Balls

Target balls are small rounded balls the approximate size of a Major League baseball and were initially hand blown into a three-piece mold. Another type of target ball is the range ball that was often as small as a golf ball and placed on top of a metal pole as a stationary target.

Most of the common balls have a sheared or sharp-edged neck caused by tearing the ball from the blowpipe before the ball had properly cooled. Then the balls were filled with confetti, ribbon, or other materials such as sawdust or wood shavings. Also, the color differences happened when the batch of glass used in the previous day's production was not entirely used and cleaned properly, and the next day's glass color would be tinted from the previous batch of glass. In addition, clear glass wasn't popular since it

Two target balls, "NB Glassworks Perth - NB Glassworks Perth," green aqua, 2-5/8", rough sheared top, 1880-1900, English; and a diamond pattern target ball, yellow amber, 2-5/7", rough sheared top, German, 1880-1900, $150-200 each.

was hard to see when projected into the air. Some of the most popular colors were amber, various shades of light blue, purple (amethyst), and green.

Used for target practice from the 1850s to early 1900s, they gained considerable popularity during the 1860s and 1870s in exhibitions and Wild West shows with Buffalo Bill Cody and Annie Oakley until the 1920s. During one summer, the Bohemian Glass Works manufactured target balls at the rate of 1,250,000 over a six-month period. Others, such as Adam H. Bogardus and Ira Paine's, had their target balls manufactured by various glassmakers throughout the country as well as in Europe and especially England.

Around 1900, clay pigeons started to be used in lieu of target balls. Because target balls were made to be broken, they are extremely difficult to find and have become rare, collectible, and valuable.

Bogardus Glass Ball Patd. Apr. 10th 1877 Light pink amethyst, 2-5/8" dia., rough sheared lip, number 8 in diamond above center band, scarce in this color, English, 1877-1900.	**$1,800-2,000**	
Bogardus Glass Ball Patd. Apr. 10th 1877 Light blue green with swirl of olive color in lower half, 2-5/8" dia., rough sheared lip, rare color, English, 1877-1900.	**$900-1,000**	
Bogardus Glass Ball Patd. Apr. 10th 1877 Yellow amber, 2-5/8" dia., rough sheared lip, larger letter B before Bogardus, American, 1877-1900.	**$350-400**	
Charlottenburg – Glasshutten Dr. Frank Yellow olive, 2-5/8" dia., rough sheared lip, German, 1880-1900.	**$250-300**	
Composite Pitch Target Ball, "Sept 199 1879, March 9, 1880" in circle around C.T.H. Pat Co. Black pitch material, 3" dia., possibly made by Carver Target Ball Co. of Greenville, Pennsylvania, American, 1870-1800.	**$150-200**	
Dr. A Frank – Charlottenburg – Glasshutten Yellow olive, 2-3/4" dia., rough sheared top, American, 1880-1890.	**$200-250**	
Gevelot (Serpentine Line) Paris – (Serpentine Line) Deep cobalt blue, 2-3/4" dia., diamond pattern, ground mouth, extremely rare, French, 1880-1900.	**$900-1,000**	
E. Jones Gunmaker Blackbourne Lancs Light sapphire blue, 2-5/8" dia., rough sheared lip, English, 1880-1900.	**$200-250**	

Target ball, C. Bogardus Glass Ball Patd. Apr. 10th 1877, yellow amber, 2-5/8"dia., rough sheared top, American, 1877-1900, $200-250.

Target ball (depiction of man shooting inside circle on two sides), medium cobalt blue, 2-5/8"dia., English, 1880-1900, $350-400.

Target ball, Ira Paine's Filled Ball Pat. Oct 23 1877, yellow with amber tone, 2-5/8"dia., rough sheared top, American, 1877-1890, $200-250.

Target ball (depiction of man shooting inside circle on two sides), moss green, diamond pattern, rough sheared top, 2-5/8"dia., English, 1880-1900, $250-300.

Target ball, brilliant cobalt blue, blown in five-piece mold, rough sheared top, 2-5/8"dia., American, 1880-1900, $100-125.

Gurd & Son 185 Dundas – Street London Ont. Yellow "old" amber, 2-5/8" dia., rough sheared lip, scarce, Canadian, 1880-1900.	$1,000-1,100	
Ira Paine's Fillled – Ball Pat. Oct. 23, 1877 Cobalt blue, 2-5/8" dia., rough sheared lip, rare in cobalt blue, American, 1877-1900.	$2,000-2,200	
Ira Paine's Fillled – Ball Pat. Oct. 23, 1877 Yellow amber, 2-5/8" dia., rough sheared lip, American, 1877-1900.	$350-400	
L. Jones Gunmaker Blackburn Lancashire Light sapphire, 2-5/8" dia., rough sheared mouth, embossed X on base, blown in three-part mold, English, 1870-1895.	$200-250	
Mauritz – Widfords Yellow amber, 2-5/8" dia., sheared lip, Scandinavian, 1890-1900.	$700-800	
Target ball Medium moss green, 2-5/8" dia., unembossed center band with overall diamond pattern, rough sheared lip, English, 1880-1900.	$350-400	
Target ball Yellow amber, 2-5/8" dia., four-pointed star pattern, rough sheared lip, rare, American, 1880-1900.	$1,000-1,200	

Target ball Cobalt blue, 2-5/8" dia., seven horizontal rings pattern, rough sheared lip, American, 1880-1900.	**$250-300**	
Target ball – unembossed center band Yellow amber, 2-5/8" dia., diamond pattern, rough sheared and ground lip, German, 1880-1900.	**$250-300**	
Target ball Deep cobalt blue, 2-5/8" dia., rough sheared lip, blown in five-part mold, American, 1880-1900.	**$150-200**	
Target ball – Man shooting shotgun inside embossed circle/identical embossing on opposite side Pale amethyst with subtle streaks of deeper amethyst swirled throughout, 2-5/8"dia., rough sheared lip, English, 1880-1900.	**$300-350**	
Target ball – Man Shooting shotgun inside embossed circle/identical embossing on opposite side Clear glass, 2-5/8" dia., rough sheared lip, English, 1880-1900.	**$250-300**	
Target ball – N B Glass Works Perth – N B Glass Works Perth Pale green aqua, 2-5/8" dia., overall diamond pattern, rough sheared lip, English, 1880-1900.	**$175-200**	

Target ball – N B Glass Works Perth – N B Glass Works Perth Light cobalt blue, 2-5/8" dia., overall diamond pattern, rough sheared lip, variant with backward "S's" and upside-down "P," English, 1880-1900.	$150-175	
Target ball Dark amethyst, 2-5/8" dia., rough sheared lip, blown in three-part mold, rare color, American, 1880-1900.	$250-300	
Target ball Yellow amber, 2-5/8" dia., rough sheared lip, raised "pimple" pattern on front and back with horizontal lines on side, referred to as "Stars and Bars," American, 1880-1890.	$1,400-1,500	
Target ball Yellow amber, 2-5/8" dia., rough sheared lip, blown in three-part mold, American, 1880-1900.	$250-300	
Target ball Deep cobalt blue, 2-5/8" dia., overall square pattern, rough sheared top, French, 1880-1900.	$100-125	
Target ball Deep cobalt blue, 2-5/8" dia., diamond pattern, rough sheared top, French, 1880-1895.	$100-150	
Target ball Yellow amber, 2-3/4" dia., overall pattern of squares, rough sheared unfinished lip, rare—can also be found in cobalt blue, Australian, 1880-1900.	$900-1,000	
Terra-cotta target ball, Model 2001 (on slightly raised panel) Red terra-cotta clay, 2-7/8" dia., two-piece mold seam, possibly American, 1880-1900.	$200-300	

Target ball, IRA Paines Filled Ball Oct 23. 1877, cobalt blue, 2-5/8" dia., American 1877-1895, $2,000-2,100.

Target ball (motif of man shooting on two sides), medium amethyst, 2-5/8" dia., English 1877-1895, $200-250.

Van Cutsem – A ST. Quentin Deep cobalt blue, 2-5/8" dia., diamond pattern, rough sheared top, French, 1880-1895.	**$100-125**
Wide-mouth target ball Deep cobalt blue, 2-3/4" dia., molted pattern, sheared and ground 1" wide mouth, 362 of these balls were discovered in an old barn in Essex, England, in 2005; each group of balls were in their original shipping box marked "E. Barton & Sons, Stourbridge, Purveyors of Fine Glass Shooting Targets," English, 1890-1910.	**$650-700**
Wide-mouth target ball Medium turquoise blue, 2-3/4" dia., molded pattern and sand grain, sheared and ground 1" wide mouth, 362 of these balls were discovered in an old barn in Essex, England, in 2005; each group of balls were in their original shipping box marked "E. Barton & Sons, Stourbridge, Purveyors of Fine Glass Shooting Targets," English, 1890-1910.	**$550-650**
W.W. Greener St. Marys Works – Birmm & 68 Haymarket London Sapphire blue, 2-1/2" dia., rough sheared mouth, English, 1880-1895.	**$200-250**

Warner

The Warner bottle was named for H. H. Warner, who sold a number of remedies developed by a Dr. Craig. Warner developed his bottle for those and other cures and began producing great volumes and varieties (over 20) in 1879 in Rochester, New York. In addition, Warner bottles were marketed and sold in major cities in Europe such as London, Melbourne, Frankfurt, and Prague.

Warner bottles, which can be categorized in the following varieties, can frequently be found with their original labels and boxes, giving additional value to these already expensive and rare pieces.

- Warner's Safe Kidney & Liver Remedy
- Warner's Safe Diabetes Remedy
- Warner's Safe Cure
- Warner's Safe Bitters
- Warner's Safe Rheumatic Cure
- Warner's Safe Cure (around shoulders – rare)
- Log Cabin Cough & Consumption Remedy
- Log Cabin Hop & Buchu Remedy
- Log Cabin Sarsaparilla
- Log Cabin Scalpine (hair tonic)
- Log Cabin Scalpine
- Long Cabin Extract, Rochester, N.Y.
- Log Cabin Rose Cream (rare)

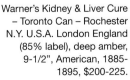

Warner's Kidney & Liver Cure – Toronto Can – Rochester N.Y. U.S.A. London England (85% label), deep amber, 9-1/2", American, 1885-1895, $200-225.

Warner's Safe Remedies Co. – Trade Mark – Rochester, N.Y., 9-3/4", and Warner's Safe Remedies sample bottle, 4-5/8", American, 1880-1895, $100-200.

Old Bottles

Warner's – Safe – Nervine (motif of safe) – London Aqua, 6-7/8", half-pint, smooth base, tooled lip, one of the rarest Warner safe bottles, not listed in aqua color in *Warner's Reference Guide* by Ojea/Stecher, English, 1890-1910.	$4,500-4,800	
Warner's – Safe – Nervine (in slug plate) – (motif of safe) – Frankfurt A/M (in slug plate) Deep green, 7-1/8", smooth base, applied top, German, 1890-1905.	$900-1,000	
Warner's – Safe – Nervine (in slug plate) – (motif of safe) – Frankfurt A/M (in slug plate) Emerald green, 7-3/8", half-pint, smooth base, applied blob top, rare, German, 1890-1900.	$1,900-2,000	
Warner's – Safe – Nervine (motif of safe) Frankfurt A/M Medium amber, 7-1/2", smooth base, applied top, rare, German, 1890-1910.	$500-600	
Warner's – Log Cabin – Extract – Rochester, N.Y. Amber, 8-5/8", perfect unopened condition with the original labels, instruction wrapper, metal ring pull and box, smooth base (Patd. Sept 6, 1887), tooled lip, American, 1887-1895.	$900-1,000	

Warner's – Log Cabin – Extract – Rochester, N.Y. Amber, 7", smooth base (Pat. Sept 6th, 1887), tooled top, 100% original label, instruction wrapper, neck and mouth label and box, American, 1887-1895.	$300-325	
Log Cabin – Scalpine – Rochester, N.Y. Medium amber, 8-7/8", smooth base (Patd Sept – 6 87) applied blob top, rarest bottle in Log Cabin Series, American, 1880-1895.	$500-600	
Warner's – Log Cabin – Sarsaparilla – Rochester, N.Y. Medium amber, 9", smooth base, applied top, 98% original label, contents, and box, American, 1887-1895.	$500-600	
Warner's – Safe Cure – (motif of safe) – Frankfurt A/M Yellow olive green, 9-3/8", smooth base, applied blob top, German, 1885-1890.	$200-250	
Warner's – Safe – Nervine (motif of safe) – London / And a Warner's – Safe – Nervine (motif of safe) – Melbourne Aus. – London, Eng. – Toronto, Can. –Rochester, N.Y. U.S.A. Yellow topaz, 9-3/8", smooth bases, applied blob tops, English and New Zealand.	$400-500	

Old Bottles

Warner's – Safe Cure (motif of safe) – Rochester, N.Y. (on slug plate) Medium emerald green, 9-3/8", smooth base, applied top, German, 1890-1900.	$400-450	
Warner's – Safe – Diabetes – Cure (motif of safe) – Rochester, N.Y. – U.S.A. – London-England – Toronto-Canada Deep amber, 9-1/4", smooth base, tooled double collar top, hard to find Canadian variant, Canadian.	$400-500	
Warner's – Safe – Diabetes – Cure (motif of safe) – Rochester, N.Y. – 90% label rear panel reads: Safe Diabetes Cure, etc. and partial label on base reads: Warner's Safe Pills, etc. Medium amber, 9-5/8", smooth base, tooled top, American, 1880-1895.	$150-200	
Warner's – Safe Cure (motif of safe) – London Medium pink topaz, 9-1/2", smooth base, applied blob top, rare in this color, English, 1885-1900.	$150-200	
Warner's – Safe – Medicines (motif of safe) – Melbourne Amber, 9-1/2", smooth base, tooled blob top, Australian, 1890-1900.	$150-200	

Warner's – Safe – Tonic – (motif of safe) – Rochester N.Y. (in slug plate) Amber, 9-1/2", smooth base, applied double collar top, American, 1875-1890.	$400-500	
Warner's – Safe – Nervine (motif of safe) – Rochester-N.Y. U.S.A. – London-England – Toronto-Canada Amber, 9-1/2", smooth base, applied double collar top, extremely rare – one of only two known examples, English or Canadian.	$300-400	
Warner's – Safe – Diabetes – Cure (motif of safe) – Rochester, N.Y. (in slug plate) Red amber, 9-3/4", smooth base (A.&D.H.C.), applied double collar top, American, 1875-1880.	$300-400	
Log Cabin – Hops and Buchu – Remedy Medium amber, 10", smooth base (Patd Sept – 6 87), applied blob top, American, 1880-1895.	$200-225	

Whiskey

Whiskeys, sometimes referred to as spirits, come in an array of sizes, designs, shapes, and colors. The whiskey bottle dates back to the 19th century and provides the avid collector with numerous examples of rare and valuable pieces.

In 1860, E. G. Booz manufactured a whiskey bottle in the design of a cabin embossed with the year 1840 and the words "Old Cabin Whiskey." One theory has it that the word booze was derived from his name to describe hard liquor. The Booz bottle is also given credit for being the first to emboss a name on whiskey bottles.

After the repeal of Prohibition in 1933, the only inscription that could be found on any liquor bottles was "Federal Law Forbids Sale or Re-use of This Bottle," which was continued through 1964.

Handled whiskey – Bininger's Knickerbocker – A.M. Bininger & Co – No. 19 Broad St. N.Y., medium yellow amber, 6-5/8", open pontil, applied tapered collar top, 1860-1870, $450-500.

Handled whiskey – Star Whiskey – New York – W.B. Crowell Jr (inside embossed seal), dark amber, rib-pattern, 8-1/8", open pontil, applied double collar top, 1865-1875, $1,000-1,200.

A.M. Bininger & Co. – No. 19 Broad St. – New – York Yellow amber, 8", handled jug, smooth base, applied double collar top, American, 1860-1870.	**$500-600**	
Barkhouse Bros. & Co. (embossed horse) Gold Dust – Kentucky – Bourbon (in slug plate) – John Van Bergen & Co. – Sole Agents Medium to deep amber with orange tint, 11-7/8", smooth base, applied top, American, 1871-1874.	**$10,000-11,000**	
Beiser & Fisher – N.Y. Yellow amber, 9" long, figural pig, smooth base, applied double collar top, American, 1865-1875.	**$900-1,000**	
Bennett & Carrol – 120 Wood St. – Pittsburg Medium yellow amber, 9-1/2", barrel shape, smooth base, applied square collar top, rare, American, 1855-1870.	**$1,400-1,500**	
Binninger's – Peep-O-Day – No. 19 – Broad St. N.Y. Amber, 7-5/8", flask, smooth base, applied double collar top, American, 1860-1870.	**$600-700**	
Binninger's – "Night Cap" – No. 17 Broad St. N.Y. Yellow amber, 7-3/4", flask, smooth base, applied double collar top, American, 1860-1870.	**$1,000-1,300**	

Boulevard Bourbon – Buneman Mercantile Co. – Sole Agents – S.F. CAL. Medium amber, 12", smooth base, tooled top, American, 1909-1919.	$230-250	
Buchanan – BCD (monogram) – Distillery (all inside shield with deer and rampart on each side) "Hand Made Sour Mash Whiskey" (inside banner) Amber, 9", figural cannon, smooth base, applied top, American, 1860-1870.	$250-300	
Callahan's – Old Cabin – Whiskey (on front and back panels) – Patented – 1865 – Pittsburgh, PA (on both side panels) Medium amber, 9", cabin shape, smooth base, applied top, according to Don Denzin, author of *Antique Eastern Whiskey Bottles*, "This is the most sought after of all antique whiskey bottles," American, 1865-1870.	$19,000-20,000	
Charles White – Rectifier – N 255- W. 15th St – N.Y. Medium amber, 9-5/8", smooth base, applied top and handle, American, 1855-1870.	$200-225	
Chapin & Gore (on shoulder) – Sour Mash – 1867 Olive yellow, 8-1/2", barrel shape, smooth base (H. Franks Patd. Aug. 1872), applied top with internal screw threads, correct embossed (Pat. Aug. 6) amber glass screw thread closure, rare, American, 1867-1875.	$200-250	

Crane & Brigham – San Francisco (inside leaf) Medium yellow amber, 10-1/4", smooth base, applied ringed top, American, 1880-1890.	$500-600	
Crown Distilleries – (crown and shield) – Company Red amber, 12", smooth base, applied top with original inside screw closure, American, 1899-1902.	$350-400	
J.H. Cutter – Old – Bourbon (crown) E. Martin & Co. – Sole Agents Medium amber, 11-3/4", smooth base, applied top, scarce, American, 1871-1877.	$350-400	
Cutter OK Whiskey (in circle) – J.H. Cutter – Old – Bourbon – Trade Mark – (embossed crown and whiskey barrel) C.P. Moorman-Manufacturer – Louisville, KY (front) A.P. Hotaling's O.K. Whiskey (back) Medium amber, 11-7/8", smooth base applied top, rare, American, 1883-1896.	$200-225	

Pure Malt Whiskey – Bourbon Co. – Kentucky, medium amber, 9", open pontil, applied ring top and handle, 1860-1870, $1,000-1,200.

Old Bourbon – Whiskey For Medicinal Purposes – Wilson, Fairbank & Co. – Sole Agents, green aqua, 9-7/8", applied tapered collar top, 1865-1875, $250-300.

Lilenthal & Co. – S.F., yellow amber, 8-1/2", applied double collar top, 1872-1880, $450-550.

J.F. Cutter – Extra Trade (five-pointed star inside embossed shield) Mark – Old Bourbon, yellow amber, 12", applied top, 1877-1885, $500-600.

Whiskey Cylinder – Dyottville Glass Works Phila (on base), medium cherry puce, 11-1/2", applied tapered collar top, 1855-1870, $200-250.

Applied seal handled chestnut whiskey – Ambrosial – B.M. & E.A.W. & CO. (on applied seal), medium amber, 8-7/8", open pontil, applied top, 1855-1870, $275-350.

Mo Cocktail – E.H. Co. – Mo Cocktail – E.H. Co., medium olive amber, 9-3/4", tooled top, 1880-1895, $350-450.

Dr. Girard's – London Ginger Brandy (on applied seal), yellow amber, 9-3/8", 1855-1865, $700-800.

Cutter – OK – Whisky – J.H. Cutter – Old Bourbon – Trade (crown on top of whisky keg) Mark – J.H.C. (inside keg) – C.P. Moorman – Manufacturer – Louisville, KY. – A.P. Hotaling's – OK – Cutter Whisky, yellow amber, 12", applied top, 1875-1880, $350-400.

Old Bottles

Durkin – Wholesale And Retail – Wines And Liquors – Sprague and Wall – Spokane, Wash Amber, 13-3/8", megaphone shape, smooth base, tooled top, American, 1895-1910.	$250-300	
E.G. Booz's – Old Cabin – Whiskey – 1840 – E.G. Booz's – Old Cabin – Whiskey – 120 Walnut St. – Philadelphia Amber, 8", cabin shape, smooth base, applied tapered collar top, Whitney Glass Works, Glassboro, New Jersey, American, 1865-1875.	$1,300-1,400	
E. P. Middleton & Bro – 1825 – Wheat Whiskey Yellow green, 12-1/4", half-gallon cylinder, smooth base, applied double collar top and seal, rare, American, 1855-1875.	$400-450	
131 – F" (inside diamond panel) – Bourbon Medium amber, 9-5/8", smooth base, applied double collar top and handle, extremely rare, American, 1860-1870.	$250-300	
Fitzpatrick & Co. Amber, 9-1/2", figural ear of corn, smooth base, applied tapered collar top, American, 1865-1875.	$1,900-2,000	

| Forest – Lawn – J.V.H.
Medium olive green, 7-1/2", iron pontil, applied double collar top, Jacob Van Horn was an early New York distributor, American, 1855-1870.	$500-600	
George Noar – Louisville – KY. – Bourbon Coy – Whisky
Amber, 8-7/8", jug, iron pontil, applied blob top and handle, extremely rare, American, 1855-1865.	$700-800	
Greeting – Theodore Netter – 1262 Market St. – Philada, PA
Cobalt blue, 6", barrel shape, smooth base, tooled lip, American, 1885-1900.	$600-700	
J.F.T. & Co. – Philad. (inside embossed seal)
Golden yellow amber, 7-1/8", rib-pattern bulbous shape, open pontil, applied double collar top, handled, American, 1855-1870.	$700-800	
J.N. Kline & Cos – Aromatic – Digestive Cordial
Medium amber, 5-5/8", tear drop pocket flask, smooth base, applied top, American, 1870-1880.	$350-400	
Jacob A. Wolford – Chicago – Wolford – Z-Whiskey
Orange amber, 8-3/4", barrel shape, smooth base (A.&D.H. Chambers Pittsburg, PA. – Pat. Aug. 6th 72) applied internal screw thread top missing stopper, American, 1872-1875.	$300-400	

Old Bottles

G.O. Blake's – Bourbon Co – Ky. – Whisky – More, Reynolds, & Co – Sole Agent's – For – Pacific Coast Golden amber, 11-3/8", smooth base, applied top, American, 1875-1880.	**$3,900-4,000**	
G.O. Blake's – KY – Whiskey (two barrels, one with Go Blake's Bourbon Co. – KY – Whisky (on one end) – Adams Taylor & Co. – Proprietors – Boston & Louisville – G.O Blake's – Whiskey- 98% label on reverse side Bright yellow amber, 11-1/4", smooth base, tooled double collar top, American, 1885-1900.	**$700-800**	
Goldwater – Schnapps – Schiedam Yellow olive green, 9-1/4", smooth base, applied tapered collar top, rare, American, 1860-1875.	**$275-300**	
Griffith Hyatt & Co. – Baltimore Medium olive green, 7-1/4", bulbous shape, pontil scarred base, applied top and handle, American, 1855-1870.	**$700-800**	
Hall, Luhrs & Cos – Snow Flake – Whiskey (in square slug plate) Medium amber, 12", smooth base, applied top, American, 1881-1886.	**$1,400-1,500**	

Hopatkong – Whiskey – J.S. Hess & Coi. Phila Deep cobalt blue, 10-1/2", lower half of bottle with 12 side panels, smooth base, applied ring top, American, 1860-1875.	**$500-600**	
IXL – Valley – Whiskey E. & B. Bevan – Pittston – PA (seven side panels have embossed five-point stars) Amber, 7-3/8", bulbous shape, pontil scarred base, applied double collar top, American, 1860-1870.	**$3,000-3,500**	
Full Half Gallon – Aneuberger – The Full Measure House – Portland, Ore. – Return Bottle And Get 10cents Clear glass with amethyst tint, megaphone shape, smooth base, tooled lip, American, 1895-1910.	**$75-100**	
Label Under Glass Whiskey – Hanlen's – Pure – Wine & - Liquor Products – Sherry – Hanlen Bros. – Sole Man'f's – Harrisburg, Pa. Clear glass, 11", background label with black lettering and gold trim, smooth base (Patnd. 1902), tooled lip, original contents, American, 1900-1915.	**$2,000-2,500**	
Lediard – New York Medium to deep puce, 11-1/8", six-sided, smooth base, applied top, American, 1860-1875.	**$600-700**	

Old Bottles

L. Lyons – Pure Ohio – Catawba Brandy – Cini. Deep amber, 13-1/2", smooth base, applied ring top, American, 1865-1875.	$300-350	
M. Gruenberg & Co. – Old – Judge – Ky. – Bourbon – San Francisco Medium amber, 11-3/8", smooth base, applied top, American, 1879-1881.	$300-350	
Mist of the Morning – S.M. – Barnett & Company Yellow amber, 10-1/8", barrel shape, smooth base, applied top, American, 1865-1875.	$350-400	
Miller's – Extra – Trade (in banner) Mark (in banner) E. Martin & Co. – Old Bourbon Light yellow amber, 11-7/8", smooth base, applied top, American, 1871-1875.	$5,500-6,000	

Myers & Company Dist's – Pure – Fulton – Whiskey – Patap. – Covington, KY. U.S.A. Aqua, 9-1/8", smooth base, tooled top, American, 1885-1895.	$100-150	
Nabob (in circle) Bright yellow amber, 10-7/8", smooth base, applied top, kick-up, American, 1882-1885.	$400-450	
Old Bourbon – Whiskey – For Medicinal – Purposes – Wilson Fairbank & Co. – Sole Agents Blue aqua, 10", smooth base, applied top, American, 1865-1875.	$150-200	
Patrick Smith – 1313 – Sec. Ave. – NW Corner 69th St. – New York – One Half-Pint – Full Measure Amber, half pint flask, smooth base (L & MC – 182 Fulton St. – N.Y.) tooled top, American, 1890-1910.	$100-125	

Old Bottles

Redington & Co – R &CO (monogram) San Francisco Medium yellow amber, 10-1/4", smooth base, applied ringed top, American, 1880-1890.	$500-600	
S.S. Smith Jr. & Co. – Cincinnati, O. Medium cobalt blue, 9-3/4", semi-cabin shape, smooth base, applied top, American, 1865-1875.	$3,200-3,500	
S.S. Smith Jr. & Co. – Cincinnati, O. Golden amber, 9-5/8", semi-cabin shape, smooth base, applied top, American, 1865-1875.	$600-700	
Simmond's Nabob (in circle) Medium amber, 10-3/4", smooth base, applied top, kick-up, four-piece mold, American, 1879-1885.	$100-125	

Full 1/2 Gallon – Star Wine Co. – Wholesale & Family – Wines & Liquors – Los Angeles, CAL. Medium amber, 13-3/4", eight-sided, megaphone shape, smooth base (1894 – I.P.G. Co.), tooled lip, American, 1895-1910.	$450-500	
Sunflower – Pennsylvania Rye – Spuance, Stanley & Co. – San Francisco, CAL. Dark amber, 10-1/4", smooth base, tooled top, American, 1900-1905.	$150-175	
T.J. Flack & Sons - Premium – Baltimore Golden amber, 7-1/4", pint flask, smooth base, applied double collar top, American, 1860-1875.	$200-225	
Applied Seal Whiskey Cylinder – Thos. H. Jacobs & Co. (on applied seal) - 99% original label reads: Old Jamaica Spirits, Thomas H. Jacobs & Co., Philadelphia Deep blue green, 11-5/8", iron pontil, applied tapered collar top, American, 1850-1865.	$2,800-3,000	
Star Whiskey – New-York – W.B. Crowell Jr. (inside embossed seal) Bright yellow amber, 8-1/4", rib-pattern cone shape, open pontil, applied top with hand tooled pour spout, handled, American, 1855-1870.	$500-600	

Old Bottles

That's the Stuff Golden amber, 10", barrel shape, pontil scarred base, applied top, rare barrel-shaped whiskey, American, 1865-1875.	$1,500-1,600	
Thos. Taylor & Co. – Sole Agents For – P. Vollmers – Old Bourbon – Louisville, KY. (all in square slug plate) Red amber, 12", smooth base, tooled top, American, 1880-1886.	$450-500	
Bottled For – Truet Jones - & - Arlington – Eichlberger – Dew Drop – 99% label reads: Superior – Old Rye – Whiskey Amber, 10", smooth base, applied top, rare Civil War-period bottle, American, 1860-1875.	$450-500	
Unembossed handled whiskey Amber, 8-1/2", bell shape, smooth base, open pontil, applied double collar top and handle, American, 1855-1875.	$500-600	
V. Olmstead & Co. – Constitutional – Beverage – New York Yellow olive, 10-1/4", semi-cabin shape, smooth base, applied top, American, 1865-1875.	$2,700-3,000	

Vidvard - & - Sheehan Medium yellow green, 9-7/8", smooth base, applied top and handle, hand-crimped pour spout, considered to be one of the top 10 handled whiskey bottles, American, 1860-1875.	$2,800-3,000	
W.F. & B – N.Y. Dark amethyst, 11", six-sided, smooth base, applied top, American, 1865-1875.	$700-900	
WM. H. Spears & Co. – Pioneer Whiskey (depiction of walking bear) – Fenkhausen & - Braunscheweiger – Sole Agents, S.F. Yellow amber, 11-3/4", smooth base, applied top, American, 1878-1882.	$5,000-6,000	
Wake Up – Wake Up Olive green, 11-5/8", triangular shape, ponil scarred base, applied top, American, 1855-1865.	$900-1,000	
Wharton's – Whisky – 1850 – Chestnut Grove Cobalt blue, 5-5/8", teardrop flask, smooth base, applied double collar top, American, 1860-1870.	$275-300	

Back Bar Bottles

Bourbon Clear glass, Fifth, swirled neck and body, light white enamel lettering, smooth base, tooled top, American, 1900-1915.	**$175-200**	
Capitol – B.B.B. – Bourbon Whiskey – Roth & Co. Agents SF Clear glass, 9-1/2", smooth base, original glass stopper, American, 1890-1915.	**$250-300**	
Chas Rebstock & Co. – Stonewall – Whiskey – St. Louis Mo. Clear glass, 11", Minnesota Brandy-style bottle, red, white and blue enamel, unique top and neck, white enamel lettering, rare, American, 1890-1915.	**$1,400-1,500**	
Chicken Cock (standing rooster) Bourbon Clear glass with amethyst tint, 7", smooth base, tooled lip, American, 1890-1915.	**$1,900-2,000**	

Cream- Pure – Rye Clear glass, 10-1/2", white enamel lettering, smooth base, tooled top, American, 1890-1915.	**$100-125**	
Cyrus – Noble Clear glass, fifth, gold enamel lettering, original cork closure, nine-sided panels, American, 1900-1920.	**$100-125**	
Elk Speed – depiction of running elk Clear glass, 11", smooth base, includes hand blown shot glass, fluted shoulders and base, corset-waist shape, tooled top, American, 1885-1910.	**$450-500**	
Fountain – Spring Clear glass, quart, smooth base, white enamel lettering, tooled top, American, 1890-1920.	**$130-140**	

Golden Age – Rye Clear glass, 10-3/4", three color paint enamel and gold paint design, smooth base, tooled top, unique mouth and neck, American, 1890-1915.	**$600-700**	
Guckenheimer – Rye Clear glass, 10-1/2", smooth base, white enamel lettering, gold paint and enamel design, tooled top, American, 1890-1915.	**$300-350**	
Imperial (gold enameled crown) – MC.D & C Clear glass, quart, gold enamel lettering, tooled top, American, 1890-1915.	**$100-130**	

Iroquois Club (torso of Indian) – Rye Clear glass, 8-7/8", polished pontil, cut glass flutes around neck and body, tooled lip, American, 1890-1915.	$1,300-1,400	
Kentucky – Reserve Clear glass, quart, white enamel lettering, smooth base, tooled top, American, 1900-1915.	$100-125	
Keystone – Rye Amber, 12", quart, smooth base, white enamel lettering and gold paint, tooled top, American, 1890-1910.	$350-400	
Label under glass back bar bottle: Jam – Rum – depiction of woman Clear glass, smooth base, enamel lettering, includes original 25-cent stopper, gold trim, American, 1890-1915.	$1,000-1,200	
Lacy (product of Crown Distilleries Company) Clear glass, fifth, gold enamel lettering, smooth base, tooled top nine-sided panels, American, 1900-1915.	$100-125	

Old Bottles

Liberty – depiction of flying eagle Clear glass, 11-1/4", smooth base, five-color enamel, eagle, and American flag with two stars, includes original metal shot glass, American, 1885-1920.	$1,500-1,600	
Mammoth Cave (scene of cave opening with forest background) Clear glass, 6-1/4", pinch bottle, smooth base, tooled lip, American, 1885-1890.	$250-300	
Metropolis – Whiskey Clear glass, fifth in smaller size, swirled neck, white enamel lettering, tooled top, American, 1899-1915.	$100-125	
Clover Leaf – Maryland – Club Clear glass, 11-1/2", smooth base, white enamel lettering, green enamel clover, fluted shoulders and base, includes metal shot glass, American, 1885-1915.	$400-450	

Old – Hickory Clear glass with tint of amethyst, 11-1/2", smooth base, white enamel lettering, tooled top, American, 1890-1920.	$250-300	
Richland – Whiskey Clear glass, pinch waist style, gold enamel lettering, smooth base, original cut glass stopper, American, 1885-1910.	$75-100	
Royal – Velvet Clear glass, quart, fluted base and shoulders, white enameled lettering, smooth base, tooled top, American, 1900-1920.	$125-150	
Rum (recessed oval panel with label under glass with picture of woman) Cobalt blue, 11-3/4", smooth base, applied ring top, American, 1875-1885.	$800-900	

Old Bottles

Label under glass back bar – Sherry (photo of pretty woman) Clear glass, 11", quart, smooth base, tooled top, American, 1885-1915.	$1,400-1,500	
Label under glass back bar – (photo of pretty woman holding beverage) Clear glass, 11-1/2", quart, multi-colored graphics, smooth base, tooled top, American, 1900-1915.	$600-700	
Stomach – Bitters Clear glass, 10", white enamel lettering, fluted shoulders and mug base, tooled top, American, 1890-1915.	$125-150	

Unembossed back bar bottle Cobalt blue, 11-3/8", cylinder, smooth base, applied ring top, raised oval front panel, blown in three-part mold, American, 1870-1880.	$375-475	
Unembossed back bar decanter Clear glass, 9-1/4", corset waist shape with cut shoulder and neck panels, shallow recessed wording "Buffalo Club" with depiction of "Brown Buffalo," polished pontil, tooled lip, original sided cut glass stopper, American, 1890-1910.	$300-400	
Target – Maryland – Rye Amber, 12", smooth base, tooled lip, raised white enamel lettering outlined in gold with gold top, neck, shoulder, and side of base bands, American, 1880-1900.	$700-800	
Yellowstone (depiction of waterfall scene) Whiskey - Yellowstone 100 Proof Kentucky Straight Bourbon Whiskey, Yellowstone, Inc. Louisville, KY. Clear glass, 11-3/4", smooth base, eight cut panels around shoulder and neck, tooled top and rim, metal cage stopper with teal and white spiral core marble, rare.	$3,500-4,000	

New Bottles

Post-1900

T he bottles in this section have been listed by individual categories and/or type since the contents hold little interest for the collector. New bottles covered in this section are valued for their decorative, appealing, and unique designs.

The objective of most new-bottle collectors is to collect a complete set of items designed and produced by a favorite manufacturer. With reproductions, like the bottles Coca-Cola has released, or with new items, such as those made by Avon, the right time to purchase is when the first issue comes out on the retail market, or prior to retail release if possible. As with the old bottles, the following listings provide a representative cross section of new bottles in various price ranges and categories rather than listing only the rarest or most collectible pieces.

The pricing shown reflects the value of the particular item listed. Newer bottles are usually manufactured in limited quantities without any reissues. Since retail prices are affected by factors such as source, type of bottle, desirability, condition, and the possibility the bottle was produced exclusively as a collector's item, the pricing can fluctuate radically at any given time.

Avon

The cosmetic empire known today as Avon began as the California Perfume Co. It was the creation of D.H. McConnell, a door-to-door book salesman who gave away perfume samples to stop the doors from being slammed in his face. Eventually, McConnell gave up selling books and concentrated on selling perfumes instead. Although based in New York, the name "Avon" was used in 1929, along with the name California Perfume Co. or C.P.C. After 1939, the name Avon was used exclusively. Bottles embossed with C.P.C. are rare and collectible due to the small quantities issued and the even smaller quantity that has been well preserved.

Today Avon offers collectors a wide range of products in bottles shaped like cars, people, chess pieces, trains, animals, sporting items (footballs, baseballs, etc.), and numerous other objects. The scarcest and most sought after pieces are the pre-World War II figurals, since few were well preserved.

To those who collect Avon items, anything Avon-related is considered collectible. That includes boxes, brochures, magazine ads, or anything else labeled with the Avon name. Since many people who sell Avon items are unaware of their value, collectors can find great prices at swap meets, flea markets, and garage sales.

While this book offers an excellent detailed cross-section of Avon collectibles, I recommend that serious collectors obtain Bud Hastings' 18th edition of *Avon Products & California Perfume Co. Collector's Encyclopedia*, which offers pricing and pictures on thousands of Avon and California Perfume Co. products from 1886 to present.

A Man's World Globe on stand, 1969.	**$7-10**
A Winner Boxing gloves, 1960.	**$20-25**
Abraham Lincoln Wild Country aftershave, 1970-1972.	**$3-5**
Aftershave on tap Wild Country.	**$3-5**
Aladdin's Lamp 1971.	**$7-10**
Alaskan moose 1974.	**$5-8**
Alpine flask 1966-1967.	**$35-45**
American Belle Sonnet cologne, 1976-1978.	**$5-7**
American buffalo 1975.	**$6-8**
American eagle pipe 1974-1975.	**$6-8**
American eagle Windjammer aftershave, 1971-1972.	**$3-4**
American Ideal perfume California Perfume Co., 1911.	**$125-140**
American schooner Oland aftershave, 1972-1973.	**$4-5**
Andy Capp figural England, 1970.	**$95-105**

Talcum powder, 3.5 oz metal cans
(different types of caps on each can),
1912-1915, $300-360.

Angler Windjammer aftershave, 1970.	**$5-7**
Apple Blossom toilet water 1941-1942.	**$50-60**
Apothecary Lemon Velvet Moist lotion, 1973-1976.	**$4-6**
Apothecary Spicy aftershave, 1973-1974.	**$4-5**
Aristocat Kittens soap Walt Disney.	**$5-7**
Armoire decanter Charisma bath oil, 1973-1974.	**$4-5**
Armoire decanter Elusive bath oil, 1972-1975.	**$4-5**
Auto lantern 1973.	**$6-8**
Auto, Big Mack truck Windjammer aftershave, 1973-1975.	**$5-6**

Sachet, glass bottle with metal cap, two-piece gold label, 1908, $100-135.

Aromatic Bay Rum, 4 oz., metal cork embossed stopper, 1927-1929, $100-125.

American Ideal powder sachet, large-size bottle with brass cap, 1912-1915, $75-100.

Auto, Cord, 1937 model Wild Country aftershave, 1974-1978.	$7-8		**Auto, MG, 1936** Wild Country aftershave, 1974-1975.	$4-5
Auto, Country Vendor Wild Country aftershave, 1973.	$7-8		**Auto, Model A** Wild Country aftershave, 1972-1974.	$4-5
Auto, Duesenberg Silver, Wild Country aftershave, 1970-1972.	$8-9		**Auto, red depot wagon** Oland aftershave, 1972-1973.	$6-7
Auto, dune buggy Sports Rally bracing lotion, 1971-1973.	$4-5		**Auto, Rolls Royce** Deep Woods aftershave, 1972-1975.	$6-8
Auto, Electric Charger Avon Leather cologne, 1970-1972.	$6-7		**Auto, Stanley Steamer** Windjammer aftershave, 1971-1972.	$6-7
Auto, Hayes Apperson, 1902 Model Avon Blend 7 aftershave, 1973-1974.	$5-7		**Auto, station wagon** Tai Winds aftershave, 1971-1973.	$7-8
Auto, Maxwell 23 Deep Woods aftershave, 1972-1974.	$5-6		**Auto, Sterling 6** Spicy aftershave, 1968-1970.	$6-7

New Bottles

Auto, Sterling Six II Wild Country aftershave, 1973-1974.	$4-5
Auto, Stutz Bearcat, 1914 model Avon Blend 7 aftershave, 1974-1977.	$5-6
Auto, Touring T Tribute aftershave, 1969-1970.	$6-7
Auto, Volkswagen Red, Oland aftershave, 1972.	$5-6
Avon Calling, phone Wild Country aftershave, 1969-1970.	$15-20
Avon Dueling Pistol II Black glass, 1972.	$10-15
Avonshire Blue cologne 1971-1974.	$4-5
Baby grand piano Perfume glace, 1971-1972.	$8-10
Baby hippo 1977-1980.	$4-5
Ballad perfume 3 drams, 3/8 ounce, 1939.	$100-125
Bath urn Lemon Velvet bath oil, 1971-1973.	$4-5
Beauty bound black purse 1964.	$45-55
Bell Jar cologne 1973.	$5-10

Benjamin Franklin Wild Country aftershave, 1974-1976.	$4-5
Big game rhino Tai Winds aftershave, 1972-1973.	$7-8
Big whistle 1972.	$4-5
Birdhouse Power bubble bath, 1969.	$7-8
Bird of Paradise cologne decanter 1972-1974.	$4-5
Blacksmith's anvil Deep Woods aftershave, 1972-1973.	$4-5
Bloodhound pipe Deep Woods aftershave, 1976.	$5-6
Blue Blazer aftershave lotion 1964.	$25-30
Blue Blazer Deluxe 1965.	$55-65
Blue Moo Soap on a Rope 1972.	$5-6
Blunderbuss pistol 1976.	$7-10
Bon Bon, black Field Flowers cologne, 1973.	$5-6
Bon Bon, white Occur cologne, 1972-1973.	$5-6

Bon Bon, white Topaze cologne, 1972-1973.	$5-6
Boot, gold top Avon Leather aftershave, 1966-1971.	$3-4
Boot, western 1973.	$4-5
Boots and saddle 1968.	$20-22
Brocade deluxe 1967.	$30-35
Buffalo nickel Liquid hair lotion, 1971-1972.	$4-5
Bulldog pipe Oland aftershave, 1972-1973.	$4-5
Bunny puff and talc 1969-1972.	$3-4
Bureau organizer 1966-1967.	$35-55
Butter candlestick Sonnet cologne, 1974.	$7-8
Butterfly Fantasy egg First issue, 1974.	$20-30
Butterfly Unforgettable cologne, 1972-1973.	$4-5
Butterfly Unforgettable cologne, 1974-1976.	$1-2

Cable car aftershave, 1974-1975.	$8-10
Camper, Deep Woods aftershave, 1972-1974.	$6-7
Canada goose Deep Woods cologne, 1973-1974.	$4-5
Candlestick cologne Elusive, 1970-1971.	$5-6
Car Army Jeep, 1974-1975.	$4-5
Casey's Lantern Island Lime aftershave, 1966-1967.	$30-40
Catch a fish Field Flowers cologne, 1976-1978.	$6-7
Centennial Express 1876 Locomotive, 1978.	$11-12
Chevy '55 1974-1975.	$6-8
Christmas ornament Green or red, 1970-1971.	$1-2
Christmas ornament Orange, bubble bath, 1970-1971.	$2-3
Christmas tree Bubble bath, 1968.	$5-7
Classic lion Deep Wood aftershave, 1973-1975.	$4-5

New Bottles

Thomas Jefferson handgun, 10" l, 2-1/2 oz, dark amber glass with gold and silver plastic cap, 1978-1979, $11.

Station wagon, 6 oz, green glass car with tan plastic top, 1971-1973, $14.

Club bottle 1906 Avon lady, 1977.	$25-30		**Covered wagon** Wild Country aftershave, 1970-1971.	$4-5
Club bottle 1st annual, 1972.	$150-200		**Daylight Shaving Time** 1968-1970.	$5-7
Club bottle 2nd annual, 1973.	$45-60		**Defender Cannon** 1966.	$20-24
Club bottle 5th annual, 1976.	$25-30		**Dollars 'n' Scents** 1966-1967.	$20-24
Club bottle Bud Hastin, 1974.	$70-95		**Dutch girl figurine** Somewhere, 1973-1974.	$8-10
Club bottle CPC Factory, 1974.	$30-40		**Duck aftershave** 1971.	$4-6
Collector's pipe Windjammer aftershave, 1973-1974.	$3-4		**Dueling Pistol 1760** 1973-1974.	$9-12
Colt revolver 1851 1975-1976.	$10-12		**Dueling Pistol II** 1975.	$9-12
Corncob pipe Aftershave, 1974-1975.	$4-6		**Eight ball decanter** Spicy aftershave, 1973.	$3-4
Corvette Stingray '65 1975.	$5-7		**Electric guitar** Wild Country aftershave, 1974-1975.	$4-5

Enchanted frog cream sachet Sonnet cologne, 1973-1976.	$3-4
Fashion boot Moonwind cologne, 1972-1976.	$5-7
Fashion boot Sonnet cologne, 1972-1976.	$5-7
Fielder's choice 1971-1972.	$4-6
Fire alarm box 1975-1976.	$4-6
First Class Male Wild Country aftershave, 1970-1971.	$3-4
First down Soap on a Rope, 1970-1971.	$7-8
First down Wild Country aftershave.	$3-4
First volunteer Tai Winds cologne, 1971-1972.	$6-7
Fox hunt 1966.	$25-30
French telephone Moonwind foaming bath oil, 1971.	$20-24
Gatnet bud vase To a Wild Rose cologne, 1973-1976.	$3-5
Gavel Island Lime aftershave, 1967-1968.	$4-5

George Washington Spicy aftershave, 1970-1972.	$2-3
George Washington Tribute aftershave, 1970-1972.	$2-3
Gold Cadillac 1969-1973.	$7-10
Gone fishing 1973-1974.	$5-7
Grade Avon hostess soap 1971-1972.	$6-8
Hearth lamp Roses, Roses, 1973-1976.	$6-8
Hobnail decanter Moonwind bath oil, 1972-1974.	$5-6
Hunter's stein 1972.	$10-14
Indian chieftain Protein hair lotion, 1972-1975.	$2-3
Indian head penny Bravo aftershave, 1970-1972.	$4-5
Inkwell Windjammer aftershave, 1969-1970.	$6-7
Iron horse shaving mug Avon Blend 7 aftershave, 1974-1976.	$3-4
Jack-in-the-box Baby cream, 1974.	$4-6

Jaguar car 1973-1976.	$6-8
Jolly Santa 1978.	$6-7
Joyous Bell 1978.	$5-6
King Pin 1969-1970.	$4-6
Kodiak bear 1977.	$5-10
Koffee Klatch Honeysuckle foam bath oil, 1971-1974.	$5-6
Liberty Bell Tribute aftershave, 1971-1972.	$4-6
Liberty dollar Aftershave, 1970-1972.	$4-6
Lincoln bottle 1971-1972.	$3-5
Lip Pop Colas Cherry, 1973-1974.	$1-2
Lip Pop Colas Cola, 1973-1974.	$1-2
Lip Pop Colas Strawberry, 1973-1974.	$1-2
Longhorn steer 1975-1976.	$7-9
Looking glass Regence cologne, 1970-1972.	$7-8

American Beauty fragrance jar liquid, 4 oz, cork stopper, 1921, $100-125.

First Class Male, 4-1/2" h, 4 oz, blue glass with red cap, 1970-1971, $10.

Mallard duck 1967-1968.	$8-10
Mickey Mouse Bubble bath, 1969.	$10-12
Mighty Mitt Soap on a Rope, 1969-1972.	$7-8
Ming cat Bird of Paradise cologne, 1971.	$5-7
Mini bike Sure Winner bracing lotion, 1972-1973.	$3-5
Nile blue bath urn Skin So Soft, 1972-1974.	$3-4
Nile blue bath urn Skin So Soft, 1972-1974.	$4-6

Avon

Seahorse, clear glass, 6 oz, gold cap, 1970-1972, $10.

Gaylord Gator, 10" l, green and yellow rubber soap dish with yellow soap, 1967-1969, $3 gator only, $10 set.

No Parking 1975-1976.	**$5-7**
Old Faithful Wild Country aftershave, 1972-1973.	**$4-6**
One Good Turn Screwdriver, 1976.	**$5-6**
Opening Play Dull golden, Spicy aftershave, 1968-1969.	**$8-10**
Opening Play Shiny golden, Spicy aftershave, 1968-1969.	**$14-17**
Owl Fancy, Roses, Roses, 1974-1976.	**$3-4**
Owl Soap dish and soaps, 1970-1971.	**$8-10**
Packard roadster 1970-1972.	**$4-7**

Pass play decanter 1973-1975.	**$6-8**
Peanuts Gang Soaps, 1970-1972.	**$8-9**
Pepperbox pistol 1976.	**$5-10**
Perfect drive decanter 1975-1976.	**$7-9**
Pheasant 1972-1974.	**$7-9**
Piano decanter Tai Winds aftershave, 1972.	**$3-4**
Pipe Full decanter, brown, Spicy aftershave, 1971-1972.	**$3-4**
Pony Express Avon Leather aftershave, 1971-1972.	**$3-4**
Pony post "Tall," 1966-1967.	**$7-9**
Pot belly stove 1970-1971.	**$5-7**
President Lincoln Tai Winds aftershave, 1973.	**$6-8**
President Washington Deep Woods aftershave, 1974-1976.	**$4-5**
Quail 1973-1974.	**$7-9**

Rainbow trout Deep Woods aftershave, 1973-1974.	$3-4	Spark plug decanter 1975-1976.	$2-5
Road Runner motorcycle.	$4-5	Spirit of St. Louis Excalibur aftershave, 1970-1972.	$3-5
Rook Spicy aftershave, 1973-1974.	$4-5	Stagecoach Wild Country aftershave, 1970-1977.	$5-6
Royal coach Bird of Paradise bath oil, 1972-1973.	$4-6	Tee off Electric pre-shave, 1973-1975.	$2-3
Scent with Love Elusive perfume, 1971-1972.	$9-10	Ten-point buck Wild Country aftershave, 1969-1974.	$5-7
Scent with Love Field Flowers perfume, 1971-1972.	$9-10	Twenty-dollar gold piece Windjammer aftershave, 1971-1972.	$4-6
Scent with Love Moonwind perfume, 1971-1972.	$9-10	Uncle Sam pipe Deep Woods aftershave, 1975-1976.	$4-5
Side-wheeler Tribute aftershave, 1970-1971.	$4-5	Viking horn, 1966.	$12-16
Side-wheeler Wild Country aftershave, 1971-1972.	$3-4	Western boot Wild Country aftershave, 1973-1975.	$2-3
Small World perfume glace Small World, 1971-1972.	$3-4	Western saddle 1971-1972.	$7-9
Snoopy Soap dish refills, 1968-1976.	$3-4	Wild turkey 1974-1976.	$6-8
Snoopy's bubble tub 1971-1972.	$3-4	World's Greatest Dad Decanter, 1971.	$4-6

Ezra Brooks

The Ezra Brooks Distilling Co. began to issue figurals in 1964, 10 years after the Jim Beam company, and quickly became a strong competitive rival due to the company's effective distribution, promotion techniques, unique design, and choice of subjects.

While many of the Brooks bottles depict the same themes as Jim Beam (Sports and Transportation series), they also produced bottles based on original subjects. One of these is the Maine lobster that looks good enough to put on anyone's dinner table. The most popular series depicts antiques such as an Edison phonograph and a Spanish cannon. Yearly new editions highlight American historical events and anniversaries. One of my favorites is the Bucket of Blood (1970) from the Virginia City, Nevada saloon by the same name, which is a bucket-shaped bottle.

While these bottles are still filled with Kentucky bourbon, most are bought by collectors.

Alabama Bicentennial 1976.	$12-14		**Auburn 1932** Classic car, 1978.	$30-35
American Legion, 1971 Distinguished embossed star emblem from World War I.	$30-40		**Baltimore oriole wildlife** 1979.	$20-30
American Legion, 1972 Salutes Illinois American Legion 54th National Convention.	$50-60		**Bare knuckle fighter** 1971.	$35-40
American Legion, 1973 Salutes Hawaii, which hosted the American Legion's 54th National Convention.	$20-25		**Baseball Hall of Fame** 1973.	$20-22
			Baseball player 1974.	$20-25
American Legion Miami, 1974.	$15-20		**Bear** 1968.	$10-12
American Legion Denver, 1977.	$15-20		**Beaver** 1972.	$10-15
American Legion Chicago, 1982.	$20-25		**Bengal tiger wildlife** 1979.	$20-30
American Legion Seattle, 1983.	$30-35		**Betsy Ross** 1975.	$15-20
AMVETS Polish Legion, 1973.	$14-18		**Bicycle** Penny-Farthington, 1973.	$10-15
AMVETS Dolphin, 1974.	$10-15		**Big Bertha** Nugget Casino's very own elephant with raised trunk.	$10-13
Antique Cannon 1969.	$10-12		**Big Daddy Lounge, 1969** Salute to South Florida's state liquor chain and Big Daddy Lounges.	$10-12
Antique Phonograph 1970.	$20-25			
Arizona, 1969 Man with burro in search of lost Dutchman mine.	$20-25		**Bighorn Ram** 1972.	$18-20
			Bird Dog 1971.	$12-14

Bordertown, 1970 Salutes Borderline Club on border of California and Nevada.	$10-15
Bowler 1973.	$15-20
Bowling Tenpins 1973.	$9-12
Brahma bull 1972.	$10-12
Bronco buster 1973.	$15-20
Bucket of Blood, 1970 Salutes famous Virginia City, Nevada saloon, bucket-shaped bottle.	$15-20
Bucking bronco Rough Rider, 1973.	$10-12
Bucky Badger No. 1 Boxer, 1973.	$30-35
Bucky Badger No. 2 Football, 1974.	$30-35
Bucky Badger No. 3 Hockey, 1974.	$30-35
Buffalo hunter 1971.	$10-12
Bulldog, 1972 Mighty canine mascot and football symbol.	$10-14
Bull moose 1973.	$12-15
Busy beaver.	$4-7

Cabin still.	$20-35
Cable car 1968.	$5-6
California quail 1970.	$8-10
Canadian honker 1975.	$9-12
Canadian loon wildlife 1979.	$25-35
Cardinal 1972.	$20-25
Casey at bat 1973.	$75-80
Ceremonial dancer 1970.	$20-25
CB convoy radio 1976.	$5-9
Charolais beef 1973.	$10-14
Cheyenne shoot-out, 1970 Honoring Wild West and its Cheyenne Frontier Days.	$10-12
Chicago Fire 1974.	$20-30
Chicago water tower 1969.	$8-12
Christmas decanter 1966.	$5-8
Christmas tree 1979.	$13-17

Churchill, 1970 Commemorating "Iron Curtain" speech at Westminster College by Churchill.	$5-9	**Club bottle** Distillery.	$9-12
Cigar store Indian 1968.	$10-12	**Club bottle, 1973** Third commemorative Ezra Brooks Collectors Club in shape of America.	$14-18
Classic firearms, 1969 Embossed gun set consisting of Derringer, Colt 45, Peacemaker, over and under flintlock, and pepper box.	$15-19	**Clydesdale horse** 1973.	$8-12
Clowns, Imperial Shrine 1978.	$30-35	**Colonial drummer** 1974.	$10-15
Clown Bust No. 1 Smiley, 1979.	$30-35	**Colt Peacemaker flask** 1969.	$5-10
Clown Bust No. 2 Cowboy, 1979.	$30-35	**Conquistadors, 1971** Tribute to great Drum and Bugle Corps.	$10-15
Clown Bust No. 3 Pagliacci, 1979.	$30-35	**Conquistadors Drum and Bugle** 1972.	$12-15
Clown Bust No. 4 Keystone Cop.	$30-35	**Corvette Indy Pace Car** 1978.	$45-55
Clown Bust No. 5 Cuddles.	$30-35	**Corvette 1957 Classic** 1976.	$110-140
Clown Bust No. 6 Tramp.	$30-35	**Court jester.**	$10-15
Clown with accordion 1971.	$30-35	**Dakota cowboy** 1975.	$30-35
Clown with balloon 1973.	$30-35	**Dakota cowgirl** 1976	$30-35
Club bottle Birthday cake.	$9-12	**Dakota grain elevator** 1978	$20-30
		Dakota Shotgun Express 1977.	$18-22

Dead wagon, 1970 Made to carry gunfight loser to Boot Hill.	$5-7
Delta Belle 1969.	$6-7
Democratic Convention 1976.	$10-16
Derringer flask 1969.	$5-10
Dirt bike Riverboat, 1869.	$10-16
Distillery, 1970 Reproduction of Ezra Brooks distillery in Kentucky.	$10-12
Duesenberg.	$24-33
Elephant 1973.	$7-9
Elk Salutes organizations that practiced benevolence and charity.	$20-28
English setter Bird dog, 1971.	$14-17
Equestrienne 1974.	$15-17
Esquire Ceremonial dancer.	$10-16
Farmer Iowa, 1977.	$30-35
Farthington bike 1972.	$6-8

Fire engine 1971.	$14-18
Fireman 1975.	$30-35
Fisherman 1974.	$15-18
Flintlock, 1969 (two versions) Japanese. Heritage.	 $10-15 $10-15
Florida "Gators," 1973 Tribute to University of Florida Gators football team.	$9-11
Foe Eagle 1978.	$15-20
Foe Flying Eagle 1979.	$20-25
Foe Eagle 1980.	$35-40
Foe Eagle 1981.	$35-40
Football player 1974.	$20-25
Ford Mustang Pace Car, 1979.	$25-35
Ford Thunderbird – 1956 1976.	$70-80
Foremost astronaut, 1970 Tribute to major liquor super mart, Foremost Liquor Store.	$5-7
Fresno decanter.	$5-12

New Bottles

Fresno grape with gold.	$48-60	**Go Tiger Go** 1973.	$10-14
Fresno grape 1970.	$6-11	**Grandfather clock** 1970.	$10-12
Gamecock 1970.	$9-13	**Greater Greensboro Open** 1972.	$25-30
Go Big Red – football-shaped bottle No. 1 with football, 1972. No. 2 with hat, 1971. No. 3 with rooster, 1972.	$20-28 $18-22 $10-14	**Greater Greensboro Open golfer** 1973.	$25-30
Golden antique cannon, 1969 Symbol of Spanish power.	$10-12	**Greater Greensboro Open map** 1974.	$40-45
Golden eagle 1971.	$18-22	**Greater Greensboro Open cup** 1975.	$25-30
Golden grizzly bear 1970.	$10-12	**Greater Greensboro Open cup** 1976.	$25-30
Golden horseshoe, 1970 Salute to Reno, Nevada's Horseshoe Club.	$15-20	**Greater Greensboro Open club and ball** 1977.	$25-30
Golden Rooster No. 1 Replica of solid gold rooster on display at Nugget Casino in Reno, Nevada.	$35-50	**Great Stone Face** Old Man of the Mountain, 1970.	$10-14
Gold prospector 1969.	$10-12	**Great white shark** 1977.	$8-14
Gold seal 1972.	$12-14	**Hambletonian** 1971.	$13-16
Gold turkey.	$35-45	**Happy goose** 1975.	$12-15
Golfer 1973.	$25-30	**Harold's Club red dice** 1968.	$20-25

Hereford 1971 and 1972, each:	$12-15		**Iowa farmer** 1977.	$55-65
Historical flask Eagle, 1970.	$5-10		**Iowa grain elevator** 1978.	$25-34
Historical flask Flagship, 1970.	$5-10		**Iron horse locomotive.**	$8-14
Historical flask Liberty, 1970.	$5-10		**Jack O'Diamonds** 1969.	$4-6
Historical flask Old Ironsides, 1970.	$5-10		**Jay hawk** 1969.	$6-8
Hollywood Cops 1972.	$12-18		**Jester** 1971.	$6-8
Hopi Indian 1970, Kachina doll.	$15-20		**Jug** Old Time 1.75 liter.	$9-13
Hopi Kachina 1973.	$50-75		**Kachina doll No. 1** 1971.	$80-100
Horseshoe Casino Gold.	$8-10		**Kachina doll No. 2** 1973.	$75-85
Idaho – Ski the Potato, 1973 Salutes the state of Idaho.	$8-10		**Kachina doll No. 3** 1974.	$80-90
Indianapolis 500.	$30-35		**Kachina doll No. 4** 1975.	$40-45
Indy Pace Car 1978.	$50-60		**Kachina doll No. 5** 1976.	$50-55
Indian ceremonial 1970.	$13-18		**Kachina doll No. 6** 1977.	$50-55
Indian hunter 1970.	$12-15		**Kachina doll No. 7** 1978.	$55-60
			Kachina doll No. 8 1979.	$85-90

Kachina doll No. 9 1980.	**$30-35**
Kansas Jayhawk 1969.	**$4-7**
Katz Cats, 1969 Siamese cats are symbolic of Katz Drug Co. of Kansas City, Kansas.	**$8-12**
Katz Cats Philharmonic, **1970** Commemorating its 27th annual Star Night.	**$6-10**
Keystone Cops 1980.	**$32-40**
Keystone Cops 1971.	**$70-75**
Killer whale 1972.	**$15-20**
King of clubs 1969.	**$4-6**
King salmon 1971.	**$18-24**
Liberty Bell 1970.	**$5-6**
Lincoln Continental Mark I, 1941.	**$20-25**
Lion on the rock 1971.	**$5-7**
Liquor Square 1972.	**$5-7**

Little Giant, 1971 Replica of first horse-drawn steam engine to arrive at Chicago fire in 1871.	**$11-16**
Maine lighthouse 1971.	**$18-24**
Maine lobster 1970.	**$15-18**
Mako shark 1962 and 1979.	**$15-20**
Man-O-War 1969.	**$10-16**
M & M brown jug 1975.	**$15-20**
Map USA Club Bottle, 1972.	**$7-9**
Masonic fez 1976.	**$12-15**
Max, The Hat, **Zimmerman** 1976.	**$25-30**
Military tank 1971.	**$15-22**
Minnesota hockey player 1975.	**$18-22**
Minuteman 1975.	**$15-20**
Missouri mule Brown, 1972.	**$7-9**
Moose 1973.	**$20-28**

Motorcycle.	**$10-14**
Mountaineer, 1971 One of the most valuable Ezra Brooks figural bottles.	**$40-55**
Mr. Foremost 1969.	**$7-10**
Mr. Maine Potato 1973.	**$6-10**
Mr. Merchant 1970.	**$10-12**
Mule.	**$8-12**
Mustang Indy Pace Car 1979.	**$20-30**
Nebraska – Go Big Red!	**$12-15**
New Hampshire State House 1970.	**$9-13**
North Carolina bicentennial 1975.	**$8-12**
Nugget Classic Replica of golf pin presented to golf tournament participants.	**$7-12**
Oil gusher.	**$6-8**
Old Capital 1971.	**$30-40**
Old Ez No. 1 Barn owl, 1977.	**$25-35**
Old Ez No. 2 Eagle Own, 1978.	**$40-55**

Old Ez No. 3 Show owl, 1979.	**$20-35**
Old Man of the Mountain 1970.	**$10-14**
Old Water Tower, 1969 Famous landmark, survived Chicago fire of 1871.	**$12-16**
Oliver Hardy bust.	**$40-45**
Ontario 500 1970.	**$18-22**
Overland Express 1969.	**$17-20**
Over-under flintlock flask 1969.	**$6-9**
Panda Giant, 1972.	**$12-17**
Penguin 1972.	**$8-10**
Penny Farthington High-wheeler, 1973.	**$9-12**
Pepperbox flask 1969.	**$5-10**
Phoenix bird 1971.	**$20-26**
Phoenix Jaycees 1973.	**$10-14**
Phonograph	**$15-20**
Piano 1970.	**$12-13**

Pirate 1971.	**$15-20**
Polish Legion American vets 1978.	**$18-26**
Portland Head Lighthouse, 1971 Honors lighthouse that has guided ships safely into Maine harbor since 1791.	**$18-24**
Pot-bellied stove 1968.	**$5-6**
Queen of Hearts, 1969 Playing card symbol with royal flush in hearts on front of bottle.	**$5-10**
Raccoon wildlife 1978.	**$30-40**
Ram 1973.	**$13-18**
Razorback hog 1969.	**$12-18**
Razorback hog 1979.	**$20-30**
Red fox 1979.	**$30-40**
Reno arch, 1968 Honoring biggest little city in the world, Reno, Nevada.	**$10-12**
Sailfish 1971.	**$7-11**
Salmon Washington King, 1971.	**$20-26**

San Francisco cable car 1968.	**$4-8**
Sea captain 1971.	**$15-20**
Sea lion Gold, 1972.	**$11-14**
Senators of the U.S., 1972 Honors senators of United States of America.	**$10-15**
Setter 1974.	**$10-15**
Shrine Fez, 1976.	**$10-15**
Shrine Clown, 1978.	**$25-30**
Shrine King Tut guard, 1979.	**$20-25**
Shrine Golden pharaoh.	**$35-40**
Silver dollar 1804, 1970.	**$8-10**
Silver saddle 1973.	**$22-25**
Silver saddle 1972 (platinum-plated).	**$28-30**
Silver Spur Boot, 1971 Cowboy boot-shaped bottle with silver spur buckled on, "Silver Spur – Carson City Nevada" embossed on side of boot.	**$15-20**

Simba 1971.	$9-12		**John L. Sullivan** 1970.	$15-20
Ski boot 1972.	$5-7		**Syracuse** New York, 1973.	$11-16
Slot machine, 1971 Replica of original nickel Liberty Bell slot machine invented by Charles Fey in 1895.	$20-25		**Tank Patton, 1972** Reproduction of U.S. Army tank.	$16-20
Snowmobiles 1972.	$8-11		**Tecumseh, 1969** Figurehead of U.S.S. Delaware, this decanter is an embossed replica of the statue at the United States Naval Academy.	$8-15
South Dakota Air National Guard, 1976.	$20-25		**Telephone, 1971** Replica of old-time upright handset telephone.	$16-19
Spirit of '76 1974.	$5-7			
Spirit of St. Louis 1977, 50th anniversary.	$6-11		**Tennis player** 1972 and 1973.	$20-25
Sprint car racer.	$30-40		**Terrapin** Maryland, 1974.	$14-16
Stagecoach 1969.	$10-12		**Texas longhorn** 1971.	$18-22
Stan Laurel bust 1976.	$40-45		**Ticker tape** 1970.	$8-12
Stock market ticker, 1970 A unique replica of ticker-tape machine.	$8-11		**Tiger on stadium, 1973** Commemorates college teams that have chosen the tiger as their mascot.	$12-17
Stonewall Jackson 1974.	$30-35		**Tom Turkey.**	$18-24
Strongman 1974.	$20-25		**Tonopah** 1972.	$15-20
Sturgeon 1975.	$20-28		**Totem Pole** 1972 and 1973.	$20-25

New Bottles

Tractor, 1971 Model of 1917 Fordson made by Henry Ford.	$9-11
Trail-bike rider 1972.	$10-12
Trojan horse 1974.	$15-18
Trojans USC football, 1973.	$10-14
Trout & Fly 1970.	$7-11
Truckin' & Vannin' 1977.	$7-12
Vermont skier 1972.	$10-12
VFW Veterans of Foreign Wars, 1973.	$10-15
VFW Veterans of Foreign Wars, 1974.	$10-12
VFW Veterans of Foreign Wars, 1982.	$25-30
VFW Veterans of Foreign Wars, 1983.	$25-30
Virginia Red cardinal, 1973.	$10-15
Walgreen Drugs 1974.	$16-24
Weirton Steel 1973.	$15-18

Western rodeos 1973.	$17-23
West Virginia Mountaineer, 1971.	$65-75
West Virginia Mountain Lady, 1972.	$20-25
Whale 1972.	$14-20
Wheat Shocker, 1971 The mascot of Kansas football team in fighting pose.	$5-7
Whiskey flasks, 1970 Reproduction of collectible American patriotic whiskey flasks of 1800s: Old Ironsides, Miss Liberty, American eagle, Civil War commemorative.	$12-14
Whitetail deer 1974.	$18-24
White turkey 1971.	$20-25
Wichita.	$4-8
Wichita Centennial 1970.	$4-6
Winston Churchill 1969.	$7-10
Zimmerman's Hat, 1968 Salute to "Zimmerman's – World's Largest Liquor Store."	$5-6

Jim Beam

The James B. Beam distilling company was founded in 1778 by Jacob Beam in Kentucky and now bears the name of Col. James B. Beam, Jacob Beam's grandson. Beam whiskey was popular in the South during the 19th and 20th centuries, but not produced on a large scale. Because of low production, the early Beam bottles are rare, collectible, and valuable.

In 1953, the Beam company packaged bourbon in a special Christmas/New Year ceramic decanter—a rarity for any distiller. Because the decanters sold well, Beam decided to redevelop its packaging, leading to production of a number of different series in the 1950s. The first was the Ceramics Series in 1953. In 1955, the Executive Series was issued to commemorate the 160th Anniversary of the corporation. In 1955, Beam introduced the Regal China Series, issued to honor significant people, places, and events with a concentration on America and Contemporary situations. In 1956, political figures were introduced with the elephant and the donkey, as well as special productions for customer specialties made on commission. In 1957, the Trophy Series honored various achievements within the liquor industry. The State Series was introduced in 1958 to commemorate the admission of Alaska and Hawaii into the Union. The practice has continued with Beam still producing decanters to commemorate all 50 States.

In total, over 500 types of Beam bottles have been issued since 1953. For further information, contact the International Association of Jim Beam Bottle and Specialties Clubs, PO Box 486, Kewanee, IL 61443, 309-853-3370, www.beam-wade.org.

New Bottles

AC Spark Plug 1977, replica of a spark plug in white, green, and gold.	$22-26
AHEPA 50th Anniversary 1972, Regal China bottle designed in honor of AHEPA'S (American Hellenic Education Progressive Association) 50th Anniversary.	$4-6
Aida, 1978 Figurine of character from the opera Aida.	$140-160
Akron Rubber Capital 1973, Regal China bottle honoring Akron, Ohio.	$15-20
Alaska 1958, Regal China, 9-1/2", star-shaped bottle.	$55-60
Alaska 1964-1965, re-issue of the 1958 bottle.	$40-50
Alaska Purchase 1966, Regal China, 10", blue and gold bottle.	$4-6
American Samoa 1973, Regal China, reflects the seal of Samoa.	$5-7
American Veterans.	$4-7
Antique clock.	$35-45
Antioch 1967, Regal China, 10", commemorates Diamond Jubilee of Regal.	$5-7

Antique coffee grinder 1979, replica of a box coffee mill used in mid-19th century.	$10-12
Antique globe 1980, represents the Martin Behaim globe of 1492.	$7-11
Antique telephone (1897) 1978, replica of an 1897 desk phone, second in a series.	$50-60
Antique Trader 1968, Regal China, 10-1/2", represents Antique Trader newspaper.	$4-6
Appaloosa 1974, Regal China, 10", represents favorite horse of the Old West.	$12-15
Arizona 1968, Regal China, 12", represents the state of Arizona.	$4-6
Armadillo.	$8-12
Armanetti Award Winner 1969, Honors Armanetti, Inc of Chicago as "Liquor Retailer of the Year."	$6-8
Armanetti Shopper 1971, reflects the slogan, "It's Fun to Shop Armanetti-Self Service Liquor Store," 11-3/4".	$6-8
Armanetti vase 1968, yellow-toned decanter embossed with flowers.	$5-7
Bacchus 1970, issued by Armanetti Liquor Stores of Chicago, Illinois, 11-3/4".	$6-9

Barney's slot machine 1978, replica of the world's largest slot machine.	$14-16
Barry Berish 1985, Executive Series.	$110-140
Barry Berish 1986, Executive Series, bowl.	$110-140
Bartender's Guild 1973, commemorative honoring the International Bartenders Assn.	$4-7
Baseball 1969, issued to commemorate the 100th anniversary of baseball.	$18-20
Beam pot 1980, shaped like a New England bean pot, club bottle for the New England Beam Bottle and Specialties Club.	$12-15
Beaver Valley Club 1977, a club bottle to honor the Beaver Valley Jim Beam Club of Rochester.	$8-12
Bell scotch 1970, Regal China, 10-1/2", in honor of Arthur Bell & Sons.	$4-7
Beverage Association NLBA	$4-7
The Big Apple 1979, apple-shaped bottle with "The Big Apple" over the top.	$8-12

Bing's 31st Clam Bake Bottle 1972, Commemorates 31st Bing Crosby National Pro-Am Golf Tournament in January 1972.	$25-30
Bing Crosby National Pro-Am 1970.	$4-7
Bing Crosby National Pro-Am 1971.	$4-7
Bing Crosby National Pro-Am 1972.	$15-25
Bing Crosby National Pro-Am 1973.	$18-23
Bing Crosby National Pro-Am 1974.	$15-25
Bing Crosby National Pro-Am 1975.	$45-65
Bing Crosby 36th 1976.	$15-25
Bing Crosby National Pro-Am 1977.	$12-18
Bing Crosby National Pro-Am 1978.	$12-18
Black Katz 1968, Regal China, 14-1/2".	$7-12

Duck Unlimited (American Widgeon Pair), 1989, $65; Football, 1989, $50; American Brands, 1989, $300; Nutcracker, 1989, $50; Nutcracker, 1989, $100.

Blue Cherub executive 1960, Regal China, 12-1/2".	$70-90		**Bobby Unser Olsonite Eagle** 1975, replica of the racing car used by Bobby Unser.	$40-50
Blue Daisy 1967, also know as Zimmerman Blue Daisy.	$10-12		**Bob DeVaney.**	$8-12
Blue gill fish.	$12-16		**Bob Hope Desert Classic** 1973, first genuine Regal China bottle created in honor of the Bob Hope Desert Classic.	$8-9
Blue goose order.	$4-7			
Blue jay 1969.	$4-7		**Bob Hope Desert Classic** 1974.	$8-12
Blue goose 1979, replica of blue goose, authenticated by Dr. Lester Fisher, Dir. of Lincoln Park Zoological Gardens in Chicago.	$7-9		**Bohemian girl** 1974, issued for the Bohemian Cafe in Omaha, Nebraska, to honor the Czech and Slovak immigrants in the United States, 14-1/4".	$10-15
Blue Hen Club.	$12-15		**Bonded gold.**	$4-7
Blue slot machine 1967.	$10-12		**Bonded mystic** 1979, urn-shaped bottle, burgundy colored.	$4-7

Bonded silver.	$4-7		**California Retail Liquor Dealers Association** 1973, designed to commemorate the 20th anniversary of the California Retail Liquor Dealers Association.	$6-9
Boris Godinov With base, 1978, 2nd in opera series.	$350-450		**Cal-Neva** 1969, Regal China, 9-1/2".	$5-7
Bourbon barrel.	$18-24		**Camellia City Club** 1979, replica of the cupola of the State Capitol building in Sacramento.	$18-23
Bowling proprietors.	$4-7			
Boys Town of Italy 1973, created in honor of the Boys Town of Italy.	$7-10		**Cameo blue** 1965, also known as the shepherd bottle.	$4-6
Bowl 1986, Executive Series.	$20-30		**Cannon** 1970, bottle issued to commemorate the 175th anniversary of the Jim Beam Co. Some of these bottles have a small chain shown on the cannon and some do not. Those without the chain are harder to find and more valuable, 8", with chain.	$2-4
Broadmoor Hotel 1968, to celebrate the 50th anniversary of this famous hotel in Colorado Springs, Colorado "1918-The Broadmoor-1968."	$4-7			
Buffalo Bill 1971, Regal China, 10-1/2", commemorates Buffalo Bill.	$4-7		Without chain.	$9-13
Bull dog 1979, honors the 204th anniversary of the United States Marine Corps.	$15-18		**Canteen** 1979, replica of the exact canteen used by the Armed Forces.	$8-12
Cable car 1968, Regal China, 4-1/2".	$4-6		**Captain and mate** 1980.	$10-12
Cabose 1980.	$50-60		**Cardinal (Kentucky cardinal)** 1968.	$40-50
California Mission 1970, this bottle was issued for the Jim Beam Bottle Club of Southern California in honor of the 20th anniversary of the California Missions, 14".	$10-15		**Carmen** 1978, third in the opera series.	$140-180

New Bottles

Carolier bull 1984, Executive Series.	$18-23
Catfish.	$16-24
Cathedral radio 1979, replica of one of the earlier dome-shaped radios.	$12-15
Cats 1967, trio of cats; Siamese, Burmese, and Tabby.	$6-9
Cedars of Lebanon 1971, this bottle was issued in honor of the Jerry Lewis Muscular Dystrophy Telethon in 1971.	$5-7
Charisma 1970, Executive Series.	$4-7
Charlie McCarthy 1976, replica of Edgar Bergen's puppet from the 1930s.	$20-30
Cherry Hills Country Club 1973, commemorating 50th anniversary of Cherry Hills Country Club.	$4-7
Cheyenne, Wyoming 1977.	$4-6
Chicago Cubs Sports Series.	$30-40
Chicago Show bottle 1977, commemorates 6th Annual Chicago Jim Beam Bottle Show.	$10-14
Christmas tree.	$150-200

Churchill Downs – pink roses 1969, Regal China, 10-1/4".	$5-7
Churchill Downs – red roses 1969, Regal China, 10-1/4".	$9-12
Circus wagon 1979, replica of a circus wagon from the late 19th century.	$24-26
Civil War North 1961, Regal China, 10-1/4".	$10-15
Civil War South 1961, Regal China, 10-1/4".	$25-35
Clear Crystal Bourbon 1967, clear glass, 11-1/2".	$5-7
Clear Crystal Scotch 1966.	$9-12
Clear Crystal Vodka 1967.	$5-8
Cleopatra, rust 1962, glass, 13-1/4".	$3-5
Cleopatra, yellow 1962, glass, 13-1/4", rarer than Cleopatra rust.	$8-12
Clint Eastwood 1973, commemorating Clint Eastwood Invitational Celebrity Tennis Tournament in Pebble Beach.	$14-17
Cocktail shaker 1953, glass, fancy bottle, 9-1/4".	$2-5

Julian McShane bottle, 1983, $60; Noel Executive, 1983, $50; Stein, 1983, $19; Zimmeran Liquors 50th Anniversary, 1983, $25; 1904 "100 Digit" Dial Telephone, 1983, $46.

Coffee grinder.	$8-12	**Collector's Edition Volume II** 1967, a set of six flask-type bottles with famous pictures: George Gisze, Soldier and Girl, Night Watch, The Jester, Nurse and Child, and Man on Horse (each).	$2-5
Coffee warmers 1954, four types are known: red, black, gold, and white.	$7-12		
Coffee warmers 1956, two types with metal necks and handles.	$2-5		
Coho salmon 1976, offical seal of the National Fresh Water Fishing Hall of Fame is on the back.	$10-13	**Collector's Edition Volume III** 1968, a set of eight bottles with famous paintings: On the Trail, Indian Maiden, Buffalo, Whistler's Mother, American Gothic, The Kentuckian, The Scout, and Hauling in the Gill Net (each).	$2-5
Colin Mead.	$180-210		
Cobalt 1981, Executive Series.	$18-23		
Collector's edition 1966, set of six glass famous paintings: The Blue Boy, On the Terrace, Mardi Gras, Austide Bruant, The Artist Before His Easel, and Laughing Cavalier (each).	$2-5	**Collector's Edition Volume IV** 1969, a set of eight bottles with famous paintings: Balcony, The Judge, Fruit Basket, Boy with Cherries, Emile Zola, The Guitarist Zouave, and Sunflowers (each).	$2-5

Collector's Edition Volume V 1970, a set of six bottles with famous paintings: Au Cafe, Old Peasant, Boaring Party, Gare Saint Lazare, The Jewish Bride, and Titus at Writing Desk (each).	$2-5
Collector's Edition Volume VI 1971, a set of three bottles with famous art pieces: Charles I, The Merry Lute Player, and Boy Holding Flute (each).	$2-5
Collector's Edition Volume VII 1972, a set of three bottles with famous paintings: The Bag Piper, Prince Baltasor, and Maidservant Pouring Milk (each).	$2-5
Collector's Edition Volume VIII 1973, a set of three bottles with famous portraits: Ludwig Van Beethoven, Wolfgang Mozart, and Frederic Francis Chopin (each).	$2-5
Collector's Edition Volume IX 1974, a set of three bottles with famous paintings: Cardinal, Ring-Neck Pheasant, and the Woodcock (each).	$3-6
Collector's Edition Volume X 1975, a set of three bottles with famous pictures: Sailfish, Rainbow Trout, and Largemouth Bass (each).	$3-6

Collector's Edition Volume XI 1976, a set of three bottles with famous paintings: Chipmunk, Bighorn Sheep, and Pronghorn Antelope (each).	$3-6
Collector's Edition Volume XII 1977, a set of four bottles with a different reproduction of James Lockhart on the front (each).	$3-6
Collector's Edition Volume XIV 1978, a set of four bottles with James Lockhart paintings: Raccoon, Mule Deer, Red Fox, and Cottontail Rabbit (each).	$3-6
Collector's Edition Volume XV 1979, a set of three flasks with Frederic Remington's paintings: The Cowboy 1902, The Indian Trapper 1902, and Lieutenant S. C. Robertson 1890 (each).	$2-5
Collector's Edition Volume XVI 1980, a set of three flasks depicting duck scenes: The Mallard, The Redhead, and the Canvasback (each).	$3-6
Collector's Edition Volume XVII 1981, a set of three flask bottles with Jim Lockhart paintings: Great Elk, Pintail Duck, and the Horned Owl (each).	$3-6
Colorado 1959, Regal China, 10-3/4".	$20-25

Colorado Centennial 1976, Replica of Pike's Peak.	$8-12	**Convention Number 6** Hartford, 1976, commemorates the annual convention of the Jim Beam Bottle Club in Hartford, Conn.	$5-7
Computer Democrat or Republican, 1984.	$12-18		
Convention bottle 1971, commemorates the first national convention of the National Association of Jim Beam Bottle and Specialty Clubs, hosted by the Rocky Mountain Club, Denver, Colorado.	$5-7	**Convention Number 7** Louisville, 1978, commemorates the annual convention of the Jim Beam Bottle Club in Louisville, KY.	$5-7
		Convention Number 8 Chicago, 1978, commemorates the annual convention of the Jim Beam Bottle Club in Chicago, IL.	$8-12
Convention Number 2 1972, honors the second annual convention of the National Association of Jim Beam Bottle and Specialty Clubs in Anaheim, Calif.	$20-30	**Convention Number 9** Houston, 1979, commemorates the annual convention of the Jim Beam Bottle Club in Houston, TX.	$20-30
		Cowboy, beige. Cowboy, in color.	$35-45 $35-45
Convention Number 3 Detroit, 1973, commemorates the third annual convention of Beam Bottle Collectors in Detroit.	$10-12	**Convention Number 10** Norfolk, 1980, commemorates the annual convention of the Jim Beam Bottle Club at the Norfolk Naval Base.	$18-22
Convention Number 4 Pennsylvania, 1974, commemorates the annual convention of the Jim Beam Bottle Club in Lancaster, Pennsylvania.	$80-100	Waterman, pewter. Waterman, yellow.	$35-45 $35-45
Convention Number 5 Sacramento, 1975, commemorates the annual convention of the Camellia City Jim Beam Bottle Club in Sacramento, Calif.	$5-7	**Convention Number 11** Las Vegas, 1981, commemorates the annual convention of the Jim Beam Bottle Club in Las Vegas, NV.	$20-22
		Showgirl, blonde. Showgirl, brunette.	$45-55 $45-55

Convention Number 12 New Orleans, 1982, commemorates the annual convention of the Jim Beam Bottle Club in New Orleans, LA	$30-35
Buccaneer, gold.	$35-45
Buccaneer, in color.	$35-45
Convention Number 13 St. Louis, 1983, stein, commemorates the annual convention of the Jim Beam Bottle Club in St. Louis, MO.	$55-70
Gibson girl, blue.	$65-80
Gibson girl, yellow.	$65-80
Convention Number 14 Florida, King Neptune, 1984, commemorates the annual convention of the Jim Beam Bottle Club in Florida.	$15-20
Mermaid, blonde.	$35-45
Mermaid, brunette.	$35-45
Convention Number 15 Las Vegas, 1985, commemorates the annual convention of the Jim Beam Bottle Club in Las Vegas, NV.	$40-50
Convention Number 16 Boston, Pilgrim woman, 1986, commemorates the annual convention of the Jim Beam Bottle Club in Boston.	$35-45
Minuteman, color.	$85-105
Minuteman, pewter.	$85-105

Convention Number 17 Louisville, 1987, commemorates the annual convention of the Jim Beam Bottle Club in Louisville, KY.	$55-75
Kentucky Colonel, blue.	$85-105
Kentucky Colonel, gray.	$85-105
Convention Number 18 Bucky Beaver, 1988.	$30-40
Portland rose, red.	$30-40
Portland rose, yellow.	$30-40
Convention Number 19 Kansas City, 1989, commemorates the annual convention of the Jim Beam Bottle Club in Kansas City, MO.	$40-50
Cowboy 1979, awarded to collectors who attended the 1979 convention for the International Association of Beam Clubs.	$35-50
CPO open.	$4-7
Crappie 1979, commemorates the National Fresh Water Fishing Hall of Fame.	$10-14
Dark Eyes brown jug 1978.	$4-6
D-Day.	$12-18
Delaware Blue Hen bottle 1972, Commemorates the State of Delaware.	$4-7

Delco Freedom Battery 1978, Replica of a Delco battery.	$18-22
Delft Blue 1963.	$3-5
Delft Rose 1963.	$4-6
Del Webb Mint, 1970 Metal stopper. China stopper.	$10-12 $50-60
Devil Dog.	$15-25
Dial Telephone 1980, fourth in a series of Beam telephone designs.	$40-50
Dodge City 1972, issued to honor the centennial of Dodge City.	$5-6
Doe 1963, Regal China, 13-1/2".	$10-12
Doe Reissued, 1967.	$10-12
Dog 1959, Regal China, 15-1/4".	$20-25
Don Giovanni 1980, the fifth in the Opera series.	$140-180
Donkey and Elephant ashtrays 1956, Regal China, 12" (pair).	$12-16
Donkey and Elephant boxers 1964 (pair).	$14-18

Donkey and Elephant clowns 1968, Regal China, 12" (pair).	$4-7
Donkey and Elephant Football Election bottles 1972, Regal China, 9-1/2" (pair).	$6-9
Donkey, New York City 1976, commemorates the National Democratic Convention in New York City.	$10-12
Duck 1957, Regal China, 14-1/4".	$15-20
Ducks and Geese 1955.	$5-8
Ducks Unlimited Mallard 1974.	$40-50
Ducks Unlimited Wood Duck 1975.	$45-50
Ducks Unlimited 40th Mallard Hen 1977.	$40-50
Ducks Unlimited Canvasback Drake 1979.	$30-40
Ducks Unlimited Blue-Winged Teal 1980, the sixth in a series, 9-1/2".	$40-45
Ducks Unlimited Green-Winged Teal 1981.	$35-45

Ducks Unlimited Wood Ducks 1982.	$35-45	**Eldorado** 1978.	$7-9
Ducks Unlimited American Widg pr 1983.	$35-45	**Election** Democrat, 1988.	$30-40
Ducks Unlimited Mallard 1984.	$55-75	**Election** Republican, 1988.	$30-40
Ducks Unlimited Pintail pr 1985.	$30-40	**Elephant and Donkey Supermen** 1980, (set of two).	$10-14
Ducks Unlimited REDHEAD 1986.	$15-25	**Elephant** Kansas City, 1976, commemorates the National Democratic Convention in New York City.	$8-10
Ducks Unlimited Blue Bill 1987.	$40-60	**Elks.**	$4-7
Ducks Unlimited Black Duck 1989.	$50-60	**Elks National Foundation.**	$8-12
Eagle 1966, Regal China, 12-1/2".	$10-13	**Emerald Crystal Bourbon** 1968, green glass, 11-1/2".	$3-5

Santa Claus, 1983, $60; Santa Claus paperweight, 1983, $30; Gibson Girl (blond), 1983, $60; Gibson Girl (brunette), 1983, $60, Thirteenth Convention Stein, 1983, $60.

Emmett Kelly 1973, likeness of Emmett Kelly as sad-faced Willie the Clown.	$18-22
Emmett Kelly Native Son.	$50-60
Ernie's Flower Cart 1976, in honor of Ernie's Wines and Liquors of Northern Calif.	$24-28
Evergreen Club Bottle.	$7-10
Expo 1974, issued in honor of the World's Fair held at Spokane, Wash.	$5-7
Falstaff 1979, second in Australian Opera Series, limited edition of 1,000 bottles.	$150-160
Fantasia Bottle 1971.	$5-6
Father's Day card.	$15-25
Female cardinal 1973.	$8-12
Fiesta Bowl Glass.	$8-12
Fiesta Bowl 1973, the second bottle created to the Fiesta Bowl.	$9-11
Figaro 1977, character Figaro from the opera Barber of Seville.	$140-170
Fighting Bull.	$12-18

Fiji Islands.	$4-6
First National Bank of Chicago 1964, commemorates the 100th anniversary of the First National Bank of Chicago. Approximately 130 were issued, with 117 being given as mementos to the bank directors with none for public distribution. This is the most valuable Beam bottle known; beware of reproductions.	$1,900-2,400
Fish 1957, Regal China, 14".	$15-18
Fish Hall of Fame.	$25-35
Five Seasons 1980, club bottle for the Five Seasons Club of Cedar Rapids honors the State of Iowa.	$10-12
Fleet Reserve Association 1974, issued by the Fleet Reserve Association to honor the Career Sea Service on its 50th anniversary.	$5-7
Florida shell 1968, Regal China, 9".	$4-6
Floro De Oro 1976.	$10-12
Flower Basket 1962, Regal China, 12-1/4".	$30-35
Football Hall of Fame 1972, reproduction of the new Professional Football Hall of Fame Building.	$14-18

Foremost – Black and Gold 1956, first Beam bottle issued for a liquor retailer, Foremost Liquor Store of Chicago.	$225-250	**Gem City** club bottle.	$35-45
Foremost - Speckled Beauty 1956, the most valuable of the Foremost bottles.	$500-600	**George Washington Commemorative Plate** 1976, commemorates the U.S. Bicentennial, 9-1/2".	$12-15
Fox 1967, blue coat.	$65-80	**German Bottle** Weisbaden, 1973.	$4-6
Fox 1971, gold coat.	$35-50	**German Stein.**	$20-30
Fox Green coat.	$12-18	**Germany** 1970, issued to honor the American Armed Forces in Germany.	$4-6
Fox White coat.	$20-30	**Glen Cambell 51st** 1976, honors the 51st Los Angeles Open at the Riviera Country Club in February 1976.	$7-10
Fox On a dolphin.	$12-15	**Golden Chalice** 1961.	$40-50
Fox Uncle Sam.	$5-6	**Golden Jubilee** 1977, Executive Series.	$48-12
Fox Kansas City, blue, miniature.	$20-30	**Golden Nugget** 1969, Regal China, 12-1/2".	$35-45
Fox Red distillery.	$1,100-1,300	**Golden Rose** 1978.	$15-20
Franklin Mint.	$4-7	**Grand Canyon** 1969, honors the Grand Canyon National Park 50th Anniversary.	$7-9
French Cradle Telephone 1979, third in the Telephone Pioneers of America series.	$20-22	**Grant Locomotive** 1979.	$55-65
Galah Bird 1979.	$14-16	**Gray Cherub** 1958, Regal China, 12".	$240-260

Great Chicago Fire Bottle 1971, commemorates the great Chicago fire of 1871 and salutes Mercy Hospital, which helped the fire victims.	$18-22
Great Dane 1976.	$7-9
Green China Jug 1965, Regal Glass, 12-1/2".	$4-6
Hank Williams, Jr.	$40-50
Hannah Dustin 1973, Regal China, 14-1/2".	$10-12
Hansel and Gretel Bottle, 1971.	$44-50
Harley Davidson 85th Anniversary Decanter.	$175-200
Harley Davidson 85th Anniversary Stein.	$180-220
Harolds Club – Man-in-a-Barrel 1957, first in a series made for Harolds Club in Reno, Nevada.	$380-410
Harolds Club - Silver Opal 1957, commemorates the 25th anniversary of Harolds Club.	$20-22
Harolds Club - Man-in-a-Barrel 1958.	$140-160

Harolds Club - Nevada (gray) 1963, created for the Nevada Centennial, 1864-1964, as a state bottle. This is a rare and valuable bottle.	$90-110
Harolds Club - Nevada (silver) 1964.	$90-110
Harolds Club – Pinwheel 1965.	$40-45
Harolds Club - Blue Slot Machine 1967.	$10-14
Harolds Club - VIP Executive 1967, limited quantity issued.	$50-60
Harolds Club VIP Executive, 1968.	$55-65
Harolds Club Gray Slot Machine, 1968.	$4-6
Harolds Club VIP Executive, 1969, this bottle was used as a Christmas gift to the casino's executives.	$260-285
Harolds Club Covered Wagon, 1969-1970.	$4-6
Harolds Club 1970.	$40-60
Harolds Club 1971.	$40-60
Harolds Club 1972.	$18-25

Harolds Club 1973.	$18-24	**Hawaii** 1959, Tribute to the 50th state.	$35-40
Harolds Club 1974.	$12-16	**Hawaii** Reissued, 1967.	$40-45
Harolds Club 1975.	$12-18	**Hawaii** 1971.	$6-8
Harolds Club VIP, 1976.	$18-22	**Hawaii Aloha** 1971.	$6-10
Harolds Club 1977.	$20-30	**Hawaiian Open Bottle** 1972, honors the 1972 Hawaiian Open Golf Tournament.	$6-8
Harolds Club 1978.	$20-30	**Hawaiian Open** 1973, second bottle created in honor of the United Hawaiian Open Golf Classic.	$7-9
Harolds Club 1979.	$20-30		
Harolds Club 1980.	$25-35	**Hawaiian Open** 1974, commemorates the 1974 Hawaiian Open Golf Classic.	$5-8
Harolds Club 1982.	$110-145	**Hawaiian Open Outrigger** 1975.	$9-11
Harp Seal.	$12-18		
Harrahs Club Nevada – Gray 1963, this is the same bottle used for the Nevada Centennial and Harolds Club.	$500-550	**Hawaiian Paradise** 1978, commemorates the 200th anniversary of the landing of Captain Cook.	$15-17
		Hemisfair 1968, commemorates the "Hemisfair 68-San Antonio."	$8-10
Harry Hoffman.	$4-7	**Here Brothers.**	$22-35
Harvey's Resort Hotel at Lake Tahoe.	$6-10	**Hobo** Australia.	$10-14
Hatfield 1973, the character of Hatfield from the story of the Hatfield and McCoy feud.	$15-20	**Hoffman** 1969.	$4-7

Holiday-Carolers.	$40-50
Holiday-Nutcracker.	$40-50
Home Builders 1978, commemorates the 1979 convention of the Home Builders.	$25-30
Hone Heke.	$200-250
Honga Hika 1980, first in a series of Maori warrior bottles. Honga Hika was a war chief of the Ngapuke tribe.	$220-240
Horse (Appaloosa).	$8-12
Horse (black).	$18-22
Horse (black) Reissued, 1967.	$10-12
Horse (brown).	$18-22
Horse (brown) Reissued, 1967.	$10-12
Horse (mare and foal).	$35-45
Horse (Oh Kentucky).	$70-85
Horse (pewter).	$12-17
Horse (white).	$18-20
Horse (white) Reissued, 1967.	$12-17
Horseshoe Club 1969.	$4-6

Hula Bowl 1975.	$8-10
Hyatt House Chicago.	$7-10
Hyatt House New Orleans.	$8-11
Idaho 1963.	$30-40
Illinois 1968, Honors the 1818-1968 Sesquicentennial of Illinois.	$4-6
Indianapolis Sesquicentennial.	$4-6
Indianapolis 500.	$9-12
Indian Chief 1979.	$9-12
International Chili Society 1976.	$9-12
Italian Marble Urn 1985, Executive Series.	$12-17
Ivory Ashtray 1955.	$8-10
Jackalope 1971, honors the Wyoming Jackalope.	$5-8
Jaguar.	$18-23
Jewel T Man 50th Anniversary.	$35-45

John Henry 1972, commemorates the legendary Steel Drivin' Man.	$18-22
Joliet Legion Band 1978, commemorates the 20th national championships.	$15-20
Kaiser International Open Bottle 1971, Commemorates the 5th Annual Kaiser International Open Golf Tournament.	$5-6
Kangaroo 1977.	$10-14
Kansas 1960, commemorates the "Kansas 1861-1961 Centennial."	$35-45
Kentucky Black Head – Brown Head, 1967: Black head. Brown head. White head.	 $12-18 $20-28 $18-23
Kentucky Derby 95th Pink, red roses, 1969.	$4-7
Kentucky Derby 96th Double rose, 1970.	$15-25
Kentucky Derby 97th 1971.	$4-7
Kentucky Derby 98th 1972.	$4-6
Kentucky Derby 100th 1974.	$7-10

Key West 1972, honors the 150th anniversary of Key West, Florida.	$5-7
King Kamehameha 1972, commemorates the 100th anniversary of King Kamehameha Day.	$8-11
King Kong 1976, commemorates Paramount's movie release in December 1976.	$8-10
Kiwi, 1974.	$5-8
Koala Bear 1973.	$12-14
Laramie 1968, commemorates the Centennial Jubilee Laramie, Wyo., 1868-1968.	$4-6
Largemouth Bass Trophy Bottle 1973, honors the National Fresh Water Fishing Hall of Fame.	$10-14
Las Vegas 1969, bottle used for customer specials, Casino series.	$4-6
Light Bulb 1979, honors Thomas Edison.	$14-16
Lombard 1969, commemorates "Village of Lombard, Illinois-1869 Centennial 1969."	$4-6
London Bridge.	$4-7

St. Louis Glass Convention Bottles, 1983, bourbon, vodka, scotch, gin, brandy, tequila, Canadian whiskey, $5 each.

Louisville Downs Racing Derby 1978.	$4-6
Louisiana Superdome.	$8-11
LVNH Owl.	$20-30
Madame Butterfly 1977, figurine of Madame Butterfly, music box plays "One Fine Day" from the opera.	$340-370
The Magpies 1977, honors an Australian football team.	$18-20
Maine, 1970.	$4-6
Majestic, 1966.	$20-24
Male Cardinal.	$18-24
Marbled Fantasy 1965.	$38-42

Marina City 1962, commemorates modern apartment complex in Chicago.	$10-15
Marine Corps.	$25-35
Mark Antony 1962.	$18-20
Martha Washington 1976.	$5-6
McCoy 1973, character of McCoy from the story of the Hatfield and McCoy feud.	$14-17
McShane Mother-of-Pearl, 1979, Executive Series.	$85-105
McShane Titans, 1980.	$85-105
McShane Cobalt, 1981, Executive Series.	$115-135

McShane Green pitcher, 1982, Executive Series.	$80-105
McShane Green bell, 1983, Executive Series.	$80-110
Mephistopheles 1979, figurine depicts Mephistopheles from the opera Faust, music box plays "Soldier's Chorus."	$160-190
Michigan Bottle 1972.	$7-9
Milwaukee Stein.	$30-40
Minnesota Viking 1973.	$9-12
Mint 400 1970.	$80-105
Mint 400 1970.	$5-6
Mint 400 1971.	$5-6
Mint 400 1972, commemorates the 5th annual Del Webb Mint 400.	$5-7
Mint 400 1973, commemorates the 6th annual Del Webb Mint 400.	$6-8
Mint 400 1974.	$4-7
Mint 400 7th annual, 1976.	$9-12

Mississippi Fire Engine 1978.	$120-130
Model A Ford 1903 (1978).	$38-42
Model A Ford 1928 (1980).	$65-75
Montana 1963, tribute to "Montana, 1864 Golden Years Centennial 1964."	$50-60
Monterey Bay Club 1977, honors the Monterey Bay Beam Bottle and Specialty Club.	$9-12
Mortimer Snerd 1976.	$24-28
Mother-of-Pearl 1979.	$10-12
Mount St. Helens 1980, depicts the eruption of Mount St. Helens.	$20-22
Mr. Goodwrench 1978.	$24-28
Musicians on a Wine Cask 1964.	$4-6
Muskie 1971, honors the National Fresh Water Fishing Hall of Fame.	$14-18
National Tobacco Festival 1973, commemorates the 25th anniversary of the National Tobacco Festival.	$7-8

Nebraska 1967.	$7-9
Nebraska Football 1972, commemorates the University of Nebraska's national championship football team of 1970-1971.	$5-8
Nevada 1963.	$34-38
New Hampshire 1967.	$4-8
New Hampshire Eagle Bottle 1971.	$18-23
New Jersey 1963.	$40-50
New Jersey Yellow, 1963.	$40-50
New Mexico Bicentennial 1976.	$8-12
New Mexico Statehood 1972, commemorates New Mexico's 60 years of Statehood.	$7-9
New York World's Fair 1964.	$5-6
North Dakota 1965.	$45-55
Northern Pike 1977, the sixth in a series designed for the National Fresh Water Fishing Hall of Fame.	$14-18
Nutcracker Toy Soldier 1978.	$90-120
Ohio 1966.	$5-6
Ohio State Fair 1973, in honor of the 120th Ohio State Fair.	$5-6
Olympian 1960.	$2-4
One Hundred First Airborne Division 1977, honors the division known as the Screaming Eagles.	$8-10
Opaline Crystal 1969.	$4-6
Oregon 1959, Honors the centennial of the state.	$20-25
Oregon Liquor Commission.	$25-35
Osco Drugs.	$12-17
Panda 1980.	$20-22
Paul Bunyan.	$4-7
Pearl Harbor Memorial 1972, honoring the Pearl Harbor Survivors Association.	$14-18
Pearl Harbor Survivors Association 1976.	$5-7

Pennsylvania 1967.	$4-6
Pennsylvania Dutch Club Bottle.	$8-12
Permian Basin Oil Show 1972, commemorates the Permian Basin Oil Show in Odessa, Texas.	$4-6
Petroleum Man.	$4-7
Pheasant 1960.	$14-18
Pheasant 1961, reissued; also '63, '66, '67, '68.	$8-11
Phi Sigma Kappa (Centennial Series) 1973, commemorates the 100th anniversary of this fraternity.	$3-4
Phoenician 1973.	$6-9
Pied Piper of Hamlin 1974.	$3-6
Ponderosa 1969, a replica of the Cartwrights of "Bonanza" TV fame.	$4-6
Ponderosa Ranch Tourist 1972, commemorates the one millionth tourist to the Ponderosa Ranch.	$14-16
Pony Express 1968.	$9-12

Poodle Gray and white, 1970.	$5-6
Portland Rose Festival 1972, commemorates the 64th Portland, Oregon Rose Festival.	$5-8
Portola Trek 1969, bottle was issued to celebrate the 200th anniversary of San Diego.	$3-6
Poulan Chain Saw 1979.	$24-28
Powell Expedition 1969, depicts John Wesley Powell's survey of the Colorado River.	$3-5
Preakness 1970, issued to honor the 100th anniversary of the running of the Preakness.	$5-6
Preakness Pimlico 1975.	$4-7
Presidential 1968, Executive Series.	$4-7
Prestige 1967, Executive Series.	$4-7
Pretty Perch 1980, 8th in a series, this fish is used as the official seal of the National Fresh Water Fishing Hall of Fame.	$13-16
Prima-Donna 1969.	$4-6
Professional Golf Association.	$4-7

Queensland 1978.	$20-22	**Rennie the Runner** 1974.	$9-12
Rabbit.	$4-7	**Rennie the Surfer** 1975.	$9-12
Rainbow Trout 1975, produced for the National Fresh Water Fishing Hall of Fame.	$12-15	**Reno** 1968, commemorates "100 Years – Reno."	$4-6
Ralph Centennial 1973, commemorates the 100th anniversary of the Ralph Grocery Co.	$10-14	**Republic of Texas** 1980.	$12-20
		Republican Convention 1972.	$500-700
Ralphs Market.	$8-12	**Republican Football** 1972.	$350-450
Ram 1958.	$40-55	**Richard Hadlee.**	$110-135
Ramada Inn 1976.	$10-12	**Richards - New Mexico** 1967, created for Richards Distributing Co. of Albuquerque, New Mexico.	$8-10
Red Mile Racetrack.	$8-12		
Redwood 1967.	$6-8	**Robin** 1969.	$5-6
Reflections 1975, Executive Series.	$8-12	**Rocky Marciano** 1973.	$14-16
Regency 1972.	$7-9	**Rocky Mountain** Club Bottle.	$10-15
Reidsville 1973, issued to honor Reidsville, North Carolina, on its centennial.	$5-6	**Royal Crystal** 1959.	$3-6
		Royal Di Monte 1957.	$45-55
Renee the Fox 1974, represents the companion for the International Association of Jim Beam Bottle and Specialties Club's mascot.	$7-9	**Royal Emperor** 1958.	$3-6

Royal Gold Diamond 1964.	$30-35		**SCCA** Etched.	$15-25
Royal Gold Round 1956.	$80-90		**SCCA** Smoothed.	$12-18
Royal Opal 1957.	$5-7		**Screech Owl** 1979.	$18-22
Royal Porcelain 1955.	$380-420		**Seafair Trophy Race** 1972, commemorates the Seattle Seafair Trophy Race.	$5-6
Royal Rose 1963.	$30-35		**Seattle World's Fair** 1962.	$10-12
Ruby Crystal 1967.	$6-9		**Seoul – Korea** 1988.	$60-75
Ruidoso Downs, 1968 Pointed ears. Flat ears.	$24-26 $4-6		**Sheraton Inn.**	$4-6
Sahara Invitational Bottle 1971, introduced in honor of the Del Webb 1971 Sahara Invitational Pro-Am Golf Tournament.	$6-8		**Short Dancing Scot** 1963.	$50-65
			Short-Timer 1975.	$15-20
			Shriners 1975.	$10-12
San Bear – Donkey 1973, Political Series.	$1,500-2,000		**Shriners – Indiana.**	$4-7
Samoa.	$4-7		**Shriners Pyramid** 1975, issued by the El Kahir Temple of Cedar Rapids, Iowa.	$10-12
San Diego 1968, issued by the Beam Co. for the 200th anniversary of its founding in 1769.	$4-6		**Shriners Rajah** 1977.	$24-28
San Diego – Elephant 1972.	$15-25		**Shriners Temple** 1972.	$20-25
Santa Fe 1960.	$120-140		**Shriners Western Association.**	$15-25

Sierra Eagle.	$15-22
Sigma Nu Fraternity 1977.	$9-12
Sigma Nu Fraternity Kentucky.	$8-12
Sigma Nu Fraternity Michigan.	$18-23
Smiths North Shore Club 1972, commemorating Smith's North Shore Club, at Crystal Bay, Lake Tahoe.	$10-12
Smoked Crystal 1964.	$6-9
Snow Goose 1979.	$8-10
Snowman.	$125-175
South Carolina 1970, in honor of celebrating its Tri-Centennial, 1670-1970.	$4-6
South Dakota Mount Rushmore, 1969.	$4-6
South Florida Fox on Dolphin, 1980, bottled sponsored by the South Florida Beam Bottle and Specialties Club.	$14-16
Sovereign 1969, Executive Series.	$4-7
Spengers Fish Grotto 1977.	$18-22

Sports Car Club of America.	$5-7
Statue of Liberty 1975.	$8-12
Statue of Liberty 1985.	$18-20
St. Bernard 1979.	$30-35
St. Louis Club Bottle.	$10-15
St. Louis Arch 1964.	$10-12
St. Louis Arch Reissue, 1967.	$16-18
St. Louis Statue 1972.	$8-10
Sturgeon 1980, exclusive issue for a group that advocates the preservation of sturgeons.	$14-17
Stutz Bearcat 1914 1977.	$45-55
Submarine Diamond Jubilee.	$35-45
Submarine Redfin 1970, issued for Manitowoc Submarine Memorial Association.	$5-7
Superdome 1975, replica of the Louisiana Superdome.	$5-8

Swagman 1979, replica of an Australian hobo called a swagman who roamed that country looking for work during the depression.	$10-12
Sydney Opera House 1977.	$9-12
Tall Dancing Scot 1964.	$9-12
Tavern Scene 1959.	$45-55
Telephone No. 1 1975, replica of a 1907 phone of the Magneto wall type.	$25-30
Telephone No. 2 1976, replica of an 1897 desk set.	$30-40
Telephone No. 3 1977, replica of a 1920 cradle phone.	$15-20
Telephone No. 4 1978, replica of a 1919 dial phone.	$40-50
Telephone No. 5 1979, replica of a pay phone.	$25-35
Telephone No. 6 1980, replica of a battery phone.	$20-30
Telephone No. 7 1981, replica of a digital dial phone.	$35-45
Ten-Pin 1980.	$8-11

Texas Hemisfair.	$7-11
Texas Rose 1978, Executive Series.	$14-18
Thailand 1969.	$4-6
Thomas Flyer 1907 1976.	$60-70
Tiffany Poodle 1973, created in honor of Tiffiny, the poodle mascot of the National Association of the Jim Beam Bottle and Specialties Clubs.	$20-22
Tiger Australian.	$14-18
The Tigers 1977, issued in honor of an Australian football team.	$20-24
Titian 1980.	$9-12
Tobacco Festival.	$8-12
Tombstone.	$4-7
Travelodge Bear.	$4-7
Treasure Chest 1979.	$8-12
Trout Unlimited 1977, to honor the Trout Unlimited Conservation Organization.	$14-18

Truth or Consequences Fiesta 1974, issued in honor of Ralph Edwards radio and television show.	$14-18
Turquoise China Jug 1966.	$4-6
Twin Bridges Bottle 1971, commemorates the largest twin bridge between Delaware and New Jersey.	$40-42
Twin Cherubs 1974, Executive Series.	$8-12
Twin Doves 1987, Executive Series.	$18-23
US Open 1972, Honors the US Open Golf Tourney at Pebble Beach, Calif.	$9-12
Vendome Drummers Wagon 1975, honored the Vendomes of Beverly Hills, Calif.	$60-70
VFW Bottle 1971, commemorates the 50th anniversary of the Department of Indiana VFW.	$5-6
Viking 1973.	$9-12
Volkswagen Commemorative Bottle Two colors, 1977, commemorates the Volkswagen Beetle.	$40-50
Vons Market.	$28-35

Walleye Pike 1977, designed for the National Fresh Water Fishing Hall of Fame.	$12-15
Walleye Pike 1987.	$17-23
Washington 1975, a state series bottle to commemorate the Evergreen State.	$5-6
Washington - The Evergreen State 1974, the club bottle for the Evergreen State Beam Bottle and Specialties Club.	$10-12
Washington State Bicentennial 1976.	$10-12
Waterman 1980.	$100-130
Western Shrine Association 1980, commemorates the Shriners convention in Phoenix, Arizona.	$20-22
West Virginia 1963.	$130-140
White Fox 1969, issued for the 2nd anniversary of the Jim Beam Bottle and Specialties Club in Berkley, Calif.	$25-35
Wisconsin Muskie Bottle 1971.	$15-17

New Bottles

Woodpecker 1969.	$6-8		**Zimmerman** Blue Daisy.	$4-6
Wyoming 1965.	$40-50		**Zimmerman Cherubs** 1968.	$4-6
Yellow Katz 1967, commemorates the 50th anniversary of the Katz Department Stores.	$15-17		**Zimmerman** Chicago.	$4-6
Yellow Rose 1978, Executive Series.	$7-10		**Zimmerman** Eldorado.	$4-7
Yellowstone Park Centennial.	$4-7		**Zimmerman** Glass, 1969.	$7-9
Yosemite 1967.	$4-6		**Zimmerman** Oatmeal Jug.	$40-50
Yuma Rifle Club.	$18-23		**Zimmerman** The Peddler Bottle, 1971.	$4-6
Zimmerman Art Institute.	$5-8		**Zimmerman** Two-Handled Jug, 1965.	$45-60
Zimmerman Bell 1976, designed for Zimmerman Liquor Store of Chicago.	$6-7		**Zimmerman Vase** Brown.	$6-9
Zimmerman Bell 1976.	$6-7		**Zimmerman Vase** Green.	$6-9
Zimmerman Blue Beauty, 1969.	$9-12		**Zimmerman** 50th Anniversary.	.$35-45

Automobile and Transportation Series

Chevrolet

1957 Convertible Black, new.	**$85-95**		**Camaro** 1969, green.	**$100-120**
1957 Convertible Red, new.	**$75-85**		**Camaro** 1969, orange.	**$55-65**
1957 Black.	**$70-80**		**Camaro** 1969, Pace car.	**$60-70**
1957 Dark blue, PA.	**$70-80**		**Camaro** 1969, silver.	**$120-140**
1957 Red.	**$80-90**		**Camaro** 1969, yellow, PA.	**$55-65**
1957 Sierra gold.	**$140-160**		**Corvette** 1986, Pace car, yellow, new.	**$60-85**
1957 Turquoise.	**$50-70**		**Corvette** 1984, black.	**$70-80**
1957 Yellow hot rod.	**$65-75**		**Corvette** 1984, bronze.	**$100-200**
Camaro 1969, blue.	**$55-65**		**Corvette** 1984, gold.	**$100-120**
Camaro 1969, burgundy.	**$120-140**			

Corvette (black), 1989, $95; Corvette (bronze), 1989, $110; Corvette (gold), 1989, $110; Nineteenth Convention bottle, 1989, $40.

New Bottles

Corvette	
Corvette 1984, red.	$55-65
Corvette 1984, white.	$55-65
Corvette 1978, black.	$140-170
Corvette 1978, Pace car.	$135-160
Corvette 1978, red.	$50-60
Corvette 1978, white.	$40-50
Corvette 1978, yellow.	$40-50
Corvette 1963, black, PA.	$75-85

Corvette	
Corvette 1963, blue, NY.	$90-100
Corvette 1963, red.	$60-70
Corvette 1963, silver.	$50-60
Corvette 1955, black, new.	$110-140
Corvette 1955, copper, new.	$90-100
Corvette 1955, red, new.	$110-140
Corvette 1954, blue, new.	$90-100
Corvette 1953, white, new.	$100-120

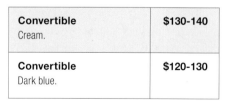

Duesenberg Convertible Coupe, 1983, $250-275.

Duesenberg

Convertible Cream.	$130-140
Convertible Dark blue.	$120-130

Convertible Light blue.	$80-100
Convertible Coupe, gray.	$160-180

Ford

International Delivery Wagon Black.	$80-90		**Model A** 1928.	$60-80
International Delivery Wagon Green.	$80-90		**Model A Fire Truck** 1930.	$130-170
Fire Chief 1928.	$120-130		**Model T** 1913, black.	$30-40
Fire Chief 1934.	$60-70		**Model T** 1913, green.	$30-40
Fire Pumper Truck 1935.	$45-60		**Mustang** 1964, black.	$100-125
Model A Angelos Liquor.	$180-200		**Mustang** 1964, red.	$35-45
Model A Parkwood Supply.	$140-170		**Mustang** 1964, white.	$25-35
Model A 1903, black.	$35-45		**Paddy Wagon** 1930.	$100-120
Model A 1903, red.	$35-45		**Phaeton** 1929.	$40-50
			Pickup Truck 1935.	$20-30

Ford Woodie (1929), 1983, $90; Police Patrol Wagon (1931), 1983, $155.

New Bottles

Police Car 1929, blue.	**$75-85**
Police Car 1929, yellow.	**$350-450**
Police Patrol Car 1934.	**$60-70**
Police Tow Truck 1935.	**$20-30**
Roadster 1934, cream, PA, new.	**$80-90**
Thunderbird 1956, black.	**$60-70**
Thunderbird 1956, blue, PA.	**$70-80**

Ford Fire Engine (1930 Model A), 1983, $205.

Thunderbird 1956, gray.	**$50-60**
Thunderbird 1956, green.	**$60-70**
Thunderbird 1956, yellow.	**$50-60**
Woodie Wagon 1929.	**$50-60**

Mercedes

1974 Blue.	**$30-40**	**1974** Red.	**$30-40**
1974 Gold	**$60-80**	**1974** Sand beige, PA.	**$30-40**
1974 Green.	**$30-40**	**1974** Silver, Australia.	**$140-160**
1974 Mocha.	**$30-40**	**1974** White.	**$35-45**

Casey Jones with Tender, 1989, $50; Casey Jones Caboose, 1989, $30.

Trains

Baggage Car.	$40-60		**Flat Car.**	$20-30
Box Car Brown. Yellow.	$50-60 $40-50		**General Locomotive.**	$60-70
			Grant Locomotive.	$50-65
Bumper.	$5-8		**Log Car.**	$40-55
Caboose Gray. Red.	$45-55 $50-60		**Lumber Car.**	$12-18
			Observation Car.	$15-23
Casey Jones with Tender.	$65-80		**Passenger Car.**	$45-53
Casey Jones Caboose.	$40-55		**Tank Car.**	$15-20
Casey Jones Accessory Set.	$50-60		**Track.**	$4-6
			Turner Locomotive.	$80-100
Coal Tender (no bottle).	$20-30		**Watertower.**	$20-30
Combination Car.	$55-65		**Wood Tender.**	$40-45
Dining Car.	$75-90		**Wood Tender (no bottle).**	$20-25

Other

Ambulance.	$18-22.
Army Jeep.	$18-20
Bass Boat.	$12-18
Cable Car.	$25-35
Circus Wagon.	$20-30
Ernie's Flower Cart.	$20-30
Gold Cart.	$20-30
HC Covered Wagon 1929.	$10-20
Jewel Tea.	$70-80
Mack Fire Truck 1917.	$120-135
Mississippi Pumper Truck 1867.	$115-140
Oldsmobile 1903.	$25-35
Olsonite Eagle Racer.	$40-35

Police Patrol Car 1934, yellow.	$110-140
Space Shuttle.	$20-30
Stutz, 1914 Gray. Yellow.	$40-50 $40-50
Thomas Flyer, 1909 Blue. Ivory.	$60-70 $60-70
Vendome Wagon.	$40-50
Volkswagon Blue. Red.	$40-50 $40-50

San Francisco Cable Car, 1983, $60.

Miniatures

When a discussion on bottle collecting begins, it's clear that most collectors focus their attention on the physically large bottles such as beer, whiskey, or maybe bitters. But there is a distinct group of collectors who eschew big finds and set their sights on the small. Their quest for that special find leads them into the world of miniatures. Until I started bottle collecting, the only miniature bottles that I knew of were the ones passengers bought on airplanes.

16 Years Old – Hunter – Medicinal Spirits, 1930-1935, $25-30.

Today, there is tremendous enthusiasm for miniature bottle collecting. Not only are there specialty clubs and dealers across the United States but throughout the world in the Middle East, Japan, England, Scotland, Australia, and Italy to name just a few. The new collector will soon discover that all miniatures are unique and fascinating in their own way. Because of the low average cost of $1 to $5 per bottle, and the relatively small amount of space required to store them, it's easy to start a collection. As is the case with the larger bottles, there are some rare and expensive miniatures.

While a number of miniatures were manufactured in the 1800s, most were produced from the late 1920 to the 1950s with peak production in the 1930s. While miniatures are still made today, some of the most interesting and sought after are those produced before 1950. The state of Nevada legalized the sale of miniatures in 1935, Florida in 1935, and Louisiana in l934.

If you are looking for a 19th century miniature, you might seek out miniature beer bottles. They are a good example of a bottle that was produced for more than one use. Most of the major breweries produced them as advertisements, novelties, and promotional items. In fact, most of the bottles did not contain beer. A number of these bottles came with perforated caps so that they could be used as salt and pepper shakers.

Old Economy Brand Whiskey, 1930-1935, $45-50.

The Pabst Blue Ribbon Beer Co. was the first brewery to manufacture a beer bottle miniature commemorating the Milwaukee Convention of Spanish American War Veterans. Pabst's last miniature was manufactured around 1942. Most of the miniature beers you'll find today date from before World War II. In 1899 there were as many as 1,507 breweries, all of which produced miniatures.

Collecting miniature liquor bottles has become a special interest for more than bottle collectors. A number of the state liquor stamps from the early 1930s and 1940s have specific series numbers that are sought by stamp collectors. As a reference for pricing, I have consulted Robert E. Kay's *Miniature Beer Bottles & Go-Withs* price guide and reference manual with corresponding pricing codes (CA-1, California, MN-1, Minnesota, etc.).

Old Kentucky Colonel
– Pure Whiskey,
1930-1935, $35-40.

"Lincoln Inn"
– Old Rye
– Whiskey,
1925-1930,
$25-35.

Beer Bottles, Pre-Prohibition, Circa 1890–1933

E. Anheuser – E. Anheuser Co. Brg. Assn. – (MO-84) St. Louis, 1877, embossed. Note: Earliest known mini-beer.	**$100-150**
Edelweiss – P. Schoenhofen Brewing Co. – Chicago (IL-3) Chicago, 1900, embossed and paper label, 5-1/8".	**$100-150**
Elgin Club – Elgin National Brewing Co. – Elgin (IL-54) Elgin, IL, 1900, paper label.	**$100-150**
Malt Sinew – The Conrad Seipp Brewing Co. – Chicago (IL-53) Chicago, 1908, embossed and paper label.	**$100-150**
Pilsner Export – F.W. Cook Brewing Co. – Evansville (IN-30) Evansville, IN, 1900, paper label.	**$100-150**
SchoenHofenbrau – P. SchoenHofenbrau Brewing Co. – Chicago (IL-57) Chicago, 1896, embossed and paper label.	**$100-150**
Theo. Hamm's Export – Theodore Hamm Brewing Co. – St. Paul (MN-44) St. Paul, 1896, paper label.	**$100-150**

Old Angler Kentucky Whiskey, 1930-1935, $35-45.

Beer Bottles, Post-Prohibtion, Circa 1933-Present

Acme Beer – Acme Breweries – San Francisco (CA-7) San Francisco, 1957, decal label, 3".	$10-20	**Country Club Beer – St. Joseph (MO-9)** St. Joseph, MO, 1950, decal label, 4-1/4".	$5-10
Arrow Beer – The Globe Brewing Co. – Baltimore (MD-5) Baltimore, 1953, foil label, 4".	$5-10	**Country Club Pilsener Beer – St. Joseph (MO-4)** St. Joseph, MO, 1941, decal label, 4-1/4".	$5-10
Ballantine Extra Fine Beer – P. Ballantine & Sons – Newark (NJ-9) Newark, NJ, 1951, paper label, 4-1/4".	$5-10		
Berghoff 1887 Beer – Berghoff Brewing Co. – Fort Wayne (IN-13) Fort Wayne, IN, 1950, foil label, 4".	$10-20		
Black River Ale – Haberle Congress Brewing Co. Inc. – New York (NY-46) New York, 1940, decal label, 3".	$30-50		
Camden Lager Beer – Camden Country Beverage Co. – Camden (NJ-2) Camden, NJ, 1952, decal label, 4".	$10-20		
Canandiagua Premium Lager Beer – George F. Stein Brewery, Inc. Buffalo (NY-12) Buffalo, NY, 1950, decal label, 4".	$10-20		

Kentucky Old Hospitality – Whiskey – Bottled In Bond, 1930-1933, $30-35.

Drewrys Ale – Drewrys Ltd. U.S.A. Inc. – South Bend (IN-4) South Bend, IN, 1948, paper label, green glass, 4-1/4".	$5-10		**Falls City Beer – Falls City Brewing Co. Inc. – Louisville (KY-6)** Louisville, 1950, paper label, 3".	$10-20
Duquesne Beer – Duquesne Brewing Co. - Pittsburgh (PA-7) Pittsburgh, 1950, foil label, 4-1/4".	$5-10		**Falstaff Beer – Falstaff Brewing Co. – St. Louis (MO-34)** St. Louis, 1953, foil label, 4".	$5-10
Edelweiss Beer – Schoenhofen Edelweiss Co. – Chicago (IL-28) Chicago, 1950, paper label, 4-1/4".	$5-10		**Falstaff Super X – St. Louis (MO-25)** St. Louis, 1936, decal label, 4-1/4".	$10-20
Esslinger's Little Man Ale., – Esslinger's, Inc. – Philadelphia (PA-9) Philadelphia, 1936, decal label, 4-1/4".	$10-20		**Fehr's Kentucky Beer – Frank Fehr Brewing Co. – Louisville (KY-3)** Louisville, 1936, decal label, 4-1/4".	$30-50

Apple Valley Inn – Kentucky Straight Bourbon Whiskey, 1930; Duffy's Tavern – Diluted Blended Whiskey, 1933; Bonded Beam – Kentucky Straight Bourbon Whiskey, 1935, $35-40 each.

Goetz Country Club Beer – M.K. Goetz Brewing Co. – St. Joseph (MO-13) St. Joseph, MO, 1958, foil label, 5-3/8".	$5-10
Gold Bond Beer – Cleveland – Sandusky Brewing Co. – Cleveland (OH-24) Cleveland, 1952, decal label, 4".	$40-50
Good Host Beer – North American Brewing Co. – Brooklyn (NY-29) Brooklyn, 1940, decal label, 3".	$75-100
Gluek's Pilsener Pale Beer – Gluek Brewing Co. – Minneapolis (MN-12) Minneapolis, 1947, decal label, 3".	$100-150
Grain Belt Beer – Minneapolis Brewing Co. – Minneapolis (MN-15) Minneapolis, 1952, foil label, 4-1/4".	$5-10
Gunther Beer – Gunther Brewing Co. Inc. – Baltimore (MD-4) Baltimore, 1958, foil label, 4".	$5-10
Gunther Beer – Gunther Brewing Co. Inc. – Baltimore (MD-4) Baltimore, 1958, foil label, 4".	$5-10
Haberle's Light Ale – Haberle Congress Brewing Co., Inc. – New York New York, 1940, decal label, 3".	$10-20

Knickerbocker Dark Beer – Jacob Ruppert – New York City (NY-33) New York City, 1955, foil label, 4".	$10-20
Lang's Bohemian Beer – Gerhard Lang Brewery – Buffalo (NY-24) Buffalo, NY, 1936, decal label, 4-1/4".	$10-20
Manru – Larger – Schreiber Brewing Co. Inc. – Buffalo (NY-22) Buffalo, NY, 1945, decal label, 4".	$100-150
Milan Springs Beer – The Milan Brewing Corp. – Milan (OH-27) Milan, OH, 1936, decal label, 4-1/4".	$50-75
Old Tap Brand Ale – Enterprise Brewing Co. – Fall River (MA-3) Fall River, MA, 1940, decal label, 3".	$10-20
Piels Real Draft – Piel Bros. – Brooklyn (NY-27) Brooklyn, NY, 1960, paper label, 4".	$5-10
Reading Premium Beer – The Old Reading Brewery, Inc. – Reading Reading, PA , 1960, paper label, 4".	$10-20
Red Top Beer – Red Top Brewing Co. – Cincinnati (OH-15) Cincinnati, 1950, decal label, 4".	$30-50
Walter's Beer – The Walter Brewing Co. – Pueblo (CO -1) Pueblo, CO, 1956, foil label, 4".	$20-30

Foreign Beer Bottles

Balboa Lager – Panama Brewing & Refining Co. – Panama (PAN-3) Panama, 1936, decal label, 4-1/4".	$30-50		**Mampe – Halb und Halb – Mampe-Berlin (GER-2)** Berlin, Germany, 1965, paper label, 4".	$5-10
Carlsberg Beer – The Carlsberg Breweries – Copenhagen (DEN-1) Copenhagen, Denmark, 1955, foil label, 4".	$10-20		**Mexicali Beer (MEX-9)** Mexican, 1950, paper label, 3".	$10-20
Cerveza Negra – San Miguel Brewery – Manila (PHIL-4) Manila, Philippines, 1965, enamel label, 4-1/4".	$5-10		**Suprema (MEX-6)** Mexican, 1950, paper label, 4".	$10-20

"Since 1788" – Whiskey – Unexcelled For Medicinal Use, 1930-1935, $45-50.

James E. Pepper – Sour Mash Whisky, 1930-1935, $30-35.

Whiskey Flasks, Circa 1925-1940

Black Hawk Whiskey 3-1/4", 1936.	$50-75
Broad Ripple – Straight Whiskey 4", 1934.	$100-125
Brown-Forman – Bottoms Up 4-1/8", 1937.	$75-100
Chevy Chase – Straight Whiskey 4", 1935.	$50-60
Grand Sire – Kentucky Straight – Bourbon Whiskey 4", 1935.	$55-75
G & W – Mountain Ridge – Bourbon Whiskey 3-5/8", 1937.	$70-80
Kentucky Pride – Kentucky Straight – Bourbon Whiskey 4", 1936.	$75-100
Mattingly & Moore – Whiskey Blend 4-3/16", 1934.	$65-85
Mint Springs – Kentucky – Straight – Bourbon- Whiskey 4", 1933.	$50-75
Old Camel – Straight - Bourbon Whiskey 4-3/16", 1936.	$75-125

Old Cask Brand – Straight Bourbon Whiskey 3-7/8", 1935.	$50-75
Old Drum Brand – Blended Whiskey 4", 1940.	$50-75
Old Medley – Kentucky Straight – Bourbon Whiskey 4-1/8", 1939.	$50-60
Old Oscar Pepper Brand 4-1/4", 1935.	$50-75
Old Tucker Brand – Straight Whiskey 4", 1934.	$60-70
Powder Horn – Malt Whiskey 4-1/8", 1940.	$75-100
Rosita – Bourbon Whiskey 4", 1937.	$50-60
Three Rivers – Straight Bourbon Whiskey 3-7/8", 1934.	$50-75
Valley Falls – Straight Bourbon Whiskey 3-15/16", 1936.	$50-75
Washington Club Brand – Bourbon Whiskey 4-1/4", 1939.	$75-100

Golden Wedding – Whiskey, 1925-1930, $35-40.

Golden Premium Whiskey, 1930-1940, $40-45.

Scotch Whiskey

Bonnie Gem – Fine Old – Scotch Whiskey.	$90-150		**Glen Grant –** 20 Years Old.	$300-400
Bonnie Piper – Scotch Whiskey.	$130-160		**Glen Oykel –** Pure Scotch – Whiskey.	$130-170
Bridge Of Allan – Fine Old – Scotch Whiskey.	$130-150		**Golden Dew –** Scotch Distillers Union.	$200-300
Cleveland Club – Fine Old Blended – Scotch Whiskey.	$125-150		**Grey Label –** Old Scotch Whiskey.	$300-400
Deanston Mill – Single Malt – Scotch Whiskey.	$300-350		**Highland Lights –** Rare Old – Blended Scotch Whiskey.	$175-250
Glenfiddich – Pure Malt – Scotch Whiskey.	$50-90		**Johnson's Rhuvaig –** Old Scotch Whiskey.	$175-250

Lord Raymond – Bourbon Whiskey, 1935; Union Club – Straight Bourbon Whiskey, 1930; Tom Taylor – Straight Bourbon Whiskey, 1937, $30-40 each.

Lorne – Rare Old – Scotch Whiskey.	$250-300		**Old Grandtully Whisky.**	$250-350
Master Gunner – Finest Old Scotch Whiskey.	$300-400		**Ross's –** Ancient & Honorable – Blended – Scotch Whisky.	$130-175
Old Anthony – Scotch Whiskey.	$130-150		**Royal Highlander –** Blended Scotch Whisky.	$90-150
Old Cellar – Scotch Whiskey.	$175-250		**Royal St. George.**	$175-250
Old Fettercairn – Fine Blended Malt – Whisky.	$175-250		**Royal Scot –** Scotch Whisky.	$130-170
Double – OO – Old Orkney – Real Liqueur Whisky.	$130-170		**Strathglass House.**	$175-250

John Smith – Bourbon Whiskey, 1940; G. & G. Special – Kentucky Straight Bourbon Whiskey, 1930; Tennessee Walker – Blended Whiskey, 1940, $30-34 each.

Scotch Whiskey

Bonnie Gem – Fine Old – Scotch Whiskey.	$90-150		**Glen Grant –** 20 Years Old.	$300-400
Bonnie Piper – Scotch Whiskey.	$130-160		**Glen Oykel –** Pure Scotch – Whiskey.	$130-170
Bridge of Allan – Fine Old – Scotch Whiskey.	$130-150		**Golden Dew –** Scotch Distillers Union.	$200-300
Cleveland Club – Fine Old Blended – Scotch Whiskey.	$125-150		**Grey Label –** Old Scotch Whiskey.	$300-400
Deanston Mill – Single Malt – Scotch Whiskey.	$300-350		**Highland Lights –** Rare Old – Blended Scotch Whiskey.	$175-250
Glenfiddich – Pure Malt – Scotch Whiskey.	$50-90		**Johnson's Rhuvaig –** Old Scotch Whiskey.	$175-250

Whiskey Nipper – Your Health, 1930s, $30-40.

Whiskey Nipper – Old Scotch, 1930s, $35-40.

Soda Pop Bottles
(3" to 5" in size, Circa 1930s-1950s)

Applied Color Painted Label (ACL)

High Spot Applied Color Label (ACL).	$10		**Squirt** Green bottle, decal label.	$15
Pepsi-Cola Decal label.	$30		**Squirt** Clear glass, decal label.	$12
Smile Embossed.	$25		**Vess** Applied Color Label (ACL).	$15
Spur Applied Color Label (ACL).	$15		**7-Up** Decal label.	$35
Spur Cola Applied Color Label (ACL).	$25			

Whiskey Nipper – A Wee Scotch –
Old Whisky, 1930s, $40-50.

Old Ripy
Whiskey,
1925-1930,
$50-60.

Soda
Applied Color Labels

Anyone who has ever had a cold soda on a hot summer day from a bottle with a painted label probably didn't realize that the bottle would become rare and collectible. Today, collecting Applied Color Label (ACL) soda bottles has become one of the fastest growing and most affordable areas of bottle collecting. This rapid growth has resulted in the Painted Soda Bottle Collectors Association, the nationwide collectors group dedicated to the promotion and preservation of ACL soda bottles.

So, what is an Applied Color Label soda bottle? The best description is this excerpt from an article written by Dr. J.H. Toulouse, a noted expert on bottle collecting and glass manufacturing in the late 1930s:

"One of the developments of the last few years has been that of permanent fused-on labels on glass bottles. The glass in a glass furnace is homogenous in character, all of one color and composition. When the bottles are ready for decoration, the color design is printed on them in the process that superficially resembles many printing or engraving processes. The color is applied in the form of a paste-like material, through a screen of silk, in which the design has been formed. The bottles,which contains the impression of that design, must then be dried and then fired by conducting it thorough a lehr, which is a long, tunnel-like enclosure through which the bottles pass at a carefully controlled rate of speed and in which definite zones of temperature are maintained. The maximum temperature chosen is such that the glass body will not melt, but the softer glass involved in the color will melt and rigidly fuse on the glass beneath it."

The first commercially sold soda was Imperial Inca Cola, its name inspired by the Native American Indian, and promoted medical benefits. The first truly successful coal drink was developed in 1886 by Dr. John Styth Pemberton of Atlanta, who called it Coca-Cola. Carbonated water was added in 1887 and by 1894, bottled Coca-Cola was

Devil Shake, $80; Dew, $8; Diamond, $15; Diet-Way, $6; Dodger, $6;
Double Cola, $20; Double Cola, $7; Double Cola, $5.

Ma's, $6; Mayville, $8; Mid-Valley, $13; Mix-Up, $7; Mission, $6; Oscar's, $8.

Lix, $33; Lane's, $5; Lucky Club, $25; Lincoln, $75; Lemmy, $25; Lift, $11; Little Joe, $11; Long Tom, $8.

in full production. The familiar configuration of the Coke bottle was designed in 1915 by Alex Samuelson. Numerous inventors attempted to ride on the coattails of Coke's success. The most successful of these inventors was Caleb Bradham, who started Brad's drink in 1890 and in 1896 changed its name to Pep-Kola. In 1898, it was changed to Pipi-Cola and by 1906 to Pepsi-Cola.

The ACL Soda Bottle was conceived in the 1930s when Prohibition forced numerous brewing companies to experiment with soda. What started out as a temporary venture saved many brewing companies from bankruptcy; some companies never looked back. From the mid-1930s to the early 1960s, with the peak production falling in the 1940s and 1950s, many small, local bottlers throughout the United States created bottle labels that will forever preserve unique moments in American history. The labels featured western scenes, cowboys, Native Americans, bi-planes to jets, clowns, famous figures, birds, bears, boats, Donald Duck, and even Las Vegas (Vegas Vic).

Since Native Americans and cowboys were popular American figures, these bottles are among the most popular and most collectible. In fact, the Big Chief ACL sodas are the most popular bottles, even more than the embossed types. These small bottlers produced the majority of the better-looking labels in contrast to the largely uniform bottles by major bottlers like Coca-Cola and Pepsi-Cola. Because these bottles were produced in smaller quantities, they are rarer and hence more valuable. While rarity will affect the dollar value, a bottle with a larger label is even more desirable for collectors. The most sought after bottles are those with a two-color label, each color adding more value to the bottle.

Unless noted otherwise, all of the ACL soda bottles listed have a smooth base and a crown top.

New Bottles

Bottles

Embossed – All Bottles Have A Smooth Base, Unless Note Otherwise.

A Treat, Allentown, PA White, 12 oz, 1952.	**$35**
Aircraft Beverages, Stratford, CT White and red, 24 oz, 1958.	**$43**
Arrowhead Famous Beverages, Los Angeles, CA White, 10 oz, 1953.	**$15**
Bauneg Beg Beverages, Springvale, ME Green and white, 7-1/2 oz, 1944.	**$15**
Belfast Sparkling Beverages, San Francisco, CA White, 10 oz, 1957.	**$10**
Big Boy Beverages, Cleveland, OH Red and white, 7 oz, 1947.	**$15**
Big Chief Soda Water, Natchitoches, LA Red and white, 8 oz, 1951.	**$20**
Big Chief Beverages, Modesto, CA Green bottle with red label, 10 oz, 1956.	**$300-400**
Blue Jay Beverages, Junction City, KN Blue and white, 9 oz, 1956.	**$45**
Capitol Club Beverages, Norristown, PA White, 7 oz, 1954.	**$15**

Champ of Thirst Quenchers, Philadelphia, PA Brown, white and yellow, 8 oz, 1960.	**$25**
Chase Flavors, Jackson/ Memphis, TN Brown and white, 10 oz, 1952.	**$15**
Cherry River Beverages, Richmond, W. VA Red and white, 10 oz, 1958.	**$20**
Chief Muskogee Fine Beverages, Muskogee, OK Red, black and white, 8-1/2 oz, 1950-52.	**$30**
Clipper Old Fashioned Root Beer, New Castle, ME Amber glass with black and white label, 10 oz, 1953.	**$35**
Daniel Boone Mix, Spencer, NC Black and white, 7 oz, 1946.	**$12**
Drink –O Delicious, Knoxville, TN Green and white, 10 oz, 1955-56.	**$40**
Duke Beverages, Alton, IL Red and white, 12 oz, 1954.	**$75**
Dumpy Wumpy Beverages, Dunbar, WV Purple and white, 6 oz, 1948.	**$150**
Excel, Breese IL Red and white, 10 oz, 1961.	**$7**

Fawn Beverage Co., Elmira, NY White, 12 oz, 1951.	$36
Fontinalis Berverages, Grayling, MI Red and white, 8 oz, 1946.	$125
Fox Beverages, Fremont, OH Red and white, 10 oz, 1963-68.	$5
Frontier Beverages, North Platte, NE Brown and white, 8 oz, 1948.	$250
Gholson Bros. Beverages, Albuquerque, NM White, 7 oz, 1953-58.	$10
Go – For Brand, Austin, MN Orange and white, 7 oz, 1948.	$15
Golden Dome Ginger Ale, Montpelier, VT Yellow and white, 28 oz, 1948/	$15
Grantman Beverages, Antigo, WS Red and white, 7 oz, 1965.	$10
Hamakua, Paauilo, HI White, 12 oz, 1941.	$15
Harris Springs Ginger Ale, Waterloo, SC Green glass with white label, 12 oz, 1938-48.	$70
Harrison 's – Heart –O-Orange, Globe, AZ Orange and white, 10 oz, 1941.	$16

Heep Good Beverages – Wenatchee Bottling Works, Wenatchee, WA Green, 7 oz, 1937.	$80
Hy-Plane Beverages, Connersville, IN Yellow, white, and red, 7 oz, 1945.	$35
Indian Mound Springs Quality Beverages- Ace of Them All, Bridgeville, PA Red and white, 7 oz, 1966.	$18
Iwana Beverages, Dover, OH Black and white, 8 oz, 1944-50.	$25
Jacks – Up, Gillespie, IL Green glass with white label, 7 oz, 1954.	$45
Jay Cola Sparkling Beverages, Oklahoma City, OK Red, black, and yellow, 10 oz, 1947.	$320
Jet Up Space-Age Beverages, Grove City, PA Red and black, 7 oz, 1960.	$15
Johnny Bull Root Beer, Wheeling, WV Green glass with red and white label, 7-1/2 oz, squat shape 1952-56.	$170
K. C. Beverages – Kit Carson Love, Muskogee, OK Red and white, 10 oz, 1957.	$35

New Bottles

Simba, $10; Sperky, $5; Smile, $27; Smile, $23; Smarty, $12;
Son-E-Boy, $11; Setzler's, $5; Stevens, $17.

TIP, $5; Top's, $10; Tecumseh, $19; Tom Tucker, $41; Ted's Root Beer, $20;
Tiny Tim, $16; Tiny Tim, $10; TNT, $22.

Golden Bride Beverages,
$8; Pa-Poose Root
Beer, $13; Tru-Treat, $9.

Polly, $7; Herby Cola (orange), $10;
Herby Cola (yellow); Elk's Beverage
(embossed), $10; Elk's (label), $8.

Big Chief, $15; Indian Club, $10;
Becher (aqua), $20;
Becher (pale green), $20.

K's Fruit Beverages, Los Angeles, CA Blue and white, 7 oz, 1944.	$20
Kelly's Cream-Top Root Beer, Mishawaka, IN Red and white, 10 oz, 1953.	$45
King Orange Soda, W. Barrington, RI / Buff, NY Red, blue, and white, 12 oz, 1941.	$15
Lammi Beverages, Iron Mountain, MI Red and white, 7 oz, 1959-1960.	$20
Land – O – Lakes Beverages, Paris, MI White, 7 oz, 1948.	$10
Lazy-B Beverages, Fremont, OH Red and white, 8 oz, 1957.	$15
Lincoln, Chicago, Ill Blue and red, 12 oz, Abe Lincoln with cabin in background, 1957.	$75
Little Joe, Perry, IA Green glass with red and white label, 7 oz, 1947.	$20
Mac Fuddy Beverages, Flint, MI Green, red, and white, 10 oz, 1963.	$25
Magic City Beverages, Birmingham, AL Red and white, 7 oz, 1947.	$150
Maple Spring Beverages, E. Wareham, MA Red, green, and white, 7 oz, 1962-67.	$15

Mingo Beverages, Williamson, WV Black and orange, 9 oz, 1922 and 1950.	$75
Mixer Man Beverages, Elkins, WV White and green, 16 oz, 1955.	$65
Nemasket Springs Beverages, Middleboro, MA Red and white, 8 oz, 1948.	$70
New Yorker Beverages, Detroit, MI White, 7 oz, 1947.	$25
Nezinscot Beverages, Turner, ME Red, white, and black, 6 oz, 1941.	$10
Nu-Life Grape – For Better Life, New Orleans, LA Black and white, 7 oz, 1947.	$75
Old Jamaica Beverages, Waldoboro, ME Red, 7 oz, 1964.	$20
Old Nassua – Pale Dry – Ginger Ale, Mineola, NY Green and white, 7 oz, 1947.	$20
Old Smoky Beverages, Greenville, TN Red and white, 10 oz, 1952-58.	$35
Out West Beverages, Colorado Springs, CO White, 10 oz, 1959-1956.	$150
PA-Poose Root Beer, Cushocton, OH Red and yellow, 12 oz, 1941-43.	$50

New Bottles

Pacific (Surfer & Surfer Girl), Honolulu, HI Green and white, 6-1/2 oz, 1950-53.	$50
Pelican Beverages, Alexandria, LA Red and white, 10 oz, 1964-70.	$30
Peter Pan – Delicious – Refreshing, Buffalo, NY Red and white, 7 oz, 1948.	$30
Polar Pak Beverages, San Diego, CA Green and white, 7 oz, 1944-46.	$25
Quality Flower's Beverages, Charlotte, NC Blue and white, 10 oz, 1969.	$7
Ralph's Beverages, Zanesville, OH Red and yellow, 10 oz, 1961.	$30
Red Arrow Beverages – Taste Better, Detroit, MI Red and white, 7 oz, 1946-47.	$15
Red Lodge Beverage Company, Red Lodge, MT Red and white, 7 oz, 1950.	$44
Rocket Beverages, Greeley, CO White, 10 oz, 1965.	$50
Royal Palm, Ft. Myers, FL Red and white, 8 oz, 1955-58.	$10
Sioux Beverages, Sioux Falls, SD Red and white, 7 oz, 9148-52.	$80
Sno-Maid, Reading, PA Green and white, 7 oz, 1966.	$25

Snow White Beverages, Saxton, PA Green and white, 12oz, 1961.	$10
T & T Beverages, Gipsy, PA White, 7 oz, 1957.	$30
Tasty Maid, Madera, CA White, 10 oz, 1968.	$20
Uncle Tom's Root Beer, San Bernardino, CA Red, white, and yellow, 10 oz, 1955.	$520
Variety Club Junior Beverages, Columbus, OH Red and white, 7 ½ oz, 1943.	$60
Vino – Pride of Florida – Punch, Wildwood, FL Red and white, 7 oz, 1960.	$25
Walker's Root Beer, Melrose, MA White, 12 oz, 1949,	$35
Western Beverages, Albuquerque, NM White, 8 oz, 1947.	$50
Zeeh's Beverages, Kingston, NY Red and white, 12 oz, 1949,	$35
Zills's Best Soda, Rapid City, SD Yellow, 7 oz, 1948.	$20
7-UP – Star Beverage Co. (Lady in bathing suit around bubbles) Amber, 7oz, crown top, American, 1920-1930.	$100-150

CHRONOLOGY OF THE GLASS PACKAGE FOR COCA-COLA, 1894 to 1975, from the archives of the Coca-Cola Company, Atlanta, Georgia.

Left to Right, top row:

A. 1894, Hutchinson-Style Bottle. Joseph A. Biedenharn, the first Coca-Cola bottler, began using this bottle in Vicksburg, Mississippi, in 1894.

B. 1899-1902, Hutchinson-Style Bottle. This bottle style was used by Coca-Cola bottlers after November 1899 and before 1903.

C. and D. 1900-1916, Straight-Side Bottle. These bottles had the trademark Coca-Cola embossed in glass. They were designed for crown closures and were distributed with the diamond-shaped label from 1900 through 1916. Both flint and amber bottles were used by Coca-Cola bottlers during this period.

E. Nov. 16, 1915, Hobbleskirt Design: This was the first glass package for Coca-Cola using the classic contour design. It was introduced to the market in 1916.

Left to Right, bottom row:

F. and G. December 25, 1923 (known as the Christmas bottle), and August 3, 1937 (Patent No. D-105529). These two successive designs with patent revisions were used between 1923 (patent date December 25, 1923) and 1951 when the 1937 patent (D-105529) expired. In 1960, the contour design for the bottle was registered as a trademark.

H. 1957. Applied Color Label (ACL). The ACL Coca-Cola trademark was incorporated on all sizes of classic contour bottles.

I. 1961. One-Way Bottle (OWB). The one-way, or no-return glass bottle was later modified for the twist top.

J. 1975. One-Way Bottle (Plastic). This experimental 10 oz. package was made in the classic contour design with twist-top cap. It was tested 1970-1975.

New Bottles

Coca-Cola

Coca-Cola – Los Angeles (embossed around lower part of bottle) Aqua, 7", crown top, American, 1910-1925.	$100-150
Coca-Cola – Los Angeles Amber, 7", crown top, American, 1910-1920.	$150-200
Coca-Cola – Richfield, Utah Clear, 9", crown top, American, 1910-1925.	$100-150
Coca-Cola Co. – Seattle Aqua, 8", crown top, American, 1910-1925.	$75-100
Coca-Cola – Ten Fl. Oz. – Bottling Works – Rochester NY – 10 Fl. Oz. Amber, 8", crown top, American, 1910-1925.	$300-400
Coca-Coal – Trade Mark Registered – Boise Idaho Aqua, 7", crown top, American, 1910-1925.	$100-200
Coca-Cola – Trade Mark Registered – Crown – Bottling Works – Contents 6 Fl. Oz – Cheyenne, Wyo Clear, 7-3/4", crown top, American, 1910-1930.	$750-950
Coca-Cola – Trade Mark Registered – Dr. J.C. Bogue – Sherman, Texas Clear, 8", crown top, American, 1915-1930.	$100-150

Coca-Cola Bottling Co- Las Cruces – Deming – New Mexico Clear, 8", ABM top, 6-panel arches, American, 1900-1915.	$100-120
Coca-Cola Bottling Works – Los Angeles (embossed around the base) Clear, 8-1/2", CCBW on base, tooled crown top, American, 1905-1915.	$100-160
Coca-Cola – Denver Clear, 8-3/4", crown top, American, 1905-1916.	$150-200
Coca-Cola – San Francisco Cal. Clear, 8", tooled top, American, 1905-1925.	$200-250
Colorado – Coca-Cola (in script) – Springs Clear, 9", crown top, American, 1910-1925.	$150-230
Indian Rock – Ginger Ale – Coca-Cola – Bottling Co. – Washington N.C. Light green aqua, 7-3/4", ten-pin shape, crown top, American, 1910-1930.	$300-500
Property of Salt Lake Coca-Cola – Bottling Co. – Coca-Cola (in script) – Salt Lake City – Registered Clear, 8", tooled top, American, 1905-1925.	$100-150

Property Of – Salt Lake – Coca-Cola (in script) – Bottling Co. – Salt Lake City Utah Blue aqua, 10", tooled top, American, 1905-1920.	**$325-425**
The Best By A Dam Site – Boulder – Products – Las Vegas Nev (Las Vegas Coke) Clear, 7-1/2", ABM top, American, 1905-1920.	**$150-200**
The – Coca-Cola – Trade Mark Registered – Bottling Co. – Denver, Colo Clear, 7", crown top, American, 1905-1920.	**$75-100**
The Salt Lake Coca-Cola Bottling Co. – Red Seal Brand Aqua, 7-1/2", ABM top, American, 1905-1915.	**$50-100**

Pepsi-Cola

Indian Rock – Ginger Ale – Richmond – Pepsi-Cola Co. – Richmond VA – 7 Fluid Ounces Clear, 7-3/4", ten-pin shape, crown top, American, 1910-1930.	**$300-500**
Pepsi-Cola (Prototype bottle) Clear, 7", crown top, American, 1906-1910.	**$900-1,000**
Registered – Pepsi Cola (In script on four of the eight panels) Clear, 8", ABM top, base reads: Ideal Bottling Works – L.A. Calif), American, 1906-1920.	**$200-400**

Violin & Banjo

While roaming the aisles of bottle and antiques shows, I have often seen a violin- or banjo-shaped bottle on a table, admired its shape and color, then set it back down and moved on to whiskey and medicine bottles. I didn't fully appreciate these uniquely shaped bottles until I attended the June 1999 National Bottle Museum Antique Bottle Show in Saratoga, New York, to participate in a book signing.

Before the show, a silent auction was held that included a spectacular display of violin and banjo bottles. At that time I had the pleasure of meeting several knowledgeable collectors and members of the Violin Bottle Collectors Association and received a short lesson and history of violin bottles. With the help of many dedicated members of the association, we've written a chapter that will assist both the veteran and the novice collector with understanding the fun and collecting of violin and banjo bottles.

While gathering the information for this chapter, it became clear that the majority of bottle and antiques collectors and dealers (including this collector) had little knowledge about violin and banjo bottles and their beginnings. Are they considered antiques? How old is a violin bottle? Why and where were they manufactured?

First, most were manufactured in the 20th century, with heavy production not taking place until the 1930s. One interesting aspect about violin and banjo bottles is that they are completely original designs and not copied from any earlier bottle types, such as historic flasks and bitters. This makes these bottles antiques, in that they are the first of their design and style.

As with other specialty groups, violin and banjo bottles have specific categories and classes, and codes with each category. For the serious collector, I recommend *The Classification of Violin Shaped Bottles*, 2nd Edition, 1999, and 3rd Edition, 2004, by Robert A. Linden (dorall114@aol.com) and *Violin Bottles, Banjos, Guitars, and Other Novelty Glass*, 1995, by Don and Doris Christensen. Information on the association can be obtained by writing to the Violin Bottle Collector's Association, C/O Meg Stevens (membership director), 13 Whipple Tree Rd., Ballston Spa, NY 12020 or at pook@nycap. rr.com or Samia Koudsi (president) at s.koudsi@mchsi.com.

Violin Bottles:
Category 1: American Styles

LV: LARGE VIOLIN-SHAPED BOTTLE (FIGURE 1)

FIGURE 1

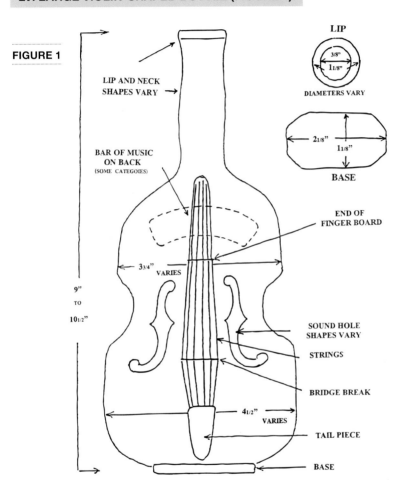

- Eight molds have been identified:
  - Molds 1, 4, and 6 - Produced at Clevenger Brothers Glass Works
  - Molds 2, 3, and 7 - Produced at Dell Glass Company
  - Mold 5 – Maker unidentified
  - Mold 8 – Produced in Japan
- Bottles had no contents and were made only for decorative purposes.
- Production began in the 1930s; first identified in the market place in the 1940s.
- Height range of 9"–10-1/4"; body width 4-1/4"-4-3/8"; 1-1/2" thick near base.
- Colors (various shades) – amber, amberina, amethyst, blue, cobalt, green, yellowish, and vaseline.

New Bottles

SV – SMALL VIOLIN-SHAPED BOTTLE (FIGURE 2)

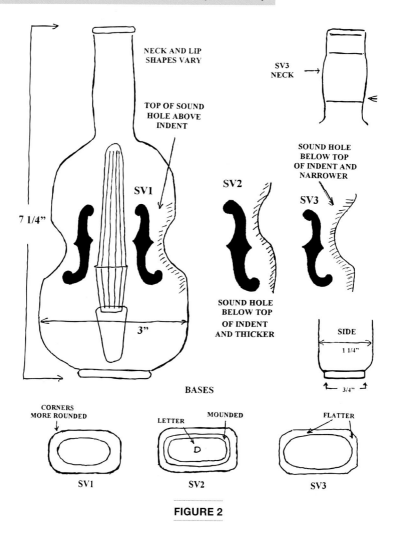

FIGURE 2

- Three molds have been identified:
  - Mold 1 – Produced at Clevenger Brothers Glass Works and Old Jersey Glass Co (a Dell Glass Company)
  - Mold 2 – Produced at Dell Glass Company
  - Mold 3 - Produced at Clevenger Brothers Glass Works
- Less common than large violin bottles.
- Bottles had no contents and were made only for decorative purposes.
- First identified in the market place in the 1940s.
- Height range of 7-1/4"; body width 3"; 1-1/4" thick near base.
- Colors (various shades) – cobalt, clear, blue, green, amber, and amethyst.

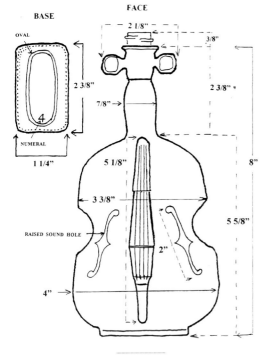

FIGURE 3

EV – VIOLIN-SHAPED BOTTLE WITH "EARS" OR TUNING PEGS ON THE NECK (FIGURE 3)

- Four molds have been identified (four neck shapes (Figure 4) represent mold pattern and numerals are cavity numbers).
- EVA1 up to EVA7 – Each has an "A" neck shape with one of seven.
- EVB1 up to EVB7 – Each has a "B" neck shape with one of seven.
- EVC1 up to EVC7 – Each has a "C" neck shape with one of seven.
- EVD1 up to EVD7 – Each has a "D" neck shape with one of seven.
- Produced at Maryland Glass Company
- ABM product (mold line goes up through neck, ears, and lip)
- Bottles had contents such as cosmetic lotion.
- Labeled as Flasks, Figural, Vases, and Cosmetic bottles.
- Production began in the mid 1930s through the mid-1950s.
- Height 8"; body width 4"
- Colors (various shades) – blue, amber, and clear.

NECK SHAPES

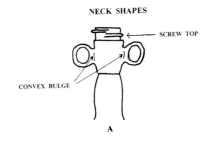

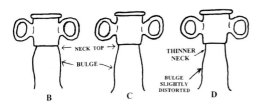

FIGURE 4

New Bottles

BV - BARDSTOWN VIOLIN-SHAPED WHISKEY BOTTLE (FIGURES 5 & 6)

During the late 1930s, bourbon whiskey was distilled in Bardstown, Kentucky, and distributed throughout the Eastern United States and Canada. Bardstown used a violin-shaped bottle, which came in several sizes depicting many attractive labels that became a common identifier until production ceased in 1940. An interesting fact is that while the violin bottle molds spanned 16 years, the molds were only used for four years. Due to the limited production, Bardstown bottles with full labels are difficult to locate.

- Two molds have been identified (produced at Owens-Illinois and Anchor-Hocking)
- Mold 1 – Cork Top
- BVC1 –11" – Quart
- BVC2 – 11" – 4/5 Quart
- BVC3 – 10-1/8" – Pint
- BVC4 – 9-5/8" – Pint
- BVC5 – 8-1/8" – Half-Pint
- Mold 2 – Screw Top
- BVS1 – 14" – Half-Gallon
- BVS2 – 9-1/2" to 10" – Pint
- BVS3 – 7-3/4"-8-1/8" – Half-Pint
- BVS4 – 4-3/4"-4-7/8" – Nip
- Only American violin figural designed and patented specifically with alcoholic content.
- Production began in the 1930s until 1940, when production ceased.
- Color – amber

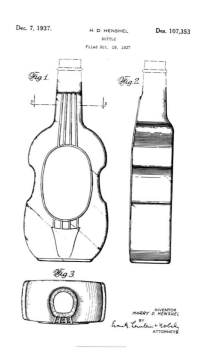

FIGURE 5

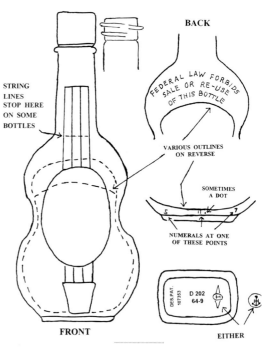

FIGURE 6

Category 2: American Styles

DV – Definitive violin-shaped bottles

FV – Violin-shaped bottle embossed "Bottles Made in France" on base.

CV – Violin-shaped bottle etched "Czecho" and "Slovakia" on base.

Category 3: Special Styles

OV – Other violin-shaped bottles including miniatures

Category 4: Banjo-Shaped Bottles (Figure 7)

LB – Large banjo-shaped bottles
- Six molds have been identified
  - LB1 – Does not have a base (mold line goes all around the body) and no embossing.
  - LB2 – Plain oval base and no embossing. Possible prototype for future models.
  - LB 3 – Only type produced to contain alcohol. LB 3 bottles have the following embossed legend "Federal Law Forbids Sale or Reuse of this Bottle," which was required from 1933 (repeal of prohibition) to 1966.
  - LB 4 – Minor changes with a "new" face and a clean reverse side.
  - LB 5 – Same as LB 4 with the famous base embossing removed and a pontil mark.
  - LB 6 – No pontil marks since snap case tools were used. Finer and more delicate string and sound hole embossing.
- All large banjos have the same discus body shape, approximate height, width, and neck measurements (height 9-1/2"; diameter 5-1/4"; 1-5/8" thick; oval base 1-1/2" long by 3/4" wide)
- Production began in 1942 and continued until 1975.
- Produced at Clevenger Brothers Glass Works, Dell Glass Company, and the Maryland Glass Company.
- Colors (various shades) – amber, green, blue, and amethyst.

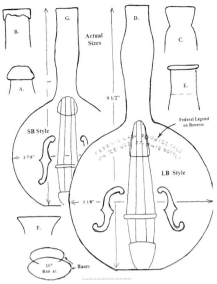

FIGURE 7

SB – Small banjo-shaped bottles
- Two molds have been identified:
  - SB 1 – Smaller version of LB; height 7"; discus diameter 3-7/8"; lady's neck 3-1/8"; oval base 1-1/8" by 3/4".
  - SB 2 – Squared sides with height 7-7/8"; discus diameter 4-1/2"; straight neck 3-1/2"; oval base 2" by 1-1/8" with a 1" kick-up in center of bottle (scarce).
- Produced at Clevenger Brothers Glass Works, Dell Glass Company, and the Maryland Glass Company.
- Colors (various shades) – amber, green, blue, amethyst.

OB – Other banjo-shaped bottles
- Three molds have been identified:
  - OB1 – Corked stopped whiskey measuring 10-3/4" tall; 5-5/8" wide; and 2-1/2" thick. Embossed on back is "Medley Distilling Company Owensboro, Kentucky 4/5 Quart." Color – clear.
  - OB2 – Produced in Italy for 8 to 12" liquor bottles. Base embossing with "Patent Nello Gori." Color – clear.
  - OB3 – Possible miniature, 4-1/2" tall, cobalt salt and pepper shakers in the image of a banjo. Produced by Maryland Glass Company in the 1930s.

Violin

LV1a1 (United Church Bandstand) Amethyst.	**$150-250**
LV1a2 (Auburn Die Company) Amethyst.	**$250-350**
LV1a3 (VBCA, 1997) Cobalt.	**$50-100**
LV1a4 (VBCA, 1999) Amethyst.	**$50-150**
LV1 (Clevenger) Blue. Green. Amethyst. Jersey green. Amber. Cobalt. Amberina.	$20-30 $20-30 $30-45 $30-45 $40-50 $50-100 $400-550
LV2 (Dell) Blue. Green. Amethyst.	$15-25 $15-25 $30-45
LV3 (Dell) Blue. Green. Amethyst.	$15-25 $15-25 $30-45
LV4 (Clevenger) Green. Amethyst. Amber. Cobalt.	$50-60 $50-60 $50-60 $80-100

Violin bottle, emerald green, 9-1/4", $60-70.

LV5 (Dell Glass)	
Royal blue.	$50-70
Clear.	$50-70
Deep green.	$90-110
Golden amber.	$100-120
Yellow.	$100-120
Fluorescing green.	$250-350

LV6 (Clevenger)	
Blue.	$20-30
Green.	$20-30
Jersey green.	$25-40
Amethyst.	$30-45
Amber.	$40-50
Clear.	$40-50
Cobalt.	$50-100
Vaseline.	$250-350

LV7 (Dell Glass)	
Light blue.	$25-35
Light green.	$25-35
Light amethyst.	$30-45
Milk glass.	$400+

LV8 (Japan)	
Light blue.	$60-80
Dark blue.	$60-80
Dark green.	$60-80
Dark amethyst.	$60-80

SV1 (Clevenger)	
Blue.	$25-35
Green.	$25-35
Amethyst.	$35-45
Jersey green.	$35-45
Amber.	$45-60
Clear.	$45-60
Cobalt.	$45-60

SV2 (Dell)	
Blue.	$15-25
Green.	$15-25
Amethyst.	$20-30

SV3 (Clevenger)	
Blue.	$25-35
Green.	$25-35
Amethyst.	$35-45
Amber.	$45-60
Cobalt.	$45-60

SV3app (Pairpoint glass)	$60+
Ruby red.	

EVs (Maryland Glass Company)	
Light cobalt.	$10-20
Dark cobalt.	$10-20
Amber.	$10-20
Clear.	$10-20

DV1 (unknown)	
Blue.	$30-50
Green.	$30-50
Clear.	$30-50
Amber.	$40-60
Red.	$80-100

DV2 (unknown)	
Clear.	$15-25
Blue.	$20-30
Green.	$20-30
Amber.	$25-40
Red.	$60-100

DV3 (unknown)	
Clear.	$15-25
Blue.	$20-30
Green.	$20-30
Amber.	$25-40
Red.	$60-100

Violin bottle, dark amber, 8", $35-40.

Violin bottle, light cobalt blue, 6-1/4", $45-60.

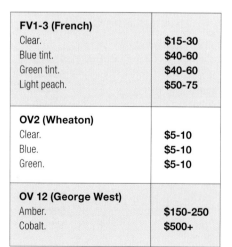

FV1-3 (French)	
Clear.	$15-30
Blue tint.	$40-60
Green tint.	$40-60
Light peach.	$50-75

OV2 (Wheaton)	
Clear.	$5-10
Blue.	$5-10
Green.	$5-10

OV 12 (George West)	
Amber.	$150-250
Cobalt.	$500+

OV14 (stumpy)	
Light blue.	$40-60
Green.	$50-80
Amethyst.	$50-80

OV16 (decanter)	
Light blue.	$150-300
Green.	$150-300
Amethyst.	$150-300
Clear.	$150-300

Large violin bottle (LV1a3), cobalt blue, $50-100.

Large violin bottle (LV1), amber, $40-50.

Large violin bottle (LV7), light amethyst, $30-45.

Large violin bottle (LV8), light blue, $60-80.

Large violin bottle (LV6), blue, $20-30, green, $20-30, amber, $40-50.

New Bottles

Small violin bottles (SV1): green, $25-35; clear, $45-60; cobalt blue, $45-60; blue, $25-35; amber, $45-60.

French violin bottle (FV1-3), blue tint. $40-60; green tint, $40-60; light peach, $50-75.

Small violin bottle (SV2), amethyst, $20-30.

Definitive violin
bottles (DV 2
and 3), ruby red,
$60-100 each.

Large violin bottle
(LV3), amethyst,
$30-45.

Large violin bottle
(LV5), yellow,
$100-120.

Violin bottle (EV) with tuning pegs
or "ears," cobalt blue, $10-20.

Special style violin bottle, amber, $150-250.

Violin bottles (EV) with tuning pegs or "ears," cobalt blue, amber, $10-20 each.

Definitive violin bottle (DV1), blue, $30-50.

Banjo

LB1, 9", no base or embossing, mottled glass, small applied tooled lip, unknown origin Green.	$75-125
LB2, 9-1/2", oval base, no embossing, unknown origin Blue. Amethyst. Green.	 $40-70 $40-70 $60-100
LB3, 9-1/2", 107 R44 41 embossed on base, "FEDERAL LAW FORBIDS SALE OR REUSE OF THIS BOTTLE" embossed on reverse. Maryland Glass pre-1966 Blue.	$60-100

LB4, 9-1/2", 107 R44 41 embossed on base, strings and sound holes, Dell Glass 1940s Blue. Amethyst. Green.	 $25-40 $25-40 $25-40
LB5, 9-1/2", no embossing on base, strings and sound holes, Dell Glass, 1940s Blue. Amethyst. Green.	 $25-40 $25-40 $25-40

Large banjo (LB4 and 5, 9-1/2"), blue, amethyst, green, $25-40.

LB6, 9-1/2", no embossing on base, strings and sound holes, Clevenger 1940s, type-e neck	
Blue.	$25-50
Amethyst.	$25-50
Green.	$25-50
Cobalt.	$75-100
Flared lip	
Blue.	$75-100
Amethyst.	$50-75
Green.	$50-75
Amber.	$150-200
LB6, 9-1/2", embossed slug plate commemoratives, no embossing on base, strings and sound holes, Clevenger, 1970s. LB6a, depiction of East Bridgewater Church, amber.	$150-250
LB6b, just the words "American Handmade, Clevenger Brothers Glass Works, Clayton, NJ," amber.	$100-150
LB6c, depiction of two glassblowers, words "Clevenger Brothers Glass Works, American Made Mouth Blown"	
Blue.	$75-100
Amethyst.	$75-100
Green.	$75-100
Amber.	$75-100

LB6d, Bicentennial "Celebrating 200 Years of Freedom 1776-1976," green.	$50-100
LB6, 9-1/2", embossed slug plate, commemoratives, no embossing on base, strings and sound holes, Pairpoint Glass, 2001. LB6e, VBCA 2000 Commemorative, cobalt.	$45-65
LB6f, VBCA blank slug plate, cobalt.	$45-65
LB6g, Chelmsford Historical Society/ Ezekial Byam Commemorative, teal.	$30-50
SB1, 7", embossed strings and sound holes, Old Jersey Glass/Dell, 1940s.	
Blue .	$25-50
Amethyst.	$25-50
Green.	$75-100
SB2, 7-7/8" with 4-1/2" diameter disc body, embossed strings, no sound holes, origin unknown	
Blue.	$35-60
Amethyst.	$35-60
Green.	$75-100

Banjo bottle, cobalt blue, 5-1/4", $45-55.

Banjo bottle,
clear, 11-1/4",
$50-60.

Small banjo (SB1-7"): amethyst, $25-50; green, $75-100; blue, $25-50.

Large banjo
(LB6b), amber,
$100-150.

Large banjo
(LB1-9"), green,
$75-125.

Reference

Trademarks

Trademarks are helpful for determining the history, age, and value of bottles. In addition, researching trademarks will give the bottle collector a deeper knowledge of the many glass manufacturers that produced bottles and the companies that provided the contents.

What is a trademark? By definition, a trademark is a word, name, letter, number, symbol, design, phrase, or a combination of all of these items that identifies and distinguishes a product from its competitors. For bottles, that mark usually appears on the bottom of the bottle and possibly on the label if a label still exists. Trademark laws only protect the symbol that represents the product, not the product itself.

Trademarks have been around for a long time. The first use of an identification mark on glassware was during the 1st century by glassmaker Ennion of Sidon and two of his students, Jason and Aristeas. They were the first glassmakers to identify their products by placing letters in the sides of their molds. In the 1840s, English glass manufacturers continued this practice using a similar technique.

Identifying marks have been found on antique Chinese porcelain, on pottery from ancient Greece and Rome, and on items from India dating back to 1300 B.C. In addition, stonecutter's marks have been found on many Egyptian structures dating back to 4000 B.C. In medieval times, craft and merchant owners relied on trademarks to distinguish their products from makers of inferior goods in order to gain buyers' loyalty. Trademarks were applied to almost everything, including paper, bread, leather goods, weapons, silver, and gold.

In the late 1600s, bottle manufacturers began to mark their products with a glass seal that was applied to the bottle while still hot. A die with the manufacturer's initials, date, or design was permanently molded on the bottles. This was both efficient and effective because cutting wasn't required, and the mark could be easily seen by the buyer.

Reference

Since the concept of trademarks spread beyond Europe, they were quickly adopted in North America as the number of immigrants grew. For many early trademark owners, protection for the trademark owner was almost nonexistent. While the U.S. constitution provided rights of ownership in copyrights and patents, there wasn't any trademark protection until Congress enacted the first federal trademark law in 1870. Significant revisions and changes were made to the 1870 trademark law in 1881, 1905, 1920, and 1946. Research indicates that registration of trademarks began in 1860 on glassware, with a major increase in the 1890s by all types of glass manufacturers.

Determining Bottle Makers and Dates

If you're able to determine the owner of a trademark, as well as when it might have been used, you will likely be able to determine the date of a piece. If the mark wasn't used long, it is much easier to pinpoint the bottle's age. If, however, the mark was used over an extended period of time, you will have to rely on additional references. Unfortunately, most numbers appearing with trademarks are not part of the trademark and, therefore, will not provide any useful information.

Approximately 1,200 trademarks have been created for bottles and fruit jars. Of these, 900 are older marks (1830s-1940) and 300 are more modern marks (1940s to 1970). Very few manufacturers used identical marks, which is amazing, considering how many companies have produced bottles.

Note: Words and letters in bold are the company's description with the trademarks as they appeared on the bottle. Each trademark is followed by the complete name and location of the company and the approximate period in which the trademark was used.

United States Trademarks

A

A: Adams & Co., Pittsburgh, PA, 1861-1891

A: John Agnew & Son, Pittsburgh, PA, 1854-1866

A: Arkansas Glass Container Corp., Jonesboro, AR, 1958-present (if machine made)

A (in a circle): American Glass Works, Richmond, VA, and Paden City, WV, 1908-1935

A & B together (AB): Adolphus Busch Glass Manufacturing Co, Belleville, IL, and St. Louis, MO, 1904-1907

ABC: Atlantic Bottle Co., New York City, NY, and Brackenridge, PA, 1918-1930

ABCo.: American Bottle Co., Chicago, IL, 1905-1916; Toledo, OH, 1916-1929

ABCO (in script): Ahrens Bottling Company, Oakland, CA, 1903-1908

A B G M Co.: Adolphus Busch Glass Manufacturing Co, Belleville, IL, 1886-1907; St. Louis, MO, 1886-1928

A & Co.: John Agnew and Co., Pittsburgh, PA, 1854-1892

A C M E: Acme Glass Co., Olean, NY, 1920-1930

A & D H C: A. & D.H. Chambers, Pittsburgh, PA, Union Flasks, 1843-1886

AGCo: Arsenal Glass Co. (or Works), Pittsburgh, PA, 1865-1868

AGEE and Agee (in script): Hazel Atlas Glass Co., Wheeling, WV, 1919-1925

AGNEW & CO.: Agnew & Co., Pittsburgh, PA, 1876-1886

AGWL, PITTS PA: American Glass Works, Pittsburgh, PA, 1865-1880; American Glass Works Limited, 1880-1905

AGW: American Glass Works, Richmond, VA, and Paden City, WV, 1908-1935

Ahrens Bottling (AB Co. in middle) Oakland Cal.: 1903-1908, listed in business directories as Diedrich Ahrens

Alabama Brewing (W over B in middle) San Francisco: 1899-1906

Albany Brewing (Trade AB Mark in middle): 1858-1918 (business ended with Prohibition)

AMF & Co.: Adelbert M. Foster & Co., Chicago, IL; Millgrove, Upland, and Marion, IN, 1895-1911

Anchor figure (with H in center): Anchor Hocking Glass Corp., Lancaster, OH, 1955

A. R. S.: A. R. Samuels Glass Co., Philadelphia, PA, 1855-1872

A S F W W Va.: A. S. Frank Glass Co., Wellsburg, WV, 1859

ATLAS: Atlas Glass Co., Washington, PA, and later Hazel Atlas Glass Co., 1896-1965

B

B: Buck Glass Co., Baltimore, MD, 1909-1961

B (in circle): Brockway Machine Bottle Co., Brockway, PA, 1907-1933

Ball and Ball (in script): Ball Bros. Glass Manufacturing Co., Muncie, IN, and later Ball Corp., 1887-1973

Baker Bros. Balto. MD.: Baker Brothers, Baltimore, MD, 1853-1905

BAKEWELL: Benjamin P. Bakewell Jr. Glass Co., 1876-1880

Reference

Baltimore Glass Works: 1860-1870

BANNER: Fisher-Bruce Co., Philadelphia, PA, 1910-1930

Beer Steam Bottling Company (WG & Son in diamond and W Goeppert & Son in middle) San Francisco: 1882-1886

BB Co: Berney-Bond Glass Co., Bradford, Clarion, Hazelhurst, and Smethport, PA, 1900

BB48: Berney-Bond Glass Co., Bradford, Clarion, Hazelhurst, and Smethport, PA, 1920-1930

BBCo: Bell Bottle Co, Fairmount, IN, 1910-1914

B.B. & Co.: 1852-1905 -Baker Bros. & Company (Proprietors of the Baltimore Glass Works)

B-C: Bartlett-Collins Glass Company, Sapulpa, OK (1914-1929)

Bennett's: Gillinder & Bennett (Franklin Flint Glass Co.), Philadelphia, PA, 1863-1867

Bernardin (in script): W.J. Latchford Glass Co., Los Angeles, CA, 1932-1938

The Best: Gillender & Sons, Philadelphia, PA, 1867-1870

B F B Co.: Bell Fruit Bottle Co., Fairmount, IN, 1910

B. G. Co.: Belleville Glass Co., IL, 1882

Bishop's: Bishop & Co., San Diego and Los Angeles, CA, 1890-1920

B & J: Oakland – Braken Felder and Jochem 1906-1907 (Beer)

BK: Benedict Kimber, Bridgeport and Brownsville, PA, 1825-1840

BLUE RIBBON: Standard Glass Co., Marion, IN, 1908

B. & M. S. Co: Bottler's & Manufacturer's Supply Company, Long Island City, NY 1904-1920. Mark seen on heel of New York City blob beer bottle.

Boca (BOB in a circle in middle) Beer: 1875-1891

BODE: Bode Extract Company, Chicago, IL. (Gustav Augustus Bode, proprietor). Mark seen on heel of Hutch Soda Bottles. Bode manufactured bottles from 1890 to 1892. He concentrated on production of extracts from 1892-1900; he passed away in 1900.

BOLDT: Charles Boldt Glass Manufacturing Co., Cincinnati, OH, and Huntington, WV, 1900-1929

Boyds (in script): Illinois Glass Co., Alton, IL, 1900-1930

BP & B: Bakewell, Page & Bakewell, Pittsburgh, PA, 1824-1836

Brelle (in script) Jar: Brelle Fruit Jar Manufacturing Co., San Jose, CA, 1912-1916

Brilliante: Jefferis Glass Co., Fairton, NJ, and Rochester, PA, 1900-1905

Buffalo Brewing Co. (Buffalo inside Horse Shoe): Sacramento, Cal. – (Beer)

C

C (in a circle): Chattanooga Bottle & Glass Co. and later Chattanooga Glass Co., 1927-present

C (in a square): Crystal Glass Co., Los Angeles, CA, 1921-1929

C (in a star): Star City Glass Co., Star City, WV, 1949-present

C (in upside-down triangle): Canada Dry Ginger Ale Co., New York City, NY, 1930-1950

Canton Domestic Fruit Jar: Canton Glass Co., Canton, OH, 1890-1904

C & Co. or C Co: Cunninghams & Co., Pittsburgh, PA, 1880-1907

C. Beck, Santa Cruz: (Big Trees Brewery), 1894-1917

CCCo: Carl Conrad & Co., St. Louis, MO, (Beer), 1860-1883

C.V.Co. No. 1 & No 2: Milwaukee, WI, 1880-1881

C C Co.: Carl Conrad & Co., St. Louis, MO, 1876-1883

C C G Co.: Cream City Glass Co., Milwaukee, WI, 1888-1894

C.F.C.A.: California Fruit Canners Association, Sacramento, CA, 1899-1916

CFJCo: Consolidated Fruit Jar Co., New Brunswick, NJ, 1867-1882

C G I: California Glass Insulator Co., Long Beach, CA, 1912-1919

C G M Co: Campbell Glass Manufacturing Co., West Berkeley, CA, 1885

C G W: Campbell Glass Works, West Berkeley, CA, 1884-1885

C & H: Coffin & Hay, Hammonton, NJ, 1836-1838, or Winslow, NJ, 1838-1842

C & I: Cunningham & Ihmsen, Pittsburgh, PA, 1865-1879

C V No 2 – MILW: Chase Valley Glass Co. No 2, Milwaukee, WI, 1880-1881

Chicago – (Trade-Mark Logo): Lager Beer – Chicago Brewing Co. – S.F. -1993-1890 (beer)

C L G Co.: Carr-Lowrey Glass Co., Baltimore, MD, 1889-1920

CLARKE: Clarke Fruit Jar Co., Cleveland, OH, 1886-1889

CLIMAX: Fisher-Bruce Co, Philadelphia, PA, 1910-1930

CLOVER LEAF (in arch with picture of a clover leaf): 1890 (marked on ink and mucilage bottles)

Clyde, N. Y.: Clyde Glass Works, Clyde, NY, 1870-1882

The Clyde (in script): Clyde Glass Works, Clyde, NY, 1895

C. Milw: Chase Valley Glass Co., Milwaukee, WI, 1880-1881

Cohansey: Cohansey Glass Manufacturing Co., Philadelphia, PA, 1870-1900

CO-SHOE: Coshocton Glass Corp., Coshocton, OH, 1923-1928

C R: Curling, Robertson & Co., Pittsburgh, PA, 1834-1857, or Curling, Ringwalt & Co., Pittsburgh, PA, 1857-1863

CRYSTO: McPike Drug Co., Kansas City, MO, 1904

CS & Co: Cannington, Shaw & Co., St. Helens, England, 1872-1916

C.V.G.CO: Chase Valley Glass Company, Milwaukee, WI, 1880-1881

D

D (in a Keystone): Denver Glass Bottle Company, Denver, CO, 1946-1951

D 446: Consolidated Fruit Jar Co., New Brunswick, NJ, 1871-1882

DB: Du Bois Brewing Co., Pittsburgh, PA, 1918

Dexter: Franklin Flint Glass Works, Philadelphia, PA, 1861-1880

Diamond: (Plain) Diamond Glass Co., 1924-present

The Dictator: William McCully & Co., Pittsburgh, PA, 1855-1869

Dictator: William McCully & Co., Pittsburgh, PA, 1869-1885

Reference

Dillon G. Co.: Dillon Glass Company, Converse, IN, and Fairmount, IN, 1990-1894

D & O: Cumberland Glass Mfg. Co., Bridgeton, NJ, 1890-1900

D O C: D.O. Cunningham Glass Co., Pittsburgh, PA, 1883-1937

DOME: Standard Glass Co., Wellsburg, WV, 1891-1893

D S G Co.: De Steiger Glass Co., LaSalle, IL, 1879-1896

Duffield: Dr. Samuel Duffield, Detroit, MI, 1862-1866, and Duffield, Parke & Co., Detroit, MI, 1866-1875

Dyottsville: Dyottsville Glass Works, Philadelphia, PA, 1833-1923

E4: Essex Glass Co., Mt. Vernon, OH, 1906-1920

Economy (in script) TRADE MARK: Kerr Glass Manufacturing Co., Portland, OR, 1903-1912

Electric Trade Mark (in script): Gayner Glass Works, Salem, NJ, 1910

Electric Trade Mark: Gayner Glass Works, Salem, NJ, 1900-1910

Erd & Co., E R Durkee: E.R. Durkee & Co., New York, NY, Post-1874

The EMPIRE: Empire Glass Co., Cleveland, NY, 1852-1877

E R Durkee & Co: E.R. Durkee & Co., New York, NY, 1850-1860

E.S. & CO.: Evans, Sell & Company, Pittsburgh, PA, 1873-1877

Eureka 17: Eurkee Jar Co., Dunbar, WV, 1864

Eureka (in script): Eurkee Jar Co., Dunbar, WV, 1900-1910

Everett and EHE: Edward H. Everett Glass Co. (Star Glass Works), Newark, OH, 1893-1904

Everlasting (in script) JAR: Illinois Pacific Glass Co., San Francisco, CA, 1904

E W & Co: E. Wormser & Co., Pittsburgh, PA, 1857-1875

Excelsior: Excelsior Glass Co., St. John, Quebec, Canada, 1878-1883

F (inside a jar outline or keystone): C.L. Flaccus Glass Co., Pittsburgh, PA, 1900-1928

F in a Hexagon: Fairmount Glass Works/Company, Fairmount, IN 1889-1906, Indianapolis, IN, 1906-1968

F in a Shield: Federal Glass Company, Columbus, OH, 1901-1980

F WM. Frank & Sons: WM. Frank & Co., Pittsburgh, PA, 1846-1966, WM. Frank & Sons, Pittsburgh, PA, 1866-1876

F & A: Fahnstock & Albree, Pittsburgh, PA, 1860-1862

FERG Co: F.E. Reed Glass Co., Rochester, NY, 1898-1947

FF & Co: Fahnstock, Fortune & Co., Pittsburgh, PA, 1866-1873

F G: Florida Glass Manufacturing Co., Jacksonville, FL, 1926-1947

FL or FL & Co.: Frederick Lorenz & Co., Pittsburgh, PA, 1819-1841

FLINT–GREEN: Whitney Glass Works, Glassborough, NJ, 1888

F. O. Brandt: Healdsburg Cal. – 1895-1912 (Ice and Bottling Works)

FOLGER, JAF&Co., Pioneer, Golden Gate: J. A. Folger & Co., San Francisco, CA, 1850-present

G

G in circle (bold lines): Gulfport Glass Co., Gulfport, MS, 1955-1970

G E M: Hero Glass Works, Philadelphia, PA, 1884-1909

G & H: Gray & Hemingray, Cincinnati, OH, 1848-1851; Covington, KY, 1851-1864

G & S: Gillinder & Sons, Philadelphia, PA, 1867-1871 and 1912-1930

Geo. Braun Bottler (C over B in arrowhead in middle) 2219 Pine St. S.F.: 1893-1906

Gillinder: Gillinder Bros., Philadelphia, PA, 1871-1930

Gilberds: Gilberds Butter Tub Co., Jamestown, NY, 1883-1890

GLENSHAW (G in a box underneath name): Glenshaw Glass Co., Glenshaw, PA, 1904

GLOBE: Hemingray Glass Co., Covington, KY (the symbol "Parquet-Lac" was used beginning in 1895), 1886

Greenfield: Greenfield Fruit Jar & Bottle Co., Greenfield, IN, 1888-1912

G.W.: Great Western Glass Company, St. Louis, MO, 1874-1886

GWK & Co.: George W. Kearns & Co., Zanesville, OH, mid-1860s–1868; 1878-1913

H

H and H (in heart): Hart Glass Manufacturing Co., Dunkirk, IN, 1918-1938

H (with varying numerals): Holt Glass Works, West Berkeley, CA, 1893-1906

H in a Circle: Hemingray Glass Company, Muncie, IN (mark used 1924-1935)

H in a Square: Hemingray Glass Company, Muncie, IN (mark used 1924-1935)

H (in a vertical diamond): A.H. Heisey Glass Co., Oakwood Ave., Newark, OH, 1893-1958

H (in a triangle): J. T. & A. Hamilton Co., Pittsburgh, PA, 1884-1943 (mark used approximately 1900-1943)

Hamilton: Hamilton Glass Works, Hamilton, Ontario, Canada, 1865-1872

Hansen & Kahler (H & K in middle) Oakland Cal.: 1897-1908

Hazel: Hazel Glass Co., Wellsburg, WV, 1886-1902

H.B.Co: Hagerty Bros. & Co., Brooklyn, NY, 1880-1900

Helme: Geo. W. Helme Co., Jersey City, NJ, 1870-1895

Hemingray: Hemingray Brothers & Co. and later Hemingray Glass Co., Covington, KY, 1864-1933

Henry Braun (beer bottler in middle) Oakland Cal.: 1887-1896

H. J. Heinz: H.J. Heinz Co., Pittsburgh, PA, 1860-1869

Heinz & Noble: H.J. Heinz Co., Pittsburgh, PA, 1869-1872

F. J. Heinz: H.J. Heinz Co., Pittsburgh, PA, 1876-1888

H. J. Heinz Co.: H.J. Heinz Co., Pittsburgh, PA, 1888-present

HELME: Geo. W. Helme Co., NJ, 1870-1890

HERO: Hero Glass Works, Philadelphia, PA, 1856-1884 and Hero Fruit Jar Co., Philadelphia, PA, 1884-1909

H F J Co (in wings of Maltese cross): Hero Glass Works, 1884-1900

HP (close together in circle): Keene Glass Works, Keene, NH, 1817-1822

HS (in a circle): Twitchell & Schoolcraft, Keene, NH, 1815-1816

Reference

IDEAL: Hod c. Dunfee, Charleston, WV, 1910

I G Co.: Ihmsen Glass Co., Pittsburgh, PA, 1855-1896

I. G. Co: Ihmsen Glass Co., 1895

I. G. Co.: Monogram, Ill. Glass Co. on fruit jar, 1914

IPGCO: Ill. Pacific Glass Company, San Francisco, CA, 1902-1926

IPGCO (in a diamond): Ill. Pacific Glass Company, San Francisco, CA, 1902-1926

IG: Illinois Glass, F inside a jar outline, C. L. Flaccus 1/2 glass 1/2 co., Pittsburgh, PA, 1900-1928

Ill. Glass Co.: 1916-1929

I G: Illinois Glass Co., Alton, IL, before 1890

I G Co. (in a diamond): Illinois Glass Co., Alton, IL, 1900-1916

Improved G E M: Hero Glass Works, Philadelphia, PA, 1868

I P G: Illinois Pacific Glass Co. San Francisco, CA, 1902-1932

I S G Co.: Interstate Glass Company, Kansas City, MO, 1902-190

I X L: I X L Glass Bottle Co., Inglewood, CA, 1921-1923

J (in keystone): Knox Glass Bottle Co. of Miss., Jackson, MS, 1932-1953

J (in square): Jeannette Glass Co., Jeannette, PA, 1901-1922

JAF & Co., Pioneer and Folger: J.A. Folger & Co., San Francisco, CA, 1850-present

J D S: John Duncan & Sons, New York, NY, 1880-1900

J. P. F.: Pitkin Glass Works, Manchester, CT, 1783-1830

J R: Stourbridge Flint Glass Works, Pittsburgh, PA, 1823-1828

JBS monogram: Joseph Schlitz Brewing Co., Milwaukee, WI, 1900

JT: Mantua Glass Works, later Mantua Glass Co., Mantua, OH, 1824

JT & Co: Brownsville Glass Works, Brownsville, PA, 1824-1828

J. SHEPARD: J. Shepart & Co., Zanesville, OH, 1823-1838

K (in keystone): Knox Glass Bottle Co., Knox, PA, 1924-1968

Kensington Glass Works: Kensington Glass Works, Philadelphia, PA, 1822-1932

Kerr (in script): Kerr Glass Manufacturing Co. and later Alexander H. Kerr Glass Co., Portland, OR; Sand Spring, OK; Chicago, IL; Los Angeles, CA, 1912-present

K H & G: Kearns, Herdman & Gorsuch, Zanesville, OH, 1876-1884

KH & GZO: Kearns, Herdman & Gorsuch, 1868-1886

K & M: Knox & McKee, Wheeling, WV, 1824-1829

K & O: Kivlan & Onthank, Boston, MA, 1919-1925

KO – HI: Koehler & Hinrichs, St. Paul, MN, 1911

K Y G W and KYGW Co: Kentucky Glass Works Co., Louisville, KY, 1849-1855

L (in keystone): Lincoln Glass Bottle Co., Lincoln, IL, 1942-1952

L (in an oval): W.J. Latchford Glass Co., Los Angeles, CA, 1925-1938

Lamb: Lamb Glass Co., Mt. Vernon, OH, 1855-1964

LB (B inside L): Long Beach Glass Co., Long Beach, CA, 1920-1933

L. G. (with periods): Liberty Glass Co., 1924-1946

L-G (with hyphen): Liberty Glass Co., 1946-1954

L G (with no punctuation): Liberty Glass Co., since 1954

LGCo.: Lindell Glass Co. 1874-1892

L & W: Lorenz & Wightman, PA, 1862-1871

Lightning: Henry W. Putnam, Bennington, VT, 1875-1890

LP (in keystone): Pennsylvania Bottle Co., Wilcox, PA, 1940-1952

L K Y G W: Louisville Kentucky Glass Works, Louisville, KY, 1873-1890

M

"Mascot, "Mason" and M F G Co.: Mason Fruit Jar Co., Philadelphia, PA, 1885-1890

Mastadon: Thomas A. Evans Mastadon Works, and later Wm. McCully & Co. Pittsburgh, PA, 1855-1887

MB Co: Muncie Glass Co., Muncie, IN, 1895-1910

M B & G Co: Massillon Bottle & Glass Co., Massillon, OH, 1900-1904

M B W: Millville Bottle Works, Millville, NJ, 1903-1930

McC & CO.: William McCully and Company – Pittsburg, PA, 1841-1909

M. Casey, Gilroy Brewery Cal.: Chicago Bottle Works, San Francisco, CA, 1896-1906

McL (in circle): McLaughlin Glass Co., Vernon, CA, 1920-1936, Gardena, CA, 1951-1956

MEDALLION: M.S. Burr & Co., Boston, MA (mfgr. of nursing bottles), 1874

M (in keystone): Metro Glass Bottle Co., Jersey City, NJ, 1935-1949

MG: Straight letters 1930-1940; slanted letters, Maywood Glass, Maywood, CA, 1940-1958

M.G. Co.: Modes Glass Company, Cicero, IN, 1895-1904

M. G. W.: Middletown Glass Co., NY, 1889

MGCo.: Mississippi Glass Co., 1873-1874

Moore Bros.: Moore Bros., Clayton, NJ, 1864-1880

MOUNT VERNON: Cook & Bernheimer Co., New York, NY, 1890

N

N (in keystone): Newborn Glass Co., Royersford, PA, 1920-1925

N: H. Northwood Glass Co., Wheeling, WV, 1902-1925

N (bold N in bold square): Obear-Nester Glass Co., St. Louis, Missouri and East St. Louis, IL, 1895

N 17: American Bottle Co., Toledo, OH, Div. of Owens Bottle Co., 1917-1929

N. B. B. G. Co: North Baltimore Bottle Glass Co., North Baltimore, OH, 1888-1995; Albany, IN, 1895-1900; Terre Haute, IN, 1900-1926

N. Cervelli (N over C in middle) 615 Francisco ST. S.F.: 1898-1906

N G Co: Northern Glass Co., Milwaukee, WI, 1894-1896

N - W: Nivison-Weiskopf Glass Co., Reading, OH, 1900-1931

Reference

O

O (in a square): Owen Bottle Co., 1919-1929

O B C: Ohio Bottle Co., Newark, OH, 1904-1905

O-D-1-O & Diamond & I: Owens Ill. Pacific Coast Co., CA, 1932-1943. Mark of Owens-Ill. Glass Co. merger in 1930

O G W: Olean Glass Co. (Works), Olean, NY, 1887-1915

O (in keystone): Oil City Glass Co., Oil City, PA, 1920-1925

OSOTITE (in elongated diamond): Warren Fruit Jar Co., Fairfield, IA, 1910

O-U-K I D: Robert A Vancleave, Philadelphia, PA, 1909

P

P (in keystone): Wightman Bottle & Glass Co., Parker Landing, PA, 1930-1951

PCGW: Pacific Coast Glass Works, San Francisco, CA, 1902-1924

PEERLESS: Peerless Glass Co., Long Island City, NY, 1920-1935 (was Bottler's & Manufacturer's Supply Co., 1900-1920)

P G W: Pacific Glass Works, San Francisco, CA, 1862-1876

Picture of young child in circle: M.S. Burr & Co., Boston, MA (mfgr. of nursing bottles), 1874

Premium: Premium Glass Co., Coffeyville, KS, 1908-1914

P in square or pine in box: Pine Glass Corp., Okmulgee, OK, 1927-1929

P S: Puget Sound Glass Co., Anacortes, WA, 1924-1929

Putnam Glass Works (in a circle): Putnam Flint Glass Works, Putnam, OH, 1852-1871

P & W: Perry & Wood and later Perry & Wheeler, Keene, NH, 1822-1830

Q

Queen (in script) Trade Mark (all in a shield): Smalley, Kivian & Onthank, Boston, MA, 1906-1919

R

Rau's: Fairmount Glass Works, Fairmount, IN, 1898-1908

Ravena Glass Works: Ravena Glass Works, Ravenna, OH, 1857-1867

R & C Co: Roth & Co., San Francisco, CA, 1879-1888

Red (with a key through it): Safe Glass Co., Upland, IN, 1892-1898

R G Co.: Renton Glass Co., Renton, WA, 1911s

R.G. & B. Co.: Rhodes Glass & Bottle Company, Massillon, OH, 1901-1919

Root: Root Glass Co., Terre Haute, IN, 1901-1932

S

S (in a star): Southern Glass Co., L.A., 1920-1929

S (in a circle): Southern Glass Co., 1919-1920

S (in an elongated diamond): Southern Glass Co., 1920-1925

S (in a triangle): Schloss Crockery Co., San Francisco, CA, 1910

S (in keystone): Seaboard Glass Bottle Co. Pittsburgh, PA, 1943-1947

SB & GCo: Streator Bottle & Glass Co., Streator, IL, 1881-1905

SF & PGW: San Francisco & Pacific Glass Works, San Francisco, CA, 1876-1900

S & C: Stebbins & Chamberlain or Coventry Glass Works, Coventry, CT, 1825-1830

S F G W: San Francisco Glass Works, San Francisco, CA, 1869-1876

SIGNET (blown in bottom): Chicago Heights Bottle Co., Chicago, Heights, IL, 1913

Squibb: E.R. Squibb, M.D., Brooklyn, NY, 1858-1895

Standard (in script, Mason): Standard Coop. Glass Co., and later Standard Glass Co., Marion, IN, 1894-1932

Star Glass Co: Star Glass Co., New Albany, IN, 1867-1900

Swayzee: Swayzee Glass Co. Swayzee, IN, 1894-1906

T

T (in keystone): Knox Glass Bottle Co. of Miss., Palestine, TX, 1941-1953

T C W: T.C. Wheaton Co., Millville, NJ, 1888-present

The Bay Bottling Co.: San Francisco, CA, 1905 (beer)

THE BEST (in an arch): Gotham Co., New York, NY, 1891

TIP TOP: Charles Boldt Glass Co., Cincinnati, OH, 1904

T W & Co.: Thomas Wightman & Co., Pittsburgh, PA, 1871-1895

T S: Coventry Glass Works, Coventry, CT, 1820-1824

U

U: Upland Flint Bottle Co., Upland, Inc., 1890-1909

U in Keystone: Pennsylvania Bottle Co., Sheffield, PA, 1929-1951

U S: United States Glass Co., Pittsburgh, PA, 1891-1938, Tiffin, OH, 1938-1964

W

WARRANTED (in arch) FLASK: Albert G. Smalley, Boston, MA, 1892

WARREN GLASS WORKS Co.: Warren Glass Works, 1880-1888

W & CO: Thomas Wightman & Co., Pittsburgh, PA, 1880-1889

W C G Co: West Coast Glass Co., Los Angeles, CA, 1908-1930

WF & S MILW: William Franzen & Son, Milwaukee, WI, 1900-1929

W G W: Woodbury Glass Works, Woodbury, NJ, 1882-1900

WILLIAM FRANK PITTSBURG: William Frank & Sons, Pittsburgh, 1866-1875

WM. FRANK & SONS, PITTS: William Frank & Sons, Pittsburgh, 1866-1875

WYETH: Drug manufacturer, 1880-1910

W. T. & Co. (in rectangle): Whitall-Tatum & Co., Millville, NJ, 1875-1885

W.T. & Co. - E (in small rectangle within big rectangle): Whitall Tatum, Millville, NJ, 1885-1895

W.T. & Co. – C – U.S.A. (in small rectangle within big rectangle): Whitall Tatum, Millville, NJ, 1891-1984

W.T. & Co. – U.S.A. (in small rectangle within big rectangle): Whitall Tatum, Millville, NJ, 1890-1901

W T R Co.: W.T. Rawleigh Manufacturing Co., Freeport, IL, 1925-1936

Foreign Trademarks

A (in a circle): Alembic Glass Industries, Bangalore, India

Big A (in center of it GM): Australian Glass Mfg. Co. Kilkenny, So. Australia

A.B.C.: Albion Bottle Co. Ltd., Oldbury, Nr. Birmingham, England

A.G.W.: Alloa Glass Limited, Alloa, Scotland

A G B Co.: Albion Glass Bottle Co., England; trademark is found under Lea & Perrins, 1880-1900

B & C Co. L: Bagley & Co. Ltd., Est. 1832, England (still operating)

AVH.A: Van Hoboken & Co., Rotterdam, the Netherlands, 1800-1898

Beaver: Beaver Flint Glass Co., Toronto, Ontario, Canada, 1897-1920

Bottle (in frame): Veb Glasvoerk Drebkau Drebkau, N. L., Germany

Crown with three dots: Crown Glass, Waterloo, N.S., Wales

Crown (with figure of a crown): Excelsior Glass Co., St. Johns, Quebec and later Diamond glass Co., Montreal, Quebec, Canada, 1879-1913

CS & Co.: Cannington, Shaw & Co., St. Helens, England, 1872-1916

CSTS (in center of hot air balloon): C. Stolzles Sohne Actiengeselichaft fur Glasfabrikation, Vienna, Austria, Hungary, 1905

D (in center of a diamond): Dominion Glass Co., Montreal, Quebec, Canada

D.B. (in a book frame): Dale Brown & Co., Ltd., Mesborough, Yorks, England

Fish: Veb Glasvoerk Stralau, Berlin, Germany

Excelsior: Excelsior Glass Co., St. John, Quebec, Canada, 1878-1883

HH: Werk Hermannshutte, Czechoslovakia

Hamilton: Hamilton Glass Works, Hamilton, Ontario, Canada, 1865-1872

Hat: Brougba, Bulgaria

Hunyadi Janos: Andreas Saxlehner, Buda-Pesth, Austria-Hungary, 1863-1900

IYGE (all in a circle): The Irish Glass Bottle, Ltd. Dublin, Ireland

KH: Kastrupog Holmeqaads, Copenhagen, Denmark

L (on a bell): Lanbert S.A., Belgium

LIP: Lea & Perrins, London, England, 1880-1900

LS (in a circle): Lax & Shaw, Ltd., Leeds, York, England

M (in a circle): Cristales Mexicanos, Monterey, Mexico

N (in a diamond): Tippon Glass Co., Ltd. Tokyo, Japan

NAGC: North American Glass Co., Montreal, Quebec, Canada, 1883-1890

NP: Imperial Trust for the Encouragement of Scientific and Industrial Research, London, England, 1907

NS (in middle of bottle shape): Edward Kavalier of Neu Sazawa, Austria-Hungary, 1910

P & J A: P. & J. Arnold, LTD., London, England, 1890-1914

PRANA: Aerators Limited, London, England, 1905

PG: Verreries De Puy De Dome, S.A. Paris

R: Louit Freres & Co., France, 1870-1890

S (in a circle): Vetreria Savonese. A. Voglienzone, S.A. Milano, Italy

S.A.V.A. (all in a circle): Asmara, Ethiopia

S & M: Sykes & Macvey, Castleford, England, 1860-1888

T (in a circle): Tokyo Seibin., Ltd. Tokyo, Japan

vFo: Vidreria Ind. Figuerras Oliveiras, Brazil

VT: Ve.Tri S.p.a., Vetrerie Trivemta, Vicenza, Italy

VX: Usine de Vauxrot, France

WECK (in a frame): Weck Glaswerk G. mb.H, ofigen, Bonn, Germany

Y (in a circle): Etaria Lipasmaton, Athens, Greece

Auction Companies

ABIC Absentee Auctions
139 Pleasant Ave.
Dundas
Ontario, Canada L9H 3T9
Phone: (519) 443-4162 or (905) 628-3433
E-mail: info@auctionsbyabc.com
Website: http://www.auctionsbyabc.com

ABCR Auctions
16 Lorikeet Crescent
Whittlesea
Victoria, Australia 3757
Phone: 61-417-830-939
E-mail: info@abcrauctions.com
Website: www.abcrauctions.com

American Bottle Auctions
915 28th Street
Sacramento, CA 95816
Phone: (800) 806-7722
Fax: (916) 443-3199
E-mail: info@americanbottle.com
Website: http://www.americanbottle.com

American Glass Gallery
P.O. Box 227
New Hudson, MI
Phone: (248) 486-0530
E-mail: jpastor@americanglassgallery.com
Website: www.americanglassgallery.com

Antique Pottery & Stoneware Auctions
Bruce & Vicki Waasdorp
P.O. Box 434
Clarence, NY 14031
Phone: (716) 759-2361
Fax: (716) 759-2379
E-mail: waasdorp@antiques-stoneware.com
Website: www.antiques-stoneware.com

Armans of Newport
207 High Point Ave.
Portsmouth, RI 02871

Robert Arner Auctioneer
153 Pinehill Rd.
New Ringgold, PA 17960
Phone: (570) 386-4586
e-mail: Lentigo&ptd.net
Website: Arnerauctioneers.com

Australian & Collectables Auctions
David Wescott
P.O. Box 245
Deniliquin NSW 2710, Australia
Phone: 011-61-35881-2200
Fax: 011-61-35881-4740
E-mail: dwescott@wescottdavid.com
Website: www.westcottdavid.com

B & B Auctions/Bottles & Bygones
30 Brabant Rd.
Cheadle Hulme, Cheadle
Cheshire, England SK8 7AU
Phone: 011-44-7931-812156
E-mail: bygonz@yahoo.com
Website: www.bygonz.co.uk

BBR Auctions
5 Ironworks Row, Wath Rd., Elsecar
Barnsley, S. Yorkshire, S74 8HJ, England
Phone: 011-44-1226-745156
Fax: 011-44-1226-361561

Bothroyd & Detwiler Online Auctions
1290 South 8th Ave., Yuma AZ
E-mail: detwiler@primenet.com
Website: http://www.primnet.com/~detwiler/
index.html

BottleAuction.Com
P.O. Box 2146
Vista, CA 92085
Phone: (760) 415-6549
E-mail: randy@bottleauction.com

Cerebro Tobacco Ephemera Auctions
P.O. Box 327
East Prospect, PA 17317
Phone: (800) 695-2235
E-mail: cerebrolab@aol.com
Website: http://www.cerebro.com

CB & SC Auctions
Rhonda Bennett
179D Woodridge Crest, Nepean
Ontario, Canada K2B 712
Phone: (613) 828-8266

Reference

Collectors Sales & Services
P.O. Box 4037, Middletown, RI 02842
Phone: (401) 849-5012
E-mail: collectors@antiquechina.com
Website: http://www.antiqueglass.com

D. Owen Grove Auctions
255 E. 7th St. (rear)
Bloomsburg, PA 17815
Phone: (570) 387-5178
E-mail: groveauctions@yahoo.com
Website: www.groveauctions.com

Daniel Auction Company
116 East Kelly Street
Sylvester, GA 31791
Phone: (229)776-3998
Fax: (229) 776-7972
Website: www.danielauctioncompany.com

Down-Jersey Auction
15 Southwest Lakeside Dr., Medford, NJ 08055
Phone: (609) 953-1755
Fax: (609) 953-5351
E-mail: dja@skyhigh.com
Website: http://www.down-jersey.com

Gallery at Knotty Pine Auction Service
Route 10, P.O. Box 96 W.
Swanzey, NH 03469
Phone: (603) 352-2313
Fax (603) 352-5019
E-mail: kpa@inc-net.com
Website: www.knottypineantiques.com

Galleria Auctions & Bottles and More Magazine
P.O. Box #6, Lehighton, PA 18235
Phone: (610) 377-1484
E-mail: rodwalck@ptd.net
Website: www.bottlemagazine.com and www.galleriaauctions.com-0%sellercommissions

Garth's Auctions
2690 Stratford Rd., Box 369, Delaware, OH 43015
Phone: (740) 362-4771
Fax: (740) 363-0164
E-mail: info@garths.com
Website: http://www.garths.com

GLASSCO Auctions
102 Abbeyhill Dr., Kanata, Ontario, Canada K2L 1H2
Phone: (613) 831-4434
E-mail: phil@glassco.com

Glass Discoveries Collector Services Auctions
Ray Klingensmith
P.O. Box 628, Parkman, OH 44080
Phone: (440) 548-5408
E-mail: ray@glassdiscoveries.com
Website: www.glassdiscoveries.com

Glass Works Auctions
Box 187, East Greenville, PA 18041
Phone: (215) 679-5849
Fax: (215) 679-3068
E-mail: glswrk@enter.net
Website: http://www.glswrk-auction.com

Glass International
134 Meeshaway Trail, Medford, NJ 08055
Phone: (609) 714-2595
E-mail: glassinternational@comcast.net
Website: www.glassinternational.com.

Gore Enterprises
William D. Emberley
P.O. Box 158, Huntington, VT 05462
Phone: (802) 453-3311

Harmer Rooke Galleries
32 East 57th St., New York, NY 10022
Phone: (212) 751-1900

Norman C. Heckler & Co.
79 Bradford Corner Rd.
Woodstock Valley, CT 06282
Phone: (860) 974-1634
Fax: (860) 974-2003
E-mail: info@hecklerauction.com
www.hecklerauction.com

James E. Hill Auctions
P.O. Box 366, Randolph, VT 05060
Phone: (802) 728-5465
E-mail: jehantqs@sover.net

Holabird's Western Americana Collections
3555 Airway Drive Suite #309
Reno, Nevada 89511
Phone: (775) 851-1859
Fax: (775) 851-1834
E-mail: info@fhwac.com
Website: www.fhwac.com

Ken Leach Auctions
1050 2nd Ave. #47
New York, NY 10022
Phone: (800) 942-0550
Fax: (917) 591-6645
E-mail: ken@perfumebottlesauction.com
Website: www.perfumebottlesauction.com

KIWI Auctions Ltd.
19A Annalong Rd., Howick
Auckland 1705, New Zealand
Phone: +64 29 206 2000
E-mail: kiwi.auctions@xtra.co.nz
Website: www.kiwiauctions.co.nz

Randy Inman Auctions, Inc.
P.O. Box 726, Waterville, ME 04903-0726
Phone: (207) 872-6900
FAX: (207) 872-6966
E-mail: Inman@InmanAuctions.com
Website: http://www.InmanAuctions.com

Richard Opfer Auctioneering
1919 Greenspring Dr.
Luther-Timonium, MD 21093
Phone: (410) 252-5035
E-mail: info@opferauction.com
Website: www.opferauction.com

Lesie's Antiques & Auctions
The American Pharmacy Auctioneer
934 Main St., Newberry, SC 29108
Phone: (888) 321-8600
E-mail: frleslie@interpath.com
Website: http://www.antiqueusa.com

McMurray Antiques & Auctions
P.O. Box 393, Kirkwood, NY 13795
Phone/Fax: (607) 775-2321

Wm. Morford
Rural Route #2, Cazenovia, NY 13035
Phone: (315) 662-7625
Fax: (315) 662-3570

E-mail: morf2bid@aol.com
Website: www.morfauction.com

Morphy Auctions
P.O. Box 8, 2000 N. Reading Rd.
Denver, PA 17517
Phone: (717) 335-3435
E-mail: morphy@morphyauctions.com
Website: www.morphyauctions.com

New England Absentee Auctions
16 Sixth St., Stamford, CT 06905
Phone: (203) 975-9055
Fax: (203) 323-6407
E-mail: NEAAuction@aol.com

North American Glass (online auctions)
Terre Haute, IN
Phone: (812) 466-6521
Email: xx78@msn.com
Website: www.gregspurgeon.com

Nostalgia Publications, Inc.
P.O. Box 4175, River Edge, NJ 07661
Phone: (201) 488-4536
Fax: (201) 883-0938
E-mail: nostpub@webtv.net

NSA Auctions/R. Newton-Smith Antiques
88 Cedar St., Cambridge
Ontario, Canada N1S IV8
E-mail: info@nsaauctions.com
Website: http://www.nsaauctions.com

Open-Wire Insulator Services
28390 Ave., Highland, CA 92346
Phone: (909) 862-9279
E-mail: insulators@open-wire.com
Website: http://www.open-wire.com

Don Osborne Auctions
33 Eagleville Rd., Orange, MA 01354
Phone: (978) 544-3696
Fax: (978) 544-8271

Howard B. Parzow
Drug Store & Apothecary Auctioneer
P.O. Box 3464, Gaithersburg, MD 20885-3464
Phone: (301) 977-6741

Reference

Pettigrew Antique & Collector Auctions
1645 Tejon St., Colorado Springs, CO 80906
Phone: (719) 633-7963
Fax: (719) 633-5035

Phillips International Auctioneers & Valuers
406 E. 79th St., New York, NY 10021
Phone: (212) 570-4830
Fax: (212) 570-2207
Website: www.phillips-auctions.com

Carl Pratt Bottle Auctions
P.O. Box 2072, Sandwich, MA 02563
Phone: (508) 888-8794

Rich Penn Auctions
Box 1355, Waterloo, IA 50704
Phone: (319) 291-6688
Fax: (319) 291-7136
E-mail: richpenauctions@aol.com\
Website: www.richpennauctions.com

Shot Glass Exchange
Box 219, Western Springs, IL 60558
Phone/Fax: (708) 246-1559

Showtime Auction Services
Michael & Lori Eckles
22619 Monterey Dr.
Woodhaven, MI 48183
Phone: (734) 676-9703
E-mail: mikeckles@aol.com
Website: www.showtimeauctions.com

Skinner Inc.
The Heritage on the Garden, 63 Park Plaza
Boston, MA 02116
Phone: (617) 350-5400
Fax: (617) 350-5429
E-mail: info@skinnerinc.com
Website: http://www.skinnerinc.com

Mike Smith's Patent Medicine Auction
Veterinary Collectibles Roundtable
7431 Covington Highway
Lithonia, GA 30058
Phone: (770) 482-5100
Fax: (770) 484-1304
E-mail: Petvetmike@aol.com

Smittendorf Auctioneers
16943 East Y Ave.
Fulton, MI 49052
Phone: (616) 729-4660
E-mail: smittendorf1@trueyellow.net
Website: www.smittendorfauctions.ypgs.net/aboutus.asp

Sotheby's Online Auctions
Website: www.sothebys.com

Steve Ritter Auctioneering
34314 W. 120th St.
Excelsior Springs, MO 64024
Phone: (816) 833-2855

Stuckey Auction Co.
315 West Broad St.
Richmond, VA 23225
Phone: (804) 780-0850

T.B.R. Bottle Consignments
P.O. Box 1253, Bunnell, FL 32110
Phone: (904) 437-2807

Victorian Casino Antiques
4520 Arville St., #1
Las Vegas, NV 89103
Phone: (702) 382-2455
E-mail: vca@lvcoxmail.com
Website: www.vcaauction.com

Victorian Images
Box 284
Marlton, NJ 08053
Phone: (856) 354-2154
Fax: (856) 354-9699
E-mail: rmascieri@aol.com
Website: www.TradeCards.com

Museums & Research Resources

Biedenharn Coca-Cola Museum
1107 Washington St.
Vicksburg, MS 39183
Phone: (601) 638-6514
Website: www.biednharn

Bottle Tree Ranch, The
24266 National Trails Hwy.
Oro Grande, CA 92368

Canadian Museum of Civilization
100 Laurier St.
Hull, Quebec
Canada J8X 4H2
Phone: (819) 776-7000 or (800) 555-5621
Website: www.civilization.com

Central Nevada Museum
Logan Field Rd.
P.O. Box 326
Tonopah, NV 89049
Phone: (775) 482-9676
Website: www.tonopahnevada.com/
centrainevadamuseum.html

Coca-Cola Company Archives
P.O. Drawer 1734
Atlanta, GA 30301
Phone: (800) 438-2653
Website: cocacola.com

Corning Museum of Glass
One Museum Way
Corning, NY 14830-2253
Phone: (607) 974-8271 or (800) 732-6845
Website: www.corningglasscenter.com,
www.pennynet.org/glmuseum

Dr. Pepper Museum
300 S. 5th St.
Waco, TX 76701
Phone: (254) 757-2433
Website: www.drpeppemuseum.com

The Glass Museum
309 S. Franklin
Dunkirk, IN 47336-1209
Phone/Fax: (765) 768-6872

Hawaii Bottle Museum
27 Kalopa Mauka Rd.
P.O. Box 1635
Honokaa, HI 96727-1635

**Henry Ford Museum
& Greenfield Village**
20900 Oakwood Blvd.
Dearborn, MI 48121
Phone: (313) 271-1620

Heritage Glass Museum
25 High St. East
Glassboro, NJ 08028
Phone: (856) 881-7468
Email: heritageglassmuseum@hotmail.com
Website: www.heritageglassmuseum.com

Historical Glass Museum
1157 Orange St.
Redlands, CA 92374-3218
Phone: (909) 798-0868
Website: www.historicalglassmuseum.com

Mark Twain's Museum and Books
111 S. C St.
P.O. Box 449
Virginia City, NV 89440-0449

The McGill Historical Drug Company
#11 Fourth St. (Highway 93)
McGill, NV 89318
Phone: (775) 235-7082

Mount Pleasant Glass Museum
402 East Main St.
Suite 600
Mount Pleasant, PA 15666
Phone: (724) 547-5929
Email: mtpleasantglassmuseum@gmail.com

Reference

**Museum of American Glass
at Wheaton Village**
1501 Glasstown Rd.
Millville, NJ 08332-1568
Phone: (856) 825 6800 or (800) 998-4552
Website: www.wheatonvillage.org.

Museum of Connecticut Glass
27 Plank Lane
Glastonbury, CT 06033-2523
Phone: (860) 633-2944
E-mail: noel.thomas@glassmusseum.org
Website: www.glassmuseum.org

National Bottle Museum
76 Milton Ave.
Ballston Spa, NY 12020
Phone: (515) 885-7589
Website: www.crisny.org/not-for-profit/nbm

National Brewery Museum
209 S. Main St.
Potosi, WI 53820
Phone: (608) 763-4002
Website: www.nationalbrewerymuseum.org

National Heisey Glass Museum
169 W. Church St.
Newark, OH 43055
Phone: (740) 345-2932

Nevada State Museum
600 N. Carson St.
Carson City, NV 89701
Phone: (775) 687-4810

New Bern North Carolina Museum
256 Middle St.
New Bern, SC 28560
Phone: (252) 636-5898
Website: www.pepistore.com

Ohio Glass Museum & Glass Blowing Studio
124 W. Main St.
Lancaster, OH 43130
Phone: (740) 687-0101

Website: www.ohioglassmuseum.org
Pahrump Valley Museum
401 E. Basin Ave.
Pahrump, NV
Phone: (775) 751-1970

Pepsi-Cola Company Archives
One Pepsi Way
Somers, NY 10589
Phone: (914) 767-6000
Website: www.pepsi.com

Philadelphia Museum of Art
26th Street and the Benjamin Franklin Parkway
Philadelphia, PA 19130
Phone: (215) 763-8100
Website: www.philamuseum.com

Pottery Museum of Red Wing
240 Harrison Street
Red Wing, MN 55066
(651) 327-2220
Website: www.potterymuseumredwing.org

Sandwich Glass Museum
P.O. Box 103
129 Main St.
Sandwich, MA 02563
Phone: (508) 888-0251
Fax: (508) 888-4941
E-mail: sgm@sandwichglassmuseum.org

Schmidt Museum of Coca-Cola
109 Buffalo Creek Drive
Elizabethtown, KY 42701
Phone: (270) 234-1100
Website: www.schmidtmuseum.com

Seagram Museum
57 Erb St. W
Waterloo, Ontario
Canada N2L 6C2
PH: (519) 885-1857
FAX: (519) 746-1673
Website: www.seagram-museum.ca

**The Museum of American
Glass in West Virginia**
230 Main Ave.
Weston, WV 26452
Phone: (304) 269-5006
Website: www.magwv.com

The New Bedford Museum of Glass
61 Wamsutta St.
New Bedford, MA 02740
Phone: (508) 984-1666
Email: knelson@nbmog.org
Website: www.nbmog.org

The Toledo Museum of Art
2445 Monroe Street
Toledo, OH 43604
Phone: (419) 255-8000
Website: www.toledomuseum.org
Email: tsharp@toledomuseum.org

Tonopah Historic Mining Park
520 McCulloch Ave.
Tonopah, NV 89049
Phone: (775) 482-9274
Website: www.tonopahnevada.com

Wheaton Arts and Cultural Center
1501 Glasstown Road
Millville, NJ 08332
Phone: (856) 825-6800 or (800) 998-4552
Email: mail@wheatonarts.org
Website: www.wheatonarts.org

Glossary

Automatic Bottle Machine: This innovation by Michael Owens in 1903 allowed an entire bottle to be made by machine in one step. ABM bottles are identified by the seam going to the top of the mouth. By 1913 all bottles were manufactured by ABMs.

Applied Color Label: A method of labeling or decorating a bottle, specifically soda pop and milk bottles, by applying borosilicate glass and mineral pigments with a low melting point to the bottle through a metal screen and baking it in a furnace. The molten glass and pigment form the painted label.

Agate Glass: A glass made from mix incorporating blasting furnace slag. Featuring striations of milk glass in off-white tints, the glass has been found in shades of chocolate brown, caramel brown, natural agate, and tanned leather. It was made from the 1850 to the 1900s.

Amethyst-Colored Glass: A clear glass that when exposed to the sun or bright light for a long period of time turns various shades of purple. Only glass that contains manganese turns purple.

Amber-Colored Glass: Nickel was added in the glass production to obtain this common bottle color. It was believed that the dark color would prevent the sun from ruining the contents of the bottle.

Annealing: The gradual cooling of hot glass in a cooling chamber or annealing oven.

Applied Lip/Top: On pre-1880s bottles, the neck was applied after removal from the blowpipe. The neck may be just a ring of glass trailed around the neck.

Aqua-Colored Glass: The natural color of glass. The shades depend on the amount of iron oxide contained in the glass production. Produced until the 1930s.

Bail: A wire clamp consisting of a wire that runs over the top of the lid or lip, and a "locking" wire that presses down on the bail and the lid, resulting in an airtight closure.

Barber Bottle: In the 1880s, these colorful bottles decorated the shelves of barbershops and were usually filled with bay rum.

Batch: A mixture of the ingredients necessary in manufacturing glass.

Battledore: A wooden paddle used to flatten the bottom or sides of a bottle.

Bead: A raised ridge of glass with a convex section encircling the neck of a bottle.

Beveled Edge: These are rectangular or square bottle shapes with a narrow flattened edge between two wider flat, perpendicular sides of a bottle.

Bitters: Herbal "medicines" containing a great quantity of alcohol, usually corn whiskey.

Black Glass: A glass produced between 1700 and 1875 that is actually a dark olive-green or olive-amber color caused by the carbon in the glass production.

Blob Seal: A way of identifying an unembossed bottle by applying a molten coin-shaped blob of glass to the shoulder of the bottle, into which a seal with the logo or name of the distiller, date, or product name was impressed.

Blob Top: A lip on a soda or mineral water bottle made by applying a thick blob of glass to the top of the bottle. A wire held the stopper, which was seated below the blob and anchored the wire when the stopper was closed, to prevent carbonation from escaping.

Blown in Mold, Applied Lip (Bimal): A bottle formed when a gather of glass was blown into a mold to take the shape of the mold. The lip on these bottles were added later and the bases often have open-pontil scars. Side seams stop before the lip.

Blowpipe: A hollow iron tube wider and thicker at the gathering end than at the blowing end. The blowpipe was used by the blower to pick up the molten glass, which was then blown in the mold or free blown outside the mold. Pipes can vary from 2-1/2 to 6 feet long.

Blow-Over: A bubble-like extension of glass above a jar or bottle lip blown so the blowpipe could be broken free from the jar after blowing. The blow-over was then chipped off and the lip ground.

Bocca: An opening on the side of the furnace where the pot was placed. The glass batch was placed in the pot where the gather was taken.

Borosilicate: A type of glass originally formulated for making scientific glassware.

Bottom Hinge Mold: A two-piece mold hinged together at the base portion of the mold.

Bruise: Identical to a "fish eye," except that some bruises may be more transparent. A faint bruise is clearer, while a bigger bruise resembles the white eye of a fish.

Bubbles/Blisters: Air or gas pockets that became trapped in the glass during the manufacturing process. The term "seed" is also used to describe these shapes.

Calabash: A type of flask with a rounded bottom. These bottles are known as "Jenny Lind" flasks and were common in the 19th century.

Camphor Glass: White cloudy glass that looks somewhat like refined gum camphor. Was made in blown, blown-mold, and pressed forms.

Carboys: Cylindrical bottles with short necks.

Casewear: Wear marks to high points of embossing, sides, or base of a bottle due to contact with others in cases being transported.

Clapper: A glassmaker's tool used in shaping and forming the footing of an object.

Closed Mold: Bottle mold in which the base, body, shoulder, neck, and lip of the bottle all form at one time.

Cobalt Colored Glass: This color was used with patented medicines and poisons to distinguish them from regular bottles. Excessive amounts resulted in "cobalt blue" color.

Codd: A bottle enclosure that was patented in 1873 by Hiram Codd of England. A small ball is blown inside of the bottle. When the ball is pushed up by carbonation, it forms a seal.

Cork Press: Hand tool designed to squeeze a cork into the required shape for use as a bottle closure.

Crown Cap: A tin cap crimped tightly over the rolled lip of a bottle. The inside of the cap was filled with a cork disk, which created an airtight seal.

Cover Groove: A groove on top of the closure or lid that receives the bail and keeps the closure from slipping.

Closed Mold: Bottle mold where the base, body, shoulder, and neck was molded and the majority of the finish conformation was molded.

Crown Cap: A metal cap formed from a tin plate to slip tightly over the rolled lip of the bottle. The inside of the cap was filled with a cork disc, which created an airtight seal.

Cullet: Clean, broken glass added to the batch to bring about rapid fusion to produce new glass.

Date Line: The mold seam or mold line on a bottle. This line can be used to help determine the approximate date a bottle was manufactured.

De-Colorizer: A compound added to natural aquamarine bottle glass to make the glass clear.

Dimple: A small molded depression or hole in a bottle neck where a lever wire or a toggle enclosure is hooked.

Dip Mold: A one-piece mold open at the top.

Embossed Lettering: Raised letters or symbols formed in a mold. They typically identify the maker, contents, and trademark.

Fire Polishing: The reheating of glass to eliminate unwanted blemishes.

Flared Lip: A bottle whose lip has been pushed out, or flared, to increase the strength of the opening. These bottles were usually made before 1900.

Flash: A very faint crack that is difficult to see. The bottle must be turned in a certain position to see the crack.

Flashing: A method of coloring glass by dipping a bottle into a batch of colored glass.

Flint Glass: Glass composed of a silicate of potash and lead. Commonly referred to as lead crystal in present terminology.

Flux: A substance that generates the fusion of glass.

Free-Blown Glass: Glass produced with a blowpipe rather than a mold.

Frosted Glass: Frosting occurs when a bottle's surface is sandblasted.

Gaffer: A master blower in early glasshouses.

Gather: The gob of molten glass gathered on the end of the blowpipe, which the glassmaker then expanded by blowing until it formed a bottle or other glass object.

Glass Pontil: The earliest type of pontil, in which a sharp glass ring remained after the bottle was broken off the pontil rod.

Glory Hole: The small furnace used for the frequent reheating necessary during the making of a bottle. The glory hole was also used in fire polishing.

Gob: A portion of molten glass that is expanded, or blown, into a bottle of other glass vessel, or gathered at the end of a blowpipe.

Green Glass: Refers to a composition of glass and not a color. The green color was caused by iron impurities in the sand, which could not be controlled by the glassmakers.

Ground Pontil: A smooth circular area of glass created after a rough pontil scar has been ground off.

Hobbleskirt: The iconic paneled shape with curved waist used to make the classic Coca-Cola bottle.

Hobnail: Pattern of pressed glass characterized by an all-over pattern of bumps that look like hobnail heads.

Hutchinson Stopper: A spring-type internal closure used to seal soda bottles,

patented by Charles Hutchinson in 1879.

Imperfections: Flaws such as bubbles, or tears, bent shapes and necks, imperfect seams, and errors in spelling and embossing.

ISP (Inserted Slug Plate): Special or unique company names, or names of people, were sometimes embossed on ale, whiskey, and wine bottles, using a plate inserted into the mold.

Improved Pontil: Bottles having an improved pontil appear with reddish or blackish tinges on the base.

Iron Pontil: The solid iron rod heated and affixed to a bottle's base created a scar as a black circular depression often turning red upon oxidation. This is also referred to as a bare iron pontil or improved pontil.

Iridescence: A stain found on an old bottle that has been dug from the ground. The stain has an opaline or rainbow color due to the minerals in the ground fusing with the glass. Therefore, this stain is very difficult to clean and usually remains in the glass.

Jack: A steel or wooden tong-like tool the gaffer used to manipulate hot glass.

Keyed Mold: A variation of a two-piece hinge mold, in which the bottom mold seam is not straight but arches up at the middle of the bottle base.

Kick-Up: The deep indentation added to the bottom of a bottle. The indentation is formed by pressing a piece of wood or metal into the base of the mold while the glass is still hot. The kickup is common on wine bottles and calabash flasks.

Laid-On-Ring: A bead of glass that has been trailed around the neck opening to reinforce the opening.

Lady's Leg: A bottle with a long curving neck.

Lehr: An annealing oven or furnace in which a new blown bottle was gradually cooled to increase its strength and reduce cooling breakage.

Lightning Closure: A closure with an intertwined wire bail configuration to hold the lid on fruit jars. This closure was also common with soda bottles.

Lipper: A wood tool used to widen lips and form rims and spouts of pitchers, carafes, and wide-mouthed jars.

Manganese: A mineral used as a decolorizer between 1850 and 1910. Manganese causes glass to turn purple when exposed to ultraviolet rays from the sun.

Melting Pot: A clay pot used to melt silicate in the process of making glass.

Metal: Molten glass.

Milk Glass: White glass formed by adding tin to the molten glass. Milk glass was primarily used for making cosmetic bottles.

Moil: Residual glass remaining on the tip of a blowpipe after detaching the blowpipe from the blown bottle.

Mold, Full-Height Three-Piece: A mold in which the entire bottle was formed in one piece. The two seams on the bottle run from the base to below the lip on both sides.

Mold, Three-Piece Dip: A mold that formed a bottle in three pieces that were later joined together. In this mold, the bottom part of the bottle mold is one piece and the top, from the shoulder up, has two separate pieces. Mold seams appear circling the bottle at the shoulder and on each side of the neck.

Mold Seam: Raised lines on the bottle body, shoulder, neck, and/or from the base of the bottle formed where the edges of different mold sections come together.

Opalescence: Opalescence is found on "frosty" or iridescent bottles that have been buried in the earth in mud or silt. The minerals in these substances have interacted with the glass to create these effects.

Open Mold: A mold in which only the base and body of the bottle is formed in the mold, with the neck and lip being added later.

Open Pontil: The blowpipe, rather than a separate rod, was affixed to the base, leaving a raised or depressed circular scar called a moil.

Owens Automatic Bottle Machine: The first automatic glass-blowing machine was patented in 1904 by Michael Owens of the Libby Glass Company, Toledo, Ohio,

Painted Label: Abbreviation for Applied Color Label (ACL), which is baked on the outside of the bottle and was used commonly used on soda pop and milk bottles.

Panelled: A bottle that isn't circular or oval and that is made with four to twelve panels.

Paste Mold: A mold made of two or more pieces of iron and coated with a paste to prevent scratches on the glass, thereby eliminating the seams as the glass was turned in the mold.

Patina: Process of weathering to the glass as a result of the natural chemical process of decomposition from water and soil. Results of this process are also referred to as patina, sick glass, stain, opalescence, and iridescence.

Pattern Molded: Glass that was formed into a pattern before being completed.

Plate Glass: Pure glass comprised of lime and soda silicate.

Pontil, Puntee, or Punty Rod: The iron rod attached to the base of a bottle by a gob of glass to hold the bottle during the finishing.

Pontil Mark: A glass scar on the bottom of a bottle formed when the bottle was broken off the pontil rod. To remove a bottle from a blowpipe, an iron pontil rod with a small amount of molten glass was attached to the bottom of the bottle. A sharp tap removed the bottle from the pontil rod, leaving the scar.

Potstones: Flaws resembling white stones created by impurities in the glass batch.

Pressed Glass: Glass that has been pressed into a mold to take the shape of the mold or the pattern within the mold.

Pucellas: Called "the tool" by glassmakers, this implement is essential in shaping both the body and opening in blown bottles.

Pumpkinseed: A small round flat flask, often found in the Western United States. Generally made of clear glass, the shape

Reference

resembles the seed of the grown pumpkin. Pumpkinseeds are also known as "mickies," "saddle flasks," and "two-bit ponies."

Punt: Term used to describe a kick-up or push-up at the bottom of a wine bottle.

Ribbed: A bottle with vertical or horizontal lines embossed into the bottle.

Rolled Lip or Finish: A smooth lip formed when the blowpipe was removed from the bottle. The hot glass at the removal point was rolled or folded into the neck to form and smooth out the top of the finish and to strengthen the neck.

Round Bottom: A soda bottle made of heavy glass and shaped like a torpedo. The rounded bottom ensured that the bottle would be placed on its side, keeping the liquid in contact with the cork and preventing the cork from drying and popping out of the bottle.

Sabot: A type of tool that holds a bottle base for finishing purposes.

Satin Glass: A smooth glass manufactured by exposing the surface of the glass to hydrofluoric acid vapors.

Scant Size: Term for a bottle (normally liquor) referred to as a "pint" or "quart" but that actually held less capacity.

Seal: A circular or oval slug of glass applied to the shoulder of a bottle with an imprint of the manufacturer's name, initials, or mark.

Seam: A mark on a bottle where the two halves meet caused by glass assuming the shape of the mold.

Servitor: An assistant to the master glassblower (gaffer).

Sheared Lip: Plain lip formed by clipping the hot glass of the neck from the bottle using a pair of scissors like shears. No top was applied, but sometimes a slight flange was created.

Sick Glass: Glass bearing superficial decay or deterioration with a grayish tinge caused by erratic firing.

Slug Plate: A metal plate approximately 2 inches by four inches with a firm's name on it that was inserted into a mold. The slug plate was removable, allowing a glasshouse to use the same mold for many companies by simply switching slug plates.

Smooth Base: A bottle made without a pontil.

Snap Case: Also called a snap tool, the snap case had arms that extended from a central stem to hold a bottle firmly on its sides during finishing of the neck and lip. The snap case replaced the pontil rod, and thus eliminated the pontil scars or marks. It sometimes left grip marks on the side of the bottle, however.

Squat: Bottle that holds beer, porter, or soda.

Tooled Top: A bottle with a top that is formed in the bottle mold. Bottles of this type were manufactured after 1885.

Torpedo: A beer or soda bottle with a rounded base meant to lie on its side to keep the cork wet and prevent air from leaking in or the cork from popping out.

Turn-Mold Bottles: Bottles turned in a mold using special solvents. The continuous turning with the solvent erased all seams and mold marks and added a distinct luster to the bottle.

Utility Bottles: Multipurpose bottles that could be used to hold a variety of products.

WCF: Wire Cork Fastener.

Wetting Off: Touching the neck of a hot bottle with water to break it off the blowpipe.

Whittle Marks: Small blemishes on the outside of bottles made in carved wooden molds. These blemishes also occurred when hot glass was poured into cold molds early in the morning, which created "goose pimples" on the surface of the glass. As the molds warmed, the glass became smoother.

Wiped Top: A bottle in which the mold lines end before the top due to the neck being wiped smooth after the top was tooled onto the bottle. This method was used before 1915.

Xanthine Glass: Yellow glass achieved by adding silver to the glass batch.

Bibliography

Books

Agee, Bill. *Collecting All Cures*. East Greenville, PA: Antique Bottle & Glass Collector, 1973.

Albers, Marilyn B. *Glass Insulators From Outside North America*, 2nd revision. Houston, TX: Self Published, 1993.

Apuzzo, Robert. *Bottles of Old New York, A Pictorial Guide to Early New York City Bottles, 1680-1925*. New York: R&L Publishing, 1997.

Ayers, James. *Pepsi-Cola Bottles Collectors Guide*. Mount Airy, NC: R.J. Menter Enterprises, 1998.

———.*Pepsi: Cola Bottles & More*. Mount Airy, NC: R.J. Menter Enterprises, 2001.

Arnold, Ken. *Australian Preserving & Storage Jars Pre 1920*. Chicago: McCann Publishing, 1996.

Babb, Bill. *Augusta on Glass*, 2007. Bill Babb, 2352 Devere St., Augusta, GA 30904.

Badders, Veldon. *The Collector's Guide to Inkwells: Identification & Values*. Paducah KY: Collector Books, Schroeder Publishing Co., 2001.

Barnett, Carl and Ken Nease. *Georgia Crown Top Bottle Book*, 2003. Georgia Soda Bottle Book, 1211 St. Andrews Drive, Douglas, GA 31533.

Barnett, R.E. *Western Whiskey Bottles*, 4th edition. Bend, OR: Maverick Publishing, 1997.

Barrett II, William J. *Zanesville and the Glass Industry, A Lasting Romance*, 1997. Self Published, Zanesville, OH.

Beck, Doreen. *The Book of Bottle Collecting*. Gig Harbor, WA: Hamlin Publishing Group, Ltd., 1973.

Berguist, Steve. *Antique Bottles of Rhode Island*, 1998. Self Published, Cranston, RI.

Binder, Frank and Sara Jean. A Guide to American Nursing Bottles, 2001, revised edition to 1992 edition. Self Published, 1819 Ebony Drive, York, PA 17402.

Blake, Charles E. *Cobalt Medicine Bottles*, 2001. Glendale, AZ. Self Published, (602) 938-7277.

Blakeman, Alan. *A Collectors Guide to Inks*. Elsecar, England: BBR Publishing, 1996.

———. *A Collectors Guide: Miller's Bottles & Pot Lids*. Octopus Publishing Group Ltd., 2002.

Bossche, Willy Van den. *Antique Glass Bottles, A Comprehensive Illustrated Guide*, 2001. Self Published, Antique Collectors Club, Wappingers Falls, NY.

Bound, Smyth. *19th Century Food in Glass*. Sandpoint ID: Midwest Publishers, 1994.

Bowman, Glinda. *Miniature Perfume Bottles*. Atglen, PA: Schiffer Publishing, Inc., 2000.

Bredehoft, Tom and Neila. *Fifty Years of Collectible Glass 1920-1970, Identification and Price Guide*, Volume I. Dubuque, IA: Antique Trader Books, 1998.

Breton, Anne. *Collectible Miniature Perfume Bottles*. Flammarion Publications, 2001.

Briel,Donald R., *Insulators – North American Glass Insulators Price Guide*, Providence, UT, (435) 753-5786, 2011

Burggraaf, Mike. *The Antique Bottles of Iowa*, Fairview, Iowa, Self Published, 1998.

———. *2010 Update to The Antique Bottles of Iowa 1846-1915*, Fairview, Iowa, Self Published, 2010.

Burnet, Robert G. *Canadian Railway Telegraph History*. Ontario, Canada, 1996: Self Published.

Burton, David, *Antique Sealed Bottles 1640-1900: And the Families that Owned Them*, Antique Collectors Club Dist, 6 West 18th Street 4B, New York, NY 10011, February 2015

Reference

Champlin, Nat. *Nat Champlin's Antique Bottle Cartoons*. Bristol, RI: Self Published, 1998.

Chapman, Tom. *Bottles of Eastern California*, 2003. Hungry Coyote Publishing, Tom Chapman, 390 Ranch Rd., Bishop, CA 93514, (760) 872-2427.

Christensen, Don and Doris. *Violin Bottles: Guitars & Other Novelty Glass*. Privately Published, 1995, 21815 106th St. E. Buckley, WA 98321.

Cleveland, Hugh. *Bottle Pricing Guide*, 3rd edition. Paducah, KY: Collector Books, 1996.

Creswick, Alice M. *Redbook Number 6: The Collectors Guide to Old Fruit Jars*, 1992. Privately Published, 8525 Kewowa SW. Grand Rapids, MI 49504.

Culhane, Phil and Scott Wallace. *Transfer Printed Ginger Beers of Canada*, 2002. E-mail: phil.culhane@rogers.com.

———. *Primitive Stoneware Bottles of Canada*, 2002. E-mail: phil.culhane@rogers.com.

D & C (Dealers & Collectors), *Auction Price Results*, 2012, Dealers & Collectors, PO Box 413, Carlisle, MA 01741

Dean, Norman L. *The Man Behind The Bottle – The Origin and History of the Classic Contour Coca-Cola Bottle As Told by the Son of its Creator,* Xlibris Publishing, 2010.

DeGraaf, Marti & Mack, Toby, *DeVilbiss Perfume Bottles: 1907-1968*, Schiffer Publishing, Ltd., October 2014

DeGrafft, John. *American Sarsaparilla Bottles*. East Greenville, PA: Antique Bottle & Glass Collector, 1980.

———. *Supplement to American Sarsaparilla Bottles*, 2004. Self-Published, John DeGrafft, 8941 E. Minnesota Ave., Sun Lakes, AZ 85248.

Diamond, Freda. *Story of Glass*. New York: Harcourt, Brace and Co., 1953.

Dodsworth, Roger. *Glass and Glassmaking*. London, England: Shire Publications, 1996.

Dumbrell, Roger. *Understanding Antique Wine Bottles.* Ithaca, NY: Antique Collectors Club, 1983.

Duncan, Ray H. *Dr. Pepper Collectible Bottles, Identification & Values*, 2004. Black Creek Publishing, 1606 CR 761, Devine TX 78016.

Eatwell, John M. and David K. Clint III. *Pike's Peak Gold*, 2002. Self Published, 2345 So. Federal Blvd, Suite 100, Denver, CO 80219.

Edmondson, Bill. *The Milk Bottle Book of Michigan*. Privately Published, 1995, 317 Harvest Ln., Lansing, MI 48917.

Edmundson, Barbara. *Historical Shot Glasses*. Chico, CA: Self Published, 1995.

Edwards, Michael, *Fragrances Of The World 2015*, 31st Edition, Self Published – Michael Edwards & Co., 2015

Eilelberner, George and Serge Agadjanian. *The Complete American Glass Candy Containers Handbook*. Adele Bowden, 1986.

Elliott, Rex R. and Stephen C. Gould. *Hawaiian Bottles of Long Ago*. Honolulu, HI: Hawaiian Service Inc., 1988.

Faulkner, Ed and Lucy. *Inks – 150 Years of Bottles and Companies.* Moseley, VA, Self Published, 2005, Faulkner@antiquebottles.com

Ferraro, Pat and Bob. *A Bottle Collector's Book*. Sparks, NV: Western Printing & Publishing Co., 1970.

Ferguson, Joel. *A Collectors Guide to New Orleans Soda Bottles*. Slidell, LA: Self Published, 1999.

Fewless, Dennis G. and Weide, Christopher A. *Soft Drink Bottlers of the United States, Volume 1 (Vermont & New Hampshire).* Jacksonville, FL, Self Published, 2009

Field, Anne E. *On the Trail of Stoddard Glass.* Dublin, NH: William L. Bauhan, 1975.

Fike, Richard E. *The Bottle Book*, The Blackburn Press, Caldwell, NJ (973) 228-7077, 2006.

Fletcher, W. Johnnie. *Kansas Bottle Book*. Mustang, OK: Self Published, 1994, (405) 376-1045

Fletcher, W. Johnnie. *A Collector's Guide to Kansas Bottles 1854-1925*. Mustang, OK.: Self Published, 2013 (405) 376-1045

Fletcher, W. Johnnie. *A Collector's Guide to Arkansas Bottles*, Mustang, OK.: Self Published, 2013 (405) 376-1045

Fletcher, W. Johnnie. *Oklahoma Drug Store Bottles*. Mustang, OK.: Self Published, 1991 (405) 376-1045.

Gardner, Paul Vickers. *Glass*. New York: Smithsonian Illustrated Library of Antiques, Crown Publishers, 1975.

Gerth, Ellen C. *Bottles from the Deep, Patent Medicines, Bitters, and Other Bottles from the Wreck of the Steamship "Republic."* Shipwreck Heritage Press, August 2006.

Graci, David. *American Stoneware Bottles, A History and Study*. South Hadley, MA: Self Published, 1995.

— — —. *Soda and Beer Bottle Closures, 1850-1910*, 2003. P.O. Box 726, South Hadley, MA 01075.

Ham, Bill. *Bitters Bottles*, 1999, supplement 2004. Self Published, P.O. Box 427, Downieville, CA 95936.

— — —. *The Shaving Mug Market*. Downieville, CA: Self Published, 1997.

Hastin, Bud. *AVON Products & California Perfume Co. Collector's Encyclopedia*, 16th edition. Kansas City, MO: Bud Hastin Publications, 2001.

— — —. *AVON Products & California Perfume Co. Collector's Encyclopedia*, 17th edition. Kansas City, MO: Bud Hastin Publications, 2003.

— — —. *Bud Hastin's Avon Collector's Encyclopedia 18th Edition, Avon and California Perfume Company Products – 1886 to Present,* Collector Books, Paducah, KY, 2008

Haunton, Tom. *Tippecanoe and E.G. Booz Too!*, 2003. Tom Haunton, 48 Hancock Ave, Medford, MA 02155.

Head, Charles David, *A Head's Up On Koca Nola*, Ron Fowler, Seattle History Co., PO Box 158, Seattle, WA 98556-0158, 2014

Heetderks, Dewey R, M.D. *Merchants of Medicine, Nostram Peddlers-Yesterday & Today*, 2003. Dewey Heetderks, 4907 N. Quail Crest Drive, Grand Rapids, MI 49546.

Higgins, Molly. *Jim Beam Figural Bottles*. Atglen, PA: Schiffer Publishing, 2000.

Holiner, Richard. *Collecting Barber Bottles*. Paducah, KY: Collector Books, 1986.

Hudson, Paul. *Seventeenth Century Glass Wine Bottles and Seals Excavated at Jamestown*, Journal of Glass Studies. Vol. III, Corning, NY: The Corning Museum of Glass, 1961.

Holabird, Fred and Jack Haddock. *The Nevada Bottle Book*. Reno, NV: R.F. Smith, 1981.

Holabird, Fred, *Nevada History Through Glass-The Nevada Bottle Book-Volume , "Embossed Sodas, Whiskey, Beer, Dairy, and Other Bottles*, Reno, NV: Sierra Nevada Press, 2012.

Hopper, Philip. *Anchor Hocking Commemorative Bottles and other Collectibles*. Atglen, PA: Schiffer Publishing, 2000.

Hudgeons III, Thomas E. *Official Price Guide to Bottles Old & New*. Orlando, FL: House of Collectibles, 1983.

Hunter, Frederick William. *Stiegel Glass*. New York: Dover Publications, 1950.

Hunting, Jean and Franklin. *The Collector's World of Inkwells*. Atglen, PA: Schiffer Publishing, 2000.

Husfloen, Kyle. *American Pressed Glass & Bottles Price Guide*, 1st edition. Dubuque, IA: Antique Trader Books, 1999.

— — —. *American Pressed Glass & Bottles Price Guide*, 2nd edition. Dubuque, IA: Antique Trader Books, 2001.

Innes, Lowell. *Pittsburg Glass 1797-1891*. Boston, MA: Houghton Mifflin Company, 1976.

Jackson, Barbara and Sonny. *American Pot Lids*. East Greenville, PA: Antique Bottle & Glass Collector, 1992.

Jarves, Deming. *Reminiscences of Glass Making*. New York: Hurd and Houghton, 1865.

Kay, Bob. *US Beer Labels, Volumes I (Western States), II (East & Southern States), III (Midwestern States),* Batavia, Il, 2009, www.bobkaybeerlables.com

Reference

Kameny, Richard. *Australia Milk & Cream Bottles and Dairy Related Items — A Comprehensive Guide for Collectors and the Curious,* New South Wales, Australia, 2009, gdaygday@optusnet.com.au

Kendrick, Grace. *The Antique Bottle Collector.* Ann Arbor, MI: Edwards Brothers Inc., 1971.

Ketchum, William C. Jr. *A Treasury of American Bottles.* Los Angeles: Rutledge Publishing, 1975.

Klesse, Brigitt and Hans Mayr. *European Glass from 1500-1800, The Ernesto Wolf Collection.* Germany: Kremayr and Scheriau, 1987.

Knittle, Rhea Mansfield. *Early American Glass.* NY: Garden City Publishing Company, 1948.

Knob, Stephen. *Conservation and Care of Glass Objects,* London: Archetype Publications/Corning Museum of Glass, 2006.

Kovel, Terry and Ralph. *The Kovels' Bottle Price List,* 11th edition, 1999. New York: Crown Publishers, Inc., 1996.

Kovill, William E. Jr. *Ink Bottles and Ink Wells.* Taunton, MA: William L. Sullwold, 1971.

Kosler, Rainer. Flasche, *Bottle Und Bouteille.* Ismaning, Germany: WKD-Druck Gmbh Publishing Company, 1998.

Lastovica, Ethleen. *An Illustrated Guide to Ginger Beer Bottles for South African Collectors.* Cape Town, South Africa, 2000, ISBN 0-620-25981-7.

Lee, Ruth Webb. *Antique Fakes and Reproductions.* Privately Published, Northborough, MA, 1971.

Lefkowith, Christie Mayer. *Masterpieces of the Perfume Industry.* Editions Stylissimo Publications, 2000.

Leybourne, Doug. *Red Book #8, Fruit Jar Price Guide.* Privately Published, P.O. Box 5417, North Muskegon, MI, 1998.

Leybourne, Doug. *Red Book #9, Fruit Jar Price Guide.* Privately Published, P.O. Box 5417, North Muskegon, MI, 2001.

Leybourne, Doug. *Red Book #10, Fruit Jar Price Guide,* Privately Published, P.O. Box 5417, North Muskegon, MI, 2008.

Leybourne, Doug. Red Book #11, Fruit Jar Price Guide, Privately Published, P.O. Box 5417, North Muskegon, MI 49445, 2015.

Linden, Robert A. *The Classification of Violin Shaped Bottles,* 2nd edition. Privately Published, 1999.

— — —. *Collecting Violin & Banjo Bottles, A Practical Guide,* 3rd edition. Privately Published, 2004.

Maust, Don. *Bottle and Glass Handbook.* Union Town, PA: E.G. Warman Publishing Co., 1956.

Markota, Peck and Audie. *Western Blob Top Soda and Mineral Water Bottles,* 1st edition. Sacramento, CA: Self Published, 1998.

— — —. *California Hutchinson Type Soda Bottles,* 2nd edition. Sacramento, CA, Self Published, 2000.

Markowski, Carol. *Tomart's Price Guide To Character & Promotional Glasses.* Dayton, OH: Tomart Publishing, 1993.

Martin, Byron and Vicky. *Here's To Beers, Blob Top Beer Bottles 1880-1910,* 1973, supplement 2003. Byron Martin, P.O. Box 838, Angels Camp, CA 95222.

McCann, Jerry. *2007 Fruit Jar Annual.* Chicago: J. McCann Publisher, 2007,5003 W. Berwyn Ave, Chicago, IL 60630-1501.

— — —. *2008 Fruit Jar Annual.* Chicago: J. McCann Publisher, 2008, 5003 W. Berwyn Ave, Chicago, IL 60630-1501.

— — —. *2009 Fruit Jar Annual,* Chicago: J. McCann Publisher, 2009, 5003 W. Berwyn Ave, Chicago, IL 60630-1501.

— — —. *2010 Fruit Jar Annual,* Chicago: J. McCann Publisher, 2010, 5003 W. Berwyn Ave, Chicago, IL 60630-1501.

McCann, Jerry & Bernas, Barry, *Dick Roller's Standard Fruit Jar Reference* (Updated), 2011, 5003 W. Berwyn Ave, Chicago, IL 60630-1501.

McCann, Jerry. *2011 Fruit Jar Annual,* Chicago, IL, J. McCann Publisher, 2011; 5003 W.

Berwyn Ave, Chicago, IL 60630-1501

McCann, Jerry. *2012 Fruit Jar Annual*, Chicago, IL, J. McCann Publisher, 2012; 5003 W. Berwyn Ave, Chicago, IL 60630-1501.

McCann, Jerry. *2013 Fruit Jar Annual*, Chicago, IL, J. McCann Publisher, 2013; 5003 W. Berwyn Ave, Chicago, IL 60630-1501.

McCann, Jerry. *2014 Fruit Jar Annual*, Chicago, IL, J. McCann Publisher, 2014; 5003 W. Berwyn Ave, Chicago, IL 60630-1501.

McCann, Jerry. *2015 Fruit Jar Annual*, Chicago, IL, J. McCann Publisher, 2015; 5003 W. Berwyn Ave, Chicago, IL 60630-1501.

McDougald, John and Carol. *1995 Price Guide for Insulators*. St. Charles, IL: Self Published, 1995.

McKearin, Helen and George S. *American Glass*. New York: Crown Publishers, 1956.

— — —. *Two Hundred Years of American Blown Glass*. New York: Crown Publishers, 1950.

— — —. *American Bottles and Flasks and Their Ancestry*. New York: Crown Publishers, 1978.

Megura, Jim. *Official Price Guide to Bottles*, 12th edition. New York: House of Collectibles, The Ballantine Publishing Group, 1998.

Meinz, David. *So Da Licious, Collecting Applied Color Label Soda Bottles*. Norfolk, VA: Self Published, 1994.

Metz, Alice Hulett. *Early American Pattern Glass*. Paducah, KY: Collector Books, 2000.

— — —. *Much More Early American Pattern Glass*. Paducah, KY: Collector Books, 2000.

Miller, Mike. *Arizona Bottle Book. 2000*. Self Published, 9214 W. Gary Rd., Peoria, AZ.

— — —. *A Collector's Guide to Arizona Bottles & Stoneware,* 9214 W. Gary Rd., Peoria, AZ, Self Published, helgramike@cox.net.

Miller, Mike. *A Collector's Guide To Arizona Bottles & Stoneware*, 9214 W. Gary Rd., Peoria, AZ 85345 2014 (helgramike@cox.net), self published.

Milroy, Wallace. *The Malt Whiskey Almanac*. Glasgow G38AZ Scotland: Neil Wilson Publishing Ltd., 1989.

Mitchell, Jim & Lynn, *Antique Bottle Auction Price Results*, 2012, Self Published, (813) 684-2834.

Monsen & Baer. *The Beauty of Perfume, Perfume Bottle Auction VI*. Vienna, VA: Monsen & Baer Publishing, 1998.

— — —. *The Legacies of Perfume, Perfume Bottle Auction VII*. Vienna, VA: Monsen & Baer Publishing, 1998.

Montague, H.F. *Montague's Modern Bottle Identification and Price Guide*, 2nd edition. Overland Park, KS: H.F. Montague Enterprises, Inc., 1980.

Morgan, Roy and Gordon Litherland. *Sealed Bottles: Their History and Evolution (1630-1930)*. Burton-on-Trent, England: Midland Antique Bottle Publishing, 1976.

Munsey, Cecil. *The Illustrated Guide to Collecting Bottles*. New York: Hawthorn Books, Inc., 1970.

— — —. *The Illustrated Guide to The Collectibles of Coca-Cola*. New York: Hawthorn Books, Inc., 1972.

Murschell, Dale L. *American Applied Glass Seal Bottles*. Self Published, Dale Murschell, HC 65 Box 2610, Arnold Stickley Rd., Springfield, WV, 1996.

Namiat, Robert. *Barber Bottles with Prices*. Radnor, PA: Wallace Homestead Book Company, 1977.

Newman, Harold. *An Illustrated Dictionary of Glass*. London: Thames and Hudson Publishing, 1977.

Nielsen, Frederick. *Great American Pontiled Medicines*. Cherry Hill, NJ: The Cortech Corporation, 1978.

North, Jacquelyne. *Perfume, Cologne, and Scent Bottles*, Revised 3rd Edition Price Guide, Atglen, PA: Schiffer Publishing, Inc., 1999.

Northend, Mary Harrod. *American Glass*. New York: Tudor Publishing Company, 1940.

Reference

Odell, John. *Digger Odell's Official Antique Bottle & Glass Price Guides*, I - 11. Lebanon, OH: Odell Publishing, 1995.

— — —. *Indian Bottles & Brands*. Lebanon, OH: Odell Publishing, 1998.

— — —. *Pontil Medicine Encyclopedia*, Lebanon, OH: Odell Publishing, 2003.

Ojea, Ed and Jack Stecher. *Warner's Reference Book*, 1999. Self Published, 1192 San Sebastian Ct., Grover Bend, CA 93433.

Olins, Evan and Gwen. *Lei in a Bottle – Collecting Hawaiian Perfume Bottles*, Self Published – Hula Moon Press, PO Box 11173, Honolulu, HI 96828, www.hulamoonpress.com, 2008.

Ostrander, Diane. *A Guide to American Nursing Bottles*. York, PA: ACIF Publications, 1992.

Padgett, Fred. *Dreams of Glass, The Story of William McLaughlin and His Glass Company*. Livermore, CA. Self Published, 1997.

Pasquale, Dan De and Peterson, Larry. *Red Wing Stoneware Encyclopedia*. Collector Books, 2009.

Pepper Adeline, *The Glass Gaffers of New Jersey*. New York: Charles Scribners Sons, 1971.

Peterson, Arthur G. *400 Trademarks on Glass*. L-W Book Sales, P.O. Box 69, Gas City, IN 46933, 2002.

Petretti, Alan. *Petretti's Coca-Cola Collectibles Price Guide*, 11th edition. Iola, WI: Krause Publications, 2001.

— — —. *Petretti's Soda Pop Collectibles Price Guide*, 1st edition. Dubuque, IA: Antique Trader Books, 2001.

— — —. *Petretti's Soda Pop Collectibles Price Guide*, 3rd edition. Dubuque, IA: Antique Trader Books, 2003.

— — —. *Warman's Coca-Cola Collectibles, Identification and Price Guide*. Iola, WI: Krause Publications, 2006.

Pickvet, Mark. *The Encyclopedia of Glass*. Atglen, PA: Schiffer Publishing, 2001.

Polak, Michael. *Antique Trader-Bottles: Identification and Price Guide*, 4th edition. Iola, WI: Krause Publications, 2002.

— — —. *Antique Trader Bottles: Identification and Price Guide*, 5th edition. Iola, WI: Krause Publication, 2005.

— — —. *Antique Trader-Bottles: Identification and Price Guide*, 6th edition. Iola, WI: Krause Publication, 2009.

— — —. *Antique Trader-Bottles: Identification and Price Guide*, 7th Edition, Krause Publication, Iola, WI 2012.

— — —. *Antique Trader-Bottles: Identification and Price Guide*, 8th Edition, Krause Publication, Iola, WI 2016.

— — —. *Pickers Pocket Guide: Bottles*, 1st Edition, Krause Publication, Iola, WI 2014.

— — —. *Warman's Bottles – Field Guide, Value and Identification*, 1st Edition, Krause Publications, Iola, WI, 2005.

— — —. *Warman's Bottles – Field Guide, Value and Identification*, 2nd Edition, Krause Publications, Iola, WI, 2007.

— — —. *Warman's Bottles – Field Guide, Value and Identification*, 3nd Edition, Krause Publications, Iola, WI, 2010.

— — —. *Official Price Guide to American Patriotic Memorabilia,* 1st Edition, House of Collectibles, New York, NY, 2002.

Putnam, H.E. *Bottle Identification*. New York: H.E. Putnam Publisher, 1965.

Rensselaer, Van Stephen. *Early American Bottles and Flasks*. Stratford, CT: J. Edmund Edwards Publisher, 1969.

Richardson, Charles G. and Lillian C. *The Pill Rollers, Apothecary Antiques and Drug Store Collectibles*, 3rd edition, 2003. Charles G. Richardson, 1176 S. Dogwood Drive, Harrisonburg, VA 22801-1535.

Ring, Carlyn. *For Bitters Only*. Concord, MA: The Nimrod Press, Inc., 1980.

Ring, Carlyn and W.C. Ham. *Bitters Bottles*. Downieville, CA, Self Published (530) 289-0809, 2000.

Roller, Dick. *Fruit Jar Patents*, Volume III, 1900-1942. Chicago: McCann Publisher, 1996.

———. *Indiana Glass Factories Notes*. Chicago: McCann Publisher, 1994.

Roller, Dick (Updated by McCann, Jerry and Bernas, Berry), *The Standard Fruit Jar Reference 2011*, McCann Publisher, 5003 W. Berwyn Ave., Chicago, IL 60630, (773) 777-0443, 2011.

Russell, Mike. *Collector's Guide to Civil War Period Bottle and Jars*, 3rd edition. Herndon, VA: Self Published, 2000.

Schwartz, Marvin D. "American Glass" Antiques, Volume 1, 1974, Blown and Molded, Princeton, NJ: Pyne Press.

Seeliger, Michael. *H.H. Warner His Company & His Bottles*. East Greenville, PA: Antique Bottle & Glass Collector, 1974.

Sloan, Gene. *Perfume and Scent Bottle Collecting*. Radnor, PA: Wallace Homestead Book Company, 1986.

Snyder, Bob. *Bottles in Miniature*. Amarillo, TX: Snyder Publications, 1969.

———. *Bottles in Miniature II*. Amarillo, TX: Snyder Publications, 1970.

———. *Bottles in Miniature III*. Amarillo, TX: Snyder Publications, 1972.

Soetens, Johan. *Packaged in Glass: European Bottles, Their History and Production*. Amsterdam: Batavlan Lion International, October 2001.

Spaid M. David and Harry A. Ford. *101 Rare Whiskey Flasks (Miniature)*. Palos Verdes, CA: Brisco Publications, 1989.

Spiegel, Walter Von. *Glas*. Battenberg Verlag, Munchen, 1979.

Spillman, Jane Shadel. *Glass Bottles, Lamps and Other Objects*. New York: Alfred A. Knopf, 1983.

Southard, Tom and Mike Burggraaf. *The Antique Bottles of Iowa*. Des Moines, IA: Self Published, 1998.

Sweeney, Rick. *Collecting Applied Color Label Soda Bottles*, 2nd edition. La Mesa, CA: Painted Soda Bottles Collectors Assoc., 1995.

———. *Collecting Applied Color Label Soda Bottles*, 3rd edition. La Mesa, CA: Painted Soda Bottles Collectors Assoc., 2002.

Taber, George, M. "To Cork or Not to Cork." Scribner: New York, N.Y. 2007.

Thompson, J.H. *Bitters Bottles*. Watkins Glen, NY: Century House, 1947.

Toulouse, Julian Harrison. *Bottle Makers and Their Marks*. Camden, NJ: Thomas Nelson Incorporated, 1971.

———. *Fruit Jars: A Collectors' Manual*. Caldwell, NJ: The Blackburn Press, 1969, republished 2005.

Townsend, Brian. *Scotch Missed (The Lost Distilleries of Scotland)*. Glasgow G38AZ Scotland: Neil Wilson Publishing Ltd., 1994.

Tyson, Scott. *Glass Houses of the 1800s*. East Greenville, PA: Antique Bottle & Glass Collector, 1971.

Tucker, Donald. *Collectors Guide to the Saratoga Type Mineral Water Bottles*. East Greenville, PA: Antique Bottle & Glass Collector, 1986.

Tutton, John. *Udderly Delightful*. Stephens City, VA: Commercial Press, Inc., 1996.

———. *Udderly Splendid*. Stephens City, VA: Commercial Press, Inc., 2003.

Umberger, Joe and Arthur. *Collectible Character Bottles*. Tyler, TX: Corker Book Company, 1969.

Van den Bossche, Willy. *Antique Glass Bottles – Their History and Evolution (1500-1850)*. Woodbridge, England: Antique Collector Club, 2001, wvdbossche@planet.nl

———. *Bibliography of Glass, From the Earliest Times to the Present*, Woodbridge England Antique Collectors' 2012 – Willy Van de Bossche, 011-44-139-438-9950.

Van, P. Dale. *American Breweries II*. North Wales, PA: Eastern Coast Breweriana Association, 1995.

Reference

Van Rensselaer, Stephen. "Early American Bottles and Flasks." Peterborough, NH: Transcript Printing Company, 1926.

Vesilind, Priit J. *Lost Gold of the Republic, The Remarkable Quest for the Greatest Shipwreck Treasure of the Civil War Era*, Shipwreck Heritage Press, 2005.

Watkins, Laura Woodside. *American Glass and Glassmaking*. New York: Chanticleer Press, 1950.

Watson, Richard. *Bitters Bottles*. New York: Thomas Nelson & Sons, 1965.

———. *Supplement to Bitters Bottles*. New York: Thomas Nelson & Sons, 1968.

Wichmann, Jeff. *Antique Western Bitters Bottles*, 1st edition. Sacramento, CA: Pacific Glass Books Publishing, 1999.

Wilson, Betty and William. *Spirit Bottles of the Old West*. Wolfe City: Henington Publishing Company, 1968.

Wilson, Kenneth M. *New England Glass and Glass Making*. New York: Thomas Y. Crowell Company, 1972.

Wood, Zang. *New Mexico Bottle Book*. Flora Vista, NM. Self published, 1998.

Yates, Don. *Ginger Beer & Root Beer Heritage, 1790-1930*, 2004. Don Yates, 8300 River Corners Road, Homerville, OH 44235, (330) 625-1025.

Young, Susan H. "A Preview of Seventh-Century Glass From The Kourin Basilica, Cyprus", Journal of Glass Studies, Vol. 35, Corning Museum of Glass, 1993.

Yount, John T. *Bottle Collector's Handbook & Pricing Guide*. Action Printery, 10 No. Main, San Angelo, TX 76901, 1967.

Zumwalt, Betty. *Ketchup, Pickles, Sauces*. Sandpoint, ID: Mark West Publishers, 1980.

Sanborn Fire Insurance Maps – Resources

EDR Sanborn Maps
Environmental Data Resources, Inc.
3530 Post Rd.
Southport, CT 06890
(800) 352-0050
Website: www.edrnet.com,
www.edrnet.com/reports.html

Chadwyck-Healy, Inc.
1101 King St.
Suite 380, Alexdria, VA 22314
(800) 752-0515 or (703) 683-4890
FAX: (703) 683-7589
E-Mail: sales@chadwyck.com
Website: www.chadwyck.com

San Jose Public Library
San Jose, CA
Website: www.sjpl.lib.ca.us, www.sjlibrary.org

Stanford University
Stanford, CA
E-Mail: seleniteman@comcast.net
Website: www.sul.stanford.edu

University of California at Berkley
Berkley, CA
Website: www.lib.berkeley.edu, www.lib.berkeley.edu/EART/sanborn.html

Vlad Shkurkin, Publisher
6025 Rose Arbor
San Pablo, CA 94806-4147
(510) 232-7742
FAX: (510) 236-7050
E-Mail: Shkurkin@ix.netcom.com

Vista
505 Huntmar Park Dr., Suite 200
Herndon, VA 20170
(800) 989-0402 or (703) 834-0600
FAX: (703) 834-0606

Periodicals

Ale Street News
P.O. Box 1125
Maywood, NJ 07607
E-mail: JamsOD@aol.com
Web site: www.AleStreetNews.com

American Digger Magazine–For Diggers and
*   Collectors of America's Heritage*
P.O. Box 126
Acworth, GA 30101
(770) 362-8671

Antique Bottle & Glass Collector
John Pastor
P.O. Box 227
New Hudson, MI 48165-0227
(248) 486-0530.

Antique Bottle Collector UK Limited
Llanerch, Carno, Caersws
Powys SY17 5JY Wales

Australian Antique Bottles and Collectibles
AABS, Box 235
Golden Square, 3555 Australia

Australian Bottle & Collectables Review, The
84 Black Flat Rd.
Whittlesea, Victoria, 3757, Australia
E-mail: travisdunn@bigpond.com.au
Website:www.abcreview.com.

BAM (Bottles and More) Magazine
P.O. Box #6
Lehighton, PA 18235

Bottles & Bygones
30 Brabant Rd.
Cheadle Hulme, Cheadlek
Cheshire, SKA 7AU England

Bottles & Extra Magazine
1966 King Springs Rd.
Johnson City, TN 37601

British Bottle Review (BBR)
Elsecar Heritage Centre
Barnsley, S. Yorkshire S74 8HJ, England

Canadian Bottle & Stoneware Collector
*   Magazine*
102 Abbeyhill Dr., Kanata
Ontario, Canada K2L 1H2
Website: www.cbandsc.com

Crown Jewels of the Wire
P.O. Box 1003,
St. Charles, IL 60174-1003

Root Beer Float
P.O. Box 571
Lake Geneva, WI 53147

The Miniature Bottle Collector
Brisco Publications
P.O. Box 2161
Palos Verdes Peninsula, CA 92074

The Soda Spectrum
A Publication by Soda Pop Dreams
P.O. Box 23037
Krug Postal Outlet
Kitchener, Ontario, Canada N2B 3V1

Treasure Hunter's Gazette (Collector's
    Newsletter)
George Streeter, Publisher & Editor
14 Vernon St.
Keene, NH 03431

Western & Eastern Treasure Magazine
PO Box 16856
North Hollywood, CA 91615
(877) 324-9967 or (818) 487-4550.

Reference

Index

Index

TOP COLLECTOR GUIDES
JUST **FOR YOU**

Whether you are just getting started or have been collecting for years, our books will help you build, identify, value, and maintain your collections.
For more information, visit **KrauseBooks.com**

Krause Publications books can also be found at many booksellers nationwide, and at antiques and hobby shops.

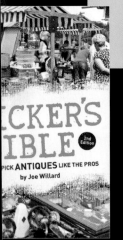

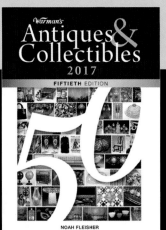

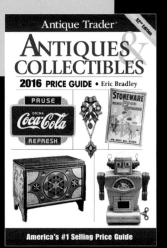